DATE DUE			

RICHARD WAGNER

RICHARD WAGNER

The Story of An Artist

By GUY DE POURTALÈS

◆◆◆◆◆◆◆◆◆◆◆◆◆◆◆◆◆◆◆◆◆◆◆◆◆◆◆◆

TRANSLATED FROM THE FRENCH
BY LEWIS MAY

ILLUSTRATED

GREENWOOD PRESS, PUBLISHERS
WESTPORT, CONNECTICUT

The Library of Congress has catalogued this publication as follows:

Library of Congress Cataloging in Publication Data

Pourtalès, Guy de, comte, 1881-1941.
    Richard Wagner; the story of an artist.

    Bibliography: p.
    1. Wagner, Richard, 1813-1883.
ML410.W1P73 1972   782.1'0924 [B]   76-138173
ISBN 0-8371-5630-0

Originally published in 1932 by Harper & Brothers,
New York

Reprinted with the permission of Harper & Row,
Publishers

Reprinted from an original copy in the collections of the
Brooklyn Public Library

Reprinted in 1972 by Greenwood Press, Inc.,
51 Riverside Avenue, Westport, Conn. 06880

Library of Congress catalog card number 76-138173
ISBN 0-8371-5630-0

Printed in the United States of America

10 9 8 7 6 5 4 3 2

LIST OF CONTENTS

PART FIVE

ILLUSTRATIONS

TRANSLATOR'S NOTE

The translator desires to thank his friend, Edwin Wareham (formerly of the Royal Opera, Covent Garden) and his daughter, Barbara Lewis May, for valuable assistance rendered during the passage of this book through the press.

Preface

SEVEN years ago I had returned from visiting, at Bayreuth, the grave where Liszt lies buried in his Franciscan habit; and just as I was about to set out for Rome, whither I was going to glimpse the form of the abbé-virtuoso on the terraces of the Villa d'Este, I inscribed the first of these romantic histories to a vehement and restless spirit indeed, but one, withal, whom the music of the heart still had a power to charm.

Now to her silent shade I dedicate this later book as I bring it to a close on the lofty plateau of le Valais, whence, a few years since, Katherine Mansfield and Rainer Maria Rilke gazed into the depths of the wide and rocky chasm which forms the valley of the Rhône. The gentle spirit of the former shuddered at the thought that death should come for her, here on this lofty eyrie, and to hasten her cure she took to weaving stories. In his Tower at Muzot, some hundreds of yards below, Rilke may perchance have heard them, for none there were so sensitive as he to catch the tales that God and children tell.

I feel a little diffident at penning here, upon these craggy heights quickened with the undying poetry of waving grasses, clouds, and the mystery of spiritual presences, a book devoted to a man and to gods whose grim and puissant race today holds sway only over the shadows of a bygone world.

For the Europe of those times, so childlike and so eloquent, that filled the years from 1830 to 1880, is dead and gone. Its romance has foundered in the sea of History and, year after year, as my work progressed, I beheld the baggage, once so seemingly formidable, which these idealist pioneers bore in their train, shrink to the dimensions of a few notebooks and bundles of old letters. Therefore it seems to me that to try to explain how I sought to trace our own ideals in the track followed by these adventurers, to make an inventory of what still survives of the ideas and sentiments which animated those eager wayfarers on their march, were as vain as to essay to weave anew Penelope's unravelled web.

Nevertheless, the mountains of Valhalla which rise up on the horizon are no extinct volcanoes. Flames still issue from them, and smoke and cavernous rumblings. And if the giants have ended their reign on earth, they have left behind them, in flowery dells and on misty summits, the sumptuous music of their dying glory. If I succeed in reawakening, in the hearts of those who may read these pages, some woodland melody, or distant trumpet call, or tragic dissonance, such as even our own humble longings are adorned withal, I shall not deem my task in vain. It may be, in the last resort, that all through my tale of Wagner's life I have only striven to appease the yearning and the pain of living to which, whatever the skill and determination with which we attempt to display an indifferent or invulnerable front to the world, we all of us are heirs.

But the sound of the bells in the valley below is a timely reminder of Rilke's story of God, whose hands had fled away to mould a human being and had thoughtlessly left him on earth before his time. "He was so impatient," they said, by way of excusing themselves. "He wanted to begin life then and there." And that tale reminds me of yet another God, seven centuries older than the first, whom you yet may see in the north doorway of Chartres Cathedral, amid a group of reliefs, in which some mediæval sculptor has carved his idea of the Creation of the World. Two of these figures have always struck me as remarkable. One shows the Eternal Father wearing Jewish headgear, resting His head in His hands and by His whole attitude revealing the disappointment which filled Him as he gazed upon His handiwork. One divines the anguish to which Jehovah is a prey at the sight of this cathedral which proclaims His glory, it is true, yet swarms with all the manifold sins and errors of His creature, Man. The other figure depicts Him with His soul behind Him, in the guise of a young and naked man.

Such, it seems to me, is the artist, leaning anxiously over the world which he has created, a world which, though scarce minted from his brain, forthwith begins to lose its form and to lapse into decrepitude and decay, ere yet the angel at his side has ceased to whisper to him of the perfection he had dreamed. Therefore it is that I place on the threshold of this work naught save the twofold symbol of Suffering and Faith.

G. de P.

Montana (Valais), August, 1932

RICHARD WAGNER

"The idea of the Past is devoid of value and significance save for him who is imbued with a passionate interest in the Future."

Paul Valéry: GLIMPSES AT THE WORLD OF TO-DAY, p. 19.

"My task it is to write the story of one of those great but ill-starred souls, too richly dowered with poetry and passion, who, like many another before him, came into this world to serve the harsh apprenticeship of genius, among men of coarser mould."

Charles Baudelaire: EDGAR POE. HIS LIFE AND WORKS.

"Some hold that on those to whom she looks for great achievements, Nature bestows a tireless energy, even as she endows with puissant vitality the trees ordained to stand as symbols of sorrow and of pain."

Ibid., p. 32.

PART ONE

Chapter I

THE POETS TAKE THE FIELD

EUROPE has never forgiven France the glory of Napoleon. That little man caused too many thrones to tremble, too much blood to flow, and subverted too many principles, not to linger even now, when a hundred years have passed, like a blood-red ember on the history. For a whole century we have been living in fear and trembling lest we should behold the great Captain of Adventure setting foot once more upon our democratic shores. However, there is no cause for alarm. Money is the ruler of your modern state, and bankers have no great liking for leaps in the dark. Napoleon has come home from St. Helena for good, and returned to the bosom of his family—the poets!

We of today have no more faith in genius, and little enough in glory. And, if it comes to that, do we even believe in the poets? I wonder—at least if we mean by the poets the gentlemen who grind out verses. For glory, for fame, we still, perhaps, retain some liking but we call it success, which, if less ethereal, is at all events something a man can lay hold of and get his teeth into. Let us, then, leave the poets alone with those who dwell apart—sad, solitary, and remote—and suffer them to unburden, one to another, the sorrows of their hearts.

The Napoleon of a hundred and fifteen years ago was unquestionably such a mighty sower of poetic seed that men's hearts sprang up like poppies beneath his iron heel, poppies incarnadined and full of song, blossoming in his track across the plains. What matters it whether love or hate was the burden of their song? They rose up and sang, and the whole of the nineteenth century reëchoes to their soaring strains. Even though it be in the foeman's breast that you kindle this heroic fire, yet the power to light that flame is none the less one of the rarest gifts the gods can bestow upon a man. Let us recall a few echoes from Chateaubriand concerning Bonaparte's last campaign in Germany:

"The battles of 1813," says he in his *Mémoires d'Outre Tombe,* "were called the Campaign in Saxony. It were better to call them the Campaign of the Poets. . . ."

"Professor Fichte was lecturing in Berlin on the subject of Duty. He spoke of the sufferings of Germany and concluded his discourse as follows: 'These lectures will be suspended until the war is over. We shall resume them when our country has won back her freedom, or we shall have laid down our lives in the struggle to regain it.' " . . . "Koerner had only one fear, the fear of dying a prosaic death. Wounded at Lutzen, he dragged himself into a wood, where he was found by some peasants; he went back to the firing-line and eventually met his death on the plains of Leipzig, when he was barely twenty-five; he had torn himself from the arms of the woman he adored and gone off to drink life and its pleasures to the lees." . . . "When these students forsook the peaceful haunts of science for the field of battle, the silent joys of study for the clamour and perils of war, Homer and the Niebelungen for the sword, what strains did they chant in answer to our hymn of blood, our songs of Revolution? Strains fulfilled of sacred love for the loyalty of the human heart." . . . "There is a tinge of the mysterious in the genius of the German race. The Germans adore freedom today, rapt in a sort of vague, indeterminate dream, even as of old they were wont to call God 'the hidden spirit of the woods.' "

I have purposely selected these passages, contained within the space of one brief chapter, because certain pictures and names are brought together therein that for us are pregnant with a sense of prophecy. You can fancy you are listening not only to the prelude of the drama of 1815, which was to mark the close of an heroic epoch, but also, in a manner, to the prologue of the Romantic revival, to the uprising of the Intellectuals and the Dreamers. After five-and-twenty years spent in pursuit of that exhausting pastime called war and revolution, a mighty shout of, "Hold! Enough!" burst from the throats of millions of men spurred on by spiritual starvation, eager to live again, to be able to call their souls their own, and, instead of drawing the map of the world anew, to read the dictates of their own hearts. It was necessary that genius should have done with its political adventure, if men were at length to have a chance of possessing their souls awhile in peace. Men were waiting for the hour to strike when they, too, could go and drink their fill of the pleasures of life. All they asked was to hang up their swords and get back again to work, to Homer and the Niebelungen. After such mighty sacrifices to the God of Hosts, the Germans, like the French and English, had but one desire, and that was to seek pardon of a deity outraged by the sins of mankind, were he but that rustic divinity "the hidden spirit of the woods."

After the manner of some lanky recruit that had drunk his fill of joy, the younger generation of the nineteenth century were eager to get back to the domestic hearth again. They were hailed as the warriors of the New Age. It was high-day and holiday for the Good, the Beautiful, and the True. People were sick to death in Europe of that monstrous captain, Reality; they longed for the urbane amenities of study and contemplation. Schiller and Goethe became the true princes of Germany, what time, in France, usury and weariness were bringing about the overthrow of the country's traditional rulers, enthroning Tragedy and her grim retinue, the passions, in her place; while England was awaiting the advent of her noblest poets. For this age, the Play, not Life, was "the thing." Finally, it was music that sent a thrill through all these young and eager hearts, freed at last from their military fetters, beckoning them onward, ever onward, to follow the path of the new and glorious destiny that was stretching out before them.

On the 21st of May, 1813, was fought the battle of Bautzen. Once again Napoleon was victorious. It was five months before Leipzig, which the Germans call the Battle of the Nations, and Chateaubriand, the Battle of the Poets. The fall of the Emperor was at hand, and proclaimed by the cosmopolitan band of artists whose universal cry was ever, "Long live liberty!" Alone perhaps of all of them, Goethe realized what a great exemplar of human worth the world was about to lose. "A madman Napoleon undoubtedly was," he confessed to Eckermann, "a madman of the first water, but such madmen as he the Greeks were wont to rank among the demigods." And then he added, "Napoleon's example will excite a certain degree of egoism in the young, for it is an object lesson to each of what he himself might become. . . . The worst of it is that you cannot expect to have another man like that straightaway. How could the Deity keep on working miracles if He did not sometimes manifest His might in individuals, at whose extraordinary powers we gaze in wonderment, never realizing whence they are derived."

In Leipzig, the day after the battle of Bautzen, little Richard Wagner was born. It was looked on as an event of very minor importance indeed. It had no great interest, even for the tenants of the second floor of the Red and White Lion on the Brühl, where the bratling had just made his entry into the world, amid the booming of the guns. Saxony had been in the occupation of the Allies for some weeks past, and Leipzig, like Dresden, was full of troops, German and Russian. The fortune of war having thus turned them into vassals of Napoleon, the Saxon citizens displayed a cautious reserve in regard to their cousins the Slavs, and their brothers the Germans, who, it was given out, had hurried to the spot to strike a blow for the universal deliverance. For suddenly, the Emperor had risen up like a tempest, hurling his thunderbolts; and the freedom of which they had caught a fleeting glimpse vanished once more from the horizon of their hopes. He gained the day at Lutzen and then at Bautzen, the very day before the wife of Friedrich Wagner, secretary to the Chief Commissioner of Police, gave birth to this untimely infant.

It may be easily imagined that its arrival was not exactly an occasion for rejoicing in the Wagner household. Eight children were burden enough in those days of military rule and household worries. What did they want with a ninth? And to put the cap on it all, the troops were pouring back again into the town. Their Majesties of Prussia and Russia were fleeing before their French conqueror. A season of Italian opera and dramatic per- formances under the management of the poet Hoffmann had been advertised to take place. Instead of the curtain going up on *Figaro and La Vestale*, the drums were beating to quarters in the streets, and all the city gates were closed. In a word, the outlook was black. Fortunately, an armistice was soon signed, and the Wagners went somewhere into the neighbouring country, where the mother was able to regain her strength. However, the peace did not endure. Napoleon had no great taste for holidays. Mr. Secretary Wagner being the only one at Police Headquarters who knew French, the family were obliged to return to town. Well, that gave them a chance to have the brat baptized. And as though the child were born for wars and battles, the day of the christening coincided with the resumption of hostilities, for the Emperor had decided he would celebrate his birthday, the 15th of August, by getting on with the war again.

On the 16th the little boy Wagner was carried into the Church of St. Thomas—Johann Sebastian Bach's church. He was chris- tened Wilhelm Richard, his father being described as Friedrich Wagner, secretary to the Commissioner of Police, and his mother as Johanna Rosina Bertz. The little ceremony was of the quietest description, only the sponsors being present. The christening over, the party returned, forthwith, to the old Red and White Lion, and resumed their customary tasks under the eyes of a few old family portraits.

These Wagners were an old and hard-working family, with- out any claim to social distinction. The Secretary's father,

Gottlob Friedrich II, had been a collector of customs dues. His grandfather, Gottlob Friedrich I, had been a theologian, and subsequently a collector of taxes. His theology must have sat lightly upon him, for his son was born out of wedlock. The great-grandfather, Samuel II, had been a schoolmaster like his father before him, who had been an organist into the bargain. And, going still further back, we come to Samuel I, born in 1643, a schoolmaster, too, and the first recorded shoot of the sturdy tree which was to produce this long succession of country dominies. There was nothing to distinguish this family from hundreds and hundreds of others. And so the birth of little Richard had no significance save for his pretty mother, the girlish-looking and comely Johanna; and perchance for yet one other, whose absence from these family festivities was keenly lamented. That was the actor, Ludwig Geyer.

Poor Geyer, however, was overjoyed to get back soon after to Leipzig, to the little stage of the Thomé Theatre, where he had scored many and many a success, but most of all to the warm hospitality of the Wagners, in whose dwelling he was apparently always welcome to bed and board. Moreover, it was this same Friedrich Wagner who, twenty years before, had given him his first start in his theatrical career. In those days he had been a painter of pictures that displayed considerable talent. But Friedrich Wagner had been quick to detect in him powers of observation and imitation so remarkable and so true to nature, that, with a passion for the stage (and Schiller's dawning fame) to spur him on, Geyer decided to try his fortune on the boards. The experiment was a complete success. He was, as we are told repeatedly, an excellent figure and very good-looking, with a mobile expression that alternated readily from grave to gay, and gay to grave. He could play Don Carlos, Hamlet, Piccolomini, and many another rôle, and he played them all with equal skill. And as he was by no means averse to novelty and change of scene, he accepted long engagements in various parts of Germany— Stettin, Magdeburg, Breslau—returning after prolonged absences to his home in Saxony. Coming back to Leipzig meant coming back to his friends the Wagners, and their home on the Brühl. It meant seeing Johanna again, so alert and active in spite of her successive confinements; and it meant resuming, once again, those long talks about poetry and the stage which he was wont to have with the Secretary, who, under the foreign occupation, had become something of a big-wig. In virtue of his knowledge of French, Friedrich Wagner, on the instructions of Marshal

Davoust, the commandant of the place, was now taking up a position of great confidence at Police Headquarters.

For some long time now things had been progressing favourably. Whenever he got back to Leipzig, Geyer bounded up the stairs that led to his friends' abode, romped merrily with the children, and got back to work on the portrait he was painting in oils of the charming Frau Wagner. And of an evening, if there were nothing doing at the theatre, there would be long and eager talks about literature and poetry. Adolf Wagner, the Secretary's brother, would sometimes put in an appearance and give the discussion a more learned turn, for Adolf was by way of being something of a celebrity in the district. First and foremost, he had been a personal acquaintance of Schiller's, a magnificent passport to popular respect. When, in 1798, he was a student in Jena, he had been to see him, and to his great confusion had heard himself singled out for praise by the man whom all young Germany revered, for some doggerel verses which he had composed and which some well-intentioned but misguided friend had, in his innocence, sent to the author of *The Brigands* for his perusal. Nevertheless, despite the absurdity of the incident, the memory of that hour, so eminently glorious, lingered like an aureole about the brow of "Uncle Adolf," as he was called. Further than that, he had been the friend and correspondent of Jean Paul, the writer who, after Goethe and Schiller, was the most considerable star in Germany. In a word, he was philologist, essayist, and critic. He had published some translations from Euripides, a work entitled *The Two Epochs of Modern Poetry Represented by Dante, Petrarch Boccaccio, Goethe, Schiller, and Wieland.* Better still, he was the author of four comedies, and of an essay which had a more direct bearing upon the subject these gentlemen so loved to discuss. It was entitled *The Theatre and the Public.* And so it came about that these meetings in the Red and White Lion were inspiring recreations for this little group of theatrical enthusiasts. Unfortunately, Geyer was perpetually having to set out on his travels again, to go to Dresden, or to Breslau, or I know not what other royal habitation. And it so happened that on the day little Richard was born, and on the day he was christened, the actor was far away from Saxony, where, amid the shock and clash of armies, his friends had their habitation. The news that came to them during the terrible year of 1813 was the reverse of reassuring; and, although the *Théâtre Français*, with Talma to lead it, had come to perform before the Emperor during the armistice, these superficial appearances deceived no one. Tidings came in swift succession of the battle of Dresden, the swift and perilous retreat of the Prussians and the Austrians, and the crushing blow dealt by Macdonald at the forces under Blücher.

In October, events hurried to a crisis. The battle was joined beneath the very walls of Leipzig. Napoleon took up his quarters in the Thomé House, the same in which the theatre was established and which was the residence-in-ordinary of the one-time Prince Elector who became a king and owed his crown to his prowess as a soldier of fortune. But the Saxons went over to the Allies. The guns thundered at the city gates and shattered all the windows in the place. The French army returned in hot haste. And Frau Wagner, hearing the clatter of mounted troops going by beneath her window, gazed out and beheld a group of generals on horseback, in the midst of whom a stoutish man, with head uncovered, trotted moodily along. She at once knew him for the Emperor.

The Romanticists had just scored a victory over the last genius of antiquity.

Chapter II

WAGNER—GEYER

THE events just recorded took place at Leipzig on the 19th of October, 1813. A few days afterwards an outbreak of typhus played havoc among the sorely tried inhabitants. A month later, on the 22nd of November, Friedrich Wagner fell a victim to the epidemic. And in the month of December of that tragic year two of the poets, the triumph of whose dreams we have just beheld, make their entry, as poets will, into the child's life, the child whose smiles were beginning to illumine the dwelling of the Red and White Lion. Now the manner of poetic intervention is always prophetic. During the night of the Feast of Saint Sylvester, Hoffmann put the finishing touch to his admirable tale of *Der Goldene Topf*; and Jean Paul wrote from his home in Bayreuth the following lines by way of preface to his friend's story: "Hitherto the God of Light flung with his right hand the gift of poetry, and with his left the gift of music, to two beings so distinct from one another that we are still waiting for the coming of him who shall be able at one and the same time to compose a complete opera." Friedrich Wagner, that great lover of the theatre, having so suddenly disappeared from the melodrama we call Life, Ludwig Geyer found himself alone with Johanna, whose tears did not avail to rob her of her comeliness. It was vain to look for help to Uncle Adolf, a man grown old before his time, buried in a den encumbered with philological treatises and the works of the poets of every age. With a high, pointed cap perched on his head, studious and solitary, he made up his mind that nothing should mar his complete independence and determined to play no part in his sister-in-law's affairs. The latter, therefore, had no one on whose devotion she could count except Geyer, and to him she did not hesitate to have recourse. Geyer was in love with her. Maybe he had loved her long, and certain it is that she loved him. Many and many a time he had come to relieve her solitude of an evening when her husband was loung-

ing about the wings of the Thomé Theatre, philandering with
the actresses there. Gossiping tongues had it that the child
Richard was the fruit of their *amours*. Well, suppose he was,
there was nothing very terrible in that. Gottlob Friedrich II, the
theologian, had he not had a natural son? And did not Johanna
give out that there was a certain mystery about her own birth;
that she came of unknown, perhaps of royal, parentage? Her
people were millers at Weissenfels, called Bertz (or Peetz). That
much everybody knew. But who was it that took her away when
she was quite small and put her to boarding-school at Leipzig?
And why did her parents maintain such a profound air of secrecy
about her? Who was it found the money for this expensive education—expensive yet rather frivolous and happy-go-lucky? And
didn't Johanna sometimes say that her real name was Perthes,
and not Peetz? And when anyone asked her about all these mysterious things, she gave out that the unseen friend who had
watched over her childhood with such fatherly care was none
other than the Prince of Weimar. This romantic genealogy was
of a nature to encourage the widow of the police official and her
friend Geyer to lose no time in uniting their destinies. They ac-
cordingly resolved to marry. Johanna was thirty-nine and Geyer
barely thirty-four. She was still as charming and active as ever,
and, as her correspondence shows, remarkably shaky in her
spelling. He was refined and sensitive, and, it seems, not very
robust. Another notable thing about him was the extraordinary
likeness he bore to Friedrich and Adolf Wagner. They might
have passed for three brothers. His family had been Protestant
for many generations, like the Wagners, with possibly a trace
of Jewish blood in their veins, though that has never been
proved. Geyer came of modest stock—civil servants, organists,
and the like; and here again was another point of resemblance
to the Wagners. The marriage, then, was merely setting the seal
of convention on an arrangement that was eminently natural
and straightforward.

Immediately after the wedding, which took place in August,
1814, the Geyers went and settled down in Dresden. The eldest
daughter, Rosalie, was put to board for the time being with
Frau Hartwig, the actress. Albert stayed on at school and the
rest of the family took up their abode in a house on the Moritz-
strasse. Geyer went back to his work at the theatre, and managed, without any undue strain, to shoulder the expenses which
his love for the Wagner family had led him to incur. He even
took up his painting again, and his studio was thronged with
people. So numerous indeed were his clients that when the

domestic establishment was enriched by the arrival of a new boarder in the person of his daughter Cecile, who was born in February, 1815, the circumstance caused him no anxiety.

Little by little, Dresden had revived the amenities and dignity appropriate to a royal city, and, after the fall of the redoubtable Emperor, kings began once more to play their regal parts. Everywhere one came across court functionaries and satellites—counsellors, purveyors, critics, men of letters, laundry-women and what not, all dependent on the court. These recipients of the royal commands inflated the whole capital with the wind of their importance. The studio of Geyer, painter to His Majesty, was no exception to the rule. Poets declaimed their poems there; actors played their parts in plays of which Geyer himself was the author, *The New Dalila*, for example, or *The Massacre of the Innocents*, and the children were encouraged to take a share in the performances; especially Louise, since she was the pupil of Hartwig, the famous actress whose charms once used to keep the secretary of police so long and so often from the domestic hearth; and Rosalie, also, whose father had definitely marked her out for the glories of a stage career. The latter made her first public appearance in a play by her stepfather on the 2nd March, 1818, two days before her sixteenth birthday. Uncle Adolf had sent her his compliments and best wishes, not unseasoned with some sage and pious admonitions, for he was a prudent man. Nevertheless, the avuncular wisdom did not prevent young Albert from throwing up his medical studies in order to become a public singer. Later on, his sister Clara also took up the stage. Clearly the family was destined for the boards. Howbeit their learned uncle did his utmost to save the three younger children, Ottilie, Richard, and Cecile, from falling victims to the contagion. But, so far, they were only up to mischief, and had given no indication of becoming infant prodigies.

Meanwhile a new planet had swum into the artistic firmament at Dresden. His name was Karl Maria von Weber, and he was sorely grieved to see that in Saxony, no less than in Vienna and Paris, the fashion in music had completely forsaken the German masters in favour of the Italians. Full of fire and energy, but lame and frail, more like a disembodied spirit than a man, he was appointed *chef d'orchestre* to the King, and forthwith started a campaign against the existing régime and its upholders. He set to work to reform the Opera and all its ways; kept a sharp lookout for fresh talent, and, as luck would have it, included Geyer among the new accessions to his staff.

Geyer had been something of a singer before this, and could still boast rather a fine tenor voice. He swiftly conceived an affection for the master, whose genius he soon discerned, and threw himself with a good heart into the work which had thus unexpectedly come his way. He sang all manner of secondary parts, still keeping up his dramatic work, and diligently plying his brush. And so it is that the name of this admirable example of versatility appears on most of the playbills in Dresden and many other towns about this time, just as it figures also on the portraits of the Queen of Saxony, of Ludwig of Bavaria and his Queen, and, lastly, in print, on the covers of his comedies.

Albert soon obtained an engagement at Breslau. Next, Rosalie quitted the family roof to take up the stage as a regular vocation. In all this concourse of actors and stage folk, the part assigned to little Richard was that of acrobat, for he was the only one of them all who could slide unerringly down the banisters, the only one who could walk on his hands. Geyer used to call him "the Cossack." They often took him to the theatre, where he had a chair in the actors' box communicating with the stage. And as it was not in the nature of things that he should wholly escape the family malady, he was given, when occasion offered, a tiny part to play. It so happened that Weber was able to find him a place in the *Vineyards by the Elbe*, in which Richard appeared as an angel with wings on his shoulders. Another time, in Kotzebuë's *Hate and Repentance*, he even had a line or two to say.

Such, then, was the nature of the family activities; for Richard, their main virtue lay in the opportunity they afforded him to neglect his lessons. He strummed a little on the piano when the fancy took him, but not with any sort of application or, apparently, with any great ardour. Geyer would have liked to make a painter of him.

When he had completed his seventh year he was sent to Possendorf, near Dresden, to board with a Herr Wetzel, a country pastor, where he learned to read *Robinson Crusoe* aloud, and a life of Mozart, who had then been dead about thirty years. But what impressed him much more vividly than all that, was hearing the pastor read the newspaper, giving accounts, interspersed with fiery comments of his own, of the fight for freedom which the Greeks were waging against their Turkish oppressors. Thus it was that Hellas and the Greek mythology burst in upon his childish mind, leaving upon it an impression that nothing ever availed to efface. Lord Byron was about to set out for Missolonghi and to meet, in a glorious death, such an end as he had coveted; while little Richard kindled the early fires of his enthusiasm as he sat and listened to the recital of these deeds of glory.

This stage in his career is worth noting. The child never regulated his life in accordance with the precepts of his elders. The real comedy of his career was the comedy he played with them and against them. Family counsel, family traditions, such successes as he won at school and elsewhere, even the experience he acquired on his own account, rarely had any determining influence on his future conduct. Much more important in their effect upon his nature and career were the accidental happenings, the chance emotions, a grave or pathetic simile, a day of enjoyment, some sort of appeal to his sensuous nature, sometimes the most abstract of ideas—anything, in short, which warmed and quickened his imagination. What kindled and gave energy to his will was the longing to recapture, the more fully to employ it, the hour in which his youthful spirit had discovered its own method of creating life.

Richard had been nearly a year with Pastor Wetzel when some one came to him one day to take him home because his stepfather was lying at the point of death. Worn out, over-worked, a chronic valetudinarian, compelled to drag himse. from town to town to fulfil his theatrical engagements, Geyei had at last come home to die. He was suffering from an acute attack of pleurisy. It was early in the autumn of 1821. They brought the child to the bedside of the dying man, his "father," as he called him. He saw him looking so exhausted, and was so terrified at the sight, that he could neither speak nor weep. His mother coaxed him to play the piano in the next room to show how well he had got on with his music, and Richard manfully attacked *Ueb' immer Treu und Redlichkeit*, and then Weber's latest air, *La Ronde des Amies de la Mariée*. The child heard the dying man murmur, "Do you think he's got a talent for music?" The words impressed him and he did not forget them. As soon as it began to grow light next morning, his mother came sobbing to his bedside. Geyer had breathed his last. "He meant to make something of you," she said. Such was the ghostly sustenance bequeathed by the dead to the living, bequeathed to this little boy of eight, who was entering into a world of which he knew nothing, save that the theatre is at once the glory and sole resource of large families.

Chapter III

ZARATHUSTRA

*I love him who desireth not
too many virtues.*
—ZARATHUSTRA

*When Zarathustra came to the neighbouring city, which was
nigh unto the woods, he met with a great host of people who
were gathered together in the market place, for it had been
bruited abroad that a tight-rope dancer was about to appear.
And Zarathustra spake unto the people, saying:
"I teach unto you the superman. Man is something that must
be surpassed. I beseech you, my brethren, keep ye faithful unto
earth and put not your trust in those who would speak to you of
things that are more than earthly. . . . Man is a cord stretched
between the beast and the superman—a cord across the abyss.
It is dangerous to pass over to the other side, dangerous to
linger on the way, dangerous to look behind—there is peril in
the halt and in the thrill.
"That which is greatest in man is that he is a bridge not a
goal; and what it behoves us to love in him is that he is a
crossing over and a sinking down. I love those who despise
greatly. I love him that labours and invents. I love him that
loveth his virtue. I love him that hath made of his virtue his
treasure and his destiny. . . . I love him whose soul spendeth
itself freely. . . . I love him that scattereth words of gold before his works and fulfilleth more than he promiseth."
But then there came to pass something that made all lips to
be silent and attracted the gaze of all the multitude. For during
this while, the tight-rope dancer had begun his task . . . he had
come forth out of a little postern gate and was walking on the
rope which was stretched between two towers, high above the
market place and the people.*

THE Wagners were now living in the Marktplatz. It is there that the travelling circuses and roundabouts take up their stand. Young Richard was still eager for these sights, and whenever an acrobat began to perform—especially if he were a tight-rope walker—he was to be seen motionless in the front row, devouring with all his heart and soul this amazing spectacle of human prowess. Head steady, limbs free, nothing but a pole to balance with, terrific will-power within—what moral lesson, what example of energy and resolution, could surpass such a sight as that? The child had made up his mind to one thing, one thing alone, and that was that he would perform this stupendous feat and walk on a rope stretched thirty feet above the heads of the crowd, straight across from side to side, without growing dizzy; that he would kill all sense of fear within him. And then how the people would grow hoarse with cheering when the thing was accomplished! Think of the name that would be his, and of the joy unspeakable of perils overcome! He practised on a rope he had put up in the courtyard at home. He climbed on to the college roof to retrieve a cap he had flung up into the gutter. He was certainly his father's "Cossack," this little Richard Geyer. What's that you say? Geyer?

That was the name in which he was entered at the Kreuzschule, where he went in December, 1822, and remained four years. His relations wanted it so, and it was not until several years later that he resumed the name of Wagner. He was a pretty sturdy child, very industrious to begin with, and, though he began at the bottom of his class, he soon worked his way to the top. He had no taste for mathematics, and none for the dead languages; but he shone in composition, essay-writing, mythology, history, and so on. He was quick-witted, merry, impressible —too much so in fact. That was doubtless due to the exclusively feminine society he encountered in his mother's house—they were all women there. If he had been asked to make a list of those he loved, in the order and degree of his affection, he would have put down his mother at the top, then his little sister Cecile, then Rosalie, then some animals (first and foremost his dog, which he had fished out of the pond one day and which, when it jumped out of a window and broke its neck, caused him the greatest of his childhood's sorrows); then he would produce from his ark, horses, birds, cats, all the living things of creation; next some friends—one or two school chums—and, finally, men. And before all other men, Karl Maria von Weber, the author of *Der Freischütz*.

There was a man if you like! A being apart, unique, super-

natural; a living example of what a man could and should become. All the rising hopes of Germany were centred upon this
cripple of genius, who sent a thrill through the hearts of all the
younger generation of 1830. "Neither king nor emperor do I
want to be," young Richard would murmur to himself as he
gazed at the conductor's marvellous skill, "but to be where he is,
standing up, head erect, conducting one's orchestra!" He practised hard at the piano, wholly and solely to be able to play the
overture to *Der Freischütz*, which gave him incomparable delights, seeming to make his whole being dilate. He lost his heart
to one Spiess, for no other reason than that the young man never
wearied of playing him that inspiring piece. It was all very well
for Maestro Humann, his music-master, to animadvert on his
pupil's unorthodox fingering; the pupil didn't care a straw and
worked away furiously, pounding into the thing, till, by sheer
strength and determination, he mastered his rebellious muscles
and compelled his fingers to do his bidding. At last a rude and
rough-hewn *Freischütz* emerged from this titanic effort.
'Twas enough. He was happy. He could now give up the piano,
since he had made it yield him what he wanted. Mozart's *Don
Giovanni*? Not very much to his taste. Rather trivial, rather
frivolous, rather effeminate sort of stuff. What remained to be
learnt—and was it not the best way to retain and assimilate his
favourite passages?—was the art of musical notation. His mother
thought twice about giving him money for so vain a purpose,
but he won her over and set to work, copying page after page,
unweariedly—*Le Chasseur de Lutzow, Oberon* (Weber and still
more Weber, Weber all the time). He goes to the Grossgarten,
where a military band plays every afternoon. And there,
planted right up against the bandstand, the urchin listens with
all his heart and soul, carried away by the joyous rhythm of the
music. His heart almost bursts at the sound of the oboe, "seeming to rouse the other instruments, like a ghostly cry." And the
rustle of the bows on the strings of the violins—yet more
ghosts!

One day, at the far end of the Ostrallee, in front of the palace
of Prince Antony, he starts back in amazement because a statue
adorned with the symbols of music suddenly begins to tune its
violin. Another time, when he was staying with Uncle Adolf at
Leipzig, his quarters were in the great Thomé House where,
once upon a time, Augustus the Strong and the Emperor Napoleon had had their apartments. Uncle Adolf and the aged
Jeanette Thomé occupied a few of its sombre and sumptuous
apartments. Old-fashioned portraits peopled the walls, over-

hanging the bed of state in which the little boy had to pass the
hours of slumber. There, too, he would wake in the middle of
the night, bathed in a cold sweat and crying aloud in terror
because the ghosts that haunted the deserted palace had come
to gaze upon him as he slept.

Everywhere in this world the ghosts of the dead start up
beneath the feet of the living. At the end of the Ostrallee a
prince carved in stone scrapes his violin as you pass. In the
Thomé House, grand lords of other days came forth from their
tarnished frames. When you come back from school of an afternoon, what shades are those on the landing but the shades of
your two fathers, Wagner and Geyer, come to strike terror into
you when you have been idle at your work? And next 'tis a pupil,
a classmate, whom death had suddenly taken off. His school-
fellows were bidden write some verses in his memory, whereof
the best was to be accorded the honours of print. It was Richard
Geyer who came out on top. Straightway he wrote another poem,
on the death of Ulysses. Then came the death of the one and
only god who had taken up his abode among mortals—Karl
Maria von Weber. It was through Weber and none other that
he had attained consciousness of himself, consciousness that he
was a German; to Weber he owed it that he came to understand
what it means to have a country of your own. And now Weber
had vanished, too. What a world of ghosts!

Is he a poet? These visitants from the world of the dead, all
these strange things that happened to him, those prizes that fell
to him at school—did not the whole seem to point to a vocation
of the spirit? That is what little Cecile affirmed, and he himself
was only too ready to believe it. So he wrote a play and animated
with life a whole theatre of marionettes. However, the experiment did not seem to him conclusive. His sisters frankly made
fun of him. "Already I can hear the prancing of your lordship's
steed!" This sentence which they kept throwing up at him got
on his nerves and made him blush, yet it is the only line in the
whole play which he was destined never to forget. It was rather
the scenery, the dresses, and the masks that stirred his fancy,
and a little bit of coloured rag or painted cardboard forthwith
transported him from reality to the land of dreams and make-
believe. We have now reached that complicated stage in the
child's life when, amid so many dawning and divergent apti-
tudes, he suddenly determines to follow this line rather than
that; this appeal of the creative imagination in preference to
that other course suggested by example or precept; this obscure
and possibly prophetic instinct rather than the easier and more

obvious pursuit of things for which he had already earned some meed of praise. "The road we travel," says Bergson, "is, as it were, strewn with the fragments of all the things we once began to be, of all the things we might have been." The child Wagner had now arrived at his first cross-roads. Equally responsive to music, to poetry, to the stage, to the fortuitous emotional experiences of the hour, fond of books and study, it only required, as it usually does in human life, a series of chances more or less convergent to set him on his destined path.

At the outset, it was Shakespeare, master of all those conceptions of the imagination that partake alike of passion and reality. So profound was his effect upon the pupil's mind that he pored over dictionary and grammar to see if he could not render, in appropriate metre, the deathless monologue of Romeo. Then came the *Odyssey*, of which he boasts of translating the first twelve books, a task which earned him the praise of his favourite tutor, Herr Sillig, whose aim it was to make a philologist of this turbulent but industrious scholar. Promotion for him was easy and rapid at school and he set to work with fiery zeal on a vast tragedy in verse concerning Herakles, after the Shakespearean model. Twenty-four persons are slain in it, most of whom, however, reappear as ghosts in the last act.

But at this point a great change took place in his family's affairs—a change that gave an entirely new direction to the careers of its several members. Rosalie obtained a long engagement in the theatre at Prague, where Clara had already been appearing as a professional singer. Albert transferred his activities from the theatre at Breslau to the theatre at Augsburg; while Louise joined the Leipzig players. Madame Geyer therefore decided to give up her house at Dresden and go and live in Prague. Richard alone stayed on for the time being in his native town, and he was put to board with some friends called Boehme, whose son Robert was a schoolfellow of Richard's at the Kreuzschule. But that arrangement did not last. In the course of this transitional period one circumstance deserves mention, because it relates to the inmost recesses of his sexual nature, and because Wagner himself thought it worth recording.

These Boehmes, who lived on quite a modest scale, were at considerably close quarters in their little house. Some girl friends came to visit the daughters, who were already grown up, and one of them, Amelie Hoffmann, made a great impression on the young lad. She was decidedly good-looking, always carefully dressed, and whenever she came into the living-room she filled young Richard with admiration. And so he took it into his head one day to pretend to be overcome with an irresistible attack of drowsiness, "in order," he tells us, "to make the young girls help me upstairs to bed, for on such occasions 1 had perceived with pleasurable surprise the delicious perturbation into which I was thrown by contact with them." We will not attach too much importance to this haunting reminiscence, but, except for the birch of Mademoiselle Lambercier, we seem to have here, in this passive surrender, something that recalls Jean Jacques Rousseau. Perhaps, after all, the advent of puberty exhibits a certain degree of similarity in all men, and is characterized by emotions in which smell and touch appear to be the principal agents. Soon after this Richard, in company with his friend, Robert Boehme, set out to walk from Dresden to Prague, where he would see his kinsfolk again. But both of the boys were terribly short of money, and money had to be got somehow. Richard didn't let it trouble him long. What is money, after all? This man has it; that man hasn't. But that makes no difference to their value as men. As he was plodding along the highway, a stylish equipage hove in sight. Without a moment's hesitation Richard stops it and addresses its occupants, what time Robert is crouching in the hedge, and asks for alms. It was not the first time he had played the beggar. Nor was it to be the last.

"I love them who despise greatly," said Zarathustra. "I love the man who lives to know and is resolved to know. I love the man who disdains to be overloaded with virtue."

These were the days when he was being taught religion, the days of his first communion. But it was only the communion that left its mark on the young man's mind. Of the catechism, he recked little, thinking himself a great deal too much of a man for such childish things. He bade adieu to the Boehmes and took up his quarters in a garret, where he set to work on a great poetic drama entitled *Leubald and Adelaide*, a thing of far greater importance in his eyes than his lessons in religion and philosophy. Nevertheless, just as he was proceeding to communion, just when the organ was playing and the young communicants were making their way in procession towards the holy table, the young rhymster was so overwhelmed with emotion, that he would never again renew the experience.

He was now full of the idea of leaving Dresden and settling down in Leipzig. In Dresden he had but few friends, few ties; whereas Leipzig, whither his mother had returned in order to be near Louise, was his birthplace, the family home, and, moreover, it could boast of being a university city. Then again, Louise charmed and attracted him. He knew less of her than of any of his other sisters, as she had always lived away from home. She was beautiful and she was twenty-two. Perhaps she would be a friend to him . . . especially when he donned his student's cap! The best way to get back to Leipzig was to secure his dismissal from the school in Dresden. That was as simple as daylight. It happened that, just then, he was smarting under a punishment he deemed unjust. What could be better or easier than to spring a lie. His family had ordered him home, he said. Splendid; the trick worked to perfection; and so in the Christmas of 1827, behold this lad of fifteen at last in the city of his heart's desire!

Stowed away in his trunk he had brought with him the first of his manuscripts, *Leubald and Adelaide*, the *summa* of his knowledge and experiences, he fondly thinks. It was, in matter of fact, much rather the *summa* of what he had read. Hamlet and King Lear were the chief characters; they were almost undisguised. They hold forth on life, on love, on revenge, under the thin disguise of Astolf and Leubald. The entire plot is but a series of crimes perpetrated by the hero in his pursuit of Adelaide, with whom he comes up at last, and embraces in her tomb, as in *Romeo and Juliet*. He found himself in terribly hot water with his people when they got to know that the total outcome of his last year's work had only been a monster like that. The youthful Richard was forthwith consigned to the Nicolaischule, where he was examined and put in "Tertia," though at Dresden he had got half way through "Secunda." This was a crushing blow to his pride. It meant giving up Homer, Shakespeare, and the rest, and going back to simple baby-reading. What greater humiliation could there be for such a youngster than this—to have to call down to earth the most sumptuous imagination just as it was essaying its initial flight? There was but one way out of this Slough of Despond, and that was by way of an act of faith in himself. Lonely and bemocked, he must do something to regain his lost prestige. A sudden light breaks in upon his soul: Music! "I knew what no one else knew, and that was that no one could really judge my work until it had been set to music. That music I made up my mind to compose myself, and to get it performed."

Chapter IV

THE MASK OF BEETHOVEN

ONE evening he betook himself to the Gewandhaus, the famous Leipzig concert-hall. They were performing Beethoven's *Symphony in A*. He heard the overture to *Egmont*. It was so great a surprise, so swift and complete a revelation, that it brought on an attack of fever. It was a little sick lad that went back home again after that unforgettable performance; but, henceforth, no more telling people about the presentiments that fill him with joy and amazement and upset his whole physical economy! The lad had emerged from his chrysalis. He had unfolded his wings; his doubts and fears had left him. Behold him free now to wander in the magic realms of sound. Side by side with his older idols a new god was enthroned. It was Beethoven. And he set to work to learn all about his life, his deafness, his works, and his death. "I pictured him a sort of superhuman being," he says. He saw him in his dreams, and spoke with him, and when he awoke his face was bathed in tears. It is remarkable, however, that he conceived no passion for any particular instrument from which to charm the sounds that enchanted him, as is the case with most musical children. The days of *Der Freischütz* and Master Humann's piano had gone by. The sole desire that consumed him now was to learn to compose. What he had within him was too complex, too powerful, to be expressed on the notes of a keyboard or the four strings of the violin. He needed all the vast and varied resources of a mighty orchestra. Secretly, unbeknown to anybody, he paid a clandestine visit to Wieck, the music-dealer, and hired on credit *La Méthode de basse chiffrée*, by Logier. "The monetary difficulties which dogged me all through life, started from that moment." The pecuniary anxiety would have sat lightly upon him, had it not been that Wieck's requests and threatening demands for payment let the cat out of the bag at home and resulted in further trouble with his family. What were they to do with a

20

young scapegrace who absconded from one school, idled away his time at another, got into debt, scribbled poetry, and threatened to let everything go hang, so only he had time to spend his days composing music? His mother saw there was only one thing for it—to let him follow his bent.

The result was that he had a few elementary lessons in fiddling with Robert Sipp, a violinist at the Gewandhaus. But he soon got sick of that. That wasn't at all what he wanted. Even then he saw that mere skill in playing an instrument, mere virtuosity, was quite a secondary and limited affair. He was then handed over to Gottlieb Müller, the organist, who instructed him in the rudiments of counterpoint and harmony. But here were further difficulties. The young man refused to see the necessity for rules, and the whole system of counterpoint seemed to him so much arid pedantry, a walled garden with so many notices against trespassers stuck about the place, that talent and originality could not get a look in. He nearly gave up the whole business in disgust. He had come to look on music as nothing but "a sublime and mystical monstrosity entirely unamenable to rules of any kind."

His sole resource in the face of these discouragements was in the lovely nights he spent diligently copying, beneath the lamp's soft glow, the works of his hero Beethoven. For there, at all events, the rules of Gottlieb Müller were magnificently disregarded. In them was life, a splendid disarray, freshness, surprise, and sometimes a sort of madness. It was like those marvellous *Tales of Hoffmann* wherein he found his daily nourishment. There was the same method in the madness, the same orderly disorder, which is the mark of everything that is really alive, really true, the same interfusion of extravagance and reason that one always finds in the things of nature. For all the differences that sundered these two men, they had a whole philosophy in common, pessimistic yet kindly, rugged, ironic and sometimes passing all understanding, but what mattered such obscurities? Moreover, is it not all for our good when a thing does not yield to us at the first blow? Uncle Adolf, too, was often enigmatic, often used strange words and involved himself in complex sentences from which he did not always find a satisfactory issue. But every mystery has its poetic value, and here, in the life of this uncle, who, the queer fellow, had just got married, having waited till he was round about fifty before he did so, there was mystery. In his work on *The Theatre and the Public*, mystery; mystery again in the war which the learned gentleman was waging in the name of Tieck, of Goethe, in defence of true but neglected art against the facile triumphs of those who were at heart only tradesmen and common hucksters. "Fortunately I've got plenty of enemies," he used to tell his nephew, "as many as I need to ensure my own growth and development." Every difficulty, every salutary obstacle he read of in the lives of people of intellect only awakened his enthusiasm. It consoled him for his early discomfiture, and sent him back to his copying, fired with renewed zeal. Needless to say the Nicolaischule had long been struck off his engagement list, and for six whole months he had not set foot inside the place. Of friends, too, he could do with few or none. His two brothers-in-law were enough for him; they impressed him by reason of their age and position. Louise, the sister he admired for her beauty, had married an influential young publisher called Friedrich Brockhaus; and Clara, the vocalist, who was achieving considerable success in Leipzig, had married Wolfram, the singer. All the same, Richard wanted some companion, some congenial person into whose ear he could pour all his schemes and wild ideas, some one out of the ordinary, some one who could understand, and his eye happened to fall on a great, lanky, hobbledehoy of a fellow he had several times observed in the different concert-rooms, a truly Hoffmannesque apparition; a very elongated body terminating in a tiny head, a strange, jerky manner of walking, and a still stranger one of talking to the members of the orchestra; but strangest of all was his habit of wagging his head and blowing out his cheeks as he listened to the music. He was clearly "touched," but why shouldn't he prove to be a musician of genius? Without the slightest hesitation Richard accosted him, discovered that his name was Flachs, went back with him to his house, and found to his joy that it was all littered with scores and manuscripts. He was, however, only a nincompoop on whom the music-dealers palmed off all their unsaleable stock. His collection included the works of Staerkel, Stanitz, Steibelt, and other nonentities, for of course Flachs hadn't a good word to say for Mozart and Beethoven. All the same he was an audience, some one to play to, and a composer forgives everything in a patient listener. So Richard played and Flachs listened, quiet and attentive, as long as needful. And one fine day it came to pass that the big Flachs took down the little Richard's airs and knocked up some sort of arrangement of them for wind instruments; and then, more wonderful still, Flachs handed the work to the band at Kintschy's Chalet Suisse, the fashionable pastry-cook's, and behold, it was played in public! What a sensation! Just think of it, the first public performance, and in a

Leipzig confectioner's, of music by Richard Wagner! The young débutant would have flung his arms about Flachs's neck had he not harboured a stray doubt or two regarding that gentleman's sanity. Doubt was turned into certainty a little while later when Flachs banged the door in his face in a fit of jealousy, jealousy not of the musician, but of the man, for Flachs, who had fallen in love with a lady of easy virtue, was afraid lest this young collegian, who had kicked over the traces of discipline, should prove a dangerous rival. Richard went off pondering deeply upon the new mystery on which he had unwittingly stumbled, the sickening mystery of the flesh and its lure.

For some temperaments there is perhaps nothing more distasteful—and therefore more suspect—than the real; nothing less fallacious—and so more authentic—than the imaginary. Such people exhibit in their composition a sort of inverted sense of values, an unconscious adaptation of the creative spirit to its secret needs. How brutally soever the world reveals itself in all its crudity to one whose soul is already stored with visions of its own, he suffers no lasting taint from the contact, but betakes himself with an added zest to the contemplation of the hidden treasures in his heart. Thus for young Wagner, the things which were most true and most real were Beethoven's death-mask, the scores of the master's works, which he had copied out by night, the purlieus of the new Theatre Royal, that universe of wings and corridors, of painted canvas, actors, actresses, music—handwritten or engraved. The false—well, that was everything else, school, the shops, Flachs's lady-love, and the thing called life. Brockhaus, who was doing well in business, had hold of the thread that leads one into the artificial world of men and women. But thanks to his sisters, particularly to Rosalie, Richard was able, when he pleased, to set foot on the *terra firma* of the theatre, where men divested themselves of their social make-believe, and lived as their hearts dictated. They played Goethe's *Faust*, Schiller's *William Tell*, Shakespeare's *Julius Cæsar*, *Macbeth*, and *Hamlet*. And now behold another planet swims into the artistic firmament and wins the applause of all, and that is Auber's *La Muette de Portici*. Who would have dreamed that such darling harmonies, a whole five act opera, a tragic theme with nothing of the "happy ending" which tradition looked on as essential, would come one day from France, where Italian music reigned supreme, with its sheepfolds, its shepherdesses, its ballets, its rose-wreathed maidens, its pompous high-priest, all surrounded by a bevy of dancing-girls in tights and muslin skirts.

La Muette de Portici presents an entire plot, or dramatic theme, developed throughout, from beginning to end, without a break, or any concession to the sentimental or the pretty-pretty, and more than that, an orchestration, a colour-scheme, a direct and dramatic use of the chorus, utterly unheard of in the history of opera up to that date. (If Auber's subsequent works failed to fulfil the anticipations of those who expected from him work of a similar calibre, the reason is that those works contained no similar passages of splendid daring; that they exhibit a return to the ordinary light-opera tradition. "What we wanted," said Wagner, later on, "was high emotion." Now that he had heard the *Symphony in A, Egmont* and *La Muette* one after another, the next thing he longed to hear was the great *Ninth Symphony.* It was said that Beethoven had composed it when he was half out of his mind and that it was the *non plus ultra*, the very limit, of the extravagant and the incomprehensible. All the more reason why he should study, and endeavour to seek out and isolate, the soul that inspired it. As soon as he succeeded in getting it into his hands, the young man felt its profound fascination, as though Fate had laid its tremendous hand on him, for in it resides, indeed, the secret of all music, the deep-sounding burden of a soul; not only of Beethoven's soul, but of Wagner's also. Forthwith he sets himself to copy out this mysterious and enigmatic *Ninth*, to steep his spirit in its scheme, and when the first beams of morning light fell upon him while yet he was buried in his task, he was seized with a kind of terror and began to shout aloud. After a few weeks of nightly toil, the child had copied out the whole of this labyrinthine score and completed a simplified version of it for the piano. Schott, the Mainz publisher, to whom he sent it, complimented him on his work, and offered him a copy of the *Missa Solemnis* in exchange.

Then came another stirring event, the memory of which never faded from his mind, and that was hearing Wilhelmine Schroeder-Devrient in *Fidelio* at the Leipzig theatre. "I remember nothing," he afterwards confessed, "that ever affected me so deeply as that performance." And there came an immense, a profound, emotional upheaval. He longed to create, to give utterance in some way, he knew not how, to the tumult that possessed him when he heard this young *prima donna* of twenty-five summers sing her glorious part. He wrote her a letter and left it at her hotel. Well for her if she remembered that obscure and commonplace name, for, one day, when that name came to signify something in the world of art, she would know it was to her that he owed the impulse which fired him to pursue his chosen path. As for seeing her, or speaking to her, the idea never entered his head. He made no attempt at critical analysis, for of the critical sense he was utterly devoid. But he felt, he arranged, he classified what he heard, and assigned it its proper rank and dignity; and the tact and judgment which so infallibly guided him herein is yet another addition to his stock of mysteries. Though his life was spent among women, woman was a closed book to him. With never a friend to call his own, it was on the dead that he lavished all the passion of his being. Since he knew not life at first hand, he must needs invent a world of his own. But who shall tell us from what hidden wells the song of an artist steals to the surface, to soar aloft at last, when the appointed day shall dawn, in melodies in which each and every one who hears them seems to be listening to himself, to the music of his own, his inmost soul!

Chapter V

STUDIOSUS MUSICÆ

SEPTEMBER of the year 1830 had not far advanced when the political storm which had been raging over Paris all through the summer began to loom ominously in the Leipzig sky. The French king, Charles X, had been driven from his throne. Once more the mob beheld La Fayette, an old man now, bestriding his charger, and shouting, as of old in 1790, "We'll win our freedom, or die to a man." The same tempestuous blast of popular insurrection suddenly arose in Saxony, where the people were bullied by a brutal police, misgoverned by a spendthrift cabinet, and treated like pawns by a magistracy whose members sought, in the stews and gambling-dens, to make up for the hard times they had suffered when Napoleon was in the saddle. News came from Dresden that the king had been compelled to appoint his nephew, Friedrich Augustus, as regent, and the latter hurriedly granted a new constitution to the people. There was a strong suspicion of gunpowder and bloodshed in the political atmosphere. It looked as if heroism was likely to become epidemic, and the names of La Fayette, Kosciuszko, and Lord Byron were often and vociferously invoked. The students of Leipzig, following the prevailing fashion, "downed tools" like the rest and threw in their lot with the workers. A few of them having been arrested in the course of the public disturbance, they all assembled in a body and, forming in procession, marched along, shouting and singing, to the prison where their comrades were confined, in order to set them free. In the event, the arrested men were set at liberty, but their friends, whose blood was now well up, were not going home without fleshing their teeth in a victim or two. Beneath their caps of many colours the students put their heads together and conceived the notion of making a descent on certain houses of ill-repute frequented by elderly gentlemen desirous of forgetting, for a few transitory moments, the burden of their years.

26

Off, then, the students rushed, through street and alley and byway, to where these haunts of senile dissipation wink and leer behind their drawn shutters. The first one they came to they carried by assault. In they burst, smashed everything they could lay their hands on, seized the women and thrashed them soundly. Among the most violent of these chastisers of vice was a little sapling of a fellow belonging to the Nicolaischule. Madder, wilder than the others, he seemed to outdo them all in fury, and the sight of the mêlée affected him like strong drink. This miserable place having been sacked from attic to cellar, the pillagers poured along like a human torrent in the direction of another similar establishment at the opposite end of the town, and there the same disorderly scenes were repeated. Again, the young collegian distinguished himself by deeds of prowess that elicited the applause of these chaste and zealous avengers of public morals. Night fell upon the scene of conflict. No blood had been shed save the blood of these young champions of social purity; and the night was dark indeed, for all the street lamps had been broken, and there was a total eclipse of the moon. When Richard awoke next morning in the room sacred to Beethoven, the first thing that caught his eye was the solitary trophy that remained in his possession to remind him of his début as a man and revolutionary; and that was a tattered shred of red curtain.

For some weeks following, the disorder waxed and waned by turns. The students had become the tutelary deities of Leipzig. They formed themselves into trained-bands and occupied the military posts. And, as generally happens, these middle-class disturbers of the peace, whose zeal was fanned by their professors, took to posing as champions of the law and as preservers of order and property. They laid down the law for the rest of the city and lived at the expense of the municipality, receiving visits from their fellow students of the universities of Halle, Goettingen, and Jena, who arrived in cartloads. Their headquarters were at the establishment of Friedrich Brockhaus, the publisher, who, by thus offering them hospitality, ensured the immunity of his hundred and twenty work-people and his printing-plant. This arrangement shed a reflected glory on Richard, and permanently established him in the good graces of these revolutionary young men. Soon, however, there came about a very decided change in public opinion. It began to dawn upon people that these students were, for the most part, just so many adventurers and parasites. A body of municipal guards was created, regular soldiers were drafted to the spot, and the students returned to their cafés.

And by the same token, Richard betook himself to school, the Thomasschule, where he was entered among the seniors. But that was no reason for giving up his music. On the contrary, he returned to his composing and soon completed an overture in B flat major. He took it to Heinrich Dorn, the young conductor of the theatre orchestra, whom he had met at Brockhaus's, and had also seen in company with his sisters. To his astonishment, Dorn said he would play it. Dorn, who favoured the new school, was a witty and cultured man with a considerable fund of dry humour to his credit. His first impression was one of amazement at the extent of young Wagner's knowledge of Beethoven's scores. No one could really come up to him in this. But what did he know besides? What was he good for? That remained to be seen. At any rate, his manuscript was remarkable for the elegance of its penmanship, and the little score he had brought with him had been executed with fastidious care. In his anxiety for neatness and clarity, he had written the string part in red ink, the wood-wind in green, and the brass in black.

The orchestra tried it over and the result was an immense burst of laughter. The older members of the band wanted to give it up; but Dorn stuck to his guns, and the night of the concert—the popular Christmas concert—the piece was performed under the title of *New Overture*, composer not stated. Richard was rather anxious about the reception it would get, and said nothing at all about the affair to anyone except his sister Ottilie, who went with him to the theatre. She joined the Brockhaus party in their box, but the little composer himself had no end of trouble to get past the barrier. In the end he had to tell the doorkeeper who he was before they would let him through, and he managed to slip in just as the band struck up the opening bars of his work. "The main theme of the allegro," Wagner informs us, "was in four time, but after every measure I had put in a fifth beat, quite independent of the melody, which interpolation was emphasized by a beat on the big drum." At first the audience were too much astonished to do anything, but when this portentous noise kept on recurring at regular intervals, they began to smile, and very soon everybody in the hall was consumed with laughter. The composer went through the torments of hell, for he knew he had marked this beat *fortissimo* all through the piece. He became oblivious to all around him and only recovered consciousness when the music ceased, like the end of "some impossible dream." The public being German and well-behaved, no hisses or protests followed, but, rather, a sensation of stupor and amazement. The composer hurried from the place, overwhelmed with confusion.

For many a youngster, such an experience would have given the *coup de grâce* to all his ambitions to shine as a composer, and would have meant farewell, a long farewell, to music. But Richard Wagner, not so easily daunted, at once set to work to write an overture to the *Fiancée de Messine*, and composed a quantity of incidental music for Goethe's *Faust*. Then a wave of enthusiasm for student life came over him again, and he started a club on the same lines as the famous *Saxonia* with its aureole of revolutionary idealism. Of course this meant sporting top-boots, white buckskin breeches, sword practice, and beer swilling *ad lib*. At the inaugural banquet he was then and there elected *subsenior*. But the experiment was severely frowned upon by the disciplinary council, and the Head informed young Wagner that, since he never attended any of the lectures, his name would be struck off the register. Thus he said good-bye to his third college, only to enroll himself—on the 23rd of February, 1831— as a student of musical art—*studiosus musicæ*—in the ancient University of Leipzig, whose easy-going rule and striking costume he had admired and coveted for many years past.

Although he was unable to matriculate in the strictly orthodox fashion, Richard Wagner was nevertheless put on the students' register. He attended the philosophy course of Professor Krug, and Weiss's lectures on æsthetics. Of Krug he pretty soon got tired. Weiss he knew personally, having heard him contending in argument with his Uncle Adolf. His features attracted him, but the extreme abstractness of his ideas and the profound obscurity of his style preyed considerably on his nerves. One thing, however, he did get out of these elucubrations, which was that "the graver problems that confront the human mind are incapable of solution by the masses." If there was such a thing as an intellectual aristocracy, it was pretty high up, soaring somewhere in the clouds. No matter; he would get there. Meantime there were other things in the world besides the speculations of the philosophers. To start with there was this famous Saxonia club, with its emblematic colours of blue and white; there were duels, and there were "sing-songs." Among the senior men—graduates of long standing in the faculty of beer-swilling —Richard came across some of the heroes of September, 1830. In particular there was Gebhardt, who could hold out a couple of men at arm's-length, one in each hand, and stop a fiacre going full tilt by catching hold of one of the wheels. And there was Degelow, who specialised in duels and affairs of the heart; Stelzer, a tenth-year's man, who posed as a decadent; and last, but not least, there was Schroeter, beloved of the Muses, a soft-mannered, daintily spoken young man, and very agreeable company. In no long time, Wagner, who concealed a bellicose temper in his little person, had four or five duels on hand. But by a succession of accidents, which rather "gives one to think," none of these meetings came off. One of his adversaries had the radial artery of his right arm severed in a previous affair; two others disappeared to evade their creditors. One Fischer, the night before he was due to fight with Wagner, had a serious affray in a house of ill-fame and had to be carted off to a hospital. Finally, the most redoubtable antagonist of them all, Degelow, who belonged to the clan of "The Giants"—that had not daunted Richard—was run through the body at Jena, and fell dead on the spot.

These sensational but abortive events were followed by revels, one of which went on for three days and three nights. Richard was the last to leave, for his motto in these things was "Nothing succeeds like excess." It was then that he discovered a new passion, a terrible and, of course, an inebriating passion, namely gambling and card-playing. To begin with, he only staked just enough to win the couple of thalers necessary to pay the expenses of this escapade. Wagner's constant and heart-breaking wrestle with fate for money began during that three-night students' orgy. For three weeks on end he tried his luck with high and low, in all the gambling-hells of Leipzig. The thing culminated in a kind of paroxysm, one of those terrific crises in which the fever consumes both itself and victim, or is conquered by the latter for good and all.

It happened that, this time, Richard had his mother's annuity cheque in his pocket. Not a second did he hesitate. He would stake it and risk the lot. It should be all or nothing. If he lost the money, which was pretty well all his people had to live on, he would clear out of the country and never return. If he won, he would pay off his debts and never touch a card again. Most of us have heard that vow before. Well, he went boldly up to the table, elbowing his way through a crowd of greedy old hags and professional crooks. He played. No luck. Well, that was so much gone! Another try. Again no luck. Every time the cards came down his little pile was lowered. And now he was down to his last crown piece. It was all he had left and he crushed it nervously in a feverish hand. However, he pushed it forward, and though he had not had a crumb to eat or a drop to drink, he was so dreadfully upset with excitement that he had to rush out of the room and be sick. When he came back, lo! another crownpiece alongside his own. Then two more! From that moment his luck turned; he went on winning. And with a superhuman effort of will he staked his all each time, knowing perfectly well that his whole future hung on the upturn of a card. At length the bank broke—cleaned out! And Richard pouched his little fortune, enough, however, to pay his mother and square up all his debts. Away he rushed, got into his quarters by climbing up a wall, and went off into a dead slumber. "From that day onward," he says, "I was never tempted again." He was delivered, and it was a new world on which he opened his eyes. As usual, after great crises in which a man's immortal soul has been at stake, there was a strong upward revulsion. It is with an older head and a clearer vision that we look out towards new ideals which a greater knowledge of ourselves holds up for our attainment. But there are other things to be done in the world than merely to gratify our desires. Wagner has a sort of intellectual reaction and now makes a really genuine and stubborn effort to conquer the secrets of harmony and counterpoint. Leipzig boasted one of those conscientious organist pedagogues who are at all times an honour to their calling. The man in question, Theodor Weinlig by name, was, as it happened, *cantor* at Saint Thomas's. He saw with half an eye that there was plenty of original, if undisciplined, ability in this little pupil of his. He must beware of cramming him with too much theory; he must give him something practical for his imagination to feed on, lead him on by easy stages to find out his rules for himself, to construct an architectural plan within whose limits he could in due time fashion his own individual style. He made his pupil begin again at the beginning, advancing step by step, from example to example, taking Bach and Mozart as his models, telling Richard that he must give form to the themes of which his head was full, that he must analyze them, chart out their way for them, amplify them, write them out in the form of a fugue or a canon, never letting anything slovenly or incorrect pass through undetected. What had hitherto seemed to Wagner mere freakishness, or unreasoning pedantry, was made clear in the soft and steady glow with which knowledge illumines the pleasures of the mind. He learnt to recognize the inner spirit of his favourite masters and then to stimulate that precision of insight, that sensitive understanding of a work which enables us to discern the hidden intentions, the delicate nuances which the composer himself has only half revealed. It was not merely the science of notes that Weinlig taught his pupil, but the art of listening to them, of weighing their values. Little did he think that he was planting in him the seeds of a critical sense which would one day make his pupil, with his deep emotional insight, an incomparable *chef d'orchestre*. Six months after his first lesson, Weinlig went to call on Madame Geyer. Quite unprepared for such a visit, the mother tremblingly asked herself what new misdeeds her Richard had been committing, that Master Weinlig had come thither to complain of him. Judge, then, of her astonishment when the *cantor* began praising her son to the skies. In short, he admitted that he had nothing more to teach him. By way of setting, as it were, the seal of approbation on his good conduct, Richard was given leave to have two of his pieces printed at Breitkopf and Haertel's, the well-known music-publishers. They were published in 1832 and consisted of a sonata for the piano in B major, and a polonaise in D major, numbered respectively, opus I and opus II. (This was the only time Wagner ever put a number to his compositions.) About the same time he composed and completed an overture in D minor, which was performed at the Gewandhaus on the 23rd of February, 1832. For the first time his name appeared on a program, and the piece was a decided success. It made up handsomely for that ill-fated experiment with the big drum solo. The critics were more than friendly, they were eulogistic, and the newspapers took good care to make a note, for future reference, of the name of this young novice who had sprung from Heaven knows where. And as this springtime was big with promise, another overture of Richard Wagner's was played in the theatre before each performance of Raupach's *King Enzio*. As if this was not enough, a third overture in C major this time, was played at the Gewandhaus, the occasion being a concert given by Madame Palazzesi, a fashionable singer from the Italian theatre at Dresden. The young composer had written it on rigidly contrapuntal lines, in strict accordance with what Weinlig had taught him. Unfortunately, Beethoven's *Egmont*, which was also on the program, offered a striking contrast to Richard's very geometrical composition. Considering the ruthless discipline he must have applied to himself to produce so very restrained a result, one can understand the shock to his feelings when, after the Beethoven overture, his mother exclaimed, "There's no getting away from it, that sort of music is a great deal more moving than those stupid fugues." From this time forth, Richard abandoned himself wholly to the promptings of the inner spirit. He felt that the imprisoned giant needed to stretch his limbs, to burst the bonds that confined him. He felt he would never discover his real self until he returned to those wild, uncultivated regions whence he drew the free harmonies, the enchanting disarray of his real master, the old, deaf wizard of the *Ninth Symphony*. Without delay he flung himself into a new work: the *Symphony in C major*. Amid all these multifarious tasks, a drama was being unfolded on the political stage in Poland which was flinging the reflection of its lurid gleams over the four quarters of the firmament. As with Chopin, it kindled in Wagner's breast fires fierce and hidden. But what in Chopin's case found dolorous utterance in the wistful melancholy that pervades his nocturnes, is in strange contrast to the volcanic convulsions which shook the bosom of Richard Wagner. After the fall of Warsaw, a whole nation of homeless people began their long trek across the broad German land. As they passed by, in wagons or on horseback, on their endless pilgrimage, their faces set towards France, young Wagner hastened forth to greet them, holding converse with them, telling of his admiration, saying that he was proud to clasp the hands of those who were "so indomitable in their suffering and sorrow."

One night, at the Gewandhaus, he observed the illustrious Count Vincent Tyskiewitsch, one of the heroes of Ostrolenka, whose bronzed visage, lofty bearing, embroidered coat, and red-velvet cap filled him with a strange sensation of satisfaction. Shortly afterwards Wagner had the supreme honour of meeting this picturesque incarnation of his new ideal at Brockhaus's, his brother-in-law's. Tyskiewitsch was sympathetically disposed towards this "intense" young man, and invited him to a *fête* which the Polish exiles were giving on the 3rd of May to celebrate the anniversary of their Constitution. The banquet soon developed into an orgy. They sang and they drank, and Richard was by no means the least excited of the party. Their patriotism found vent in songs and tears; in a word the whole thing was a colossal riot. It finished up in the garden of an inn with groups of lovers wandering about amid umbrageous groves and verdant lawns.

The insight he had lately gained into life, the desire which fires every passionate soul of twenty to pit his new-found strength against the great social machine, so slow, so unjustly logical, sometimes indeed so brutal, and yet again occasionally so docile, so tractable when a man rises up boldly and faces it, resolved to change its direction—all these considerations, obscure or guessed at, harass him and goad him on to essay a fresh escape. Vienna, the City of Music, Beethoven's garret, Vienna so harsh to the divine Mozart, was soon to behold, treading its pavements, where but a while ago the willowy form of Chopin might have been seen gliding by—was soon to behold Wagner, young Wagner, the ardent *studiosus musicæ.*

Count Tyskiewitsch himself offered the young man a lift in his famous four-horse barouche, whose prancing steeds, clattering along the cobbled streets, sent the peaceful pedestrians of Leipzig helter-skelter for refuge to the first porch or doorway that offered. The noble lord kept humming airs from *Zampa*, but his little friend had in his bag something that would beat *Zampa* into a cocked hat, and that was his symphony. A fig for *Zampa*, and Strauss and all his sugary lollipops. Yesterday he had graduated in harmony: tomorrow he was to graduate in life. Not bad for a boy of nineteen!

"For my part," says Gide, in his *Un Esprit non prévenu,* "being convinced from experience and history that the most useful forces at our command are those which at first sight look the most rebellious, and being sure of my own inner strength, I never thought of casting aside anything I fancied I could reduce to service and of which I was sure I could make good use. The things that bring trouble and perplexity today are precisely those which will prove our best friends tomorrow."

Such perplexing elements we have, so far, divined rather than observed, in young Wagner. All the same, they were there in embryo. I am putting them down by way of *marginalia* in these introductory pages of his life story, convinced that, when the time comes, he will be able to turn them to excellent account. That there was some ground for apprehension in the disorder, the unbridled appetites and violence of the boy, there is no gainsaying. But that he was already conscious of a power to dominate and direct them is what I deduce with certainty from the evidence of his growing strength of character. It is no tale of childish precocity that I have to tell, but the slow and undisciplined emergence of an artist whose greatness lies in his endless strivings towards the ideal, towards perfection; whereas the man himself, as distinct from the artist, remains to the end of the chapter imprisoned within his own shadow, intractable, imperfectible, the Satanic and almost mocking foil to his heroic ideal.

Chapter VI

PREMONITIONS: THE FAIRIES

"THE cholera was there in person before me. I saw it; I could have touched it with my hands; it crept into my bed and flung its arms about me. My limbs froze; I felt the grip of death about my heart. I don't know whether I was waking or sleeping, but when morning broke, I was amazed to find myself still alive and in perfectly good health. And so I came scathless to Vienna, and though the epidemic was raging there as well, it got no hold on me."

The cholera, or the devil, if you will, was the famous Johann Strauss, the composer of hosts of waltzes and potted honey that were being sung all over the place, from one end of the country to another. The young man took a good look at him and his orchestra, which he led to the attack, wildly waving his violin, like a captain of cavalry hurling his troopers into the mêlée, in a sort of shouting frenzy. *Zampa* and Johann Strauss were all the rage in Vienna in that sensational summer of 1832. In fact, they *were* Vienna. The spirit of Beethoven was completely overshadowed in this capital of dance and song. It did not even trouble the nineteen-year-old Wagner any longer now, so proud was he of his dawning whiskers, his tall hat and cashmere breeches. And when all was said and done, there's no doubt he did enjoy those merry evenings at the Theatre An der Wien. But the thing wouldn't have been complete without a little sentimental music, for the budding heart was anxiously awaiting the hour of its first unfolding. The hour soon came. A month later, when Richard had arrived at Pravonin, the Comte de Pachta's seat, some miles from Prague, the count's two daughters (both of them illegitimate), Jenny and Augusta Raymann, forthwith set to work to turn his head. They were friends of his sister Ottilie's. Thus Richard set foot on the path of dalliance, the only place where a man's title to fame depends on the wounds he sustains.

We need attach but a qualified significance to the flirtations of
Wagner and Jenny Raymann. A few weeks, and it was all over.
But, in the course of them, we hear the first outcries of a man
who was fated to utter many more poignant cries to which the
whole world would listen; we see his young delight, we see his
first discomfiture. "An ideal of beauty, and a glowing fancy,
there you have the whole thing in a nutshell." Thus he writes
to his friend Theodor Apel. "Looking at her through rose-
coloured glasses, I saw in her everything I wished to see; that
was the worst of it. What a struggle I had with my unruly
passions. What may wound an ardent love you may well guess.
But what can kill it outright is too horrible for words. Listen
then, and give me of your pity: she was not worthy of my
love." Rather ingenuously put, perhaps; still, with varying
degrees of taste and forcefulness, most men talk pretty much
like that. But one doesn't often find a mere youngster writing in
that strain. Such expressions are the initial symptoms of the
great malady of mankind, whose first onslaught was, in this
case, destined to determine irrevocably the course of its subsequent evolution. First of all there was this passion for wilful
idealization; then came the awakening and the inevitable blow
to his pride; after that, a storm of passionate upbraiding; and
finally, a fit of proud disdain. Directly importuned by the senses,
desperately eager to indulge them, his outraged demon punished
him for his womanish emotionalism by chastising him with the
rods of the intellect. And this was how the love of woman found
its way into the youngster's life, to the sorrow and undoing of
those who were destined to love him in the days to come. Jenny
and Augusta made excellent sport of this raw and exacting
lover. Of course they did not take him seriously, not they! They
were on the lookout for some one belonging to the neighbouring
gentry, or lesser nobility, with whom they could settle down in
comfortable security, and it is probable that they never had an
inkling of what seeds of poetry and hate they had sown in that
ardent soil.

When, after six weeks at the Château de Pravonin, he bade
adieu to these captivating damsels, Wagner could not have said
whether he was more angry than amorous, more amorous than
angry. "I grew harsh and bitter and went wandering off into
theories about the French Revolution." There was no doubt
he loved them both, and would have liked to make the pair of
them his mistresses; no doubt he hesitated as to , hether he
should adore two saints or despise a brace of wantons, from the
lofty altitudes of a spirit at once tyrannical and tender. Looking

at it from the lowest standpoint, it was an instructive interlude for a youth serving his apprenticeship to life. He thought his desire would be contagious, that it would spread to the objects of it. He had to change his tune; to yield to the convincing but unwelcome truth that women are preëminently sensitive to three things—good looks, experience, and money. Of money Wagner had not a penny; of experience, not a scrap. What, then, of his looks? The worst misfortune that can befall a man is to have big ideas in a diminutive body. What pretty girl could lose her heart to a stumpy man? His quarrel was with fate, with nature. It was just his wretched luck. However, what about Napoleon? And Beethoven? And Cæsar? Has it not always been the little men who have moulded the destinies of the world? As for money and experience—he would see to that.

Cramming his latest poetical attempts into his travelling-bag, as well as his musical MSS., he said good-bye to the stars that kissed the turrets and roofs of the Château, to the immemorial trees that adorned its park, to its aristocratic inhabitants, at once so kindly and so corrupt. From there he went on to Prague, learned the art of hitting it off with second-rate musicians, and thus contrived to secure a public performance for his *Symphony in C major*. But what he did fling himself into with frenzied eagerness was his first opera, *Die Hochzeit*, based on a libretto in verse which he had just turned out.

"Two noble families in the middle ages had long been sundered by a bitter feud. . . . A venerable chieftain, a young bride, a beloved suitor. . . . Bridal feast interrupted by tragic intrusion of a rival." *Romeo and Juliet* dished up anew, with echoes of the *Leubald and Adelaide* of bygone days. Fiery the deeds and strange the names he gave his characters: Ada, Arindal, Cadolt, Hardmer, Admund. He did not know, himself, where he got these heraldic names, all these burgraves, pale heroines, dames-in-waiting, and bearded seneschals. Needless to say, "this gloomy, sombre-sounding affair winds up with a coffin all splashed with gore. Horror upon horror, woe upon woe." A nice contrast and no mistake to Jenny's charming mouth, that "rose-wreathed porch of pearl."

His poem finished and his opera well on the way, Richard sent the whole thing to his sister Rosalie, the eldest of the family. She was his favourite now. He loved and respected her above the rest because he had found her weeping one day over her wasted youth. Secret tears, beheld by chance—they made a lasting impression on Wagner, an impression in which shyness and fear, enthusiasm and respect, were mingled in an almost mystical emotion. And he had always thought that sister the luckiest of them all. Her salary as an actress went a long way towards paying the expenses of the whole family. She had her own special apartment in their mother's house. Flattered and made much of, she was enveloped with a sort of aureole of respect and admiration, as though she were a divinity. Everyone called her *"petite âme,"* the name that Geyer had given her. Her friends, selected with care, seemed to belong to a race apart. Whatever she said was law. And it was she whom he had heard sobbing! Well, it was to her, now, that Richard dedicated his efforts. It was for her sake that he wanted to "make good," to redeem his futile past. She would restore for her whole sex the respect which those frivolous young countesses had all but made him lose. When, therefore, Rosalie returned *Die Hochzeit* to her brother, saying she could find no interest in the dismal work, he did not hesitate, but promptly and cheerfully tore his manuscript to shreds. This was the first time in his life that so formidable a reverse brought no soreness in its train. For the first time it was borne in upon him that only to him who has the strength to destroy is vouchsafed the power to create.

The power to destroy is unquestionably an asset. Tearing up his failures, rebelling against a humdrum existence, were both manifestations of the same force. What was he going to do at Leipzig, tied up to his people and living at their expense? It would be more honourable to make his own living and carve out a career for himself somewhere else. So he made up his mind to go away and remain away indefinitely, trusting to whatever luck chance might bring him. However, his family did their best to keep him. Even his sister Rosalie began to think that this queer brother of hers had a future before him, and tried hard to persuade him to settle down in Leipzig. One of his new friends, Heinrich Laube, who had founded the group of writers known as *Das Junge Europa* which began with a great flourish of trumpets, pronounced himself favourably impressed by the new composer. A few weeks after the first audition of the *Symphony in C major*, which was performed on the 10th of January, 1833, at the Gewandhaus, Laube published an article of considerable importance regarding him, predicting a striking musical career for Richard Wagner. More than that, the first wave of his Wagnerian enthusiasm carried him further still and he offered to entrust the young man with a libretto, originally intended for Meyerbeer, on the subject of Kosciuszko, the Polish patriot. But Wagner knew that his music was already too sturdy, too individual in character, to be twined like ivy in obedient tendrils round the branches of an alien tree. He set out for Wurzburg, and from there he wrote to Laube, declining his offer. This was plucky, but it was not very diplomatic. In any event, Laube took it all in good part. He, too, may have felt that the little man was quite capable of looking after his own affairs.

After Vienna, Wurzburg had but one solitary charm, and that was the charm of a quiet Old World country town. Nevertheless, it was the scene of the *Tales of Hoffmann*; moreover, Richard's brother Albert, whom he had not seen for several years, was there. Albert, now a married man with two charming little girls, united in his own person the functions of tenor, actor, and stage manager. He was true scion of this family devoted to the Muses. Well, thanks to his influence, his young brother soon got an engagement at the theatre as chorus-master. That enabled him to live in a small way, in a modest bed-sitter in the Kapuziner graben, less than a stone's throw from his brother's. The experience marks a thrilling stage in his apprenticeship, for, during the winter and spring of 1833, the company played, one after another, *Zampa, Le Porteur d'Eau, Le Vampire, Der Freischütz, Fidelio, Tancred, Fra Diavolo,* and—this was its first performance—the famous *Robert le Diable* of Meyerbeer in which Albert sang the chief part.

The more he had to do with these choral parts and new scores, the more keenly he experienced the longing to give expression to the music he felt surging up within him. Ideas, themes, ensembles, came thronging into his mind, and soon the restlessness of the creative impulse took possession of his feverish spirit. He discovered in a tale of Gozzi's, *La Donna Serpente* a subject to his hand, because it ministered alike to his fondness for the picturesque and his taste for symbolism. So he took it and moulded it to his purpose, rechristened the characters with names inspired by Ossian, and put together the poem he called *Die Feen.*

"My hero was Prince Arindal; he was beloved of Ada the Fairy who held him in thrall far from his country in her own enchanted realm. The Prince's faithful subjects go forth to seek him and at last discover where he is tarrying. To prevail upon him to return they tell him that his country has fallen into the hands of the foe. The capital alone still holds out against desperate odds. The Fairy, by whom he is beloved, herself bids him return to his own land, for a decree of fate has ordained that she should remain a fairy until her lover has proved victorious over the arduous ordeals to which she is compelled to subject him. If he emerges triumphant, she will be suffered to renounce her immortality and to become the lawful spouse of a mortal. The Prince returns to his ravaged kingdom. His heart sinks, and in his moments of deepest anguish the Fairy appears to him and essays to undermine his faith in her by enacting deeds of unheard-of cruelty. Stricken with horror, Arindal supposes that he is the victim of a sorceress who has seduced him under the guise of Ada. In order to free himself from her evil influence he lays a curse upon her. In despair, Ada falls at his feet, declaring to the unhappy man the doom that awaits them both. For having defied the commands of the fairies, she will be changed into a stone (this was how I dealt with Gozzi's metamorphosis of her into a serpent). Arindal then realises that all the abominations wrought by the Fairy were nothing but illusions. The victory over the foe, the restoration of the country's prosperity take place with marvellous rapidity. Nevertheless, Ada is dragged away by the Fairies charged with the execution of the fell decree, and Arindal is left alone, a victim to madness. His sufferings do not suffice to appease the cruel Fairies. They aim at the total annihilation of him who defied their decrees, and prevail upon him to accompany them to Hell on the pretext of showing him how he may deliver Ada from bondage. Fired with this hope, the madness of Arindal becomes a sublime enthusiasm. He follows the traitresses, but not till he has first provided himself with arms and talismans which a faithful wizard had delivered into his hands in the royal abode. The fairies were struck with amazement when they beheld Arindal lay low, one after another, the monsters of the infernal regions. All their hopes of seeing him succumb were centred on the last trial, from which, they thought, he assuredly could not emerge triumphant, since it meant moving a stone to tears, the stone which served as Ada's prison. When he found himself face to face with this petrified human form, Arindal took the lyre which the wizard had bidden him bear with him, albeit without telling him the reason. To the sounds of this instrument he chants his grief, and so touching are his melodious lamentations that the stone is moved to pity. Ada is set free and the Kingdom of the Fairies, the world of bliss, opens out before the two lovers. If Ada, by reason of her disobedience, could not become a mortal, Arindal by reason of his valour had merited immortality."

That was Wagner's own account of his text. We have quoted it word for word so that its tone and atmosphere might be preserved, and because we already discern in it a sort of philosophy of moral character, an exaltation of courage, a setting forth of the struggle between human and divine in which Fate alone is the determining factor, all of which formed the basis of his ethical system. In this overloaded, somewhat involved, poem, which was more or less of a failure, there is nevertheless apparent the germ of *Tannhäuser, Lohengrin,* and the *Tetralogy.* We observe in it that propensity for rolling a score of stories into one, that conviction that life is all a tangle of laws, aspirations, and defeats which make all action a complicated tragedy of the spirit, a conviction which this student of human destiny always tenaciously acted upon in his own life. The Fairies are a presage not only in music but in poetry. We have the absolute confidence in the power of Love. We see Music and Love interfused in one and the same genius. We have the charms, the potions, the trials, which fall to the lot of lovers; the arrival of the chosen pair in Paradise—all the things which we encounter later on more amply and more deeply exemplified in his dramas. But even here we have the rough tentative sketch or adumbration of the themes, gradations, and developments ranged like a chime of bells in that tower of many sounds which is the soul of Wagner.

By the end of 1833 the work was finished. The *studiosus musicæ* put his nose out of the window with an air of satisfaction, for he had just wound up his score with the words "Finis, Laudatur Deus, Richard Wagner." He gazed at the snowflakes falling on the roofs of Wurzburg. It was midday. There was joyousness in the air. The bells were ringing merrily. These, you see, were "signs." He wrote off to Rosalie, and, like all true dramatists, he cast the different parts and chose his singers. Come what may, he must have a Devrient for the principal rôle; the young Gebhardt girl, Eichberger, his brother Albert . . . there were such a lot of them. Just imagine it, five sopranos, three principal tenors, one barytone, four basses, not to mention incidental parts and the choruses. He had big ideas; very big. A whole nation, a whole race, a whole mythology.

The young poet at his window was incubating that strange malady which artists are heir to, a malady which compels them to be ever dying in order to bring new life to birth. Behold him now already big with those projects whose development will always bring him a joy mingled with tears and which he will one day call, in pride and fear, "the creation of a non-existent world."

Chapter VII

THE CUP OF SOCRATES

As soon as he returned to Leipzig, at the beginning of 1834, Richard endeavoured to get his new opera accepted by the theatre there. But this time he encountered a determined opposition. It was offered—this opposition—by a very sound musician, Hauser by name, the manager of the theatre, who had been brought up in the Bach tradition, and even went the length of reproaching Mozart for some of his liberties. How should he be expected to tolerate the vagaries of Wagner, for whom—though he had not as yet confessed it—the word law meant simply—licence! Hauser refused *Die Feen*. The composer, though vexed, did not lose his temper, but wrote to plead his cause. Though as yet there was no indication of the warfare he was destined later on to wage against the crass stupidity of directors and managers, Wagner put his case with force. He had been reproached for his "tendencies." They were the tendencies of the age. He had been asked why he did not orchestrate like Haydn? Because he was Richard Wagner. It was said he did not know how to use the orchestra, that he was utterly ignorant of the laws of harmony. Well, to that there was no answer. That was the sort of thing the defendant always has to put up with from the prosecution. But why could not Hauser show that he had a heart? Why not let him submit his manuscript to the conductor of the orchestra? Why not give him at least a dog's chance?

Well, they wouldn't. His opportunity was to come later. Hauser was obdurate. Richard consoled himself by going to hear Schroeder-Devrient, who had come to Leipzig to sing in Bellini's *Romeo*. Then he took up his pen and wrote his first article for the *Zeitung für die elegante Welt* run by his friend Laube. "We are not going to write like Italians, or Frenchmen or even Germans. No more German stiffness, no more science, no more deceptive fugues. What may be noble verities in Bach or Handel,

we've got to look on as absurdities in ourselves. We've got to
take our own times by the shoulders and pound them into shape."

There you have the clear, merry song of the little Saxon craftsman, rejoicing in the free play of his biceps. It is also the world-
old dithyramb chanted by the young men of every age when first
they feel the sap mounting in their veins.

So it was "On with the dance!" "What a fair and lovely
work," they cry in ecstasy, "and all our own! Cut the family
connexion! Away with our ancestors—every man Jack of them!
We are the only ones that count! We—I—will face the world
alone! Yes, I! To the deuce with the pallid Bellini! To the deuce
with the anæmic Auber! No; we'll have none of Weber, even,
and his threadbare *Euryanthe*!" But when he comes to Shakespeare and Beethoven, he pulls up, rather out of breath. Yet,
after all,. what are they to him? What do they mean to him?
Well, that remains to be seen. Meantime, let the springtide wash
us clean of all our sins, even those against the spirit, and, since
the theatre has turned down *Die Feen*, let us be off to Bohemia.
And here, in the very nick of time, comes Theodor Apel—his
father a poet of wealthy bourgeois stock—to place his purse and
a carriage at his disposal. Wagner does not refuse. His old
friend and he hire a smart turnout and so, journeying leisurely
from inn to inn, they get to Teplitz, where they make a stay of
several weeks, putting up at the King of Prussia.

Here at Teplitz it was that, one fine morning in June, ascend-
ing the Schlackenburg alone (whence you may get a bird's-eye
view of the whole town), Richard sat him down on the turf and
drew forth his notebook to jot down an idea for a new work,
Das Liebesverbot. Yet once again—but this time was the last—
it was the motley world of Shakespeare, with all its interplay of
passions, its laughter and tears, its virtues and vices, its saints
and sinners, that stirred the young man's fancy, and it was on
the sombre ground of *Measure for Measure* that he was fain to
graft his vine. To begin with, he transported the scene from
Shakespeare's wholly imaginary Vienna southwards, to sun-
drenched Palermo. Thereafter he kept close to the original argument—an incorruptible governor suddenly yielding to an onslaught of the passions and using, to attain his cruel end, all
the authority with which his position endowed him, and all the
coolly calculated machinations of a master brain. Wagner dis-
cards all secondary themes—the apparatus of the courts of
justice, the moral denunciations, and so forth, in order to con-
centrate on bringing into relief the bold and untrammelled
gratification of the senses. He had but one aim, and that was

to unmask the essential immorality of hypocrisy and all that was contrary to nature in the ruthless rigidity of the moral code. It was a typical case of repression followed by a violent outbreak which had long been ravaging a temperament famishing for an outlet to its instincts. Though he knew nothing of the passions from practical experience, he sniffed in the very breath of them and resolved that, come what might, he would proclaim the right to their free enjoyment. Among the *Junge Europa* clique, all that sort of thing was known as "emancipating the flesh." Engendered by this new turmoil of sense and sensibility, Wagner felt that strange exaltation, traversed by doubting crosscurrents, but always triumphantly resilient, which in him we call the creative mood.

Scarcely had he committed his notes to paper than he was back again in Prague. There he fell in once more with the pretty Countesses Pachta-Raymann, whose father had lately died. Irony, airy persiflage, "an antic disposition"—that was his cue this time. Not a touch of the sentimental about him now. Having thus proved that sentiment's tender floweret had swiftly withered, and that they were now most emphatically men, ripe for the serious business of life, the youngsters go back to Leipzig.

Richard's family were eagerly awaiting his return, for they had a fine piece of news for him up their sleeves, and that was that the Magdeburg Theatre, the members of which were now giving a summer season at Lauchstaedt, were looking high and low for a conductor, and were willing that he should have the post. That meant giving up all hope of getting *Die Feen* put on. But it meant a livelihood, a really good start, the first rung of the ladder.

His mind was soon made up and off he went. As soon as he arrived at Lauchstaedt, he hastened to interview the director, a little man in skull-cap and dressing-gown, whose inveterate habit it was to lubricate his ceremonious, old-fashioned eloquence with frequent nips of *schnapps*. Richard was not very favourably impressed, and became still less so when the manager informed him that everything was at sixes and sevens, that the old fellow had let everything slide, and that the orchestra simply would not rehearse, in spite of the fact that they were due to play *Don Juan* the very next Sunday. While he was telling him all this the man kept stretching his arm out of a window towards a cherry tree that was one mass of fruit. He pulled the cherries off in bunches and began to devour them, spitting out the stones. This was too much for Wagner, who, strange to say, could not bear fruit. He decided that the post was not for him. As a matter of courtesy, however, he felt bound to put in a night or two at Lauchstaedt. A young actor went with him to the quarters they had hired for his accommodation in a very nice house in the town. Just as he was arriving at his destination a young woman hove in sight whose good looks and neat attire contrasted so favourably with everything Wagner had seen that morning, that he was completely taken aback. The lady was a member of the company, who played the lead in sentimental pieces, and Wagner was at once presented by his companion to Fräulein Wilhelmina Planer. She, in her turn, surveyed with some surprise this very youthful conductor who looked as if he had just come out of his shell, while he, for his part, was lost in admiration of the lady's fresh and graceful charms and the notable reserve and dignified repose of her manner. Without more ado Richard made up his mind he would conduct *Don Juan*, after all, and accept the responsibilities of an office which, fifteen minutes earlier, he had resolutely decided to decline.

Thus it was that their lots were cast. They had but exchanged glances. Thus their paths united and the agony of alternate hatred and desire was thereafter to be their portion; yet all the long-drawn misery of their lives could not avail to quench the outbreaks of reckless and passionate affection by which they were intermittently assailed. Alternately ill-fortune and tenacity would now shatter, and then repair, the bonds of hope, until they touched the very limits of mutual compassion or disgust. Nevertheless, let no one bewail the trials that were ineluctable from the moment when these two elemental currents came thus to meet together. Who knows what Wagner would have been had he had no such obstacles to overcome, no such toils to endure? Rather let us applaud this little actress with her jealousy and her grief, and be thankful to her for goading the man she loved to such fruitful anger, to such magnificent despair. For love and material prosperity rarely go hand in hand. The great tragedy of man's life is that he can hardly progress save at the price of immolating himself or others. Few choose the former alternative. Fewer still, perhaps, have the courage to exact to the full the sufferings of another. For a long time he had the constancy of purpose to bear all, even the burden of his own frailties, his own misdeeds. And after that he crucified the woman whom he could no longer love. And so this stupendous egoist was vouchsafed the honour of draining the cup which Socrates offers only to those who confess the truth within them.

Wilhelmina Planer—Minna her friends called her—was possessed of good looks and elegant ways. Being a woman, she was a coquette, but her coquetry was somewhat of the cool and calculated order. Though not particularly stand-off, she was certainly not passionate—and she was four years Wagner's senior. This difference, hardly noticeable in such young people, before long imparted a rather maternal nuance to her attitude towards him, and the budding *chef d'orchestre* was soon somewhat surprised at the seriousness she displayed, a seriousness in marked contrast to the frivolous bearing of the other members of the company. Minna, in fact, had little to do with her colleagues. She worked away diligently in her own corner, as it were, and never showed up at the theatre except for performances or rehearsals. And as soon as they were over she would shut herself up in her own room or go and visit her particular private cronies. Being well-favoured, she had no lack of men friends, and before long Richard found himself as jealous of this woman, of whose antecedents he knew absolutely nothing, as if she had really belonged to him.

One night, coming home late, he discovered he had forgotten the front-door key and was obliged to climb the wall in order to secure an entrance. As he was making his way up, the window above was suddenly opened and Minna Planer, in her dressing-gown, stretched out a helping hand. Shortly afterwards, he had to take to his bed with an attack of erysipelas. Fräulein Planer nursed him through it, assuring him that a swollen face did not in the least disgust her. Up and about again, the only remnant of his illness was a spot on his lip, and Minna, courageous or indifferent, did not hesitate to kiss the place. "In all she did she maintained an air of quiet affection." She was a nice, homely little person, from whose ideas a *grande passion* and the thoughts of glory were equally remote. Essentially practical, simple, and sensible, what she wanted above everything else was to live a tranquil existence, free from trouble and anxiety. But being rather dull of apprehension, and singularly lacking in divination, she never guessed what an error she was making in looking forward to a future of steady work with intervals of tranquil repose in the company of her alert and active companion. Nevertheless, she hesitated, for when the players left Lauchstaedt for Rudolstadt, her reputed *fiancé*—or perhaps her lover—went with her. Richard nearly exploded with rage. But what could he do? Why, perhaps just get her to love him. This he had already resolved to do, when Minna disappeared. For weeks they did not see each other. At last they met again at Magdeburg, where the company had at length come to anchor for the winter.

Richard liked the place: sixty thousand souls, a sort of miniature capital, a theatre that was being reconstructed, and a numerous staff, the female members of which soon became interested in this eccentric director of music, for he was a bachelor, you see, and all the more attractive because he seemed to hold them cheap. They knew, however, that he was rather a gay dog, by no means indifferent to the charms of the wine-cup and up to his ears in debt. But when his creditors became too importunate, he wrote off to Theodor Apel, promised to put on his *Columbus*, and tried his hand at an art which needs a deal of skill, the art of raising money. "Oh yes, preach away; I know I deserve it, but . . . I say, do you think you could set me up again? . . . Advance me a couple of hundred thalers?" At fourteen he was holding out his hat by the roadside. At eighteen he was gambling with his mother's income. At twenty-one he was raising funds to make him a man again, as he said, he who, as yet, had never been a man at all. He had no self-discipline; no control over his desires. What *did* he desire, you ask? Why, everything—wine, food, notoriety, fine clothes, love, to go to hell and back again, to make a name for himself, to become somebody, and to seize life, like music, by the shoulders, and give it a shaking.

The money having come (it was "Thank you, my golden friend, thank you; I say no more!") Wagner forthwith set about making preparations for an impromptu party, to be held at his rooms. The cream of the company were invited; actors, actresses, wives, husbands, sweethearts, and, of course, Minna Planer, "as ladylike and well dressed as usual." Yes, and as prudent and cold and sensible as usual, too. However, the champagne and the punch *did* succeed in thawing her at last. Influenced by the "atmosphere of tenderness" that Richard managed to create, the company split up into pairs, each couple sitting apart. Even Fräulein Planer, yielding to the general example, at last ceded gracefully to the advances of her host.

All this kissing and holding of hands developed into a covenant, a regular taking-over, "to have and to hold," and promised an endless future of connubial bliss. But things which as yet had hardly entered the man's head, the woman was already seeing about and busily arranging. While he was dreaming of pleasure and dissipation, she was for getting the home together. Some time after that, Wagner, having drunk more than was good for him at a dull card party, staggered upstairs to Minna's room, delivered himself of some rather unseemly jests to a woman visitor, an old friend of Minna's, whom he found there, and finished up by dropping off into a drunken slumber on Minna's bed. Waking up sober, he realized to the full the enormity of what he had done. For among these provincial artists, such a daring nocturnal adventure could only be followed by a matrimonial engagement. Chastely, without a smile, they contemplate each other and take their breakfast side by side. The young man sees pretty clearly where this untimely mix-up may land him. What a clumsy ass he was! How stupid, loutish, and compromising his conduct had been! Minna was kindness itself; alas! too much so, too kind. Why hadn't she kicked him out? On the contrary, she had been all smiles, so gentle, so eager to wait on him hand and foot. Despite his irritation, he was very much in love with her. But suppose she had other lovers. The thought drove him to frenzy. Hadn't he gone and delivered himself gagged and bound into her hands as her accredited suitor? The whole thing made him sick. So back he plunged into his *Liebesverbot*. He prevailed on his friend Apel to come along and bring the manuscript of his *Columbus*, for which Richard wrote a powerful overture and some incidental music. The play was performed and proved a distinct success, the overture being encored. He also found means to practise the conductor's art, and in this, his first season, directed *Fra Diavolo, Oberon, The Barber of Seville, Le Porteur d'Eau, La Muette de Portici, Freischütz, La Belle Meunière*, by Paesiello. This was a first-rate practical apprenticeship, for he had to rely entirely on himself, manage the whole thing, get together his choruses, make them understand and act upon his ideas, and hammer out a style of his own. Even when he was quite a child he had been thrust like a property flower among stage settings, and he felt as if he could never breathe really comfortably anywhere but in the good old stagey atmosphere of grease-paint and pasteboard. All those wooden landscapes, those forests suspended from the ceiling by their foliage on which a mechanical contraption lets loose the tempest, those castles that a burly, stubble-bearded fairy hauls up by main force into the clouds, those Spains and Italys in sections only waiting for the leg-of-mutton fist of some Magdeburg mechanic to fit them together—such are the beauty-spots he sets out to explore, such is his countryside, such are the scenes of his travels, and here, with these people arrayed in shabby satin, cheeks besmeared with paint and plaster, throats that coo like sucking doves, he listens spellbound to the splendid dream-tales of the poets. Behind him, auditorium, a thousand gaping nonentities; before him, at the point of his bâton, souls sparkling with celestial fire. And what souls they were! There was Mme.

Schroeder-Devrient, a model of inimitable grace and perfection, who had come to give four performances at Magdeburg. This time, her little nameless admirer of Leipzig had the honour to accompany her, mingling with her voice the music of all the instruments of which he was the master and enchanter. How he feels his genius stirring within him as the trills of Bellini and Rossini, or the lyrical flights of Leonora in Beethoven's *Fidelio* fall, like cascades of purest crystal, on his amazed ear. He beholds Desdemona grief-stricken on her knees, a tragic figure indeed, her cheeks bedewed with tears, and yet it seems to him that other lamentations, more true, or which he will deem more true, will one day pour in a melodious torrent from his little frame, proudly uplifted by the creative afflatus within him. He succeeded in persuading Mme. Schroeder-Devrient to join with him in giving a concert at the Hôtel de la Ville de Londres for his own special benefit. By this means he would get clear of all his debts at a single swoop. The program included Beethoven's *Adelaide*, *La Bataille de Vittoria* and the overture to *Columbus*. The orchestra was doubled. Special contrivances were fixed up to magnify the rattle of the bullets. The brass and the drums were trebled. Despite these elaborate preparations, the room was only half filled, and when the battle attained the maximum intensity of its fury, the few people who had turned up arose and departed in dismay. Thus Wagner, worse off than before, was left to pore despondently over the considerable deficit that resulted from this, his first lyrical campaign. The theatrical company, despite the reconstruction, went bankrupt once again. The only salary its members received consisted of free tickets for next season. By hook or by crook he contrived to appease the more ferocious of his duns. He told them reinforcements were bound to reach him from Leipzig. He also had recourse to the good offices of a certain Jewish "uncle." But what was absolutely indispensable was that he himself should vanish from the scene. It was of a grief-stricken Minna he had to take his leave. She, poor soul, was doing her best to negotiate the paper given her as salary by the old gentleman of the skull-cap and dressing-gown.

At Leipzig the little great man's arrival was awaited with some anxiety. He made a clean breast of the whole thing, not even suppressing his growing indebtedness to Theodor Apel. But what gave his pride its worst fall was having once again to borrow from brother-in-law Brockhaus, that disagreeably ironic man of substance who, if he parted with his money, did not neglect to emphasize the generosity of his action. Well, he would pay when he could. He was drawing a big bill on the future, but it would all come right in time. Meanwhile his present position was denoted by a very conspicuous zero. Even his conductorship had gone. Richard Wagner's sole asset was his unfinished *Liebesverbot*—that and his dog. A brown poodle had, in fact, come home with him from Magdeburg, his first comrade among those dumb, patient creatures that attach themselves to man without expecting so much as a word in return for their unfaltering devotion.

Chapter VIII

IDEALS *VERSUS* RESPECTABILITY

AT THE Gewandhaus that season a new conductor had come upon the scene—a young man of twenty-six, elegant, well-off, rather delicate-looking, but astonishingly self-confident. No sooner did he take up office than he proceeded to a thorough overhaul of the institution. His technical ability was amazing. He did not let the grass grow under his feet. In less than no time he replaced the existing staff with younger men, recast his programs, and insisted on regular and conscientious work from each and all of his performers. Already the public had begun to think a lot of him. This pale and attractive-looking young Jew, who was himself a composer of distinction, and who, despite his youth, was known to have been an intimate friend of Goethe's, was called Felix Mendelssohn-Bartholdy. Wagner went to his concerts and was immensely delighted with the perfect ensemble work of the new combination. He entrusted his brilliant colleague with his *Symphony in C major* and asked him to keep it in his filing-cabinet. This Mendelssohn did so carefully that it never came out again, and neither then nor later did he ever make the slightest allusion to it. So here was Wagner with a fresh grievance—against Mendelssohn in particular and his native town in general. The theatre had rejected his *Fairies,* and it looked as if the Gewandhaus had no use for his Symphony; and finally Friedrich Brockhaus was always contriving to remind him of his generosity and the obligation under which it laid him. There was really only one thing to do, and that was to get away again as soon as possible; more especially as he had evaded, and proposed to go on evading, the colossal boredom of military service. True, the authorities were not so very strict in the case of members of the artistic fraternity; all the same it would be a good thing to keep out of the way for a time. Seeing, therefore, that, despite its financial difficulties, the Magdeburg Theatre was arranging to reopen in September, and that the management was relying on him to engage the necessary soloists, Richard set out on a tour of talent-hunting.

But before actually starting, he had a brief interlude with Minna Planer and one of her sisters at Dresden, and there, among the wooded valleys of Saxon Switzerland, "we spent," he says, "some delightful days full of innocent and youthful gaiety, which were only marred on one occasion by one of my fits of jealousy. There was really nothing to make me jealous, but I had it in me. It arose from my past impressions and from what I had experienced up to then in regard to women. In spite of that, the whole excursion, especially a lovely, warm, summer night at Shandau, which we spent almost entirely in the open, was about the only event of my younger days that it gave me real pleasure to remember." Perhaps he should have said the only calm event, the only one of them all which was not ruined by that strange necessity which compels jealous people deliberately to muddy the clear springs of their happiness. For Wagner was already beginning to show symptoms of that itch for self-torment which impels certain heart-hungry people with vivid imaginations, but with senses too quickly satiated, to seek the indulgence of the one luxury that never disappoints, the luxury of sorrow.

Thenceforward, Minna's beauty, her laughter, her kisses, were a music devoid of mystery. Thenceforward, too, Leipzig, its Gewandhaus, and the glory which a young composer may derive from casual applause, were become childish things in his eyes. Work, that was what was needed, hard, unremitting, intensive spade-work on this soil, the soil, that is, of his own genius, into which he aimed at striking roots so deep that, spreading far and wide, they should underlie, at last, the world and all the human race.

It was thus that, journeying to and fro between Teplitz, Prague, Nuremberg, Karlsbad, and Frankfort in search of his future singers, Wagner scans his own soul, reads his own heart.

Into his mother's ear—his mother to whom he was drawn by a strong and instinctive affection—he pours the tale of his early rebuffs. "There comes a time when separations occur automatically, when our mutual relations are only matters of external concern; when we become, one to another, mere diplomats drawn together by sentiments of friendship. . . . Now that I am far from you, I am overwhelmed with gratitude for the wonderful love you bestow upon your child; so much so that I am impelled to speak and write to you in terms of the tenderest affection. Are you not the only one in all the world who has always been

true to me, when the rest have cold-shouldered me and philo-
sophically passed by? O Mother, what if you were to die too
soon, before I had time to prove to you that you had an upright
and a grateful son. No; such a thing could not be. But from now
onward, I am a man, and I intend to stand on my own feet.
Oh, that humiliating scene with Fritz—that is buried in the
lowest depths of my heart. . . . I will pay him back to the last
penny. . . . I've done with him for ever. The greatest mistake
I ever made was to put myself in his clutches and let him get the
upper hand of me. . . . And yet how glad I am the whole trouble
happened, since it has brought me to rely on myself. Yes, I am
a man now. That was what was wanting, that was what handi-
capped me—that sort of blind, stupid reliance on external support. Well, that's all over now. I am undeceived all round, and
that's what makes me very glad. It was fated that in my weakness I should have to go through all this experience." This was
the earliest stirring, in the boy, of the man that was germinating
within him. To bring it to pass his youthful pride had had to
suffer this succession of trials: failure, poverty, humiliation, dis-
illusion. There was Mendelssohn, that over-pampered darling of
Fortune; there was Minna, the cold and passionless Minna, who
made such a drain on his emotional reserve, and then there was
that prosperous and exasperating brother-in-law with his sar-
casms and his airs of condescending superiority. Though he did
not tell himself as much, Wagner had a vague idea that adversity was somehow going to be a better school for his character
than success; that it would put a keener edge on his intelligence.
This being his mood, the journey he was undertaking appeared
to him as no light enterprise. It might bring tears in its train.
What matter! But tears there were, and in plenty.

At Frankfort one August evening, having been moping in
solitude in his hotel, he dashed off a letter to Theodor Apel and
unburdened himself of all his trials and tribulations. He had
seen Laube (of *Das Junge Europa*) looking old and worn to a
shadow, having just finished a year in prison as a political suspect. He had come across Jenny and Augusta Raymann, who
were now living under the protection of two members of the
aristocracy. And pretty Frederica Galvani, whom he had known
and been friendly with at Wurzburg, was now tied up to some
regular oaf of a fellow. Laube's staunch and manly affection for
him, and those passing love affairs, had made up pretty well all
the poetry of his youthful days. And now, while he was yet so
young, that poetry was coagulating into a dense and turgid
prose, into chilling reality. And that reality—there was no get-

ting away from it, it showed like a skeleton beneath the charming graces of the flesh—was money!

As Wagner went plodding on from town to town, trying to get
hold of an actor here, or a singer there, whom he had to lure to
Magdeburg with no better bait than promises, he realized to
the full what a sordid position he was in. It was a grim and
dismal journey; and yet there were two interludes that made a
lively and lasting impression on him, though, at a first glance,
they may seem commonplace enough. It is very difficult to
explain how it comes about that something apparently quite
trivial, some seemingly ordinary piece of scenery, or some
"jolly" evening of meaningless horseplay and racket, gets tucked
away in a corner of your memory, and you feel that, somehow
and sometime, the thing is going to have an important bearing
on your life. One such impression he got when merely passing
through a sleepy little town with its deserted palaces all about
it, in the Forests of Franconia. Its name was Bayreuth. Richard
hardly stopped any time there, but he beheld it basking in the
sunlight, and was conscious of a strange, inward peace. It would
have been good to linger there for a while; it would have been
something for his youthful imagination and passions to pasture
on. But the coach only stopped to change horses, and, a few
hours later on he was rattling into Nuremberg, where his sister
Clara and his brother-in-law Wolfram were living. He stopped
with them two days, and one night he and his brother-in-law
went out on a spree, the sort of entertainment he still had a
taste for. The scene of the revel—a tavern—was gay, and the
public boisterous. There was a carpenter fellow there who took
himself very seriously as a singer and who was the butt of the
whole company. They pitched him the yarn that Wagner was
none other than Lablache, the famous basso. Amid roars of
laughter from the audience, the carpenter fired off a few songs
in his best style. The company then escorted him home, and the
uproar roused the whole neighbourhood from its slumbers. Windows were flung open and a great deal of shouting went on.
The carpenter's wife emptied the contents of her chamber-pot
on to the crowd below, what time the moon, sailing serenely
amid the gabled roofs of the ancient city, lit up what in days to
come was to be a scene in *Die Meistersinger*, as with a glow
from out the Middle Ages. At last Wagner got back to Magdeburg. He had scraped together a few performers—Clara and
Wolfram among them—and he had spent the little bit of money
he had to spend. But Magdeburg meant his conductorship and
Minna Planer; that is to say it meant music and love. What

more could he want? With Leipzig his ties were growing more
and more slack. Uncle Adolf had just died, Uncle Adolf to
whom he owed his first intellectual awakening, who made him
acquainted with Sophocles, Dante, Calderon, and Gozzi; Uncle
Adolf who breathed the breath of the spirit into the old Red
and White Lion. Henceforward Richard, far removed in time
and space from his family and his Saxon home, came, like many
another youthful lover, to demand of his beloved that she should
make up to him for all the things of which the hazards of life
had bereft him. She became, in a way, his mother and, in a
way, his sister Rosalie. Minna was now openly his mistress, but
instinct and jealousy alike gave him warning of the risks he
would incur in making her his wife. Though he loved her passionately, violently, he thought she was always too passive, too
unlike himself. Yet he would fly into a terrible rage and utterly
lose his head the moment she showed signs of renouncing the
honours of so tyrannical a devotion. Did she guess, even then?
Did she realize that she increased her power of attraction by
holding off? And that obstacles only intensified the ardour of the
attack? What at first sight might look like very subtle tactics,
may have been nothing more than the ordinary, elementary
feminine strategy, often unconsciously, but never unsuccessfully,
applied. She left for Berlin on the grounds that she had to fulfil
an engagement at the Königstädt Theatre. Richard immediately
began to behave like a madman. Grief and terror made a clean
sweep of the last defences of his reason, and what his mistress,
when present, had implored in vain, his mistress, absent, captured at a blow. He wrote her wild and whirling words, said he
would marry her outright, and vowed that if she gave him up
he would go forthwith to rack and ruin. Back she came. Richard
hired a carriage to go out and meet her and, shedding tears of
joy, brought back to his rooms the living source of all his agony
and all his bliss.

However, the day of the wedding dawned not; in the first
place, money was still tight and one could not start housekeep-
ing on nothing. Secondly, his debts were piling up and his
creditors were beginning to look ugly. And lastly Wagner had
taken it into his head that he would produce his *Liebesverbot*
which, counting his chickens, as usual, before they were hatched,
he felt sure would float him off the rocks, moral and material, on
which his ship had stranded.

He threw himself with gusto into his task and gave in swift
succession *Fra Diavolo*, Spohr's *La Jessonda*, *La Muette de Portici* and Auber's new opera, *Lestocq*. Artistic successes all, yet

the house was never more than half full. No matter; Wagner, overflowing with youth and spirits and looking very smart in a sky-blue frock-coat, conducted away unwearied and undismayed. As the season wore on, the management got further and further in arrears with the salaries. One day a number of the soloists and members of the chorus said they would have to look out for work elsewhere. Realizing that he might founder in sight of port, Wagner determined to wind up the season with a benefit performance of his *Liebesverbot*, of which the proceeds were to go to the artists. It was the only way to keep his scheme together. He finished his work in a state of mingled triumph and disgust. The disgust arose from the venerable clap-trap he was obliged to put in to pander to the management; the triumph, from the gigantic labours which forced him to exchange the cold embraces of Minna for a mob of shouting actors and actresses, the interior of a manager's office, squabbles with contractors, and sleepless nights spent poring over his manuscripts. At length it was decided that the company were to finish up on the 1st of April. It was now the 18th of March. Ten days to get his people word perfect, rehearsed, fix up the staging and scenery, and put the thing on. But it was precisely in such titanic struggles with the impossible that Wagner realizes his strength and we his greatness. In those ten days he polished off his orchestral score, breathed new life into his cast, and made them grind up their parts. In short, he rode the whirlwind and directed the storm, and all this before the ink on his score was properly dry.

They were already in Easter week when a fresh hitch cropped up. The censor had put in his spoke. He said the title wouldn't do; it was inappropriate in the circumstances. Wagner stuck up for it, cited Shakespeare as an example, and the magistrate at last said he would pass the work provided the title was changed to *The Novice of Palermo*. It was in the middle of all these excursions and alarms that, on the 29th of March, 1836, the curtain of the theatre at Magdeburg went up on the first public performance of an opera by Richard Wagner.

His mother had promised to come. But she did not appear, nor did any of his sisters. Nor, again, did his friend Theodor Apel, though urgent whips had been sent him. Wagner stood alone, behind him a well-filled theatre, in front of him his very nervous performers. There he was with no one to help, no one to back him in tackling a work to the merits and perilous defects of which he as keenly alive. "My music was merely the reaction of my morbidly excited feelings to modern French music and (in the matter of melody) to Italian opera. Anyone who took the trouble to compare it with *The Fairies* would marvel how, in so short a space of time, such a complete development of embryonic ideas could possibly have taken place." But a further *contretemps* was about due. It punctually arrived. The tenor Freimüller, who had a poor memory, tried to compensate for his deficiency by putting in some gag which fell miserably flat. Among the women, Frau Pollert (Isabelle) came in for some applause, but it was not very hearty because no one could make head or tail of the plot. Shakespeare's argument is complicated enough, but Wagner had made it doubly obscure by dividing the interest between the daring novice and the wicked governor. The result was that the work was greeted with neither cheers nor boos, but with a sort of lukewarm friendliness—damned with faint praise, in fact. We may take it that, on the whole, the audience were bored. A second performance was advertised for the following night, for the composer's benefit (Wagner had been counting on it to get even with his creditors), but now another "incident" occurred that definitely put the extinguisher on the whole business. Just before the curtain was due to go up, a violent quarrel broke out in the wings. Herr Pollert, Isabelle's husband, "set about" the second tenor, a very personable young fellow, who was singing Claudio. Frau Pollert came rushing up, and she too received some very heavy-handed marital correction, and went off into hysterics. The whole cast now joined in the fray, taking sides for or against the outraged husband, and the stage soon became a regular shambles It looked as if everyone had chosen this unhappy evening to pay off a score or two of his own. The couple upon whom Herr Pollert had so vigorously impressed his *Liebesverbot*, not being in a fit condition to appear in public, there was nothing for it but for the manager to come before the curtain and explain that, owing to wholly unforeseen circumstances, there would be no performance that evening.

Ten days after this fiasco, Ottilie, Richard's youngest sister, was married at Dresden to Dr. Hermann Brockhaus, the distinguished philologist and Orientalist and a younger brother of Friedrich the publisher. Wagner was not at the wedding. He was too proud to acknowledge himself beaten, too haughty to eat humble pie in the presence of the great man of substance who managed his family affairs. Besides, he hadn't got a stiver to pay the fare. His creditors were "having the law" of him, and every time he went home to his lodgings on the Breiter Weg, he found a fresh summons pinned to his door. His theatrical comrades were packing up and clearing out of the town. His poor brown poodle had vanished, too, a very bad omen, he thought. And there was an eclipse of the sun, another presage of evil. Then, one day, he saw a man throw himself into the Elbe. . . . Minna alone remained at her post, busy and practical as ever. Then she managed to get a contract with the theatre at Koenigsberg, and Richard had to part with her, his sole resource in these desperate times. When he went to see her off in the *diligence*, all the inhabitants of Magdeburg were trooping out in the direction of a field hard by the city gates, where a soldier was going to be shot. A feeling of horror came over him. He had only one idea, and that was to get away as quickly as possible from a town where Death alone, it seemed, stood at the receipt of custom. Borrowing some money for the journey, he started for Leipzig to get a recharge of his moral battery from his mother and his sister Rosalie. His mind was still fickle and unstable and he needed their steadying influence. He was intensely fond of his mother and he never ceased to regard her as his ideal of human tenderness and love. And never had he forgotten how, all unawares, he had come upon Rosalie—that mysterious elder sister—and found her weeping, he knew not why. And now again she took him by the hand as she went to see him off at the conclusion of his brief visit, then swiftly turned and, gazing into the depths of his eyes, said, strangely, "God knows when I shall see you again." Yet what had she to be worried about? She had lately become engaged to Oswald Marbach, the young author, and was to marry him a few months later. But even then some dim forebodings must have shaken her heart. Wagner never saw her again. A year later she died in giving birth to her little girl.

Wandering about in search of work, any sort of work, he cared not what, Wagner came to a halt at Berlin and took up his quarters at the Hotel Kron Prinz. If his debts were soon to land him in prison, he would at least have a bit of a fling in a town which lent itself to that sort of thing. Berlin was well worth seeing, and who could say?—perhaps this capital of the *intelligentsia* would one day be his home. By great good luck it happened that his old friend Laube was there. Richard made the acquaintance of M. Cerf, the manager of the Koenigstaedt Theatre, rather an astounding person, very well in at court, and called by everyone M. le Conseiller de Commission. His wealth was great, his ignorance greater, and his professional incompetence absolutely magnificent. This cunning exploiter gave the young composer to understand that he was going to appoint him as *chef d'orchestre* for his coming "season," and that he would put on his *Liebesverbot* at the first opportunity. But it soon became obvious that all that was going to end in smoke, and the only profit that Wagner got from his first stay in Berlin was hearing a performance of *Fernand Cortez* conducted by Spontini in person. Although the singing of the principals left much to be desired, the precision of the ensembles, the majestic bearing of the old conductor (who still liked to style himself "Compositeur particulier de Sa Majesté l'Impératrice Joséphine," although for many a long year he had been Master of Music to the King of Prussia) and especially his skill with the bâton, made a profound impression upon Wagner. "I came to understand," he says, "how solemn and unique is the effect of stage performances on a grand scale, how they attain incomparable heights as a distinct form of art by the strongly marked rhythmic effect of all the several parts." These words were carefully chosen and deserve to be no less carefully pondered. They afford an early indication of the new line of development adopted by the young composer, who looked down from the altitudes of the gallery on to that instructive spectacle. Even then the massed harmonies of *Rienzi* were vibrating in his subconscious self.

But meanwhile, a man must live. He wasn't making a halfpenny and the only money he had to play with was the money Minna sent him. But where did she get it from? Somehow or other he didn't feel at all comfortable about a certain Schwabe, a successful business man of Jewish origin whom he had recently come across again at Berlin, having a little while before left him at Magdeburg. Now this Schwabe was a great admirer of Minna's; too much of an admirer, no doubt. As is always the case, jealousy fired his passion and kindled anew the dying flame. He must know the truth at all costs. Once again the idea of marriage began to stir in the dim recesses of his being. He thought that peace awaited him in the possession of the insipid charms of this sensible, but very ordinary, young woman. Had he but known, it was anything but peace. He meditates taking her by storm. Of the six letters he had written her, she had only answered two, and those answers were by far too vague. So off he goes, hot on her traces. After a few days of very uncomfortable travelling—it was the height of summer—across the Prussian Marshes, he at length arrived at Koenigsberg, where, in a dingy suburban house, he came up with his Minna, who was marketing her little stock of talent at the local theatre with her customary serenity. Wagner, now easier in his mind, drew on his stock of patience, and went the round of the theatres and managers' offices, trying to find a job.

Here, as in Berlin, the importunate place-hunter was promised a deputy conductorship in succession to Louis Schuberth, who was shortly due to return to Riga. But Schuberth did not budge. He was kept at Koenigsberg entoiled in a love-affair with the principal woman singer there. And besides that, he was a thoroughly good man at his job. At first there was a concealed rivalry between them which soon developed into open hostility. Wagner tried the effect of a diversion and went off to Memel with a company of comedians to which his mistress belonged. It was a melancholy little journey, all the way by boat, through the chain of sandy lagoons which separate the *Curish Haff* from the sea.

Dreadfully lonely and bored, the couple returned to Koenigsberg. There Richard accidentally came across the letters which Minna had been receiving from Schwabe, her commercial friend. They were a terrible revelation to him. "All my pent-up jealousy, combined with the doubts I had entertained regarding the young woman's character, made me promptly decide to leave her." That is very far from being the real truth. It was no such step as that to which his discovery, weak that he was, impelled him. These lofty but misleading words were penned thirty-five years later, under the influence of another personality. But now, carnal jealousy had him in its relentless grip. His pride had been smitten as with a dagger. He was not going to let her go, not he! He would hold on to her through thick and thin, and he would have his revenge. The only asset he had acquired during these difficult years was summed up in this woman, this rather ordinary woman. She was the daughter of a Saxon mechanic, and had been led astray at an early age by some country yokel, finding herself a mother before she was seventeen. By dint of hard work and determination she had succeeded at last in getting on to the stage, having made the most of her good looks and passionless disposition to reach the semi-bourgeois peace and comfort which it had been her aim to secure.

Well, she had almost achieved her object by sheer tenacity of purpose, doing her duty by her child—which she had palmed off as her sister—and hiding little incidental lapses which cost her nothing and brought her in a little. And so, when Wagner suddenly appeared in her path, she at once saw in him a source of something no less precious, and far more tangible, than love, and that was a respectable position in the world. That was the limit of her ambition. Not so her lover. His dreams were dreams of bliss. "I was wandering in quest of my ideal," said he. "Minna perhaps was meditating on the eligible offers she had put aside."

Thus they inaugurated the long series of future "scenes," sowing the wind whereof, in years to come, they were fated to reap the inevitable whirlwind. Richard lashed with cruel words the woman whom he loved, and she, in her underbred way, also learned the vocabulary of vituperation. From this initial disagreement both he and she might have divined how wide was the gulf that sundered them. But, as usually happens, the more formidable the gulf appears, the greater the determination of the better brain of the two to justify his actions; not to her, but to himself and to his disillusioned heart. For all these bickerings and disagreements, and for the infidelities he half-divined, there was but a single remedy. That remedy was marriage. That would put an end to doubt and give him, into the bargain, the comfortable sensation of having done the handsome thing. Wagner, then, shut his eyes and took the leap, as one might jump the crevasse of a glacier all blue with the mistiness of the unknown. Doubtless there were lovely vistas on the farther side, and again he felt that heavenly elation of spirit which makes light of hardship.

The wedding was fixed for the 24th of November of this same year, 1836. The day before the ceremony, he conducted a performance of *La Muette de Portici* given for his benefit, the proceeds of which furnished their joint dowry. Neither Frau Geyer nor Minna's relations were present. But the latter sent their nuptial blessing to their future son-in-law, Herr Musikdirektor. However, the Tragheimer Kirche was full of people—actors, actresses, musicians, singers, and all the theatre staff. The pastor delivered an address of which Richard could not understand a word. "To prepare us for times of trial—and trials would surely come—the clergyman enjoined us to have recourse to a friend whom, as yet, neither of us knew. Rather inquisitive to discover who this powerful and mysterious friend could be that chose so unusual a manner of announcing himself, I looked up enquiringly at the clergyman, who then declared to us, investing his words with a tone of solemn reprimand, that the name of this unknown friend was Jesus. I was in no way offended, but grievously disappointed. . . . At that moment I saw my whole life as in a vision. It seemed to me that I was caught between two contending currents placed one beneath the other, the upper one drawing me towards the sun, as in a dream; the nether one retaining me in a state of unaccountable anxiety."

The very next day he had to attend the court as defendant in an action brought against him by his creditors at Magdeburg. At the Town Hall he had put himself ahead a year, in order to make out that he had attained his majority (according to Prussian law, a man did not come of age till he was twenty-four; in Saxony the statutory age was twenty-one, and Wagner was in fact twenty-three and a half). At the court he put himself back a year, so as to remain a minor and gain time. Thus it was that, after a grave misreading of the compass, his new life began with a lie.

Chapter IX

THE FANFARES OF "RIENZI" AND THE STORM OF THE PHANTOM SHIP

FROM his exile in this Prussian Siberia, from this monotonous and chilly land, Wagner's imagination soon began to take flight to warmer climes where he dreamed he would be welcomed and made much of, and his creations change a land famishing for novelty, into a flowering paradise.

He had written to Scribe, who at that time was the uncontested leader of the theatrical world in Paris, to suggest that he should write a libretto to which he, Wagner, would compose the music. Although that was six months ago, he had had no reply. He therefore wrote again, proposing that the distinguished librettist should make a version of his *Liebesverbot*, referring him to MM. Auber and Meyerbeer as willing to bear witness to the musical merits of his work. This was ingenuous. But in Paris, we know, all things are possible—even the impossible; and, inasmuch as a grain of fantasy or madness seems always able to leaven the dough there, however closely compounded with tradition, why should not the kitchens of the Opéra Comique try the recipe which this young German master presented for their acceptance? Shortly afterwards a reply came from Scribe, courteously offering his services. But this project, which kept Wagner's mind strictly concentrated on Paris, had no immediate sequel, because an unforeseen event interposed to fling all his sentimental ideas into the melting-pot. On the evening of the 21st of May, 1837, six months, almost to the day, after his wedding, Richard went home to find his nest deserted. Minna had gone off with her daughter, little Natalie, taking with her all her poor stage finery, and leaving behind her not a word of explanation. Had she run away with another man? For a certain business man, Dietrich by name, had stepped into Schwabe's shoes, and it was likely enough that this individual, who styled himself "protector of the arts" was, even more, a protector of the actress. Or had she fled because she dreaded poverty and want? Or was she afraid of his outbursts of jealous fury? All these things were equally possible, and this household, where longing and tenderness seemed to have come to an end, had only been kept together by mutual repining over common disappointments. But even this bitterness, these regrets, had their sting, for the heart is still more tenacious of the things that have cost it dear, than of those that came to it unsought.

Forthwith, then, Wagner started off in pursuit of his mistress, passing through Berlin, where, through the influence of a friend, he made sure of a conductorship at Riga; then, while still keeping up the search, he lodged a petition for divorce at the Koenigsberg court. What were legal bonds to him? It is not the wife he would rediscover, but the mistress he would win again. And when at last he ran her to earth in her father's house at Dresden, all his anger fell from him and he broke down in tears as he pleaded passionately for a reconciliation. It was but an armistice, and no lasting peace. Minna had her own ideas, and kept them to herself. She quietly accompanied her husband to Blasewitz, where he had hired a room in a little hotel overlooking the Elbe. They started reading and writing together, preparing for a winter of music at Riga, where his salary as conductor would be enough to live on, pay his debts, and even permit his young wife to abandon the stage. It was Wagner's desire that Minna should henceforth have no more to do with the theatre, which he looked on as a career fraught for her (and for him) with much more danger than advantage.

This was another error on his part. Minna loved her work and was quite decently successful in it, and it may be that the husband's denunciation of the wife was easier for her to bear than the artist's indifference to the actress. But she did not complain. He spent his time burrowing in Bulwer Lytton's *Rienzi*, a long historical novel which suggested to him a wealth of ideas, an endless succession of scenic tableaux. She left him to his new craze. Then she started on a journey with a woman friend, whom she had known ever since she was a child. The days went by, and Wagner was beginning to grow a little anxious at her lengthy absence, when her eldest sister arrived and asked him for the authorisation necessary to enable Minna to obtain a passport. At the same time a letter came from his friend Moeller at Koenigsberg explaining matters. It announced that master Dietrich had left for Dresden, where he had joined Minna in a hotel, and that, by the time the letter in question reached him, the couple would be doubtless well away. . . .

Wagner went to the address indicated, found that the information was correct and that his wife had again left him. "My grief was intense," he wrote later on, "and poisoned my whole life." This is putting it too strongly. It was a long time now since his love had ceased to possess that bloom which alone causes such a betrayal to have so tragic and indelible an effect on a man's after-life. Moreover, the disappointment a man feels at an act which tears away the mystery that enveloped the beloved one, and reveals to the tortured heart the resemblances—too clearly divined—which she bears to the common herd, at once dispels the magic and destroys the charm. Wagner learnt that a woman may easily prefer to the sufferings of love, to the torments of a jealous husband, to miseries loyally and daily endured, the quiet satisfaction of humdrum pleasure and the facilities afforded by a well-lined purse. He rushed off to his sister Ottilie Brockhaus. He wept as he had rarely wept. He sweated out in blood and tears what remained in him of desire for the wife who had been totally unable to discern in her husband the still-veiled countenance of genius. But if his outward pride was broken, his inward courage was still unbowed. From that day onward, all that remained in Wagner's heart for Minna Planer was pity— and not a little vexation. He knew, now, that he was strong; he felt that he had disencumbered himself of a burden. Never again would he trip and stumble, for all the tears and all the contrition of this repentant Magdalen. Whether she turns again to him or not, she will not win him, or wring his heart with her entreaties. "There comes a time when separations happen of their own accord," he had written at the time of his quarrel with Friedrich Brockhaus. What he had been through with Minna might also be to his advantage. He was cured of that passion; his heart was strong now and he shook it from him. There was something stirring within him which was more imperious, more alluring, than fleshly love. *Rienzi* haunted him more insistently than his practical, bourgeois little wife. The face and form of the last of the tribunes, the fourteenth-century hero of Italian unity, the friend of Petrarch, kindled into rapture all the artist in his soul. He fell to weaving the web of romance about the life of this hero of Might and Order. He did what Bulwer had done. He did what Shakespeare had done for all the figures that peopled his imagination, and what, so long as the world shall last, all who have suffered betrayal or disappointment, all the poor ones of this earth shall do, in whose ears resounds the music of the unattainable.

The latter half of the summer he spent under the roof of

Hermann Brockhaus, with Ottilie, who now became, for a time, his favourite sister. The atmosphere of this youthful *ménage* did him much good. In the second half of August he had to set out for Riga, to take up his new appointment. The journey—rather a long and trying one—came to an end at last, and when he arrived the traveller was much amazed at the great, undisciplined crowds that swarmed about the famous Russian seaport. Riga, the meeting-place of East and West, is picturesque, dirty and opulent. There is a whole army of customs officials in the place, and no end of showing of passports and disbursing of tips. Fortunately, German was understood more or less everywhere. He had an encouraging reception from Charles Holtei, the manager, a poet and dramatist who hailed from Silesia. He was an adroit, intelligent, rather incalculable sort of person, a little overpowering in manner and a tremendous talker. He was pretty acute, too, for he started by knocking two hundred off the thousand rubles due to Wagner, on the grounds that the deduction was "in the higher interests of art." He made no secret of his preference for French and Italian music, and said he had placed an order for the scores of all the operas by Bellini, Donizetti, Adam, and Auber. He had a great liking for strolling players, and he would gladly have gone touring about with his whole company in a caravan. As for the orchestra, twenty-four strong, it was not at all bad. The wood-wind was good; the brass first rate. The vocalists were fair to middling. Taking it all round, there were distinct possibilities.

There was one strange thing that happened, and that was his running across Heinrich Dorn, who used to conduct the orchestra at Leipzig, the same Dorn that had once conducted the young man's *New Overture*, the work in which the prodigious beats on the big drum had sent the audience into fits of laughter. At Riga, Dorn was what was officially known as the Municipal Director of Music in Schools and Churches. He took his former colleague out to his place in the country, a little bungalow "in the greenery," which meant, it would seem, among the sand-dunes by the sea. Out in this lonely spot Wagner began to long desperately for the sun. Riga was not his sort of country. His sole resource against complete boredom was the routine business at the theatre (where he soon found himself at loggerheads with Holtei) and his own private work. He got down to his *Rienzi*, and as soon as he had the paper in front of him, with no one to interrupt, he felt that profound sensation of well-being which the free expression of one's ideas never fails to engender. "I was in a state of veritable enthusiasm, a striking contrast to the circumstances in which I was placed materially, and rather like the gaiety of a man resolved to have one last good fling before the end." The meaner and more sordid his surroundings, the nobler and more splendid his dreams and imaginative flights. The more Holtei tried to bend him to the fashionable gew-gaws of the day, the more utterly he abandoned himself to the promptings of the spirit within, growing, expanding in force and stature, piling Pelion upon Ossa.

All the same, the public liked him. They had been a little mistrustful and stand-off at first, but they soon came round. They liked the young man's dash and go. The box-office takings went up. The theatre was a huge, ramshackle place, very free and easy (the women in the gallery brought their knitting with them and also "a bit to eat" during the performance), but there were three peculiarities about it which impressed themselves on Wagner's imagination. The pit was constructed in tiers, like a circus; the auditorium was in darkness; and, lastly, the orchestra was down in a sort of hollow. If he did not realize the importance of these things straight away, the day was to come, in the distant future, when all this came back to his mind and brought about a complete revolution in the architecture of the theatre. As he had no *prima donna* in his company, it occurred to Wagner to write to his sister-in-law Amalie and ask her to fill the post. She wrote back at once from Dresden, accepting the offer and telling him, at the same time, of Minna's return to the paternal roof. "She was depressed and demoralized, and appeared to be seriously ill." The news left Wagner cold. He had begun divorce proceedings and he knew that his wife had been openly parading about with Dietrich in Hamburg; and he also knew that his domestic affairs were the theme of open, and not very flattering, comment in the theatrical world at large. No, he did not want to make it up. Then Minna herself took up the pen and "in a really touching letter frankly confessed her faithlessness." It is a pity we have not got that letter, and also the one in which Wagner wrote and told her to come back to him. Still, it is not difficult to imagine that the loneliness of his life at Riga, combined with the sensuous appeal that grief in all its forms never failed to make to his emotional nature, rendered this letter of his a profoundly moving and magnetic human document. What an exquisite and voluptuous revenge lay in the humiliation of this penitent wanderer. Abandoned by her lover, in a state of pitiable suffering, moral and material, she went down on her knees to the man whom she had always misunderstood, the man who, for all the torments he inflicted on her, was yet the ruling spirit of her life, and implored him to take her back. "And so it was that, recognizing the terrible plight in which she found herself, she came back to me, imploring my forgiveness and assuring me that now at last, and not until now, she realized the full strength of the love that bound her to me."

The two sisters arrived together at Riga and the reconciliation took place quite smoothly and without reproaches. The fact was Wagner was in a hurry to get back to a home of his own. He longed for peace, for the opportunity of steady work and for decent cooking. Well, Minna knew how to run a home, there was no doubt about that. They moved their quarters to the first floor of a house in the Faubourg de St.-Pétersbourg. On one side were two small rooms for Amalie; on the other the conjugal bedchamber; in the middle was the *Wohnzimmer*, in other words the drawing-room, transformed into a sort of musical laboratory, with a piano, a table littered with papers, two Russian heating-stoves, and red curtains at the window. If they gave a glance upwards the passersby could see, sitting a little way back from the open window, the young *Musikdirektor*, attired in dressing-gown and Turkish cap, smoking his long porcelain pipe.

It was in these humble lodgings that *Rienzi* was born. It was here that, during the two winters, 1837-38, and 1838-39, Wagner planned out all the operatic performances at the theatre: Mozart's *Don Giovanni* and *I Nozzi*; Bellini's *Norma*; Weber's *Oberon*; Méhul's *Joseph*; and Auber's *Muette*; besides a number of lesser operatic works and a whole series of concerts. "Wagner worried the life out of my staff with his interminable rehearsals," says Holtei. "Nothing was ever good enough, nothing delicate or polished enough, for him. The upshot was that the staff were for ever complaining. One after another, musicians and singers would come to me and say they really couldn't stand it. Secretly, I rather sided with Wagner, but still I couldn't let him have things all his own way. He would have been the death of all my people." Such, then, was the artistic conscience, the *Grundlichkeit*, which this little conductor of twenty-five summers had already so fully developed. There was no arguing with him, once he had got hold of a work of art. Everything had to be perfect, logical, coherent, and explicable. And the explanation had to be forthcoming even if it meant grinding up whole treatises on history, philosophy, and philology to track it down. He now took up the pen and wrote an article on Bellini for the Riga paper. "Sing, sing, sing, and yet again sing, you Germans! Since song is the means by which man expresses himself musically, no one will understand your song, your music, if it be not as well constructed and as skilfully made use of, as any other recognized mode of speech." It must not be supposed that he was in the least pedantic; but he liked acquiring knowledge and imparting it, when acquired, to others. The rather middling pupil of Dresden and Leipzig developed—and the phenomenon is not at all unusual with the self-taught—a positive passion for learning and teaching. He was in love with his work. "In the sweet exile of toil," wrote Rodin to Reiner Maria Rilke, "a man first of all learns to be patient, and patience teaches us energy; and this latter bestows upon us eternal youth, compounded of fire and meditation." Wagner was full of energy, full of sap, full of raging and tearing enthusiasms about all manner of things. Yet he was always thrown in upon himself. He was a stranger to the whole world. But this solitude, which he hated, even as the disillusionments which lay in wait for him, were the unfailing guardians of his dawning genius. Night by night they hovered above the fitful slumbers of the pale and under-nourished little man. The more forlorn and desperate his seeming plight, the more surely they distilled, drop by drop, into his heart, the elixir that was to temper his spirit and lend fire to his powers.

Wagner was not yet a great man, but he already had some of the attributes of the great; he was grim, harsh, exacting, overbearingly and unashamedly selfish. He was getting his hand in. Some laughed at him, and others trembled. He was voted a genius, but unbearable. But no one knew how insatiable he was for work and that, notwithstanding the exhausting labours involved in continuous rehearsals with chorus and orchestra, and experiments with lighting and scenery and stage effects, this visionary would sit up half the night composing an opera that was destined to sweep the old repertory off the field. Even an attack of typhoid failed to bowl him over. By the 6th of February the first act of *Rienzi* was finished; and a few months later, the second. He little suspected, however, that the very people who were so busily exploiting his energy and his talents, were also plotting his discomfiture.

But the fact was that Dorn and Holtei were conspiring to bring about his downfall; Dorn for the simple reason that he wanted his job, and Holtei because Wagner was not easy-going enough and would not understand that the theatre was not a penal settlement, but a place to enjoy oneself, to have a good time, and that in a manner not always consonant with the strictest morality. One fine day it came out that Holtei had suddenly quitted Riga in order to avoid some scandal in which he had involved himself. He would not come back; that was a cer-

tainty. But before his departure he had formally handed over
his interests to the actor Hoffmann, and appointed Dorn as the
new conductor. This twofold betrayal at first put Wagner beside
himself. Here he was once more on his beam ends, deprived of
his modest livelihood before he had been able to pay off his debts,
and interrupted in the very middle of his work on *Rienzi*. But
in point of fact, was it really such a disaster? Was it not rather
a stroke of Providence that rescued him from the drab surroundings and the boredom of a provincial town, from this two-
penny-halfpenny poultry-yard of tame, villatic art where, for
months past, he himself had been hatching an eagle's egg. Suddenly the thought of Paris flashed into his mind, Paris the very
hub of grand opera, Paris where his *Rienzi* should first dawn
upon the world. He had already written Scribe, sending him a
fair copy of his *Liebesverbot* through his sister Cecile, who was
engaged to Edouard Avenarius, head of the Paris branch of the
Brockhaus publishing establishment. He had also written Meyerbeer, "Composer, and Chevalier de la Légion d'Honneur." Did
not all these things amount to an intellectual relationship, and
constitute as it were a new mode of existence? Leave he must;
get out of this blind alley of a place, get clear of this deadly
routine that threatened to bury him alive, and try his fortune
in the finest theatre in the world, the only one commensurate
with the scope of his ideas. "When I had in my hands the letter
which Scribe wrote to Avenarius about me, I felt I had a proof
that the French writer had taken up my case and that we were
now already more or less in France. Scribe's letter also made a
great impression on my wife, who was not very demonstrative—
so great, indeed, that it completely allayed the anxiety which
the Paris adventure had been causing in her mind." With the
lightning speed which always characterized the movements of
this impulsive being, he made up his mind to be on his way to
France within four weeks. Paris lay before them like the shores
of some tropic isle; a Land of Promise, with its strange and
gifted people, its theatre with the cosmopolitan heart, under
whose ægis so many had beheld the dawning of better times.
Why should not Richard Wagner also take Paris by storm one
of these days?

He resumed his French studies with Professor Henriot, and
together they roughed out a translation of the first act of *Rienzi*,
of which Wagner made a copy in red ink on his score, so as not
to waste a day after his arrival in Paris. He sold up his furniture, gave a concert for his own benefit, and thought seriously
about paying his debts, not only at Koenigsberg, but also at

Magdeburg. . . . The trouble was, however, if he got rid of all
his cash, how in the world was he to pay for the journey?

On the advice of his old friend Moeller, the difficulty was
solved in this way: Wagner was to keep his cash, and pay his
creditors as soon as his successes in Paris provided him with
the money to do so. That was quite simple. What was considerably less so, was to get across the Russian frontier without
passports; for his remorseless creditors, alive to the possibility
of his trying to steal away, had procured a seizure of all the
necessary papers. "Well then, we shall have to do without them,
that's all," sniffed the foxy old Moeller. Nothing easier. They
would drive to a place near the frontier. Moeller had a friend
with a house just over the border, on the Prussian side. He
would lend them a hand. All they had to do was to wait till it
was dark, and then "good-bye Russia!" The whole thing sounded
splendid, with just a touch of adventure to give it an additional
spice.

And so they left Riga, as they had left Koenigsberg, without
a qualm, and without a stick—but also without any further
hitch, quite indifferent to a past that had brought them neither
money nor any real peace of mind. The only memory Richard
carried away with him was the memory of his wife's escapade,
another proof that misfortune dogs a man like the ghosts of his
dead hopes.

Side by side in their carriage, the young couple sat gazing
into space, peering into a future whose countenance they could
not read. All he had to his name was a few manuscripts and
an enormous dog of which he made a tremendous fuss. For some
time past this animal had been following him about wherever
he went. It used to wait outside the house at night until he
came home. So Wagner had made it one of the family. Just as
three years earlier he had left Magdeburg with nothing to call
his own but his *Liebesverbot*, and never a friend in the world
but his poodle Rupel, so now he departed with his *Rienzi* and
Robber, the great Newfoundland, perched up between Minna
and himself.

But negotiating the frontier was not quite so easy as it looked.
The first thing they had to do was to hide in a sort of smuggler's
den till the sun went down, and then make their way across
country to the moat that runs the whole length of the frontier,
taking care to dodge the Cossacks and the soldiers on sentry-go,
who had orders to fire at anyone or anything that looked suspicious. Then they had to get across the moat and clamber up
the opposite bank without being seen. And all this had to be done

with travelling-bags to carry, Minna almost in a state of collapse, and the embarrassing Robber, who might betray them at any moment. By a miracle, the whole thing went off without a hitch, and Moeller, who had been anxiously awaiting the fugitives on Prussian soil, wept for joy. Next day they had to make a wide détour to avoid Koenigsberg, as the place was full of sheriff's men, and make the best of their way to Arnau in an old, rattletrap wagonette. Then the driver went and upset his cargo into a clump of furze. Minna complained of pains in her inside, and they had to stay a whole day at a very uncomfortable farm. From there they managed to get to Pillau, the Prussian seaport, and contrived to get taken on board an old sailing-ship, the *Thetis*, whose captain agreed to convey the dubious-looking pair as far as London. The crew consisted of seven men, including the captain. They bundled the Wagners and their monumental dog into the hold, and wouldn't even let them up for a breath of air till they were well out to sea. The weather was dead against them; in the Baltic it was as calm as a mill pond. Richard took advantage of his enforced tranquillity to rub up his French a little by reading George Sand's *La Dernière Aldini*.

It took them one whole week to get to Elsinore, where they saw the ancient castle with its greenish bronze roof and its bare, wind-swept "platform," and thought of Hamlet and the words he uttered after he had seen his father's ghost: "There are more things in heaven and earth, Horatio, than are dreamt of in your philosophy." And thus, as ever, the poet of tragedy persisted in rising up in the path of the musician whithersoever he might choose to wander. Then came the Kattegat and the Skaggerack, and suddenly a fierce storm arose and raged with such violence that you might have thought that now Ariel, now Caliban, were striving, the one to save, and the other to drown this last surviving passenger of the enchanted ship. Twelve-score years and ten since Shakespeare died, this pale-faced exile, gazing out over the wild waste of waters, may well have thought, like Prospero, that

> . . . the best comforter
> To an unsettled fancy,

would be "some heavenly music." Everyone on board thought his last hour had come. But the captain, after trying vainly for twenty-four long hours to beat up against the howling blast, at length gave up the attempt and ran with the wind abeam to seek for shelter on the coast of Norway. At last the *Thetis*, feeling her way gingerly among the granite reefs, glided into the smooth waters of the fjord of Sandvigen, not far from Aerendal. The crew furled their sails, singing the while a cheery chanty, and the rocky shore, against which the wind was still spending its fury, echoed back the sound. Bliss followed on the heels of woe. Ariel, bright spirit of the world of thought, was victor now. Lulled by those airs that sang of perils overpast, Wagner listened to another music, the music in his heart, and caught, as it rose from its hidden depths, his own *Song of the Sailors*. Not long ago he had read in Heine that mystic story of the Flying Dutchman, whose phantom ship wanders eternally over the homeless deep. And the song of those ghostly mariners, doomed ever more to sail the seas, strikes on his ears in this theatre of naked rock, mingling its music with the salt sea-winds, the scent of the brine, and the drifting cloud wrack, and inspiring the drama which tells of the strife of man with the elements, with ineluctable, unconquerable Destiny. The Dutch mariner, that Wandering Jew of the restless ocean, on whom death can lay no hand, is doomed everlastingly to sail the seas, through storm and tempest, until he encounters the woman who shall bring him redemption from sin and rest from all his toil. *Thesis:* Music. *Antithesis:* the Drama of Life. *Synthesis:* Music and Drama, face to face. So we have Wagner armed, not only with masterful visions and a splendid legend, but with the lively elements of an ethical system. His affair is not merely with the theatre, with dramatic art, but with morality. It came to him now as a revelation that art derives its motive power from the feelings, and he noted down this aphorism, "For my part, I can only think of the spirit of music in terms of love." A new life, a philosophical ideal—the most perilous of human quests—took shape before his eyes in this fjord as he fixed his gaze on the far-flung harmonies of the setting sun. "From that moment began my poetical life. The Flying Dutchman appeared before my eyes. From my own plight he derived his moral power; and the storm, the billows of the sea, the Scandinavian rocks, and the life on shipboard supplied his physiognomy and native hue."

But Wagner's trials were not yet over. After three days in port, the *Thetis* set sail again, and ran upon a rock. They were obliged to drop anchor to see what damage the vessel had sustained. On the 1st of August they made another start. On the 6th a fresh northerly wind sprang up. By evening it was blowing a hurricane. On the 7th, about two in the afternoon, the passengers gave themselves up for lost. There came a moment of blank despair. The sailors began to look darkly at them. Only some spirit of evil in their midst could account for such a sinister series of disasters. A huge wave carried away the figurehead, a symbolical presentment of the nymph Thetis, a sure sign of divine displeasure. Minna was for casting herself overboard. She prayed that the lightning might strike her, and besought her husband to cling closely to her so that death itself should not divide them. In the howling of the wind among the shrouds they seemed to hear the wild laughter of the Dutchman, and all the mighty symphony of doom broke in a deafening diapason on their ears. But next day the violence of the storm abated; bedrenched and bruised and battered, they caught glimpses of other sails, and on the 9th, after three weeks at sea, during which they had suffered every imaginable peril, the little craft was hailed by a British pilot. Three days later she sailed into the estuary of the Thames. Richard attired himself with considerable care, shaved on deck at the foot of the mainmast, and put on all his best. He now quitted the *Thetis* with his wife and dog, and made the remainder of the journey up the Thames to London by steamboat. At last they found themselves on *terra firma*, and took their seats in one of London's narrow cabs in which there is only room for two to sit face to face. Richard sat opposite Minna, and Robber planted himself athwart the vehicle with his head out of one of the windows and his tail out of the other. In this conveyance the composer and his wife went ambling along the London streets, talking over their plans for the future, and wondering how best they could "conquer the monstrous city." The battle thus contemplated reduced itself to one week's intensive onslaught, in the course of which they visited Westminster Abbey, saw Poets' Corner and the bust of Shakespeare. Then they visited the Houses of Parliament, where Wagner hoped to find "Lord Bulwer Lytton" and personally to hand him the libretto of *Rienzi*; but "Lord Bulwer" was not there, and Wagner had to content himself with listening to a speech by the Prime Minister, Lord Melbourne, a rejoinder thereto by Lord Brougham and, by way of finale, to sit through the harangue of a man who wore his grey beaver all the time, kept his hands stuck in his pockets, and seemed on the whole a considerable bore. This was the Duke of Wellington. His attitude relieved Wagner of any exaggerated respect he may have felt for the conqueror of Napoleon.

They then decided they would go to France, and, in company with the captain of the *Thetis*, travelled for the first time in their lives in a "steam-coach." The evening of the 20th of August found them at Boulogne-sur-Mer. As luck would have it, Meyerbeer was there, too. The illustrious Berliner might well be useful to them. He already counted among the people with whom he was "in touch" since he (Wagner) had written him a letter. Besides, Meyerbeer's kindness was proverbial. He found out where the great man was staying, called, and was asked in. "I was delighted beyond all expectation." No one could have been more gracious than the composer of the *Huguenots*; moreover we know the enthusiasm with which a young poet always regards those who invite him to recite his verses. Wagner read over to Meyerbeer the first three acts of his drama, and left him the musical manuscript. What chiefly impressed Meyerbeer was the excellence of the handwriting. This little Saxon was a penman, and no mistake! He offered him letters of introduction to Duponchel, director of the Grand Opera; Habenek, the conductor; and Schlesinger, the music publisher. He introduced the young neophyte to Moschelès and Mlle. Blahedka, the celebrated *virtuosa*.

So Wagner was now in the swim, in direct relations with his peers, talking music, making music, and hearing music. On the 12th of September he completed the orchestration of the second act of *Rienzi*. And now he was burning to see Paris, to set foot at last on the famous stage which was awaiting his coming. He therefore wrote off to Edouard Avenarius, his sister Cecile's *fiancé*, addressing his missive to the *Librairie Allemande Brockhaus et Avenarius*, 60 rue de Richelieu. This letter, couched in his most engaging terms, begged the recipient to take a furnished room for him, if possible not too far away from his own bookshop. The couple then took their places in the diligence in which they were to accomplish the final stages of this interminable journey. But at the far end of that long French highway, with its endless fringe of poplars, Wagner knew that for all the trouble and obstacles he had endured and met with, and for all the energy he had expended, a fitting recompense would at last be his. At daybreak on the 16th of September they arrived at the Port Saint-Denis, where Wagner applied for his correspondence, expecting to find an answer from Avenarius about the lodgings. There was nothing, no letters at all; so on they went—man and wife and great, lumbering, good-tempered dog—in the wake of a long procession of market carts. The diligence finally deposited them at the rue Jussienne, and they hurried off to Avenarius, who, as it happened, had just fixed up a room for them near the Halles. And so they make acquaintance with this Paris of the early morning, Paris of the stubbly beard, smelling of the earth earthy; Paris that yawns still but half-awake, threading its way amongst its turnips, and slithering on its scattered cabbage leaves. Marché des Innocents, rue de la Fromagerie, de la Triperie, du Marché aux Poires, the gourmand's Mecca. Could this be the city of Méhul, the scene of Gluck's courtly love-making, the place whereof Mozart once wrote, "I am, so to speak, up to my neck in music; I am at it all day long. I must turn out a grand opera." Yet there it was, too, that the great man was so completely misunderstood and suffered so grievously in consequence. Was it not he who exclaimed, "The devil must have made this French language!" And did Wagner dream that he would succeed where Mozart failed? Was he going to finish his opera in a place like this? And would he write others in such a chaotic, confusing welter of fruit and vegetables?

At last they halted at No. 33 rue de la Tonnellerie, which links up the rue Saint-Honoré with the Marché des Innocents. So this was the place, this was the frowsy den, for which they had so long been making! Wagner already began to feel as if he had gone down a peg or two in the social scale. And yet there, on the façade of their dingy hotel, was a bust bearing the inscription, "Molière was born here." Good Heavens! Was that the sort of thing the French did with the birthplaces of their great men? Our young German friends took possession of a dismal room that looked out on to the market below where every kind of fruit and vegetable lay tumbled in disorderly profusion on the cobbled pavement. "We looked at each other with misgiving, wondering what in the world we had come there to seek." The answer was, glory—glory that lies in wait for every poet in the chance encounters of a great and populous city.

PART TWO

Chapter I

PARIS UNDER THE CITIZEN-KING

THE well-to-do, middle-class and would-be dashing France with which the young German composer was called on to make acquaintance in the Paris of 1839 was rather calculated to suit his taste. The king, Louis Philippe, whom France never thought very much of (perhaps because his features lent themselves too readily to caricature) was one of the most sagacious and prudent princes the world had ever known. He knew what it costs to play the tyrant, and regarded the ruler of a modern state as the chairman of a board of directors. He governed his country as one governs a bank, with prudence, moderation, good temper, never omitting, however, to feather his nest with whatever perquisites came his way from a satisfactory deal, and always doing his best to keep up the confidence of his customers. He adopted the "national" ticket, the day of the aristocrat being over and done with. He stood for the golden mean. He was thrifty, knew the value of money, and was determined not to jeopardize, on any field of battle, the fortunes of the New Order. Trade, commerce, manufactures, were the order of the day, and traders and manufacturers were going to wield the supreme power in the state, namely the power of the purse, and he was not going to risk all that in any sort of war. "All my life," he said, "I have detested that profound iniquity called war, whose only result is to send to their death tens of thousands of men the vast majority of whom are not in the least interested in the cause for which they are invited to lay down their lives. My enemies call me the 'peace-at-any-price king.' They are right. I am." And yet this easy-going and most highly respectable monarch, this "citizen-king," was nearly murdered over and over again because he favoured the policy of an understanding with England. They said he was a coward. But in spite of his miraculous escapes from assassination, he never shirked a public function. All the same he had lost faith in the wisdom of the people and he no longer believed in crowns. "The present attitude of the crowned heads will bring disaster on everything," he said. " 'The world shall be unkinged,' " he added, quoting Shakespeare. It was just as it had been a quarter of a century before, when Napoleon fell, and Richard Wagner was born. The prophets of the new generation were seeking to discover a synthesis between the discordant elements—political, literary, and musical—of 1839. The romantic movement had already got its slogan, which it called its "ideals," and an attempt was being made to erect into a dogma what was merely the outcome of exuberant health and high spirits. The young, however, are always more serious-minded than the middle-aged and the elderly. There was a continuous conflict between two main parties. On the one hand, there were the poets and reformers, who were full of fight and anxious to "ring out the old" and "ring in the new"; anxious to shatter everything to bits and then "remould it nearer to the heart's desire." On the other side there were the well-to-do, the comfortably-off, the people who had "got there" and were only too anxious to avail themselves of the period of peace and quiet which their sensible, easy-going king was offering them. It was a case of the individual against society. The nineteenth century was hardly in its teens, but it was penetrating the hoary winter of monarchical Europe like the dawn of a universal springtime, and a fierce feud existed between these two seasons—winter and spring—one of which could only expand by slaying the other. Meanwhile the old army veterans had all the longings that come of twenty years of playing the hero. They had been victorious on a hundred fields and clamoured for some reward for their valour, before they died in their four-posters. They were resolved to have a taste of that youth which their grandiose emperor had made them squander, chasing after glory, the fruits of which he never allowed them the leisure to enjoy. The upshot was that they actively resented the encroachment of these young romantics with their luxuriant beards and rapt expressions. But if some of the revolutionaries, like Vigny, Dumas, Victor Hugo, Lamartine, and Musset, had got themselves talked about, the real leading-lights were Villemain, Barante, Fauriel, Pichot, poets like Casimir Delavigne and Népomucène Lemercier, the brothers Deschamps, Jules Lefèvre, Viennet, Millevoye, Béranger, and those indefatigable storytellers Frédéric Soulié, Eugène Sue, Paul de Kock, Roger de Beauvoir, Legouvé, and so on. In the same category as these gentry, but attaining a still higher level, were such foreigners as Goethe, Walter Scott, and that most admirable monster,

Byron. While, far above them all, shone down, on Paris café and on German tavern, the ray divine of the immortal Shakespeare, the Great Enchanter, the King of all Romantic Drama. With Shakespeare had come the taste for the subtle interplay of light and shade, of guilt and innocence, enacting their divers parts amid the shifting shadows of the Gothic stage; that complex pattern of contrasts wherein we see the rival powers of Light and Darkness battling eternally for dominance in the soul of man. Walter Scott had rung up the curtain on his stage, and it was peopled with a wondrous company of high-born ladies, minstrels, knightly lovers, magnanimous pirates and witches, and the so-called historical novel was destined to revive a world of forgotten symbolism and antique legend. If the plants of the literary garden of 1839 were full of sap and vigour, though giving as yet no certain sign what form that garden's crowning flower would take to grace its Easter Day withal, an efflorescence still more rapid was taking place hard by, in the hothouses devoted to the cultivation of music. Paris was then the hub of the musical universe. Since 1828, one year after Beethoven's death, the Conservatoire had undertaken the study and orchestral performance of all his symphonies. The Royal Academy of Music (Grand Opera), endowed with an annual subsidy of 700,000 francs, was the most brilliant operatic theatre in Europe. The Opéra Comique, despite certain successes like *Zampa* and the *Fiancée* of Auber, had to give precedence to the Italian Opera, which for thirty years became the centre of all the wealth and fashion. It took up its quarters in 1841 in the Salle Ventadour. Auber, Adam, Hérold, Halévy, were the great French names that figured conspicuously in its programs. Their music was good sound stuff, bright and attractive. It had no exaggerated ambitions, and its immediate object was to please. It was exactly suited to the intellectual capacity of the worthy middle-class folk who came and planked down their half-crowns and expected a little gaiety and a modicum of sentiment in return. In 1839 Auber had been appointed *Directeur des Concerts de la Cour*, or Master of the King's Music. One of his strokes of genius was his discovery of that amazing librettist, Eugène Scribe, who, when he died, had no less than seventy-six theatrical works to his credit. One of Auber's sayings was: "I loved music till I was thirty, a regular young man's passion. . . . Music was all very well as a mistress; but as a wife, well . . ."

Halévy's muse was graver, more austere. Four years earlier he had produced his masterpiece, *La Juive*, which he conceived one night as he was strolling about in Scribe's garden. It was

Nourrit, the famous tenor who wrote the words for the air that
was then all the rage, words which Marcel Proust again called
back to life, *"Rachel, quand du Seigneur, la gloire tutélaire"*
(Rachel, when the light of the Lord's protecting ray . . .).

Adam was a strange creature. He had been born with a taste
for science and dry-as-dust research, and then, when he composed *Le Chalet*, he suddenly found himself the possessor of
quite a different sort of gift. Thereafter it never took him more
than a few days, or at the most a few weeks, to bring an opera
to birth. *Le Postillon de Lonjumeau* was good theatre *à la mode*,
and the one-time little pedantic apprentice now declared: "My
one and only ambition in composing music for the stage is to
write clear, understandable things, that will entertain the public.
I just put down the ideas that come into my head, and they keep
on coming, the dear young things."

The two outstanding Italian composers were Rossini and
Spontini. They were in a different class altogether. A pupil of
Gluck and Mozart, Spontini introduced orchestral devices and
massed scenic effects that were an absolutely new departure.
Inventive, with plenty of daring, he came to grief in Berlin, as
he had come to grief in Paris, by reason of his exacting and
uncompromising temper. In spite of all, he held on his way
undaunted, snapping his fingers at the whole gang of "contrapuntal duffers," and laughing at all these "young note-weavers
who are about as capable of understanding what is really great
in musical art as the doorkeepers who begat them." *La Vestale*
created an uproar, and just as, a few years before, Fernand
Cortez had opened the gates of an unknown world to Richard
Wagner, so *La Vestale* took Berlioz's breath away and "made
him stagger." Spontini was a downright revelation to these two
young composers. As for Rossini, although he had given up composing some long time ago, he was still the *illustrissimo maestro*,
"The Great Jove of Music," "a man," as Stendhal said, "whose
fame was coextensive with civilization itself." But the Swan of
Pesaro, on whom the mellowing years were descending, had
already described from afar the changes that the future had in
store, changes which, in the world of music, foreshadowed a
revolution no less profound than in the world of politics. And if
he had remained silent since that memorable night which, ten
years ago, had witnessed the first performance of his *William
Tell*, may it not have been that he was conscious of the growth
of those "new theories which aimed at making music a literary
art, an art of imitation, a mode of giving musical expression to
philosophical ideas?" (From a letter to Rossi, director of the

Milan Conservatoire.) Little did he, the man of runs and trills, of *il bel canto*, the melody-at-any-price man, dream that in a modest "bed-sitter" at the Hôtel Molière, a young man was elaborating a theory of art which would not have it that music should be wooed as a man might woo a maid, with langorous looks, or dashing airs; but rather insisted that it should be treated as a system, a plan, an architectural structure, a higher form of life; not as a pastime, a diversion, but as drama, the very stuff of life itself.

Well then, among the young musicians of the new school, who was the one that was going to count? Was it Marliani, the author of *Xacarilla*, a little opera of which M. Scribe, of course, furnished the libretto? Was it M. Gounod, who carried off the first prize offered for competition by the Académie des Beaux-Arts with a cantata for three voices? The papers said, "This young man's work has warmth and inventiveness, it promises a composer of distinction. . . . But his cantata lacks melody and tunefulness, though it is written with ability and correctness." Or was it this strange Hector Berlioz, whose *Harold en Italie* had moved Paganini to such a pitch of enthusiasm that he had flung himself on his knees before the composer, in the presence of the whole orchestra? Berlioz already had his *Symphonie fantastique*, the *Requiem*, and *Benvenuto Cellini* to his credit, and he had then just recently been conducting, at the Conservatoire, his *Roméo et Juliette*, a symphony with choruses, solos, and a choral recitative. But if he himself was chanting the pæan of victory, the critics were not exactly showering bouquets upon him. One animadverted on the symphonic form he had given to his work. Another gave it as his opinion that the *Queen Mab* scherzo was nothing but a funny little noise that reminded him of a lot of twittering canaries. At any rate, he was not to be daunted, and he stuck at nothing. He wrote for the full orchestra, choruses, harmonicas, two pianos, twenty basses in unison, and even for three orchestras at once. And so his musical monstrosities, "born into the world with all their teeth, like Richard III," as their sire declared, occasionally met with some "terrifying" successes. No matter, this leader of the younger school, this flamboyant romantic, was a power, an authority. There was more real stuff in him than in all those melody-mongers put together, and that was why Richard Wagner devoted one of his first free evenings to *Roméo et Juliette*. It amazed him much as *La Vestale* had amazed Berlioz. The skill of the orchestration, the wealth of sublime harmonies, came upon him with something of a shock, sweeping all personal considerations utterly away. There was no question of metaphysics here. It was not merely a statement, a presentation of intellectual ideas, but a whole symphonic drama. Despite a few banalities, despite a certain feeling of oppression which Wagner could never wholly throw off when listening to the overwhelming volume of sound in Berlioz's music, he immediately recognized the native grandeur and energy of that incomparable artist. These *dissonances des consonances* (particularly the discords in the seventh major to which he was especially addicted) endow his music with a mystical quality and a freedom of orchestration which were destined to have a lasting effect on Wagner. "We must honour Berlioz," he afterwards declared, "as the true redeemer of the world of music."

That consoled him a little for the operas of his compatriot, Meyerbeer; for all Meyerbeer did was to exploit the methods of Spontini and Rossini, falsifying and distorting them; and so, despite the welcome he had received from him at Boulogne, Wagner was hostile to him. "I cannot exist, or feel as an artist in my own eyes or in my friends', without telling myself and everyone that Meyerbeer and I are poles asunder." But perhaps at bottom, in the unplumbed depths of his soul, this animosity was engendered by a kind of similarity, a sort of kinship, spiritual and physical, of which Wagner was dimly conscious, between himself and Meyerbeer. He was a German like Maître Jacob (the name appeared as Giacomo on the posters). Perhaps, though he never avowed it even to himself, he also had in his veins a trace of that Oriental blood to which many a man from the land of Israel is indebted for the sensitiveness of his perceptions. . . . Perhaps, too, they had in common a leaning towards the dramatic romanticism of the younger musical generation, disencumbered of its elaborate vocal arabesques, but steeped all the same in that Viennese Italianism for which Mozart was responsible. Lastly, the creator of *Robert le Diable* and *The Huguenots* may have impressed him with the authoritativeness that attends on success, with his thorough knowledge of everything connected with the theatre, his skill in stagecraft, his dramatic sense, his mastery of detail. Unlike the general run of French authors, he left nothing to chance or to the inspiration of the moment. He was years working up an opera, experimenting with the movements, choosing the cast, and when at length the curtain did go up on a new work of his, the thing had been brought to such a pitch of perfection, its success was so certain, that an unbroken run of a hundred nights could confidently be predicted for it. That, too, was scientific, sober business. Although Wagner, fired by the youthful ardour of his convictions, despised this straining after effect and was very much disposed to regard it as utterly worthless, he *did* learn from M. Meyerbeer one absolutely essential lesson, and that was the need a composer has to discover, even though it be in spite of himself, or at least without any conscious intention, a really poetical situation; by which I mean a scene, or a speech, proceeding from the heart which shall inspire the composer with the divine afflatus, and so enable him to obtain all that is richest, noblest, and most moving in musical expression. And Wagner cites as an illustration of his contention, the love-scene from *The Huguenots*, "that heaven-sent melody, in G flat major, that miracle of expression. . . . Even among the most perfect productions of the musical art, there are few things to be compared with it." But so perfect a consonance between the imagination of the poet and the creative genius of the musician is too much a matter of chance not to be exceptional. Anything, therefore, in the nature of a sustained collaboration between the composer and the librettist is clearly out of the question. The fallacy of opera is precisely here: the means, namely music, has been made the end; and the end, namely the drama, has become the means. This truth, though as yet still dim and undefined, is essential to the development of opera. Though ordinary opera is a hybrid and almost absurdly unnatural combination, music-drama, that dream of a new world, may nevertheless arise from it. And Wagner knew full well that the sorrows and triumphs of the new birth thus foreshadowed were stirring within him.

As often happens with artists, their enthusiasm for forms of art parallel with their own, tends to diminish in proportion as their knowledge of themselves increases. Things that once moved them to delight begin to lose their charm, and finally become positively hateful to them. To begin with, they seek nurture for their spirit from extraneous sources, but as soon as they begin to find themselves, they turn away and take their leave of regions wherein their sojourn was but transitory. The world must needs be examined anew, and fashioned anew ere they find a suitable habitation for their souls. They are like those wayward and intelligent children who refuse to conform to rules of conduct based on conventions whose validity they deny. They exalt injustice to the level of a duty, and forge their ideal in the fires of revolt. The more fierce their resistance, their refusal to submit, the greater the man and the greater the work that emerges from the conflict. So Wagner seldom went to the theatre. His first weeks in Paris were taken up with efforts, both wearisome and fruitless, to derive some practical advantage from the introductions with which Meyerbeer had furnished him. It dawned on him at length that, though these Frenchmen always seemed in a hurry, their actual rate of progress was disconcertingly slow. Duponchel, the director of the Opéra, received him courteously, and, eyeglass in eye, glanced through Meyerbeer's letter, which he put in his pocket, and with a few friendly remarks showed his visitor to the door. From that source Wagner never heard another word. Then he went to call on Schlesinger, the music-publisher, who was just as polite and just as indifferent. Having composed a barytone setting to Heine's *The Two Grenadiers*, a lullaby and a little song to Ronsard's *Mignonne, allons voir si la rose*, he took them to M. Dupont, third tenor at the Opéra, who told him that, the words being in old French, it wouldn't stand a chance. M. Géraldy, a teacher of singing, to whom he next applied, declared that his song *The Two Grenadiers* (composed six months before Schumann's) would never go down because the accompaniment wound up with a suggestion of the *Marseillaise*, a song which was never heard in those days, save as an obbligato to gun fire and street fighting. Wagner got to know a M. Dumersan, who turned out little sketches for the stage, and he wrote French words to some passages out of the *Liebesverbot* to serve as specimens for a preliminary audition which he hoped to obtain at the Renaissance. And, better still, he managed to get hold of three well-known singers, one of whom was Pauline Garcia, a sister of La Malibran, a star that had just taken her place in the galaxy of Boulevard favourites. He thought this meant an engagement, success at last. But things dragged on in the most disconcerting manner. Wagner called on the famous Lablache, for whom he had written a grand bass tune with chorus, to be included in his rôle of Oroviste in *Norma*. But Lablache would have nothing to do with such an unorthodox proceeding, and Wagner withdrew covered with blushes and confusion.

Then he went to see Scribe. That potentate received him with the most perfect courtesy, and made an appointment for an audition in the Foyer des Artistes at the Opéra. On the due date, Scribe appeared, in company with M. Edouard Mounais, acting director of the Royal Academy of Music, and Wagner played the piano accompaniment to the three airs which he had selected as examples of his work. Both these gentlemen pronounced the music "charming." Scribe, as usual, said he would be delighted to do the necessary with the text. But this promise, like all its predecessors, was barren of result, and at last the composer, thinking that, after all, this rather neglected score was perhaps a little unworthy, decided to abandon the work upon which he had reared so many soaring castles—in Paris!

The one paltry satisfaction that fell to his lot during these long months was the performance of his overture to *Columbus* at the Conservatoire concert rehearsals. Habenek, a conductor with a European reputation, had promised to do that much for him, and he kept his word. This was the first time Wagner's name appeared in a French paper. "An Overture by a young German composer of very remarkable ability has just been rehearsed by the orchestra of the Conservatoire and received with unanimous applause. We look forward to hearing this work very shortly, and shall give it most careful attention" (*Revue et Gazette musicales de Paris*, 22nd of January, 1840). This auspicious event was the occasion of an emotional experience which exerted a profound effect upon his whole life. That same evening he heard the famous orchestra play Beethoven's *Ninth Symphony,* a work which his compatriots described as the unintelligible ravings of a madman. But for Wagner it came with all the tragic force of a sudden and blinding revelation, and imparted a decisive bent to his artistic orientation. "I suddenly beheld, before my very eyes, the image that I had but half-divined in my youthful dreams. There it was, as clear as the sunlight, and I could touch it with my hands. My period of decadence, which had commenced with the perturbation into which I had been thrown by hearing the performance (in Germany) of Beethoven's work, and which had developed so disastrously during the barren days of my theatrical conductorship, came to a sudden end, amid shame and contrition. . . . I may compare this experience with the emotion I felt as a boy of sixteen when I heard Mme. Schroeder Devrient in *Fidelio.*"

But if, in Wagner's eyes, the Choral Symphony symbolizes the tragedy of despair, it is also the defile through which the artist must needs adventure if he would make his way "into the world of light upon whose soil the music of humanity raises itself to heaven." Thus it was that he came to the threshold of that period of hardship and discouragement which was, as it were, the first circle of the inferno into which he must descend ere he finds the path that is to lead him to himself, that shall reveal to him his own ego.

He went roaming about Paris, resolutely, almost savagely, alone; a stranger in a city of strangers, wondering how, from one day to another, he was going to win his bread. No managerial antechambers opened their doors to this nameless alien.

No publisher cared a straw about his work. Some of the less ungracious among them advised him to write "gallops," or else to go back home again. He hurries from the Guignol of the Champs Elysées to the fowl-run of the Comédie Française and stakes his last remaining cash on schemes that come to naught. Some one points him out the pawnshop. He had seen the sign already, but hadn't understood what it meant. His watch goes first, his little silver knick-knacks, his poor wedding presents, then Minna's trinkets, and finally her theatrical wardrobe. Meanwhile he sticks to his work, but henceforth he is not going to be told by anyone; he recognizes no man as master here, in this city that never yielded to any but the strong. His will was indomitable; nothing could break it; and he started on an Overture to *Faust* mainly with the idea of buttressing up his self-respect, and for his motto he chose those lines of Goethe which describe how he who has lived so long on the breath of enthusiasm, for the first time gives utterance to his hate:

> *Der Gott der mir im Busen wohnt*
> *Kann tief mein Innerstes erregen,*
> *Der über allen meinen Kräften thront,*
> *Er kann nach aussen nichts bewegen;*
> *Und so ist mir das Dasein eine Last,*
> *Der Tod erwünscht, das Leben mir verhasst.*

Chapter II

THE SCHOOL OF HATE

In the shop of Messrs. Brockhaus and Avenarius, in the rue de Richelieu, under the very shadow of the Bibliothèque Royale, and a few steps from the rue Le Peletier, where stands the Opéra, the stronghold of his adversaries, Richard Wagner found a friend. He was a man of about fifty who hailed from Bonn, and had some little pettifogging job in the great Paris Library. This sage and learned musicographer, who was equally devoid of energy and ambition, had for some time past been wearing out his days in the spacious halls of the City of Books, through which he flitted to and fro, noiseless as a moth of darkness. No one knew aught of this mysterious toiler in the realms of erudition, save that he was a philosopher who, in his pilgrimage through life, had shed, one by one, all his dreams, all his illusions, even his very name. True, he was known as Mr. Anders, but that—which meant Mr. Otherwise—was a pseudonym which he invented the better to conceal a past which, if Avenarius was to be believed, had been a brilliant one. He had once been rich, but all his wealth had disappeared, all save his books, the which, in their cherished bindings, garnished the walls of his little lodging in the rue de Seine and softly illumined it from floor to ceiling. This fellow-countryman and zealous admirer of Beethoven, conceived an affectionate regard for the youthful newcomer from the Saxon land, and, erelong, brought his second self to see him, Mr. Anders II, namely the philosopher Lehrs. Now, Lehrs was a German, too, of Jewish blood, whose parents had saddled him with the romantic prenomen of Siegfried. However, he was commonly called Samuel, an appellation much more becoming to this distinguished but retiring Hellenist, whose labours consisted in the compilation of learned commentaries for editions of Homer, Hesiod and Nicander, which were then appearing under the imprint of the House of Didot. Philologist and musicographer lived together as industrious and thrifty as

men could be, both as ignorant of the world and all its ways
as the Pons and Schmucke of Balzac's tale. You might well
believe that Balzac had taken them for his models. Despite the
privations he had to endure there, Lehrs would have it that there
was no place in the world where he could possibly live but Paris.
He worked all day, and when the evening came he would go the
round of the bookstalls on the quays, after which he and Anders,
who hobbled along leaning on a stick and an umbrella, would
struggle up as far as the Wagners' humble lodging. And straightway they would all fall to discussing plans for the future, for
these two poor souls, who nourished no loftier ambition for
themselves than to end their days still working on their humble
tasks, were no sooner brought into contact with Richard's passionate idealism than they felt all the old ardours, which long
ago had warmed their simple hearts, kindling anew within them.
They were both ill and worn out (Lehrs succumbed to phthisis
shortly afterwards) ; but a plan of campaign for the "conquest
of Paris" took shape, just as, a few months earlier, the plan for
the "conquest of London" had been carefully elaborated. At one
end of the table on which these imaginary stakes were being
put to the hazard, Minna would prepare a scanty meal, whereof
the mighty Robber—of whom Anders was in mortal dread—
would scarcely so much as smell the leavings. Alas! Robber disappeared a little later on. Perhaps he did not get enough to eat;
perhaps he got lost or stolen. For many a week this faithful
friend had been the joy of the children that haunted the Palais
Royal, his favourite recreation-ground, where he would run and
fish out of the pond the things which the children flung therein
for him to retrieve. One day he failed to come home, and despite
all efforts to discover him, was never found again. It was a
terrible blow to Wagner, who got it into his head that it was an
evil omen.

However, Lehrs and Anders had so strong a faith in the
future of their *protégé* that they urged him to quit his present
hovel and move into more cheerful rooms in the rue du Helder.
To get on in Paris, Lehrs assured him, it was necessary to keep
up appearances. Richard was only too easily persuaded to spend
money, for debts had no terrors for him ("one always contrives
to scrape through somehow or another") and a little comfort in
his private surroundings was becoming an absolute necessity.
Some decent furniture, a few things to delight the eye—surely
this was just as much a necessity as food. Besides, Dumerson
seemed more and more confident about the Théâtre de la Renaissance. And then Laube had appeared on the scene again—Laube

of the *Journal du monde élégant*, the Laube of Dresden and Berlin—and, thanks to him, a little band of well-to-do Leipzig people combined to make young Wagner a small monthly allowance.

On the 15th of April, 1840, they moved into their new quarters on the fourth floor of No. 25 rue du Helder, fifty yards or so from the Boulevard des Italiens, the most elegant artistic and literary quarter in Paris. The very day of the move, Lehrs brought news of a great disaster—the Théâtre de la Renaissance had gone bankrupt. Wagner was knocked all of a heap. He now began to wonder whether Meyerbeer, who was always in the know about everything, had put him on to this theatre in order to shunt him off the Grand Opéra. But he was not one to give way under misfortune, and with the spontaneous energy he always displayed in times of crisis he plunged into his *Rienzi*, determined that this time he would get through with it. In all this he obeyed the instincts of the true artist, who, when anything occurs to disturb the balance of his life, automatically proceeds to redress it by an act of creation. And it should not be in Paris that he would get his work performed, but in Dresden, where Semper, the architect, had been commissioned to build a new theatre. Meanwhile he had got to live. He therefore betook himself to Schlesinger, who published the *Gazette Musicale*, and the works of Liszt, Chopin, and a host of other composers, and suggested that he should publish his *Two Grenadiers*. Schlesinger would only agree on condition that he put down fifty francs by way of deposit. As Wagner had not got fifty francs, Schlesinger told him he could work it off by writing some articles for his *Gazette*. So Wagner went home and turned scribe. But as he could not possibly write in French, he had to employ the services of a translator, of course at his own expense. Oh, well; it could not be helped. Then and there he sat down and dashed off a longish dissertation "On German Music." It attracted attention. Schlesinger said he would like more, and in the course of two months Wagner sent him "The Executant's Task and the Composer's Independence," "A Visit to Beethoven," and "A German Composer in Paris." In these articles Wagner avenged himself for the snubs he had received.

"Poverty and privation, unfailing comrades of the German artist, it is to you that, in recording these sacred memories, it behoves me to address my initial invocation." Such were the opening words of his "Visit to Beethoven." The visit, be it remarked, was wholly imaginary and symbolical, for Wagner never beheld his deity. But here, in these glowing pages, he gives a vivid impression of the great man's genius, of his rustic ways, of his loneliness. And, making him speak of *Fidelio* and *Adelaide*, he puts into the mouth of Beethoven his own confession of faith concerning the office of the voice in music. "The human voice is nobler and more beautiful than any other instrument. It is the direct interpreter of the human heart, and gives utterance to our subjective and individual experiences. Its domain is therefore essentially limited, but its manifestations are always clear and precise. Well then, unite the two elements; express the vague and rugged sensation of wild nature by the language of instruments (the orchestra), in contrast to the positive ideas of the spirit, represented by the human voice, and the latter will exercise a luminous influence on the former by controlling their exuberance and moderating their violence. Thus the heart, unfolding itself to these complex emotions, exalted and expanded by this infinite and delicious expectancy, will welcome with enthusiasm and conviction the inward revelation of a supernatural world." Such, in a few words, was the Wagnerian doctrine, in which hardship and the spirit of revolt had, in the space of a few brief months, wrought so deep a transformation. Never had he felt himself so near as now to the glorious and incomparable master who pointed out to him the rock from whose summit one learns to gaze forth undazzled on the world and its temptations. He would not sell himself, he would not debase himself, nor pander to the grovelling public taste, nor play the sycophant to the second-rate. He spared neither himself nor poor Minna, now sunk to the level of a maid-of-all-work, for she scrubbed the floors and did the housework and the cooking for a pair of German ladies, "paying guests," to whom they had been compelled to sublet their best rooms. When, after a few months' stay, these ladies took their departure, the Wagners managed to fill the gap with a commercial traveller who, unfortunately, was accustomed to employ his leisure in practising the flute. But we have got to put up with all sorts of things in this life. From Richard's bed to his writing-table was but a couple of steps; to eat his meals, he had merely to swing round in his chair, which he never quitted till far on into the night to turn into bed again. Every four days he took the air and went for a brief outing either with Lehrs or with two new friends who had now arrived to complete the colony. One was a painter named Ernest Kietz, who was studying under Paul Delaroche, the fashionable portraitist; the other, Friedrich Pecht, also a painter and a pupil of Delaroche. Kietz was a sort of big undisciplined child, who had had very little schooling.

He was rather like Robber in his good-humoured playfulness, but he was endowed with a gift for harmless repartee that made him most amusing company. He seemed to think that an artist had fifty or sixty years in front of him in which to learn to mix his paints. So he spent all his time studying how to prepare his palette and his brushes. This took him the whole day, so that when he was at last ready to begin his picture, the light would already be failing and the work had to be put off till the following morning. As, next day, the same process had to be gone through all over again, he deplored the brevity of life, and said that his models "were dying beneath his brush"! All the same, he did get through a portrait of Richard in a flowered dressing-gown, owing to the fact that he spent a good part of his day in the Wagners' rooms in order to amuse Minna. This gave him the opportunity of painting his landlord and so working off his rent.

Such was the little brotherhood of German bohemians, the first, in date, of all the Wagnerian groups. When occasion offered—when, that is, any of them had a windfall that enabled him to play the host—they all foregathered at Brocci's, an Italian restaurant opposite the Opéra, where the most brilliant of all these voluntary exiles, Heinrich Heine, was the centre of attraction. Things were then going very well with Heine: brilliant success as a writer in France, as in Germany; in looks and manner a dilettante eighteenth-century abbé; a charming young woman for a help-meet, surpassing even Minna in looks; and a snug little allowance from an uncle in Hamburg, not to mention a subsidy of six thousand francs granted him by M. Guizot from the secret funds of his department.

Of course Wagner regarded this brilliant person with deferential interest, the more so as he discovered that in one of his books (*Mémoires de M. de Schnabele-Wopski*) he had dealt with a theme which, as long ago as his voyage on the *Thetis*, had fired him with musical inspiration, the story of *The Flying Dutchman*. He was no less taken with the irony of Heinrich Heine, who, in the German tongue, but with a most Parisian wit, mocked at the managers of the Opera who had the happy inspiration so to bedazzle the eyes of the spectators that they were quite able to put up with the music. Heine also said of Meyerbeer that he would be immortal as long as he lived, and even a little longer because he had paid for it in advance. . . .

But Wagner was seldom seen in theatre or café; it cost too much. He was anxious to write music for his *Flying Dutchman*, and so hastened to have done with *Rienzi*. Nevertheless, his penury was growing more agonizingly acute than ever, and kept dragging him away from his proper work. He had to undertake the most ludicrous tasks, those horrible, humiliating pot-boilers that make one blush to think of them, whose tragi-comedy is only discernible when you come in after-years to look back on them. For example, Schlesinger got him to write "fourteen pieces for the cornet," the instrument which was then all the rage with the younger generation. (Schlesinger said when they were done, that they were all written in too high a key; so Wagner had to go through them all again, which took away half the profit.) Anger and anxiety sometimes made him weep reluctant tears. He put down the dates on which this happened in his little diary, the secret witness of this distressful summer.

23rd June, 1840. Just now, tears that I could not restrain came to my eyes again. Is a man cowardly, or merely to be pitied, who thus finds relief in weeping? A German workingman came to see me a little time ago. He was ill, and I invited him to come back to lunch. But Minna said we should have to use up all the money we had to buy bread. Poor soul! She is right; things are going ill with us. When I let my thoughts dwell on it all, the only thing I can foresee with certainty is misery, unimaginable misery. To keep on smiling in spite of all would be a shame, if I had to tell myself that all I had to rely on henceforth was gifts of money—alms!

29th June. What we are going to do next month I do not know. I've only got twenty-five francs left. On the 1st, I shall cash a draft for 150 francs, but then on the 15th, I have the rent to pay. I keep on hiding the position from my poor wife—but when the 15th, comes she will be bound to know.

30th June (evening). Went for a walk with my wife just now and told her the whole business. I pity the poor soul from the bottom of my heart. 'Tis a dismal outlook for the pair of us. What I've got to do is work.

And work he does—with a vengeance. It was in the very middle of all these worries that he put the finishing touches on *Rienzi*, never for a moment dreaming that he had written the vastest of his operas, the most "martial" of all his works, and the first to fling out across the world the passionate cry that told of the will to dominate with which his soul was filled. Is it the malady of an age that is dying, and is Wagner only the standard-bearer in its last, desperate rear-guard fight? Or is it the promise of things to come, and is Wagner the herald of them? He knows not. He asks not—even of himself. He did not perceive that he had put into this prodigious score all the harvest of his wanderings among the works of Weber, Beethoven, Auber, Donizetti, Spontini, and that he had now set foot on the path that was to lead him to—Richard Wagner! At last the work was finished.

Now the question was, how was it to be got going? He sent it, together with a whole battery of letters, to his friends in Dresden; to Mme. Schroeder-Devrient the famous singer, to Tichatschek the tenor, to the King of Saxony himself. If only they would realize that he was worth backing. If only Theodor Apel would come to his assistance, Theodor Apel, who, like himself, had been drilled in the school of adversity, for the news had come to him that Apel had met with a riding accident which had left him blind. But he was a poet still . . . still good and kind . . . he would have pity . . . he would come to the rescue!

Not a word from any of them. Then Minna herself wrote a letter to the blind man. Minna, too, had been tutored by misfortune, and her letter was a noble one. It needed, she said, but a gesture, a sigh, to save an artist who was like to drown himself—to save him from despair. She begged and prayed and flung herself at Apel's feet, for that very morning, the 28th of October, her husband had been arrested and imprisoned for debt. No effort had been spared to move the compassion of the pitiless creditor (a German, too, more shame to him!). Lehrs, Anders, Kietz offered everything they had to their name. But nothing could ward off the blow. Yet dire as were their straits, the Wagners were too proud to apply to Brockhaus to help them in their extremity.

At last, from the blind poet, his ransom came. Wagner returned to his home and put the finishing touches on the opera which he had brought with him all the way from Riga, preserving it from the winds and waves in the Baltic and the North Sea, and which he had submitted to Meyerbeer, putting his signature to the final page the very day that he came out of prison, the very day that his "Visit to Beethoven" appeared in the pages of the *Gazette Musicale*. But as though this first ray of hope were at last the herald of a brighter day, Schlesinger, one morning in December, came bustling into his room in the rue du Helder and, with the air of one who has news of immense importance to communicate, wrote down the following on a sheet of paper: "*La Favorite*, arrangement for piano with words; arrangement without words, for two hands, ditto for four hands, arrangement for quartette, ditto for two violins, ditto for cornet. Total amount payable: 1,100 francs of which 500 are payable in advance."

This was the repercussion of Donizetti's triumph at the Opéra. Wagner fully realized the moral anguish this job was going to cause him; but he also saw, and very plainly, the 500 francs. He agreed to do it, and went to pocket the cash. He came home, piled the money up on the table, counted it over and over again. And thus the hard labour began anew. So many hours a day devoted to this game of patience, and the little that was over given to the orchestration of his Overture to *Faust*. It is a remarkable thing how, despite all these harassing occurrences, Wagner brought himself to give free and generous expression to his views on the subject of dramatic music in France and Germany. "Both these nations," said he, "have but one music. From their intimate union and from the habitual interchange of their most conspicuous talents, there has resulted for art in general a splendid twofold inspiration and richness of production of which we have had many wonderful manifestations. We can only hope that this noble alliance will be ever more and more closely cemented, for where shall we find two races, two countries, whose union and fraternal accord could furnish a more brilliant augury for the future of music?"

But the gloom of these long and difficult autumn days soon settled down again. It was about this time that Wagner had a most sensational encounter, which he put down as one of the most extraordinary incidents in his career. He went out one day, very early in the morning, on urgent business. He had to see some creditors of his who held some bills which he had signed and which it was necessary for him at all costs to renew. He was bound for the establishment of one of these gentry, a cheesemonger in the *Cité*. Beneath the folds of a very inadequate cloak he was carrying a metronome which some one had lent him to mark the *tempi* in his *Rienzi*, and which he was now about to restore to its owner. The streets were full of fog. He had not gone many yards from his house when there came towards him, out of the murk, the phantom of an enormous dog. For a moment man and beast stood face to face, for they had recognized each other immediately. But whether Robber—for it was he—was afraid of a beating from his former master, whom he may have taken for a being bereft of his soul, or whether he thought he saw in this apparition the spaniel of Mephistopheles, they approached each other with about as much friendliness as the devil and Dr. Faustus. Wagner made towards Robber with arms outstretched, while Robber slowly backed. Then he turned, and both began to run. Whenever he turned a corner the dog would come to a halt and look furtively about him; then, as soon as he saw the man emerge from the fog, he started off again faster than ever. For a long time they kept up the running. Now the quarry was lost to sight, now he came into view again. At last he disappeared entirely and Wagner saw him no more.

By this time he had reached the Church of Saint-Roch. He pulled up, gasping for breath, still clutching the metronome. He felt mortally sick at heart, and in this meeting and vain pursuit, saw yet a further presage of disaster. It was evening before he got in, foiled and utterly exhausted. Minna had been waiting for him. She had raised a modest loan from their boarder, the flute-player, to get her husband an appetizing repast. . . . Alas, when he got back there was nothing left for him but to get on with his "arrangements" and his writing, and that was precisely what he did. He wrote "A Musician's End in Paris, the Story of a Man's Last Hours." And yet, in spite of its despair, it was the testament of a believer. Vanquished by this City of Hope, dying with all his illusions destroyed, a German musician makes his confession of faith ere he renders up his last breath: "I believe in God, in Mozart, in Beethoven and in all their disciples and apostles. I believe in the Holy Spirit and in the truth of an Art, one and indivisible; I believe that this Art proceeds from God and lives in the hearts of all enlightened men. I believe that all people may be made blessed by this Art and that it is there-fore permitted to each one to die of hunger while confessing it. I believe that on earth my life has been a discord which will find in death a pure and a triumphant resolution."

Chapter III

A NEW WORLD

THE year 1841 promised to be little better than its predecessor. Wagner began it with a fiasco at a concert held under the auspices of the *Gazette Musicale*, at which his Overture to *Columbus* formed part of the program. But the brass in Valentino's orchestra produced such a terrific din that the indignant public included both performers and composer in one sweeping anathema. There was actually a certain amount of hissing. Minna very nearly fainted. Berlioz, who had been present at the rehearsal, did not commit himself, merely remarking with a sigh that "everything was very difficult in Paris." The friends were much upset at this reverse. Richard alone was more or less unaffected by it, and a little supper having been arranged in the rue du Helder to celebrate the event, he did the honours gaily and the festivities wound up with songs and speeches.

Nevertheless, a thought came to him that evening which was destined to stick in his mind, and that was the uselessness of staying on in Paris, and, its corollary, the desirability of getting back to Germany—unless, of course, they went off to America. . . . Unfortunately, whatever plan they might fix upon needed money for its execution, and poverty showed no sign of loosening its grip. On the contrary, it was tighter than ever.

Of course, there was Franz Liszt, whose generosity was proverbial. Why not go and try him? The idea seemed sound. Wagner called at the hotel at which the famous pianist usually put up. However, although he was received by the young man in question (he was just two years older than Wagner and already famous throughout the world) with the stateliest and most consummate courtesy, Wagner could not bring himself to play the needy suppliant. Liszt offered him a couple of tickets for the concert he was giving in aid of the Beethoven memorial. Wagner accepted them, went to the concert a few weeks later, and wrote rather a severe account of it for the Dresden *Abend-*

zeitung. Seven more years were destined to elapse before these two men, so diverse in temperament, were suddenly to realise that they had at last come to know each other. But now, in the spring of 1841, how should any common ground have been discovered between the most brilliant of pianists and this piece of flotsam cast up by the sea of misery? "What could Liszt be," cried the latter, "unless it were a celebrity, in other words, a slave?" And how should he have forgiven the *virtuoso*, called back ten times to make his bow, for sitting down again at the piano to play his *Fantasia* on *Robert le Diable*, saying aloud as he did so, "I am, I need not say, the servant of the public." It was not merely a clash of characters, but a difference in mentality, a complete divergence in their intellectual and æsthetic outlook. And in Wagner's view there was no forgiveness for sins against art and against the spirit. . . .

The mere mention of Beethoven always made him thrill with enthusiasm—and indignation; and since chance had turned him into a writer, why should he not devote his time and knowledge to writing a life of Beethoven, a scholarly presentment, a romantic version on high, artistic lines? Anders urged him to the task —Anders who had collected together an enormous mass of unpublished material concerning the master that left little or no room for further gleaning. Surely that would be better than these journalistic pot-boilers, "The Dead Musician," "Diversions in Paris," "The Parisian Whirligig," "The Musician and the Press" and all the things he turned out for the *Gazette Musicale* and the German papers, as "from our Paris Correspondent." Moreover, the work would be a lasting monument in its way; it would contain the first complete chronological list of the master's compositions, with musical examples and careful analyses. A year's work, with Anders' vast collection to go upon—it was obviously a tempting enterprise. He wrote to three of the leading publishers in Germany, and all three, as by a preconcerted arrangement, replied in the negative. Yet again the hand of fate brought him back to his destined task of composition.

Once more, therefore, he fell back on the idea of *The Flying Dutchman*, of which he had made a rough sketch for the Director of the Opéra, M. Leon Pillet, and took it to show him. He was so pleased with it that he then and there entrusted the task of composing the music of it to a M. Dietsch, one of his regular purveyors of operatic trifles. It would be impossible to give Wagner himself any commission for at least seven years, as the management was full up with commitments. Besides, M. Paul Foucher, a relative of M. Victor Hugo, had declared that the

plot of *The Flying Dutchman* was no novelty in France, and
that the wisest course would be to give it up altogether.
M. Foucher, however, offered to give the young foreigner 500
francs for his rights. Now there was a flattering, generous
offer—a windfall if you like! Wagner hesitated an instant. He
saw clearly that his hopes of getting an opera of his own put on
in Paris were passing into the limbo of chimeras. So he agreed
to the terms. All the same, he swore he would be even with these
parasites, swore he would write his poem and compose the music,
for a German theatre. Anger, disappointment, bitterness brought
him back in an instant to himself and fired him to grasp again
at a talent which he deemed he had lost but which, during these
few months of daydreaming, had only been coming to maturity
in the hard soil which had been watered with his tears and
swept with his laughter.

Wagner was now a changed man. Paris had taught him
something more than the tragedy that lay in the struggle for
daily bread; it had taught him a certain lofty disdain, combined
with the critical sense, which is called irony. And this irony
had given an edge to his understanding, soothed his *amour-
propre*, and mellowed his character. He no longer appeased his
indignation with Paris by putting into the mouth of *Rienzi* the
imprecations uttered by that tribune against Rome. He had now
acquired the indulgence which the weak display towards the
strong. He had come to understand that eloquence is not necessarily pompous, that grace has its value, the comic its beauties,
and even suffering its cheerful reticences. Wagner was now no
longer the melodramatist of *Rienzi*; he had become the poet of
The Flying Dutchman.

He was about to surrender his keys to the estate agent, when
he learned to his amazement that the requisite period for giving
notice had been exceeded by one day and that the landlord would
accept no excuse, but held him responsible for his tenancy for
another whole year. After endless anxiety and trouble, the
concierge managed to get hold of a family of foreigners who
agreed to take the place over as Wagner's sub-tenants. The
Wagners then began to look out for some modest retreat outside Paris. They heard of a queer sort of place that belonged to
an old artist in the suburbs, somewhere between Bellevue and
Meudon. They viewed it and liked it, although the walls were
covered with hideous paintings, the works of the owner,
M. Jadin. They moved in at once, taking along with them their
flute-playing boarder, M. Brix. His plight was now as desperate
as their own, but they refused to leave him in the lurch. This, of

course, only added to their difficulties. Things had come to such
a pass that, one day, Richard went wandering about all over
Paris to try and rake up five shillings. He did not succeed and
there was nothing for it but to trudge all the way back to
Meudon, where Minna was on the lookout for him, seated at the
window as she had so often sat before, awaiting his return, in
the rue du Helder. They had to persuade the local grocer to let
them have some things on credit. As good luck would have it,
the 500 francs promised by Paul Foucher for *The Flying Dutchman* arrived like a godsend in the midst of these embarrassments. He could now pay up the tradesmen and even hire a
piano, a thing he had had to do without for months past.

The principal parts of the poem he had already got down
on paper, and he made up his mind to start on the music without delay, but, somehow, he felt afraid to open the piano lest
he should find his head was empty and his heart a void. But no
sooner had he got down to the work than the song of the Pilot
came to him in a flash, and then, no less readily, the song of the
Spinning Maidens. "I went wild with delight when it was borne
in upon me that I was still able to compose." What a load off
his mind it was! He felt a new man, for he had now got hold of
the plan of his building, both music and poetry: the reality
of the unreal, the supernatural made natural and tangible by the
heavenly alchemy of art. In ten days the text was written out
in full; and in seven weeks the music was completed. He raced,
for very joy, about the woods, gathered a harvest of mushrooms,
and composed a poem in honour of Minna, who had given him a
grand pair of green shoes for his birthday. For one brief moment
all the world smiled upon him, his poor neglected wife, his dead
love, these suburban Parisians, even Meyerbeer, whom he had
unjustly suspected, seeing that he had put in a good word with
the intendant of the theatres in Saxony in favour of *Rienzi*, and
in July he received the overwhelming news that his opera had
been accepted in Dresden and that it was hoped to put it on at
the Theatre Royal during the coming winter.

What cared he for privation and penury, and all the snubs and
setbacks he had had to put up with in France, now that the
sun was rising once again in Germany? The trumpets of *Rienzi*
sound afar, and the music of his native land awakens in his
heart. The intendant's letter meant Wagner's return to the
bosom of his thankless country. He wrote to his mother after
years of silence. He told her all about his life, about the things
he was doing, his irresistible vocation, and all that he had had to
suffer. He brought no charge against anyone, not even against

Paris, where he had at least come to the knowledge of himself. And now Dresden—Dresden which he had deserted yet still adored—should be the taking-off ground whence he would try his fortune anew.

Everything beguiled and enchanted him during these weeks of mental convalescence, even old Jadin, his landlord, an octogenarian of Royalist and Legitimist convictions, who loathed Louis-Philippe, performed his ablutions stark naked in a bath he had fitted up in his garden, and made his own wigs, of which he possessed a wide assortment, ranging from the locks of a fair-haired lad to a white-polled grandsire. Unfortunately, he was given to playing a kind of harpsichord of his own invention, even as Brix would insist on playing his flute. Another trial to put up with!

But autumn came and with it gloom and penury once more. Foucher's money was all gone and the old problem of keeping the wolf from the door confronted them again. So terrible were their straits that when he had finished recopying the score of *The Flying Dutchman* he signed it with these despairing words: "In the depth of night and misery. *Per ardua ad astra*. Amen." This time it was the excellent Kietz who kept them afloat, coming along in the nick of time with 200 francs, obtained from heaven knows where. It was enough to pay their debts and get them back to Paris. They would have to hang on there till it was time to start for Dresden. With the last few sticks of their rue du Helder furniture coming on behind, they trundled off to some little lodgings at No. 14 rue Jacob. And here again Kietz provided the needful, thanks to the five- and ten-franc pieces he contrived to extract, one at a time, from the clutches of a miserly uncle. "During that period I often displayed with joyous pride those shoes of mine, which were shoes no longer, for the soles had entirely disappeared." Alas! that that birthday offering should have come to such a pass!

Meanwhile, the little company, for all their poverty, did not neglect their reading. Lamennais' *Paroles d'un Croyant* was a work they keenly discussed, and still more keenly, Proudhon's *Qu'est-ce que la propriété?* the author of which, curiously enough, was to succeed them in the tenancy of their rooms in the rue Jacob—where penury dwelt cheek by jowl with her rebellious victims.

Richard now resumed those hideous tasks that had dealt his *amour-propre* so staggering a blow—his letters for the *Abendzeitung*, the arrangement of operas for the piano. Halévy had just scored an unexpected success with his *Reine de Chypre*. It was necessary, to make the most of its vogue, that the *Reine* should be served up with all manner of musical sauce. Anyhow, to get to know the composer personally was a considerable satisfaction, for Wagner had an admiration for the quiet vigour of his work; a very different thing from Donizetti's syrupy stuff. He went to call, and happened to arrive just as he was having lunch. He gave one to understand that he found fame rather boring and accused Schlesinger of having engineered the whole thing just to torment him. The two composers were in perfect agreement regarding the decadence of the contemporary stage and the decline in public taste. As a result of this visit, Halévy always displayed a friendly attitude towards the work of the young composer. Unfortunately, this interest was consistently platonic, and life in the rue Jacob continued to be as calamitous as it had been in the rue du Helder.

Wagner could not even get taken on in the chorus at the Opéra, where he applied for a job, hoping to get the three francs per night which was the usual rate of pay. Not one in the little colony but knew to his cost what it was to do battle with the world. Encouraged by Lehrs, Wagner started getting up early German history in the works of Raumer, and immediately a whole host of subjects for operas came thronging to his brain. He thought of setting to music the story of Manfred, the son of the Emperor Friedrich II of Hohenstaufen. But he soon gave up that idea because Lehrs lent him the old poem about the Tourney on the Wartburg, the War of the Singers (*Sängerkrieg*), as well as the legends of Tannhäuser and Lohengrin. "A new world dawned upon my vision!"

This, then, at all events, he owed to Paris, this chance reading, this fortuitous encounter between the artist in whose veins the creative sap was seething, and the subject matter which was to awaken his powers to triumphant life; and so he could rightly sing the pæan of his wretchedness now over and done with. "Oh, Paris! Oh, place of joy and suffering! . . . We bless the sorrows you inflicted, for they brought forth splendid fruit!" (Letter dated September 1842.)

Never was his longing to get back to Germany more pathetic than in this, his last, winter in Paris. And although the performances of *Rienzi* were continually being postponed from month to month, he kept on writing to the manager, chorus-master, stage-manager, the *kapellmeister*, and the vocalists of the Dresden Theatre. He offered them his *Flying Dutchman*; he offered it at Breslau and Leipzig. It was turned down all round. Munich said it was unsuitable for Germany. Then he wrote to

Friedrich Wilhelm IV of Prussia, to whom he proposed to dedicate the work. No answer. No doubt he wrote too much and too
often. These officials did not care a straw about his work, and
he tired them out in advance with his questions, his fussiness
about details, his endless reccmmendations on this point and on
that. He kept pestering them with lists of things which, he said,
really must be seen to, in a way calculated to discourage even
the most whole-hearted of his well-wishers. In short, he committed, in one solid block, all the faults against modesty and
moderation which people in authority are slow to tolerate in a
newcomer. But then his self-respect, his ambition, his very existence were at stake. All his artistic future, which he felt quickening within him, he put to the hazard. He left no stone unturned
to achieve the two ends which he assigned himself as the only
possible justification for the years of preparation he had spent
at Koenigsberg, Riga, and Paris, *viz.*, the full-dress performance
of *Rienzi* and the acceptance of *The Flying Dutchman.*

At last, word came to him from Count Redern that his *Flying
Dutchman* had been accepted by the Berlin Theatre "in token of
their appreciation of music that was so rich in invention and
effect." That was Meyerbeer's influence again. Wagner felt that
the time had now come to take advantage of the flowing tide and
get back to Germany. His brother-in-law, Avenarius, who had
many a time befriended the needy pair himself, had written
Louise Brockhaus, urging her to send her brother some money
from time to time. Wonders will never cease! The little-expected
relief arrived not once, but twice. The first time, it took the form
of a five-hundred-franc note. This Richard stuffed into the beak
of a goose which he presented to his wife with his own hands,
the day after Christmas. Then a second accession to his funds
enabled him to pay off some of his debts and to make arrangements for departing during Holy Week.

The hour of deliverance sounded at last. Springtime, loud with
the twittering of the Paris sparrows, filled the heart of Wagner
with a sense of gratitude, not unalloyed with sadness, for a city
in which, in the twenty-ninth year of his age, he had attained his
spiritual majority. He had nothing to regret, save leaving the
modest friends whom the City of Good Hope had, for close on
three years, made the sharers of his humble lodgings. All of
them were deeply moved, almost overcome, indeed, when the
time came to say good-bye to the youngest and most ardent of
their party. It was the 7th of April, 1842. Anders was bowed
down like an old man whose end was not far off. Lehrs, too,
knew he was under sentence of death, and it was with the cer-

tainty that he would never see them again that he bade farewell to this little *ménage* so rich in illusions and so confident in their star. Kietz, too, was there, a great, big-bearded, warm-hearted boy. At the last moment he slipped a five-franc piece—the only coin he had—into Wagner's pocket. It might buy him some little luxury on the journey which he would otherwise have had to go without. At last the diligence got under way.

This time again Wagner's valise was stuffed full of papers— rough copies of his arrangements of *Robert le Diable*, *Les Huguenots*, *Zanetta*, and *La Reine de Chypre*, which he had not yet finished and for which he had to account to Schlesinger. The heavy old vehicle lumbered across the bridges, rolled along the sunlit boulevards, and passed through the city gates. "And we saw nothing of it all, for our eyes were blinded with tears."

Chapter IV

THE LAURELS OF "RIENZI"

ONE of the most outstanding examples of man's inconsequence—
and one of the most natural—is the honour he pays to his
sorrows, the value he sets upon his tears. Joy leaves but a slender
trace behind it and makes but a faint impression on our recollection. But suffering lends an amplitude to our memories, increases
our self-esteem, and ennobles our miseries with an aureole of
poetry.

Scarcely had they bidden it farewell than this same Paris,
where such hardship and misfortune had fallen to their lot,
appeared to Wagner's eyes like some enchanted land of freedom,
friendship, and fruitful toil. "I said to myself that French folk
returning home from Germany did well to unbutton their great-
coats and inhale the air, as if they were passing out of winter
into spring. . . . Never was it so hard for me to say good-bye."
As for Minna, she wept continuously, could speak of nothing
save of going back again to France, and hoped her husband's
operas would prove an utter failure, so that there might be an
excuse for their returning to Paris.

The reception, however, which awaited them from their rela-
tives in Leipzig was more cordial than they had anticipated.
Madame Geyer was now an old lady, tenderly watched over and
made much of by her Brockhaus children. There was a great
set-out to greet the prodigal's return. They were quite friendly
towards his wife, despite her humble origin and her thirty-four
or thirty-five years. There was great rejoicing at the good news
about *Rienzi*, and the family put their heads together and
arranged to advance 200 thalers to the needy couple until they
got into smooth water again. But in spite of all this, Richard,
one night when he was dining at the Brockhaus's, burst into a
flood of tears. "My excellent sister who, five years before, had
realized all the misery of my untimely marriage, looked as if
she understood." As long as they were living a life of exile,

Minna had displayed both courage and devotion, and her husband's repeated failures hardly permitted him to play the critic. But now that he was home again in the old familiar surroundings, the kind of mirage in which one seems to live abroad melted into thin air, and Richard suffered cruelly from his contact with reality. Minna's shortcomings were brought out into strong relief; and Richard's also. As I let my thoughts dwell on these two beings united in a common misfortune, I cannot help thinking of that traveller of Claudel's who returns to his own home as a guest. He is a stranger to all, and all to him is strange. "Serving-woman, hang up the traveller's cloak, but put it not away."

In such a case the proper thing is work. We must seek refuge from our thoughts in action. He went to Berlin to see about *The Flying Dutchman*, caught a fleeting glimpse of Meyerbeer, Mendelssohn and the Count von Redern, the intendant-general of the theatres. But, despite the happy auguries, it did not seem as though things were going to progress very rapidly. He returned by way of Halle, paid a brief visit to his brother Albert (the Wurzburg brother), who was now attached, though in no very exalted capacity, to the local theatre. His daughter Johanna, whose voice bade fair to prove a very fine one, sang to him, to his great delight. Then he took up his quarters with his mother and wife at Teplitz, the charming watering-place where, eight years before, the idea for the ill-fated *Liebesverbot* had come into his mind. Well, it was a joy to plunge again into the very heart of nature. How soothing to his overwrought nerves! No; he wanted neither Paris, nor Leipzig, nor Berlin, nor any town at all. "I imagine," he wrote to the Lehrs, "that I cannot become attached to any town on this earth. My heart finds no delight in men, nor in the works of men. What it needs must have is nature and friends." He departed for a solitary walking tour in the mountains, putting up at the little inn at Schreckenstein, and went for daily rambles in the heart of the Wostrai. Once, as he was making his way round a little glen in this most romantic of regions, he came suddenly upon a shepherd lad blithely whistling some country dance or other. In a moment Wagner pictured himself taking part in a procession of pilgrims passing through these solitary groves. The Venusberg of the Tourney on the Wartburg came to his mind. He roughed out a sketch then and there, and made a note of the principal *motifs*. The country was decidedly favourable to imaginative flights. What, then, is inspiration? Perhaps nothing more than the exhilarating consciousness of one's strength, a subtle synchronization of event and attendant circumstances. When one feels one's senses all alert and receptive, there falls by chance upon the ear a sound which wakes an answering rhythm in the soul. And so he returned to Dresden rich with these latest spoils and all on fire for work.

At last the rehearsals of *Rienzi* began in earnest and Wagner plunged into the world of singers, musicians, and intrigue, a world which he had always felt was the only one in which he was fated to thrive. It was his native air, the world which he could and would mould to his own designs. "Nature" right enough, but nature refashioned, dream-cities, enchanted forests, and those artists wholly submissive to his will, who shall give form and speech to all the living beings which people his imagination. With that instinct for command and organization which is the complement of real power, Wagner examined the forces at his disposal, noted the weak spots in his army, and decided how they were to be set right.

At the very top of the ladder there was Herr von Luttichau, the general manager, a kindly man, a high official, and a prudent administrator. Stage-manager, scene-painter, and costumier: Ferdinand Heine, an old friend of the Wagners', of the Geyers', a squat, gnome-like personage, but useful and thoroughly loyal and devoted. In him Richard found that sympathy and affection which were so essential to him. Chorus-master: Wilhelm Fischer, an old man, but what a man! So full of ardour and enthusiasm that the very first day Wagner went to see him he came rushing to meet him with eager outstretched arms. A greeting like that transported Wagner "into an atmosphere of hope." The conductor was Reissiger, a man of about forty-four, a composer fertile in banalities who had turned out a number of second-rate operas, of which *Weber's Last Waltz* is the only thing that has escaped oblivion. It was hardly to be expected that Reissiger should view with satisfaction the arrival of so youthful a colleague in his theatre, and, as he was a very indolent person, Wagner had much ado to devise a stratagem that would compel him to work. Reissiger was anxiously hunting about for a libretto to use with a "melody" which he had written, but could not find anything to suit him. Wagner, however, promised him he should have a page of verse for every pianoforte rehearsal. He kept his word and turned up regularly with the promised instalment, which he tore out of an old libretto he had once written round Koenig's novel, *The Noble Bride*. The orchestra was middling, seventy instrumentalists; but the strings lacked that richness and power which made the Parisian ensembles so remarkable. However, the two principal vocalists, Tichatschek the tenor, and Mme. Schroeder-Devrient, were really splendid, and justified the highest hopes.

Tichatschek was an admirable musician and the possessor of a magnificent voice. Unfortunately, he was just as lazy as Reissiger and never learnt his words. But it was hoped that his glorious voice would compensate for all shortcomings. From the very first he was fired with enthusiasm for his part, and Richard had no anxiety so far as he was concerned. As for Mme. Schroeder-Devrient, she was an old acquaintance, and when he saw her again he was simply transported with joy and excitement. He had been thrilled by her when he was a lad of sixteen, and had sent her his schoolboy's vow that they would meet again some day. He had, indeed, seen her at the time of the Magdeburg fiasco; but this time they met on a level, and negotiated as one great power with another. In the intervening thirteen years her voice had lost a little and her body, alas! had gained much. There was no denying that; her movements had become slow and heavy, and her acting had grown uncomfortably stagey. But although Richard was by no means blind to these defects, her fire, her ardour, filled him with exultant delight. And so the rehearsals went on, in an atmosphere of extraordinary tension and excitement, which increased steadily in proportion as the ensemble work came nearer to perfection and the great movements of the chorus and orchestra fell into their appointed orbits. Before long, everyone became convinced that success was assured. In spite of the terrific amount of work he had to do, Richard let nothing slide and fulfilled all his engagements. He wrote to Avenarius, to the friends in Paris, sent Schlesinger the "arrangement" of the *Reine de Chypre* which he had promised him, and deplored the death of the Duc d'Orléans. "Paris remains unforgettable," he said, "and whatever our sufferings may have been, they impress us less than the glorious recollection of the life we led there." He even felt the lack of Minna, who had stayed on for a part of the summer at Teplitz, the lack, that is to say, not so much of the mistress but of the *hausfrau*, the good manager and the trusty comrade in times of stress. As usual, he was irked by the interruption of a long-standing habit.

All through August and September the rehearsals went on. Wagner worked like a slave, making cuts and patching up the gashes, keeping Reissiger up to the scratch, flinging himself into the breach, rushing here, there, and everywhere, coaching now this one and now that, wherever he saw a weak spot. Finally, about the beginning of October, all was ready. Everyone was in a fever of excitement and Wagner himself had caught it. All the personnel, down to the humblest little employee, loved and worshipped him and looked upon him as a sort of demigod. Though they may not have realized how great and glorious he was one day to become, they all—actors and supers—felt a tremendous accession of energy from their contact with this little man with the great head. He literally fascinated them. So much so that, one day, one of his singers stopped him in the street, gazed at him in speechless admiration, and finally stammered out that he wanted "to take stock of a man for whom so glorious a destiny was in store." Wagner felt a little dizzy as he took in this rather heady liquor on an empty stomach (it is a fact that sometimes he had only one meal a day). He felt "as one inebriated with some mysterious power. I jest; yet, I really thought there must be something in me." Something in him! What was it, then? What sinister spell, or what beneficent miracle, was it that was to be revealed to him? He had just written these words to his brother-in-law, Avenarius, "Yes, my dear Edward, on the 19th the devil will be let loose, amid thunder and lightning." The devil? "No," whispered Mme. Schroeder-Devrient in his ear; "not the devil, your genius!"

On the 20th of October, 1842, the curtain went up for the first time on *Rienzi*, "A Grand Tragic Opera in Five Acts, by Richard Wagner." Clearly this youthful scion of the Heroic Muse has little in common with what we call historic truth. But Rienzi's life was compounded of the very stuff to fire the imagination of a youth who himself longed to figure as a great reformer. "Never, perhaps, has the energy and effect of a single mind been more remarkably felt," says Gibbon, referring to the tribune, in his *Decline and Fall of the Roman Empire*; and he portrays him as a prodigious stage-manager (like all politicians), a man who had staged the revolution as one would stage a play, and whose sole dominion was the human heart. Now Wagner also deemed that revolution should be set in motion through the heart, so he made free with history as well as with Bulwer Lytton's novel, and laid all the emphasis on the moral aspect of the drama, framing it in a fresco of epic magnificence. He telescoped Rienzi's two terms of office into one, and confined the action solely to Rome. In contrast to Bulwer, Wagner assigns no wife to his hero, but represents him as concentrating all his love upon the Eternal City. It is to his sister Irene, the incarnation of the tribune's ideals, that is vouchsafed the honour of voluntarily laying down her life for the sake of the royal and imaginary country of her visionary aspirations. . . . The saviour of Rome, therefore, had, of course, to be the messenger of impossible ideals, his soul must needs be unmarred by any stain or weakness; he was, in other words, a star of the first magnitude in the operatic firmament. Nevertheless, he had all the dazzling and seductive radiance of a dream of heroism and romance. The work, moreover, was brocaded with a wealth of fanfares and processions, adorned with a ballet, and intersected with preludes and finales à la Meyerbeer and Spontini, and punctuated with those *leit-motifs* wherein the public, wrought up to the highest pitch of excitement, were destined to find the old sensations which they expected, and some new ones which they did not, but of which, though they did not straightway comprehend them, they dimly felt the charm. The unexpected and the conventional were mingled cheek by jowl, and each in its way contributed to the triumph.

The composer took up his position in a box facing the stage, together with his wife and his sister, Clara Wolfram. He was neither anxious, nor excited. It seemed to him that it was some one quite different that all the pother was about, and that he himself was now only an astral body, an unincarnate spirit. He listened to the buzz of conversation among the audience without daring to look about him, and sat huddled up in the darkest corner of the box, thinking of all the weak spots in his score and how insufferably it dragged from time to time. He was not even conscious that he had stood up at the end of the first act, or that he had been pushed on to the stage, and all this clapping and cheering that grew more deafening than ever at the sight of an unknown young man who, a moment since, had leapt into fame. How strange and mystifying it all seemed! What could it mean? It couldn't possibly be for him, all this applause, for him, the unlucky one, for him who had nothing to his name, who seldom had enough to stay his hunger, who hadn't even got the wherewithal to tip the stage hands—no luck, no position, nothing, a man who had nothing to call his own save this inordinately long opera, which would collapse, just as his overtures, his concertos, his *Liebesverbot*, just as his Paris dreams, his wife's love, and even his dog's, had melted away and come to naught. Tichatschek, it is true, had an irresistible fire about him, and Mme. Schroeder-Devrient was still the incomparable singer and *tragédienne* she had ever been. But was not the whole thing a piece of well-meant legerdemain, a kind of conjuror's transformation scene designed to deceive the author and cover up his failure? They had begun at six, and the thing was still going on at ten—at eleven. It would be midnight and past before they got through with the five acts. Yes, old Fischer was right about the cuts. Would he had taken his advice! However, the theatre was still packed for the final scene. Then, at long last, down came the curtain. Once more he had to show himself on the stage with the whole cast, happy but utterly exhausted, all about him. "A scene from fairyland!" The audience were in the seventh heaven. "Greater than Donizetti!" said fat old Count Solms, one of the *cognoscenti*. There was a thirteen-year-old schoolboy in the theatre who had a passionate love of music. So overcome with emotion was he that all through one act he had been stricken with deafness. He came to from his trance with his face all bathed in tears, and swore eternal allegiance to the strange, brown-clad musician who had cast the spell upon him. That boy was Hans von Bülow.

Wagner went to bed a famous man. He slept as he had never slept before, and never so much as noticed that poor Minna had strewn the bed with laurel.

There is assuredly no date so important in the history of an artist as the date when his first great work obtains public recognition, and when his hitherto nameless countenance suddenly takes on the significance with which posterity is to invest it. Vague in outline it is as yet, however, and time has still to stamp it with its imprint; but even now society was scanning the visage of its young contemporary, seeking therein some image of itself that it might learn to love. This shy, elusive nimbus encircling the brows of a man till yesterday unknown, what was it but the patent of a dignity which the world would seal and ratify? It is a sort of mystic burden the tragic weight of which the world can never realize. For either the world bends its favourite to its will and, having wrested from him the secret of his mastery, consigns him to oblivion; or else, taken aback by his force, it will combat its own elect, essay to mould him to its own designs, and never yield to him until, as the price of his greatness and his solitude, it has bereft him of all his happiness and peace of mind. The story of genius is one long record of give and take.

If, after this performance of the 20th of October, 1842, Wagner had written a second *Rienzi*, as his admirers urged him to, we should today be reduced to hunting for his name among the disciples of Spontini and Meyerbeer. But he had composed *The Flying Dutchman*, he had joined battle with himself. He felt the uprush within him of a violent appetite for pleasure and, at the very same time, a paradoxical disgust for all the delights which he had so long and so ardently desired. He craved

for life, yet never did he feel so imperious within him the need
to get on with his work. Even now he felt he must correct and
prune the work which, but a few days since, had won him so
crude and garish a triumph, felt that he must shear away its
tawdry bedizenments and disencumber it of all its padding. Off
he tore to the copyists, blue-pencilled whole pages. Then he
rushed away to Tichatschek at the theatre and said he was going
to curtail his part on the spot. But the singer protested, "I won't
be robbed of a note . . . it's divine." Hearing all these testi-
monies to a success in which he could still scarcely bring himself
to believe, made him feel curiously strong—and ridiculous. Was
it his own judgment, he asked, or other people's, that he had to
go by? The manager, von Luttichau, sent him an official letter of
thanks. They paid him 300 thalers for his opera, which was
exceptional, the usual author's rights being twenty pounds. The
king and the princesses came to hear the opera about which
everyone was now talking. The management tried splitting the
performance into two parts so as to bring it within the compass
usual for such entertainments, for fear the audience should be
fatigued. But so great was the public impatience that, after
trying this experiment three times, they had to revert to playing
the opera in its entirety every evening.

Of course, in view of this success, there could be no longer
any question of allowing *The Flying Dutchman* to be given in
Berlin. It was brought back again to its Dresden home and put
into rehearsal straightaway. This time Mme. Schroeder-Devrient
had full scope for her voice and talents as an actress. Richard
was utterly carried away, for it was not only into the art of the
theatre that this queen of passion gave him such an insight, but
into the drama of life itself, the tragedy of love. She took
Wagner into her confidence, told him all about her love-affairs—
they were really rather lurid—and confessed that she was living
under the protection of a man whom Wagner considered utterly
unworthy of a woman with such a lofty soul as hers. (How
young this man of thirty still remained!) But her very caprices
inspired the musician with an extraordinary interest, so new
and penetrating was the light they threw upon the female heart.
Mme. Schroeder-Devrient's sole means of escape from her passionate infatuation was work, and she rehearsed the rôle of
Senta with such fire and intensity that on one occasion Richard
leapt from his stool to beseech her to husband her strength.
She assured him that all was well, and to show him how strong
she was contracted and relaxed the muscles of her powerful
frame. No, her strength was proof against everything, and pas-

sion, so far from exhausting her energy, did but enlarge the sphere of its activity. "I was obliged to recognize the remarkable fact that the actress's infatuation for a very commonplace man was all to the advantage of my Senta." Such a gift for seeing things in their true light was a rarity in the young artists of those days. Love, then, can derive sustenance from the most vulgar encounters—that he plainly saw—even when it is impossible for an intelligent person to remain under any delusion as to the quality of his sentiments. Does, then, the sole advantage of love—and its *raison d'être*—reside in its intensity, in its power to stimulate the will, in the increase of strength it imparts to those who experience it? To give it any spiritual justification, then, it must be sublimated and transported into a higher, a nobler region, "which must shine pure, chaste, virginal, inaccessible. . . . It must elude the present and lose itself in an infinite and unearthly love." Such was the doctrine which was beginning to blossom in Wagner's soul.

The days immediately following the success of *Rienzi* were devoted to making plans for the future, and to letter-writing (for of course Avenarius, Kietz, Lehrs, and Anders had to be kept duly posted). But if the world about him had completely changed, if he had suddenly become the man of the moment, all this excitement was purely professional. No adventure with the sex lured him on. All his thoughts were centred on getting his *Flying Dutchman* under way. Moreover, this work appeared to him superior to *Rienzi*, smoother, better worked-out. Nor had he any doubts of its success, the enthusiasm of the actors, orchestra, manager, and staff continuing at the same high level. Was it, then, a further triumph for him when, on the 2nd of January, 1843, scarcely ten weeks after *Rienzi*, *The Flying Dutchman* was performed for the first time? Yes, and no. Anyhow it was a different kind of triumph. Wagner fully realized that he was drawing much more heavily on the imagination of his audience, since the subject matter of his opera was vaguer and, as it were, dissolved in an atmosphere of legend. And then again, he had done away with all the well-worn cheap effects. He had created a *genre* which excluded all the old familiar devices—the big ensembles, the choruses and finales. He had put himself up as a wizard, a wonder-worker. *Rienzi* was but a high, adventurous flight designed to give the tenor an opportunity to display his dazzling virtuosity, against a background of tragedy and ruin. But *The Flying Dutchman* embodied his latest theory of mysticism and enchantment, of the wizardry of the heart. He had done now with the supernatural *à la* Mozart, which was merely a symbolical presentment of the heavenly powers. Wagner's is a human sorcery, in which the marvellous is within reach of all, and is contagious, like a sickness. His work is the first passionate initiation into that madness whence the spirit returns for ever unfitted for the hard, unmusical world of reality and fact.

The public, though interested, seemed rather at sea, and were certainly more impressed by Mme. Schroeder-Devrient's admirable interpretation, than thrilled by the composer's theories and experiments. Let us say, then, that it was a *succès d'estime*. Rather a doubtful compliment. As a matter of fact, the affair was the first milestone along the lonely road, the artist's first stage on the solitary path which was to lead him away from the multitude and to bring him to the realization of himself, of his own soul.

Four performances sufficed to satisfy the curiosity of the music-loving public. Wagner, however, was by no means depressed at this diminishing interest in his work. He bolstered himself up with the reflection that there was "a singular divergence between his inward aspirations and his outward successes." Three circumstances afforded positive proof that his fame was established. First, the absolute, unshakable confidence of Mme. Schroeder-Devrient in his future; next an avalanche of dunning letters from Magdeburg, Koenigsberg, Riga, and Paris; and finally, the offer of the conductorship-in-chief at the Dresden Theatre Royal.

As regards the wretched debts which had dogged him for so many years, Wagner discharged them all, thanks to a loan from the kindly Mme. Schroeder-Devrient. (What joy to be able to pay back poor old Kietz the 600 francs he had borrowed!) As to the conductorship, Wagner was in two minds. Of course the pay was good (1,500 thalers a year), there was no doubt about that; but, somehow, he was afraid it would be hanging the old millstone round his neck again and courting a renewal of the old trials and tribulations, the scar of which eight years had not sufficed to obliterate. Was he to begin all that over again? Was he to throw away the liberty he had won at the price of all the privations he had gone through in Paris? People will say it was the path of fate to which he was for ever being brought back. Always the same terrible conductor's desk, the boards, the icy draughts, the cellar-like smells, the threadbare velvet, the paint, the pasteboard, the tinsel, and the powder—all the "decadence of the modern theatre." But his sisters whisper in his ear that he really must have some regular means of subsistence; and the manager tells him it will give him the opportunity of trying out his future works. Madame Karl Maria von Weber, the popular composer's widow, said, "Think what I shall have to tell Weber when I see him; fancy my having to say that the work he loved so dearly has been left to go to rack and ruin." And lastly there was Minna sighing joyfully: "Ah, what a relief to have a home of our own, plenty to live on, and the king at the back of us. Ah! what an honour to be the wife of the chief court *kapellmeister*!"

All that, however, would not have sufficed to persuade him. But, overtopping all these voices, came a phrase that brought him to heel, for he recognized it for his own—"to create the impossible!" His optimism won the day. And so it came to pass that, on the 2nd of February, in the offices of the Intendance Royale, and in the presence of von Luttichau and his staff, the royal decree was formally recited. Richard Wagner was received in audience by His Majesty King Friedrich of Saxony, attired for the occasion in full court dress, and duly took the oath.

And now behold him a prisoner once more, back again in the vicious circle into which he was always fated to be lured, from which he was ever trying to escape and in which he was so long fated to fight a losing battle. It was because he knew not the secret of his nature, with its call of death—death to which, like his mariner condemned eternally to roam the seas in quest of his "redemption," he stretched out his arms in vain. But as yet Wagner knew not that the name of the siren whose songs of love above all others sounded most drowningly in his ear was Death.

Chapter V

"TANNHÄUSER," THE FLOWER WHOSE
SCENT WAS DEATH

"IN PARIS it is a common error, whenever German music is in question, to drag the slow movements and accelerate the quick ones a great deal too much, and of this fault Herr Wagner was guilty throughout the whole opera (*Don Juan*). His *tempi* were characteristically French."

"Herr Wagner conducts in a painstaking and intelligent manner, but he lacks thoughtfulness and repose. His eager temperament has not yet thoroughly adapted itself to his over-sudden and over-favourable turn of fortune."

"Richard Wagner has ushered in a new era in music; an ebb and flow of vibrant volumes of sound which are seldom rounded off into a satisfying and comprehensible melody."

"A chaos of sounds." "A puzzle." "A step further and there would be no more music at all." "A dramatic poet, maybe; a composer, I think not. . . ."

Such were some of the opinions of which the critics delivered themselves about the capabilities of Dresden's new conductor. He pretended not to notice them. Like Berlioz, he consoled himself with the plaudits of the public and vaunted the praises showered on him by the directors of the theatre, by his friends abroad, and especially by Schumann. Nevertheless, Schumann averred that he found in the scoring of *Rienzi* more than one reminiscence of Meyerbeer. . . . How utterly absurd! Laube, in spite of a handsome biographical article in his journal, had, it must be confessed, but a very imperfect understanding of Wagner's music. Reissiger, smarting from the outrage to his *amour-propre*, was even now bestowing on him the Judas kiss. The black humours gathered in the depths of Wagner's heart, fermented there and distilled the first drop of the poison that was destined to become chronic with him, namely the delusion of persecution. It was not precisely neurasthenia, but just that

115

touch of restless anxiety that makes the weak man tremble for his safety and fortifies the strong man in his revolt against the restraints of routine and authority. His soul would grate and grind sometimes, as though the grit had got into it, and he looked in vain for oil to make its running smooth. There was none, save only music! Yet men looked to Wagner to put new life into the theatre. He was referred to as Weber's successor. But only the public, the uninstructed public, spoke like that; not his colleagues, not his peers. Here is an example. Berlioz came to Dresden to direct two concerts. He heard *Rienzi* and *The Flying Dutchman* and confided his impressions to his friend Ernst: "After suffering in Paris all the hardships and privations inseparable from a situation of penniless obscurity, Richard Wagner, on returning to his native Saxony, had the audacity to attempt, and the good fortune to achieve, an opera in five acts, for which he wrote both words and music. The work was a brilliant success in Dresden. I remember a beautiful prayer chanted by Rienzi in the last act, and a triumphal march of excellent workmanship with nothing slavishly imitative about it. The orchestration of *The Flying Dutchman* impressed me, owing to its sombre colour scheme and certain storm effects in perfect harmony with the subject. At the same time one is bound to condemn an abuse of the tremolo, which is the more regrettable in that I had already been struck by it in *Rienzi*. It may, therefore, be taken as indicating in the author a certain passivity of spirit against which he does not take sufficient precautions." Now the tremolo, against which these animadversions were directed, that inward throbbing of the orchestra, is nothing more or less than the forerunner of the harmonic gradations interfused with chromatic changes which, later on, were to blossom forth so triumphantly in *Tristan*. But Berlioz, who belonged to a generation already growing outmoded, was unable to understand the unprecedented complexity of these new sound relations where all musical elements are employed in combination as a means of expressing the finer shades of emotional feeling. He probably failed to understand the novel effects which this innovator obtained from the complementary harmony by a sequence of contrasts. All the new relief-work was calculated to pass unnoticed by the crowd, or to shock it, and not only that, but also to incur the disapprobation of the experts, whose ear refused to admit, without further preparation, these dazzling "accidents" produced by an harmonic sound-scheme made up of the most skilful and cunningly devised discords. And who would have recognized in the Wagner of those days the lineal descendant of the Greek dramatists or have perceived in the rare efflorescence of *The Flying Dutchman*, a legitimate outcome of its modification and development by Monteverdi, Gluck, and Weber? Besides, a wholly impartial and objective musical criticism cannot exist, inasmuch as criticism depends not on a theoretic consideration of ideas, but on a conflict of temperaments.

As for Berlioz, this is Wagner's comment on his visit: "The success of my operas has been an abomination in his sight. He is an unhappy man." Had, then, Berlioz betrayed a lack of enthusiasm? Most decidedly not. But Richard had grown mistrustful. He was for scenting out adversaries. He would have them powerful, so that there should be the greater honour in the combat. "We composers cannot be Europeans. We have got to choose whether we will be Germans or Frenchmen." In his heart, he believed nothing of the kind. But the memory of Paris, the harsh and thankless Paris, remained like a thorn in his flesh. He said, too, that Mendelssohn hated him, and for this reason: The illustrious conductor of Leipzig and Berlin also wanted to compose an opera, and so the brilliant success achieved by *Rienzi* had, of course, made him green with envy. He it was who prevented Schumann from coming to Dresden. A "clique" was beginning to collect round the prosperous Jew, and that clique would, of course, be anti-Wagner. With vicarious intrepidity, these gentlemen urged Moritz Hauptmann to lead the attack. Hauptmann was the editor-in-chief of the *Journal Universel de la Musique*, and a militant Mendelssohnian, and therefore, needless to say, contra Wagner, since "he who is not for me is against me." All this animosity, all this underhand intriguing, tended to magnify the importance of the adversary against whom it was directed. Richard felt himself all the more impregnable for having been made the target of these potent signors and their servile press. Nevertheless, he renewed his advances to Schumann, invited him to Dresden, and sent him the scores of *Rienzi* and *The Flying Dutchman*. They were not acknowledged.

Thereupon Wagner got down to work again. Minna and he installed themselves in some very tolerable quarters, No. 6 Ostrallee, overlooking the Zwinger (the same Ostrallee in which, when a little boy, he had heard a statue tuning up its violin). Unfortunately, fresh funds had to be borrowed and his future royalties discounted to enable them to get what was necessary— and superfluous, the Philistines would add—in the way of furniture, namely a piano by Breitkopf, a "majestic" bureau, and the Cornelius engraving that was to serve as a frontispiece to the *Niebelungen*. But how should the good folk of Dresden be expected to know what was necessary to fire the imagination of an artist! Add to that an extensive and well-chosen collection of books among which, besides the Greek, Latin, French, and Italian classics, an excellent Shakespeare and the modern poets, early German literature was abundantly represented. There were even some rare and costly treasures in the collection, such as the *Roman des douze Pairs*, and other legends of the Middle Ages.

Thus equipped, Richard imagined himself in a posture to brave all the vexations which his new duties had in store for him. They came—not single spies! For not only were his own works the object of criticism, but his interpretation of *Don Juan*, the *Enlèvement au Sérail*, *Euryanthe*, *Der Freischütz*, the *Pastoral Symphony*, on all of which he had lavished such careful study in order to discover the authentic movements. In Gluck's *Armide*, however, Wagner reveals himself an exceptional master of the orchestra and for a long time the appellation "Gluckist" was the finest feather in his cap.

There were some friendships, however, that consoled him for these professional discomfitures. Among others there was August Roeckel, eighteen months his junior, who had been sent from Weimar to Dresden to act as deputy director of music. Roeckel knew both English and French, played the piano perfectly, read scores at sight, and claimed to be something of a composer. But as soon as he heard Wagner's music and took stock of the man, he knew him for a master and lowered his flag. This is the first in date of those devoted and energetic friends who generously took upon themselves the burden of "voluntary servitude," as La Boëtie expresses it, the first of those henchmen of whose passionate devotion Wagner so dexterously availed himself. But if he had a sort of genius for making use of these planetary influences, he also, in his turn, irradiated them with the warmth of his own fire. Friendship, as he understood it, was always whole-hearted and uncalculating, and of all the obligations by which a man is bound, he always put friendship first. "The nearer I grew to man's estate, the more impossible I found it to conceive of a friendship without love." Thus his friendship exposed him to as much suffering as his loves. The death of Lehrs, which occurred about this time, affected him so deeply that for a long while he was incapable of thought or action.

By May, the poetical version of *Tannhäuser* was completed, and during the summer holidays they went back again to their beloved Teplitz, where Wagner treated the gastric trouble he had contracted in his damp lodgings in the rue Jacob, Paris, in rather a novel manner. Every morning he went for a run, armed with a bottle containing the medicinal waters and a huge one-volume edition of Grimm's *German Mythology*. This book always put him in a state of violent excitement and, despite its lack of arrangement and rather elementary scholarship, it never failed to give Wagner access to a world which, it seemed to him, had always been his home—a world of legend in which he lived and moved far more at his ease than in the realms where trills and *il bel canto* were the fashion of the day and whence his contemporaries drew their inspiration. But here, in this world of legend, he found the material for a German opera ready to his hand. Back again in Dresden, there was happiness almost unalloyed in his charming retreat in the Ostrallee. If only he had had "his Parisians" with him there, his cup of joy would have been full. And so he hates Paris that keeps his favourite sister, Cecile, away from him; he hates Vienna, the city of Donizetti. Is Dresden then the city of his heart? No; the city of his heart lies in that world of dreams in which he has now begun to dwell again, it lies in the world of Tannhäuser.

November 1843. He wrote this date on the first sheet of a ream of white paper. It was the date of a new birth, the birth of something that would sum up all the wild welter of ideas that were now besieging him. But the interruptions were unending. Performances of *The Flying Dutchman* at Cassel, at Riga (Riga, where his name was by this time completely forgotten save by his creditors), the *première* of the same opera at Berlin, where it might well be expected that the rising talent of this young Saxon, of whom so many contradictory things were being said, would have its due measure of appreciation. Nothing of the sort. At Berlin, despite an atmosphere charged with electricity, despite the rare and mysterious *Stimmung* with which the composer enveloped his whole first act, in order to hypnotize his audience, despite the flattering presence of the King of Prussia, its merits were violently disputed. Writing home to his wife, Richard blares forth his triumph *à la* Berlioz. It was even greater than *Rienzi*. Not a member of the audience, from floor to ceiling, who was not shouting with enthusiasm. They had him before the curtain times without number. Unprecedented! Incomparable! If only Mme Schroeder-Devrient can keep well! How came it, then, that the press was hostile? That terrible fellow, Rellstab, had the effrontery to say in print that the work gave evidence of great talent and great mistakes; "not a piece of real music," "a laborious work, full of harsh discords," "the composer had turned exception into rule." Had, then, some evil spirits got into the theatre? Mendelssohn's pale features had, indeed, been in evidence in one of the front boxes—the Devil in gala dress, out of a Tale of Hoffmann.

The second performance was little better. Hisses drowned the faint applause. After the performance, Wagner went with two friends to seek oblivion in alcohol. Returning a little unsteadily to his hotel, he was confronted there by a gentleman who had long been waiting for him and who now greeted him with a ceremonious bow. Richard begged to be excused; surely his visitor could see that he was not in a fit state to attend to business. But the latter would not take the hint, and insisted on entering into conversation. So they sat down in the icy bedroom, where, by the light of a single candle, Professor Werder announced his name and qualities, and then declared that he had caught a glimpse that evening of the splendid future which such a work as *The Flying Dutchman* assured to German art. Richard could not make it out. Was it a sequel to some Tale of Hoffmann that he had begun a while ago? He could hardly articulate a word and requested the strange enthusiast to write his name on a sheet of paper. Then he flung himself on the bed and fell asleep. Next day he returned to Dresden. There the features of Professor Werder came back to him as in a dream. Was it not a remarkable thing that his work should call forth such bitter condemnation from the professional critics, and yet so move a cultivated listener to enthusiasm that he was obliged to come in the middle of the night and give the derided composer the profoundest—and most disturbing—assurance of his admiration.

At Hamburg *Rienzi* had a greater success than *The Flying Dutchman* at Berlin. But the performance—showy and vulgar—so displeased the composer that the director, knowing Wagner's fondness for pets, gave him a beautiful parrot to make up for it. Minna welcomed her husband and the magnificent bird with enthusiasm, for she regarded the parrot as a palpable proof that Richard was destined to make a name in the world.

"It was in a state of agonizing, uncontrollable excitement, which kept my blood and nerves in a boiling fever, that I sketched out and composed the music for *Tannhäuser*." Wagner had come across references to the story in an old book, in Heine, in Tieck's *Faithful Eckart*, in *Der Sängerkrieg*, by E. T. A. Hoffmann, and in the German legends of the brothers Grimm. From these various sources, to which we might add two old poems of the thirteenth and fourteenth centuries, he obtained the material for his great lyrical ballad. With the unerring insight which characterizes the great dramatists, he saw at once what he could get from each, welding together the two legends of *The War of the Singers* and *Tannhäuser* and linking up the stories of Saint Elisabeth of Hungary with the legend of the Accursèd Knight; a stained glass window with five or six tableaux displaying, in contrast or in combination, the blue of Faith, the white of Purity, the bright or sombre red of Passion and Voluptuousness. In this sequence of pictures Wagner contrived to convey, in a manner wellnigh prophetic, not only certain peculiarities of his future musical art, but also the interwoven strands of his desires, his temptations, his mysticism, his bouts of sensuality, and his homesickness for the things of the spirit. Though he went for the idea and the setting of his story to popular legend, or to a poem of Heine's, its inward development was wholly his own. Properly to understand the drama of Wagner's life, to fill in its outlines, we have but to attune our ears to the message of Tannhäuser.

For seven years, this adventurous knight had lived a willing thrall of Venus, dwelling alone with her on her enchanted mountain. Howbeit, a day came at length when his mind turned with the wistful sadness of the satiated voluptuary to the ennobling sufferings of the sons of men. He dreams that he hears the bells of his native land, he thrills with the half-glimpsed hope that he may yet repent and be forgiven, he longs for regeneration and calls on death to come to him. Locked in fierce combat with the goddess who has robbed him of his soul and holds him still in thrall, he suddenly frees himself by calling on the name of Mary. The spell is broken. The restless world of pleasure closes its gates against the fugitive, and he awakens at the foot of the happy mountain of his boyhood days. The frustrate longings of his youth, his journeyings, his exile, the ashes of his burnt-out love scattered to the winds—all this belongs to the Past, and now the poet breathes in the pure air of his spiritual home which he has found once more. The Venusberg fades from his memory, while, far away, rise up the familiar outlines of the fortress of Wartburg. A shepherd lad is playing on his pipe, greeting the return of spring that clothes the earth in fresh attire. In the distance is heard the chanting of a choir. They are pilgrims on their way to Rome to seek absolution for their sins, and hymning the praises of Jesus and Mary as they go. Tannhäuser stands lost in a trance from which he is aroused by the sudden breaking in upon the scene of the Landgrave of Wartburg, his barons and troubadours. They recognize their old friend, make much of him, and besiege him with questions. Whence comes he, after so many years of mysterious silence? The

Lover of Love returns no answer, but fares along with the brilliant company until they reach the castle. There, for seven years, the Landgrave's niece has been awaiting the return of the poet who, in days gone by, had kindled the flame of love in her heart. Radiant, with arms outstretched, she hastens forth to greet him. . . . Yet no word of plighted troth passes between those twain who of yore began to love, only a look of trust and hope untroubled by desire. The bond, though deep, is not all-powerful, since it avails not to render the knight Tannhäuser deaf to the call of the Venusberg. Perhaps the bitterest curse which weighs on man is the fierce energy with which he essays to enfold in one embrace that which a single body never brings—graciousness of spirit and the ardours of the flesh. To celebrate the traveller's return, the Landgrave commands that a poetic tournament shall be held in which the task assigned shall be the definition of love, and Wolfram von Eschenbach forthwith begins the contest. He sings of pure love, love that is dutiful, reposing in the fear of God, inaccessible virginity, the wondrous fountain which no one dares approach lest he befoul it. But already the music grows tremulous with the distant incantation of Venus, and as Tannhäuser, thrilled at the memory of pangs he loved too well, gives ear to the sound, there rise to his lips, despite himself, half-stifled moans of pleasure. A little while and he contains himself no longer, breaking forth into one long cry of passionate regret. Then other poets intervene, the contest grows fiercer and more exultant, while Elisabeth, beneath her canopy—what a homage to the women who love—signs her approval of his madness. Flinging aside all prudence, regardless of the threats of the other courtiers, Tannhäuser reveals his true feelings ever more and more, discloses his love's retreat, proclaims the cult of pleasure, and chants his hymn to Venus. He is answered by a general shout of indignation. The barons draw and rush upon the Accursèd Knight who has tasted the joys of hell, when Elisabeth flings herself in their way to protect him with her purity. "Back! I fear not death . . . I whose heart he has filled with joyfulness, I implore you, spare him! Let him atone and repent. . . . I pray for him. . . ." Tannhäuser sees in a flash to what depths he has sunk. He falls at the feet of the sainted one and kisses her robe, and, as though any expectation of a new life could only express itself in two short words, he cries to the assembled multitude, "To Rome!"

From that time forth, we feel it, the knight of love's agony can only be saved by death. He has but one yearning, and that is to die that he may live. Led away and maddened by Venus, he

tore himself from her embrace to return to men and their sufferings. And when he beheld that suffering in the sorrowing
eyes of woman, he betakes himself to God. But God will not
suffer a repentance that is soiled with passion. The pilgrim then
returns from Rome the following year with his robe of repentance which the Church did not deem sufficiently pure. Elisabeth,
meanwhile, is awaiting him by the wayside in prayer, with all
the trustfulness of her innocent spirit. But she does not see him
in the procession of the pardoned. In despair, she offers her life
to God as a sacrifice. Thus the pilgrim, who is following the
saintly cohort afar off, finds but a wilderness empty of delight.
Then he tells Wolfram of the various stages of his fruitless
journey and breaks forth into imprecations and bitter railing.
Since his repentance was in vain he will fare forth again to the
Venusberg and seek once more the goddess without a soul. Even
as he speaks the air is filled with unearthly music, and through
the mists of dawn appears a naked figure, the symbol of oblivion.
Then Wolfram utters the name of Elisabeth, at whose sound all
evil spirits flee away. Tannhäuser stands rooted to the spot,
transfixed with awe and wonder. And, lo! in the distance the
sound of men chanting a hymn to celebrate the deliverance of
the sainted one. The evil vision fades away as the mists disperse,
and a funeral procession comes into view. It is the corse of the
blessed one which they are bringing to lay at the feet of the
man she has saved by her willing sacrifice. Then Tannhäuser, in
his turn, breathes his last, just as his grief and repentance give
him the certainty of divine pardon, and his pilgrim's staff, on
which the Pope had laid his ban, bursts forth anew with springtide blossom, in token of the eternal miracle of faith.

This narrative, in which pagan delights and the Paradise of
Mary are brought face to face, is the youthful testament of a
man who can only sing of his yearning for suffering and death.
"Until the final unfolding of the flower whose scent is death,"
he said, significantly, "until the annihilation of the spirit of
self. . . ." When he returns from Rome, Tannhäuser's only
feelings are those of rage against a world which, because of the
sincerity of his repentance, has forbidden him the right to live,
and it is no desire for enjoyment and pleasure that prompts him
to go back to the Venusberg, but detestation of the world, to
which he must needs give proof of the disdain and despair which
urge him on his course. . . . It is thus that he loves Elisabeth,
and such is the love with which he requites her. She has achieved
that which the whole world was powerless to achieve, and Tannhäuser, in his death, renders her thanks for that sublime testi-

mony of her love. But none there are who are not compelled to envy him his fate, and the whole universe, nay, God Himself, must needs proclaim him blessèd.

Like all great souls pursuing the quest of the supreme good, Wagner is haunted by the idea of death, "The flower whose scent is death"—it is with a mystic ecstasy that he inhales its perfume. Henceforth, that flower alone will yield him the inspiration of his life, all his music, all his fiery outbursts of prophecy or love. Tannhäuser is the first true picture of himself that it was given him to limn, the symbol of the fight within between his craving for pleasure and his horror of those indulgences that trail the wingèd spirit in the mire. Sorrow alone is real, thus thought he, even as Schopenhauer, who was soon to take him for his guide. In the very same year in which he composed his *Tannhäuser*, and in that same Saxon land, was born his disciple that was to be, who, when forty-four more years had passed, spoke these words of Wagner: "Behold a musician unrivalled in the art of giving utterance to the sufferings, the burdens, and the tortures of the soul. . . . The Orpheus of all the sorrows of the heart."

But at this time the composer of *The Flying Dutchman* and *Tannhäuser* had only begun to find himself. He still surveyed life with a young man's wonder, and a shade of disdain, nay, even perhaps of dilettantism, from the standpoint of an age that looked frowningly on art, an age in which religion was entering upon its death throes. Out of all these mingled elements he builds up his Hymn to Oblivion, oblivion and death whereon he meditates like a Buddhist, as on the supreme and sole serenity. And it is in his hatred of the world that he now proceeds to plant the earliest seeds of his love for humanity.

The year 1844, which was wholly devoted to the composition of *Tannhäuser*, was marked by certain notable occurrences. To begin with, there was the publication, now for the first time undertaken, of Wagner's works by Meser of Dresden; then his niece Johanna's appointment at the Royal Opera; next the translation of Weber's ashes from London to Dresden, and finally Spontini's visit to the latter city. This publication business, on which he had rather thoughtlessly embarked, soon became a fresh source of worry. His idea had been to undertake it at his own expense, thanks to yet another loan promised him by Mme. Schroeder-Devrient. She, however, took it into her head to involve herself in a liaison with an officer of the Guards, whose first step was to insist on looking into her affairs, and this methodical and prudent gentleman would not hear of her putting her money into anything so risky. Wagner was therefore obliged to have recourse to professional money-lenders in order that no time might be lost in bringing out the three operas which he considered would form the nucleus of his fortune, and seeing that the first two were now in demand in the principal cities in Germany and that their vogue was increasing every day, there was nothing obviously extravagant in Wagner's idea. As for Johanna, Albert Wagner's child, they liked her voice the first time they heard it, and her uncle had no difficulty in securing her appointment. It at once occurred to him that she might create the rôle of Elisabeth. But the most amazing and instructive event of the season was the performance of *La Vestale*, with Spontini himself as conductor.

The old *maestro*, who for years had been putting up with all manner of worries and humiliating vexations, was at last about to say good-bye to Berlin, and von Luttichau, the director, and Wagner had jointly invited him to come to Dresden and conduct his work in person. In a "majestic" reply, addressed to the young composer, who had referred to himself as his disciple, the old fellow signified his acceptance with an air of benevolent condescension. As the famous Mme. Schroeder-Devrient herself was to figure among the interpreters, as the theatre was still brand-new and the chorus thoroughly up to the mark, the orchestra could surely furnish an adequate number of capable instrumentalists, *the whole set off with a dozen good double basses*. Those last words, with their implication of elaborate technical requirements, created such alarm in the bosoms of the organizers that they decided to cancel the invitation. But on the day originally fixed a carriage drew up at Wagner's door, and the venerable *maestro* alighted, looking very imposing in a frock-coat of blue broadcloth. There was a tremendous commotion in the managerial department. Still, there was nothing for it but to bow to the will, and perform the dictates, of the irascible old "spoilt child." He was therefore entrusted with the task of conducting the ensemble rehearsals, which, however, seemed to cause him no little perturbation. He asked to see the bâton which Richard used for conducting, fussed and fumed, and swore he would never be able to command his troops unless he could have an ebony bâton with a big ivory knob at each end. The staff carpenter was therefore commissioned to turn out this drum-major's sceptre with all possible speed, as the "Spanish grandee" would never appear at his desk without it. The man got it done in the stipulated time, and work started next day.

The first thing Spontini did was to regroup the orchestra according to his own notions. He distributed the quartet of stringed instruments equally among the whole band, separated the brass and the big drums so as to have them one on each wing of the orchestra, while the wood-wind formed a chain between the violins. Wagner profited by this lesson and adopted the same principle, which was quite contrary to the old German usage of grouping the strings and the wind in separate bunches. "I conduct merely with a look," said Spontini. "My left eye is the first violin, my right eye the second. But to do this you must never wear spectacles, as second rate conductors do, even when you are short-sighted. Why, I can hardly see a yard in front of me, and yet I get all I want by a look!" So saying, he seized his bâton by the middle, like a field marshal, and began the manœuvres. They were all at sixes and sevens. The stage-manager was furious because Spontini insisted on the chorus performing with the same military precision as he got from his Prussian singers. Ten times he made them begin over again. At last the composer mounted the stage himself, whereupon the cast, with their nerves very much on edge, slunk off into the wings, leaving the stately old septuagenarian to lecture to a group of lighting and stage hands, on the true art of the theatre. Richard, however, was amazed at the old man's energy. It made him understand how it had enabled Spontini to strive after and obtain one of the aims of theatrical art which, in our day, has been almost completely lost sight of.

Despite his eccentricities and his extraordinary German, Spontini fascinated both orchestra and players. They soon got over their alarm and, in the subsequent rehearsals, were his to a man. The actual performance of *La Vestale*, however, was little more than a *succès d'estime* for the illustrious composer, who came on the stage all bestarred with decorations. As good luck would have it, an event occurred that spread a soothing balm on this fresh wound to his *amour-propre*. News came to Spontini at Dresden that the Pope had created him a Count of Saint Andrew, and that the King of Denmark had conferred on him the Order of the Elephant. Banquets were held in his honour, and in the course of them he let fall a few oracles from the lofty eminence of his childlike vanity. Mme. Schroeder-Devrient and Mme. Spontini (a daughter of Erard, the famous piano-maker), were talking and laughing when the old man pulled them up sharply, saying: "I will not have people laughing in my presence. I never laugh myself, and I like people to be serious." Then, turning to Wagner, he remarked, "When I heard your

Rienzi, I said: 'That is a man of genius, but he has already done more than he can do. . . .' After Gluck, it was I who brought about the great revolution, with *La Vestale.* In *Cortez* I made a great step forward, then three more in *Olympia* and a hundred in *Agnes von Hohenstaufen,* in which I made the orchestra serve as a perfect substitute for the organ. How can you suppose that anyone can invent anything new when I, Spontini, declare that I can in no way improve upon my previous works, more especially as I am advised that, since I wrote *La Vestale,* no one has written a note that has not been borrowed from my scores? In *La Vestale* my subject was Roman, in *Cortez* Spanish-American, in *Olympia* Græco-Macedonian, and, finally, in *Agnes von Hohenstaufen* German. The rest don't count. Oh, mark my words, there was some hope for Germany when I was Emperor of Music in Berlin. But now that the King of Prussia has handed it over to the two wandering Jews he has imported, there is no more hope for it."

Doubtless this allusion to Meyerbeer and Mendelssohn made Wagner smile, and he always kept a soft spot in his heart for Spontini.

Shortly after his departure, when the year was drawing to a close, Wagner put the finishing touches on *Tannhäuser.* It was the 29th of December. It now only remained for him to finish the orchestration, and the management placed an order with Desplechin & Company of Paris for some special scenic devices. At last, on 13th April, 1845, he was able to date and sign the completed work, each page of which had been lithographed as soon as finished. Praiseworthy foresight in an author, this; but expensive. It cost 500 thalers! Clearly he would have to tackle the practical side of the matter. That is to say, he would have to see about getting it staged and advertised. Rehearsals were begun in the autumn and difficulties cropped up at the very start. There was no doubt that Mme. Schroeder-Devrient would make rather a corpulent Venus, but it was clearly impossible to do without her. "For Heaven's sake," said she, "tell me what I'm to wear as Venus. It'll have to be more than a waist-band, that's certain. I shall get myself up in carnival attire. You will like that, I'm sure." Tichatschek hadn't an inkling of the deeper implications of his rôle, but, as usual, they trusted that his voice would make up for all his other shortcomings. No doubt Johanna was very young for Elisabeth, but her girlish bloom would compensate for her lack of experience. But the best of the bunch was Mitterwurzer, the barytone, who was to sing Wolfram. He was the only one of them all who understood what was in the composer's mind, and acted as he was intended to act. He made up his mind that he would have to jettison the old-fashioned recitative. He saw that old ideas would have to go by the board and that what opera, in the modern sense, really meant was drama.

The *première* took place on the 19th of October, 1845, three years, all but a day, after the opening night of *Rienzi*. It was another blank; there was no getting away from that. The *Dutchman* had not come up to *Rienzi*, and now *Tannhäuser* was a long way behind the *Dutchman*. Rather a disquieting decrescendo! Richard was perfectly well aware that there were defects in the work, though even he probably did not realize how far-reaching they were. It seemed to him that the Prologue to Act I was too vague, the part of Venus too sketchy, and that his score lacked grip and precision. Tichatschek was very disappointing, especially in Act III, where his total inability to convey the idea of grief rendered the psychological development of the character almost unintelligible. Johanna, too, failed to get any hint of passion into Elisabeth's prayer. To put the whole thing in a nutshell, the opera missed fire from start to finish. The audience simply did not understand it. It was all very well for people to applaud the final septet of Act I, the festal march, the star-song, the pilgrims' chorus, but it was not on any of these passages, with their strong family likeness to the old-fashioned artificial bravura, that Wagner relied to convey his real idea. His authentic gospel, on the contrary, was to be sought in the inward development of the general movement, culminating in the adagio of the second finale and in the long story narrated by Tannhäuser on his return from Rome. Now, it was precisely Elisabeth's eagerness to sacrifice her life, and the pathos of her heroic intervention, no less than the final monologue, that the public were unable to grasp. That a composer should go out of his way to play the philosopher, and a pessimistic one at that, was altogether too unorthodox for them to swallow. What music was for was to entertain people and cheer them up, not to make them think. What the crowd wanted was plenty of dancing and singing, and Wagner gave them "dramatic action." Not one of his ideas had caught on, and so much was this the case that the singers, despite the multitudinous composer's notes with which their script was interlarded, played the whole thing to the gallery so as to maintain at least some sort of contact with the audience. It would have taken a complete libretto, notes and all, to explain the spiritual nuances through which the composer designed to guide his listeners. It would have been necessary to show them

that orchestra, voices, declamation, action, scenery, and costumes, in a word the whole tragedy in its divers forms of expression, was in reality but one single movement, one compact
entity, from which no single fragment could be abstracted without impairing the integrity of the whole. It was not merely a new
æsthetic, but a new ethic that he was propounding, a subordination of the individual to the group, of the interpreters to the
creator; it was, if the truth be told, a stern but splendid lesson
in humility, impressing upon man the duty of effacing himself
for the good of the cause.

But all this, being new, was lost sight of. Wagner found himself obliged to make several cuts for the subsequent performances, to plane down and French-polish some of the handsomest
knots in his wood work. He did it without a twinge, but trying
all he knew to keep his original plan unimpaired. It was not
until several years later that the work, after undergoing manifold changes and developments, was given its final and definitive
form. But the week during which he was busy on these tentative
revisions, and the work which they entailed, was absolute torture
to him, and constituted an episode of outstanding importance in
his life-story. It was not merely his pride that was wounded this
time; but that from the intellectual point of view he had suffered a grievous disappointment. What it meant, as he now saw
plainly enough, was that the public were not sufficiently educated
to absorb his ideas; that his art, his aims, all his reformative
notions, were addressed to an ideal audience which had no existence in fact; that it might perhaps be years before these smug
bourgeois were capable of being aroused to the consciousness,
however dim, of the truth that the enlightened enjoyment of a
work of art presupposes in the recipient a profound interest
in his own destiny, in the mystery of his *whence* and *whither*.
It followed that these ideal, but non-existent, spectators would
have first to be brought into being, if the prophet was not to
perish before the god whose messenger he was had proclaimed
his laws. The reform, then, which he was called on to undertake
contemplated a sphere that extended far beyond the precincts
of the Dresden Theatre Royal. He would strike the old rock of
experience, and the waters of enlightenment should gush forth.
He must show his flock that art regarded as a mere pastime was
a thing for *crétins*, a wholly misleading will-o'-the-wisp, the
lamentable symptom of an impotent and degenerate age. For
the health of the world is based upon two things, and two things
only, on love and on suffering—unless, perchance, one should
add renunciation. Therefore it is in the love-impulse that man

will discover the energy by which he shall win through to his complete redemption. Soaring high above the world like an omen of things to come, a hero of the future is endowed alike with a soul divine and a body torn by passion.

Roeckel was one of those who knew these things. In spite of the very lukewarm success of *Tannhäuser*, he stood firm in the faith. He held that his friend was indomitable. He had seen, in sober truth, "the stars about his head." As for the critics, they had the time of their lives, and Wagner's moral isolation was more complete than ever, notwithstanding that he was now on friendly terms with all the artists in the place—with Ritschl and Haenel, the sculptors; Gutzkow the poet and playwright; Semper the architect; and Auerbach. But somehow admiration and sympathy do not seem to work so actively as malice and uncharitableness. "The poetical defects of the work are glaring," remarked the *New Musical Review*. "The overture is unintelligible and as devoid of any general colour-scheme as the work itself." But Richard did not read the letters that passed between Schumann and Mendelssohn, in which they compared notes on the lithographed score which Wagner had sent them. "A clever fellow, there's no getting away from that," said the composer of *Manfred* and *The Carnival*, "but upon my word he can't write four decent bars on end, let alone four beautiful ones. It is in harmony and in the chorales for four voices that he is especially at sea, like all the rest of them. The music isn't a shade better than *Rienzi*: in fact, it's not so good, it's duller and more forced." It was not until some time afterwards, when he had actually heard *Tannhäuser*, that Schumann changed his tune and confessed that he had been completely held by the dramatic quality of the music. Well, it is precisely in that power to "hold," to "grip," the hearer that lay the significance of the new art and the hopes of bringing forth a new kind of opera from the ashes of the old. And there, too, lay hid the deadly germ that was destined to overrun the realms of pure music—the music of Bach and the Beethoven quartets—and to bear it away from the airy regions of the spirit, to make it the bondslave of the passions. The fact, however, is that Schumann and he never really hit it off together. "Wagner is impossible," said Schumann; "he talks the whole time." "Schumann is impossible," said Wagner; "he never talks at all." Wagner was provided with special antennæ that enabled him to sense a foe; and his own particular persecution-complex was in this instance only too completely justifiable. He did not take it lying down. He returned to his books on mediæval Germany and put into rehearsal for the grand concert, held annually on Palm Sunday in the old Opera House, the *Ninth Symphony* of Beethoven. That took some pluck, when one remembers how Beethoven's major work was then decried. He found himself at once at loggerheads with the management, with Reissiger, and even with the orchestra, who sent a deputation to wait on him because they all thought that the mere fact of such a piece being chosen would ruin the booking prospects. Richard, therefore, made it a point of honour to prove them wrong. Hidden away in his study, he pored and pored over those "mysterious" pages, the very sight of which, in Flachs's time, would send him off into a trance. And straightway, as though some occult influence dwelt in the pages, Wagner felt himself again beneath the spell. All his misgivings were dispersed, all his faith restored. What in his youth he had seen but with the eye of the soul, now came home to him enriched with all the vibrant thrill of life, the riper dignity of knowledge, the splendid sorrows of one who had "voyaged through strange seas of thought—alone!" So when Herr Kapellmeister Wagner fell a-weeping as he contemplated this stupendous and soul-ravishing work, it was because he had come to maturity in the space of a few brief nights, because he was now in the fullest sense of the word a master. He must needs fling himself wholly free from the letter and henceforth see but the spirit alone. From cover to cover of the work he must track the idea, grasp the continuity of the melody, and bring himself to realize that if the Symphony was reputed to be unplayable, it was because Beethoven did not write for the Mozartian orchestra of his day, but for the great instrumental ensembles of a future age. We may take it that with Beethoven, when his deafness had come upon him, the sound pattern impressed itself so vividly upon him that he lost sight of the dynamic possibilities of the orchestra, and demanded of it effects that were until then undreamt of. In order to grasp and bring out the ideas with the requisite strictness, he would have to neglect the printed indications which were necessarily conditioned "by the structure of the horns and natural trumpets," which were the only kind then known to the manufacturers, and replace them by directions appropriate to the chromatic instruments of the day. Nay, he would even go so far in his audacity as to transfer to the trumpets the fanfare that was written for the wood-wind at the beginning of the second movement. Only thus was it possible clearly to convey the "tumultuous outburst of a wild despair" and show how part was linked with part. Then the light dawns and the speech assumes the commanding significance of a last, supreme appeal. Wagner sought a commentary on the Beethoven drama in Goethe's *Faust* and drew up an explanatory program for the benefit of the public. "A combat, in the most exalted sense of the word, a combat between the soul battling for joy and happiness against the influence of that hostile power which ever interposes between ourselves and earthly bliss—such, I take it, is the basic idea of the first movement." He printed the following line by way of a motto to illustrate the main theme:

Renounce thou must: renounce thou shalt.

That was the very slogan of Tannhäuser-Wagner. "With the second movement a wild delight takes hold of us and bears us onwards toward a happiness beyond our ken. In the third, the tumult is allayed, all is still and hushed in breathless expectation of the coming of love." It looks as if Beethoven and Goethe both regarded love not wholly as an agent of kindness and affection, but as a stimulus to the creative impulse.

Ein unbegreiflich holdes Sehnen
Trieb mich durch Wald und Wiesen hinzugeh'n,
Und unter tausend heissen Thränen
Fühlt' ich mir eine Welt ensteh'n.

Finally the fourth movement, opening as with a sort of cry, forsakes the purely instrumental character, and gives forth that moving recitative in the bass which seems to be feeling its way onward as though seeking for a voice, and culminates in a tempestuous climax expressive of triumphant possession. "Then, with the clear-cut meaning of the spoken word, we hear the sound of a human voice, and know not which to admire the more, the master's daring inspiration, or his grand simplicity of soul, when he makes this voice address the instruments and say: '*Ihr Freunde, nicht diese Töne. . . .*' It is as though the joyous truth had been made clear to us by revelation from on high, the truth, namely, that every man is born to be happy."

A thought like that, flashing a sudden light on the soul of "The Orpheus of all the Sorrows," sheds no less a light on this same Wagner who has now arrived at one of the psychological milestones of his career. The man who conducted the *Ninth Symphony* on that Palm Sunday of 1846 has nothing in common, save a faint and far-off memory, with the man who composed *Rienzi*. He is now the finished artist, shaped and moulded, the poet of *Lohengrin*, to which he has already set his hand, the creator of a whole world of music which he bears within him like some dread secret of which he fears the "hatch and the disclose." But the dizzy vision he beheld, if it sundered him for

good and all from the crowd, established in him an unshakable
faith in his mission and drew him yet closer to the one and only
model which he had elected to follow. Not only did he understand Beethoven, but he so completely fathomed his ideas as to
be able to amend the errors in printing or interpretation which
marred the perfection of his work; of substituting intentions of
his own; of assigning to the choir, instead of the everlasting
sung notes in every case, spoken appeals as though a sort of
ecstatic declamation.

The announcement of the Symphony had a sensational effect
on the prospective audience and the musical world in general.
Music-lovers, professional musicians, and conductors came flock-
ing in from Leipzig, Freiberg and the whole of Saxony to see
the tomb opened and the Symphony, which had so long been
buried therein, arise to live anew. The stage of the old Opera
House had been turned into an amphitheatre for the occasion,
and the chorus was augmented by students from the Kreuzschule, of which Richard Geyer had formerly been a pupil. And
this time the public realized that in this man, with his virile
sense of values, his ardent energy, his yearning for what he
believed to be the truth, there smouldered the hidden fire of
the revolutionary. It was a dangerous possibility, and it had
led Wagner himself to declare that the day would come when
art would have to be put under police supervision. Little did
he dream how true a prophet he was. Yet even at this date,
young folk passing along the Ostrallee, where dwelt the Master who could thus exalt them to the seventh heaven, would
raise their hats as a token of loyalty to the man whom they
looked on as their leader.

Chapter VI

THE CRAFTSMAN OF THE IDEAL—
LOHENGRIN

MIGHT it not be truly said that the more isolated a man is, the more he is likely to engage the sympathy of those who watch him as he battles for a cause which they themselves hold dear. Let there be a slighted or slandered politician, or a neglected philosopher, or an artist uncomprehended of the multitude, who is labouring for the national, moral, or spiritual welfare of his age, though such an one be unheeded by the crowd, the younger generation will be swift to note him down as one of themselves, one who reflects their own tastes and voices their own grievances.

The strange orchestral conductor who plied his task in Dresden now wielded a power which it would have puzzled the police to put under arrest. He was a queer combination of man and wizard. His personal magnetism was beginning to exert its influence, and that not merely on a few colleagues of the theatre or the orchestra, like August Roeckel and Theodor Uhlig, but on people he did not know at all, women not excluded. He was the recipient of those timid tokens of admiration and respect which constitute a poet's recompense for all his hours of solitude and silence.

At Gross-Graupe, in an out-of-the-way corner of Saxon Switzerland, a youngster came one day asking to be directed to the house in which the *kapellmeister* of the court was wont to spend his summer holidays. They pointed out a farm at some little distance from the village, where Wagner rented a large room, the sole furniture of which consisted of a grand piano and a sofa. What time the student is making a mental note of these details, behold the master in person is seen returning from the forest, wearing an immense straw hat, his dog Peps following along behind. The visitor makes himself known. He is Hans von Bülow, a sixteen-year-old student, passionately fond of

music and a profound admirer, and so on and so forth. Thus
there came into Wagner's life a youth seventeen years his junior,
whose master and tormentor he was destined to become.

"Have you encountered on the sea that ship with the red
sails and the black mast? On her deck stands the master pale
and wan, scanning the watery waste unweariedly. Hist! How
the wind whistles in the shrouds! Howbeit, one day perchance
the man shall win deliverance, if haply he falls in with a woman
who shall remain faithful unto him till death. Ah, thou wan-
faced mariner, when wilt thou meet her?" Thus sings Senta in
The Flying Dutchman, and to her song the Mariner in these
words makes reply: "That gloomy fire whereby I feel myself
consumed—am I to call it love? Ah no, alas! 'tis the restless
longing for deliverance. . . ." Erik and the Mariner scan each
other's face for the first time, here in this sylvan land of sunshine, where Richard is at work upon his *Lohengrin*. As with
Tannhäuser, as with *The Flying Dutchman*, so also with *Lohengrin*, the idea had come to him in the bosom of nature as he
roamed the Marienbad countryside, in the summer of the year
before. From the books he always carried in his pocket two
poetic ideas had come into his mind: the tale of Lohengrin and
the tale of the Meistersingers of Nuremberg. Torn betwixt one
and the other, he knew not to which he would first give ear.
Now it was the legend of the swan that held him captive, now
the rugged features of Hans Sachs, the supreme incarnation of
the popular genius. The whole comedy sprang into life before
his inward eye and he rapidly sketched it out from beginning to
end. And then behold that selfsame day, while he was in his
bath, the story of Lohengrin came back to him once more, and
to free his mind of it he must needs commit it to paper also.
Then everything had had to stand aside for the rehearsals of
Tannhäuser and the *Ninth Symphony* and all the manifold worries of the long, long winter. But now at last, in this pleasant
Saxon land, he had set about putting the finishing touches to
Lohengrin, the poem that sang of severance and renunciation.
For to this man, who hitherto has loved so little and to such
little purpose, the ultimate truth about love is that it remains
eternally unattainable. Its sole value depends on the reaction of
the lovers to the obstacles in their path. The true significance
of the tale of Lohengrin lies in these words: The contact of
human nature with the supernatural can be but brief. "God
would be better advised to spare us such revelations, because
He must not go counter to the laws of nature. Nature takes her
revenge and brings these revelations to naught." Thus he wrote

from Gross-Graupe to Dr. Hermann Franck, a friendly critic—
one of the few—who sang the praises of his work in the *Augs-burg Gazette*. Franck would have liked *Lohengrin* to have a less sombre ending. But Wagner felt something within him that prompted him to stand his ground. So *Lohengrin* remained as he had wished it to remain, the story of a pilgrim soul. The mystery of the why and wherefore of the feelings, of the origins of love, none can unravel, for it is the insubstantial fruitage of a charm; and that charm itself, like music, like love, like *Lohengrin*, melts into thin air the instant we essay to explain it. It is the immemorial adventure of Zeus and Semele, of a god in love with a mortal and compelled to destroy her to escape from love's profoundest longing, the eternal, inexhaustible yearning to know ever more and more deeply and completely.

The problem, now, from which Wagner could not escape, was this problem of the possession of a being, a longing to achieve it in the most utterly real and material sense. And as life could offer him no solution, he sought it in music. If in *Tannhäuser* he had turned instinctively to the pure and chaste as the safeguard of man, of man who had now reached the peak of isolation and the summit of human power, he longed now to plunge again into the depths, to seek the soft enfolding shelter of a woman's arms. Lohengrin then was waiting for the woman who believed in him, "who should ask not who he was, nor whence he came, but should love him for what he was and because of what he was. He sought not admiration or adoration, but the one and only thing that could deliver him from his loneliness and appease his longing, and that was love—to be loved, to be encompassed about by love. With every fibre of his being he yearned to become fully and completely a man, giving and receiving impressions and sensations with equal ardour, but a man, above all, that is to say a perfect artist, yet not a god. And so he yearned for woman; and so he came down from the solitary, sun-smitten heights, when there fell upon his ear, from the crowded haunts of humanity, the cry of that tortured heart" (Wagner).

Already we seem to hear, passing along beneath the boughs of the larches, the footfall of Zarathustra. But it is a gentler, fair-skinned Zarathustra. Not he of Portofino and Rapallo, who, borrowing the wisdom of the East, was to say, "To create is to surpass oneself," but a Nordic Zarathustra, setting foot on the shores of the Scheldt, for whom creation means to love, to live, to give oneself. Alas! an impossible gift, an impossible exchange, for Elsa is essentially the antithesis of Lohengrin, the other half of his nature, the feminine part of him. She is that unconscious self in whom Lohengrin is drawn to seek his release, "and so rooted in her jealousy that she rushes freely to her death," that amiable lovely death in which, yet once again, Wagner places the crowning ecstasy of love. "It was written," he said, "that I should slay her in order to follow the traces of the true feminine which shall bring salvation to the world and to me, by annihilating the egoism of man, how pure soever it may be. Elsa, woman, the ultimate expression of fatality, has made me a whole-hearted revolutionary. She was the spirit of the masses from whom, as an artist, I looked for my redemption."

So we behold Wagner once more a prey to two opposing currents in which his soul is struggling and of which he took cognizance on the very day of his marriage—the aspiration towards love, towards the sun, and the whirlpool which, "in an inexplicable restlessness," draws him towards all that is obscure and enigmatic in his destiny. Even his compositions now always bring him face to face with this twofold yearning, on the further side of which he sees only death. The determination to seek and to find, at last, the woman who shall "understand" him; the blind longing for that which shall allay the clamour of the senses, an artistic revolution that shall bring with it recognition of his works, a political revolution which shall abolish the antiquated officialdom on which he is dependent, a social and economical revolution which shall show him the way out of his financial embarrassments.

For his publisher was continually dunning him for money, and Mme. Schroeder-Devrient, beside herself with jealousy at the triumphs of Johanna Wagner, by whom she was being ousted more and more, had applied for a summons against her debtor. Amid all these growing preoccupations, he had none the less got to find time to stage Gluck's *Iphigénie en Aulide*, revise the score which had been grossly tampered with, get on with his studies in Greek literature and history, and lastly set to work to write the music for his *Lohengrin*. As for the management, Herr von Luttichau and the new theatrical director, Gutzkow, Wagner was now openly at war with them. All this did not tend to make his work more agreeable. To cut down expenses he decided to give up his quarters in the Ostrallee and go into smaller rooms in the old Marcolini palace in the suburb of Friedrichstadt, where he was compensated for the loss of his big rooms by the amenities of a large garden. Then, so that the publication of his works should proceed without interruption, he took out a policy on his life and raised a loan on it.

Well on in this troublous year of 1847 he turned his attention to *Lohengrin*, devoting himself to the third act. In May he wrote the first act, just when Mme. Schroeder-Devrient in *Iphigénie* was bidding farewell to the people of Dresden. Between the 18th of June and the 2nd of August he got through the second act, and on the 28th of the same month he finished his task by composing the prelude. In those few weeks Wagner had come to his full stature. True, sorrow had not yet wrought upon him with her chisel, as was later on to be his fate; still, as an artist, he had reached that decisive stage in his evolution when, freed from every otiose encumbrance, he stood up sharp and clear against the sky, a clean-cut, lonely figure standing erect and firm, henceforth solitary and inaccessible. "Freedom," he says in a letter which he wrote about this time to Roeckel— "freedom is being true to oneself. Whosoever is true and sincere towards himself, and in absolute accord with his own nature, that man is free." That was not, as some might think, a platitude. And if this talk about being true to self has since lost something of its bloom, let it be remembered that in 1847 it was far from being a commonplace. Above all, we should note that little amplification, "in absolute accord with his nature," which lends the phrase a highly Wagnerian significance. Wagner has now reached the threshold of his fame, but, in his anxiety to remain true to himself, readily runs the risk of disappointing and offending those who would see in him a "hero." Now, his concern was not with the heroism of pre-*Lohengrin* romanticism, the romanticism of Schiller and Rousseau; he was for being human, for avowing his failings, for making no secret of his egoism, aye, and if need were, for displaying his fighting quali- ties. Nevertheless, the justification for a freedom thus, and sometimes so cruelly, obtained must be the obligation of service. Service to what? To whom? That was what he had not yet made clear. But in thus turning to the masses, in thus setting his mind on a disinterested art, on the vague purity with which this lemanless lover and Godless believer invested his symbolical creations—in all this there thrilled the mighty ardour of the architect of the ideal. And that is another out-of-date phrase, yet I cannot find anything in our modern vocabulary to replace it save the word "ambition," which sees in things material what one hundred years ago men saw in things spiritual. But if, as Jean Richard Bloch has it in his *Destin du Siècle*, the mind of the twentieth century has begun to express itself in showing its contempt for things that were held so sacred in the century before—culture, intellect, sensibility, unselfishness; if it won't employ itself any more on things of the mind, but is out to destroy and rebuild in the material sphere, then the word "ideal," which, at the dawn of 1848, seemed so richly fraught with practical and soul-kindling realities, now stands drained of its life blood and is nothing more or less than one of those meaningless and obsolete signs that encumber the glossary of nations like so many dead bodies floating down the stream of time. Nevertheless, for Wagner, in 1847, it meant "following the gleam," education of the people, intellectual freedom, reforms, things that seemed urgent for the advent of the New Germany, and indispensable to Richard Wagner individually, if he was to have a right to his own thoughts and beliefs and to bring his future works into the world. And this is how it came to pass that he drew up a plan for the reorganization of the Chapel Royal to which he suggested a concert-room should be added. He also put forward a proposal for revising the *répertoire* and for a more equitable distribution of the subsidies granted to the orchestral staff. His papers were returned to him accompanied by a polite but slightly ironic note. Herr Kapellmeister had only to concern himself with his proper functions and to do what his colleagues in the past had always done and always would do until the end of time—keep things going as they were, make as much out of it all as they could—or else resign. When he's head over ears in debt a man doesn't go prating of reforms. Charity begins at home. Thus Wagner's only friends were Roeckel; Uhlig; Dr. Pusinelli; and a few unknown younger folk, among whom was the little Herr von Bülow, who was sixteen; a certain Karl Ritter, a young man of eighteen who belonged to a well-to-do family that came from Courland and had settled down in Dresden; a twenty-year-old English girl named Jessie Taylor. All these came to see him, begged for autographs, bought his music, and enveloped him with an atmosphere of deference and admiration which, as affording him at last some earnest of the world's esteem, was a perfume peculiarly to his taste. It was not a case now of the transient inebriation born of a popular success, but the lively sympathy of those who would fain penetrate the disguise he displayed to the world and read the secret of his heart. "Women are the music of life," he said in a letter to Uhlig *à propos* of this same Jessie Taylor. They catch the melody of the soul. No matter what the body, or what the countenance, they can mould it to resemble the picture in their hearts And doubtless the eyes of these adoring young people, like windows opening on the limpid depths of the soul, came fraught with a richer and a deeper implication to Wagner with his love for all comely living things, than the frothy popularity of the theatre. Then, too, there was the stirring of something revolutionary within him, emancipation from a mouldering past, a sensation of physical renewal and regeneration, of the coming of a new world, an unknown world, in which, faint and far off, he heard the voice of Elsa calling. And lastly, on young Hans von Bülow's hat, and on his father's likewise, he saw for the first time the black, red, and gold cockade of the one-time German Empire, the badge of those who hailed the dawning of the new régime.

Such, then, were the things that "bragged in the womb of time." Not here, in sleepy old Dresden, nor yet in Berlin where things went awry as usual. King Friedrich Wilhelm IV ordained that *Rienzi* should be played before him, but he never gave an audience to its author, despite his tireless efforts to secure one. For Wagner still had a great idea of monarchs, their culture, their authority, and so on. However, he saw now that they were not quite so wonderful as he thought, and that their half-baked enthusiasms soon wilted in the face of obstacles, and that one had to be content with interviewing some courtly but rather ironical old general or other whose mission it was to provide for His Majesty's minor diversions. There must be nothing out of the way. No new departures. Tieck, that grand old poet, told him on the quiet that the King of Prussia put Gluck's *Iphigénie* and Donizetti's *Lucretia Borgia* both on the same level. So, then, *Rienzi* would only be one platitude the more in the *répertoire*, and Richard himself lost interest in a performance which he knew in advance was going to be a fiasco. Had it not been for Alwina Fromann—a female admirer—and Professor Werder (the gentleman who paid him that midnight visit after the performance of *The Flying Dutchman*, and to whom he now dedicates his *Lohengrin*), his only recollection of these weeks in Berlin would have been of rain and unmitigated boredom. It was a case of professional disillusionment combined with political, for the government of Prussia, its leaders and people, showed just as much weakness—so the well-informed declared—as the other Germanic states. It was not Friedrich Wilhelm, in whom Wagner had centred all his hopes, any more than the King of Saxony, who was to be the saviour of Germany when the troubles, now everywhere brewing, at length came to a head.

The year 1847 came to an end with the sudden passing of Mendelssohn, and 1848 began with the death of Mme. Geyer. The aged and charming Johanna passed peacefully away at Leipzig on the 8th of January with all the Brockhaus family around her. At the funeral, Richard ran across Laube, who talked politics and spoke of the general condition of unrest in Europe. As he stood beside the grave into which the fragile body of his mother, the head of the family, had just been lowered, Richard felt more lonely than ever. He had now reached the halfway house in his career. Neither fame nor fortune had ever given him more than an illusory promise of favours to come. Love? His day for love was surely over. "The profoundest anxiety, the profoundest disgust." That was his balance-sheet, moral and material, just before the storm broke. Death, why shouldn't it take him, too? But at any rate he must have something to die for. You don't die of sickness of heart, or of mere indifference. Nevertheless, the heavens all round were charged with electricity. Turning his gaze about the horizon, Wagner could only see these friends of tender—too tender—years; or Roeckel, already very deeply involved with these political associations—and so a little less thick with him; or a whole crowd of colleagues and hostile chiefs. And then, in the background, a handsome, smiling visage seemed the only one to look on him with surprise and curiosity; nay, better still, with brotherly understanding; and that was the face of the pianist and composer, Franz Liszt. They had come across each other two or three times. Paris was the first occasion, but nothing further had come of that. It was when Richard's fortunes were at their lowest ebb, and Richard remembered that he had not been quite just. The next time was in Berlin when he was on a flying visit to the theatre people there in connection with his *Flying Dutchman*. Wagner was chatting with Mme. Schroeder-Devrient, in her room at the hotel, when Liszt came in. It would not have been surprising if there had been a little stiffness, seeing they must have both recalled the misunderstanding that led Wagner to write his somewhat acid comments on Liszt's concerts, but Liszt was so cordial, so disarming, that Richard was won completely over and quite forgave him his glory. The charm worked. Kindliness, good-humour, modesty, and something almost like simplicity, and then, over it all, that lofty distinction of soul which betrayed itself in gesture, smile, and expression and invested its owner with a kind of angelic grace. It was like meeting with a god.

Turning his gaze inward, there was nothing Wagner could see now save the knightly Lohengrin and the radiant pianist who had recently installed himself at Weimar. People said that he was living there with the woman of his heart, devoted to his work; and we have seen that he did everything in his power to help the composer of *Tannhäuser*. He had recently read the score and been profoundly moved. The imaginary hero whose brilliant and pathetic story Wagner was narrating, and that legendary musician, of whom he knew nothing save that Tannhäuser had overwhelmed his mighty spirit—such were the two beings with whom he was holding imaginary converse when the month of February, 1848, dawned upon the calendar.

Chapter VII

THE REVOLUTION IN DRESDEN

"THE revolution of 1848, like that of 1830, began in Paris, where people loved ideas almost as much as love, and a good deal more than they loved money or liberty. The February riots, which led to the foundation of the democratic republican state, were the natural consequence of the dual revelation of the eighteenth century which gave the educated classes freedom to think, and the working classes freedom to act, for themselves. This republican constitution was the logical outcome of that philosophical, critical, rational, liberal, or revolutionary government, whichever you may please to call it, which, originating in the upper strata of society, had undermined one by one all the beliefs on which, in the feudal, Catholic, and monarchical state, the divine right of the sovereign reposes. It may also be considered as the completest manifestation hitherto recorded of that instinctive movement which, obscurely affecting the masses, has been struggling ever since 1791 . . . to replace divine right by human right—in a word, to lay the foundations of democracy."

It was a woman of forty who penned those words and constituted herself the impromptu and eager historian of the stirring events which marched to their climax beneath her windows. She was still beautiful, but her pride and her affections had been grievously wounded by a love-affair doomed from the outset to come to naught. And now she was taking her revenge, not only on society, which had cast her off, but on the man who had so grievously underestimated the significance of her revolt. She was called the Comtesse Marie d'Agoult, and the name of her lover, who, after an intimate association of seven years, had severed relations with her, was Franz Liszt. She had formerly been a close companion of George Sand, and was still the friend and inspiration of the politicians who had recently launched the socialist movement, in which the complicated, inconsistent, and peace-at-any-price reign of Louis Philippe was to come to an end. She was unquestionably a woman of remarkable sagacity and very capable of taking an intelligent bird's-eye view of the grand political maelstrom in which Ledru-Rollin, Louis Blanc, Arago, and Lamartine were playing their several parts. Reading the introductory pages of her narrative, in which she declares her intention of tracing the origin and causes of the movement, one cannot but be struck with the soundness of her views and their remarkable application to events of which, eighty years later, we are ourselves the witnesses. "But with the return of peaceful conditions on the continent," she writes, "the aspect of things underwent a striking change. With the establishment of public security, and the growth of the population, industrial life received a vigorous impetus. Vast workshops, enormous factories, were opened in which, with the aid of newly discovered processes and marvellous machinery, the products of industry were multiplied with a speed and economy and a perfection hitherto undreamt of. The rapid fortunes amassed by the manufacturers were an astounding and dazzling phenomenon that gave rise to a spirit of wild and reckless competition. The handsome salaries paid to the workmen drew large masses of the population away from the country and into the great manufacturing districts, and over-production was thus continuously and progressively encouraged. In no long time the rate of consumption was outstripped, and the disproportion between supply and demand became very pronounced. The markets were glutted and equilibrium was destroyed." As for the old king, Louis Philippe, "obstinately bent on maintaining peace merely to bolster up a prosperity and a tranquillity that were alike fallacious; growing the more in love with his own bourgeois ideas as he saw them gaining ground around him . . . deaf to all advice, shutting himself up in an exaggerated estimation of his kingly authority, of which old age had made him jealously tenacious, this unhappy ruler ended by becoming a complete stranger alike to his country and to his generation."

Lamartine somewhere refers to the upheaval as "the revolution of scorn." It cost the Orléans family their throne; and for the second time the old régime went under in a little Paris riot. A poet took charge of the foreign affairs of France, a workingman sat in the seat of authority at the deliberations of the Ministerial Council; and, pending the arrival of some authoritative system of law and order, the Second Republic filled Europe for several months on end with a frenzy of enthusiasm that spread from Paris to Milan, Berlin, Vienna, Munich, and Dresden. Again, as in 1830, the emancipation of Poland became a sort of mystic password. But "the spirit of these European revolutions was, above everything, national. They foreshadowed the formation of those great national unifications, the Italian and the German, which were only brought about by the dismemberment of Europe as it then existed, and at the cost of great wars.

For a long time past Dresden had been filled with rumours. Not without considerable repugnance the king had found himself obliged to exchange his old advisers for a Cabinet of liberals. A parliament was elected. Patriotic unions sprang up more or less everywhere, and proclamations addressed to the people were daily and conspicuous features in the newspapers. All these wonderful occurrences, however, took place under the royal ægis and in the glare of nocturnal illuminations. The old order was departing quietly in the person of Metternich, who was compelled to leave Vienna, and King Ludwig I of Bavaria abdicated in favour of his son all the more quietly because he regarded the advantages of the throne as of much less account than the favours of Lola Montez, the dancer. Morally as well as physically the world underwent a quick change. "The mad year," people called it, when every head was more or less turned. That being so, how should artists' heads have escaped the general intoxication, seeing that this was the very turn of Fortune's wheel for which they had been waiting so long?

Roeckel plunged into the thick of the fray, Wagner after him, his pockets stuffed with poems calling princes and people to arms against the Russian tyranny. Roeckel had joined the most advanced of the political clubs, the Patriots' Union, and Wagner was allowed to attend its sittings. The moment seemed to him propitious for requesting an audience of Oberlaender, the new radical Minister, in order to give him an account of his proposed reforms, nor was he conscious of any diminution in his zeal when his friend, who had published an article on popular militias, was quietly "sacked" by the Theatre Royal. That ought to have been a warning to him; but so little was Wagner impressed by it, that he too got himself elected to the Patriots' Union. There he immediately bobbed up with suggestions for the Frankfort Assembly:

(1) The dissolution of the old *Bundestag* and the election of a new parliament.
(2) The introduction of the Swiss militia system.
(3) An alliance, offensive and defensive, with France.

Not content with this, he sent a poem entitled "Hail, People of Vienna!" to the *Austrian Gazette* which printed it over his signature. A dangerous game, but he didn't care. He wrote a leader in the *Dresden Gazette*, entitled "Republic or Monarchy," in which he lauded the idea, so dear to many liberals, of a republican monarchy. Knowing what a fine speaker he was, Roeckel got him to mount the platform at the club, and before an audience of three thousand people Wagner lectured *ex tempore* with tremendous effect, and no wonder, for his oration was nothing more or less than an onslaught of exceptional violence on the king, the aristocrats, and parliament, and an appeal for universal suffrage, so that the people alone might have power to make laws. "The poorer a man is the more he is entitled to frame the laws which are to protect him." But it was also a stern denunciation of communism by whose principles every superior brain, every exceptional talent, would be condemned to sterility. Success is heady wine. In a day, Wagner had leapt into prominence, and was more, much more conspicuous, than at his conductor's desk. The platform was new—and national—giving free scope to his ambition and a chance to get to the top of the tree. A good hit back for the cold-shouldering of *The Flying Dutchman* and *Tannhäuser* and no mistake! But if Wagner, the pamphleteer, had got a new public, Wagner, the composer, looked very much like losing his old one.

So great, in fact, was the sensation caused by his speech, that the management considered it prudent to withdraw even *Rienzi* from the bills, for fear of public disturbances. Not only this, but he had to put up with a torrent of malevolent comments in the press, hostility on the part of court officials and employees, and a challenge to a duel from the officer commanding the Communal Guard. Articles appeared in which he was held up to ridicule as "The Little Tin King" and "Doctor Richard Faust."

> We should not have heard much of the Ninth but for him,
> And the fame of the Wettins would swiftly grow dim;
> There is never his equal on earth to be seen,
> He's as noble and brave as the great Lamartine.
> So we'll harness ourselves to his glorious car,
> And bow down to show him how grateful we are.

Wagner defended himself in a letter to the king and Herr von Luttichau thought it expedient to send his fiery conductor away for a change of air; so the latter decided he would go to Vienna. A few days, however, before he left, being bothered to death by his ever-increasing pecuniary difficulties, he suddenly made up his mind to appeal for succour to that lucky Fairy Prince who, for some months past, seemed silently to have been keeping on the alert for any cry of distress that might reach him from his friend-to-be. And so it came to pass that there reached Liszt's hands the first of those famous letters—it was dated 23rd of June, 1848—in which the composer of *Tannhäuser* offered to sell him his operas, and ended by surrendering his soul. "Things are going ill with me" (he wrote), "and I often say to myself that you might come to my aid. I arranged, myself, to have my three operas published . . . the sum involved is five thousand thalers. . . . Wouldn't it be very interesting if you were to become the proprietor-publisher of my operas? Do you know what it would mean? It would mean that I should become a *man*, an artist who, as long as he lived, would never ask for another farthing. Dear Liszt, with that money you would redeem me from bondage. Do you think that, as a slave, I'm worth the price?"

While waiting for the opportunity for a personal meeting with the man who thus dwelt continuously in his thoughts, Wagner betook himself to Vienna, which was then in the midst of a revolution, one might almost say in the heyday of revolution, for it was a joyous revolution, literary, theatrical, and sartorial. Eight thousand students belonging to the Academic Legion marched past in plumed hats, "Fine men, all of them!" And what elegance, what wealth, what pretty women! At the An Der Wien (the theatre where Strauss had led his squadron of fiddlers to the charge seventeen years before) they were playing *Scenes from the Life of Napoleon*. The poet Grillparzer paraded about in official uniform. The whole city, sparkling and effervescent, went lounging about arm in arm—bandsmen, officers, workpeople, generals. Wagner was the only one at a loose end. What was he to do? He thought of a merger of five theatres, drafted the articles of association for a proposed opera syndicate; he visualized himself as an impresario. But in a few days all that had gone up in smoke. These Viennese are desperately fond of dancing and speechifying, but the higher music—oh no! They received him warmly, but he went back to Dresden, having done nothing except get through his money.

Well, then, clearly there was nothing for it but to be off to Weimar. So now behold Wagner in the Athens of Thuringia, and at the Hotel Erbprinz, where Liszt had taken up his abode. Together they strolled through the Grand Ducal Park—the pleasance that had once shadowed the love of Goethe and Frau von Stein—in the direction of the Altenburg, a lordly mansion in which the lady who had succeeded Marie d'Agoult in Liszt's affections had taken up her residence. The famous pianist was now thirty-seven, two years older than Wagner. Recently installed in Weimar, under the protection of the Dowager Grand Duchess, the Tsar's sister, he had made himself responsible for the music of the royal abode. But it was first and foremost his own education and culture that absorbed his interests. After twenty years of roaming about from place to place, the sort of rest for which he craved was studious repose. His inward life, with an energetic and devoted woman to lend it poise and direction, gave promise of yielding better, more lasting fruit than the plaudits of the throng. Wagner's thus coming into his life at the very moment he was about to begin his labours as a composer seemed to Liszt like an act of Providence, a direct interposition of Fate. For Wagner's imagination had of late been strangely haunted by the countenance of Liszt. The curious feeling of something about to happen, the feeling of strangeness which the bland amenities of his life at Weimar had imparted to his roving spirit by thus bringing it to rest, had in a measure provoked in him a kind of curiosity as to what new experience, what new mission, the Fates were about to call on him to fulfill. Well, the victor had to bow his head; had to acknowledge in this out-at-elbows little Saxon a European cast in a mightier mould than he. It was written that the fame, the wealth, the connections, the social gifts of the world's incomparable virtuoso should be enlisted in the service of this genius of the rank and file, whose originality and personality had given scandal in the world. Be it added, to the credit of the rather bohemian-looking princess who for a year past had been playing an intimate part in Liszt's life, that she promptly did her utmost to foster this budding friendship. In this first and fleeting interview between Liszt and Wagner bonds of friendship were forged which, in spite of unforeseeable moral complications which subsequently ensued, endured until death. In a word, Apollo and Marsyas had met at last. Relying on his power, the god of light had given ear to this uncouth flute-player from a world of pain and misery. And if the latter was to pay for his self-confidence by a protracted martyrdom, it was at all events his privilege to amaze and to bewilder the eternal youth who turned his startled and unpractised gaze on the spectacle of human woe. But what I consider most striking of all in this preliminary skirmish is the almost inexplicable attraction between two people so totally dissimilar, between two temperaments so pathetically divergent. The day was to come when it would be made clear to them that had they not become friends at first sight they would have been condemned to mutual hatred. No doubt that was what very nearly happened. But that day they instinctively forbore to question one another. The game they played was the very opposite to Lohengrin's and Elsa's. There was neither "how" nor "why" in their discourse. Concerning themselves they were silent, leaving it to music to weave the bonds between them, bonds destined to unite them by that spiritual essence which ever defies definition; not a matter of sentiment only, or the conjunction of two parallel activities, but rather a kind of physical and spiritual hypnosis. From the time of their first meeting, the spell was woven, and Liszt and Wagner belonged to one another. It was something certainly akin to love. And music also played its part. All this throws a further light on that aphorism of Wagner's which we have already had occasion to quote.

At Dresden, the preliminaries of the revolution were becoming more and more noticeable. Roeckel was its active agent on the proletarian side. In consequence of an appeal which he had addressed to the soldiers of the Saxon army, he had been arrested and put into prison, but had been subsequently released on bail. He started a weekly paper for popular consumption, and, taking a leaf out of Proudhon's book, proceeded to indoctrinate the masses with the socialist gospel. His main idea was to overthrow capitalism, to enthrone labour in its place, and to alter the laws of marriage, thus inaugurating a new system of morality. The Saxon electorate voted radical to a man. The royal civil-list was subjected to a strict revision, and Wagner, like many another, falsified his entry, for he believed an upheaval was at hand and that an artistic revival would immediately follow in its train. He had been through political crises before, and now, as then, he became poetically prolific and turned out, in lightning succession, a preliminary sketch for a drama on Frederick Barbarossa, another which he called *The Death of Siegfried*, and a dissertation on the Nibelungen in which he welded together in one whole the legend of the Nibelungen and the old tale of the Ghibellines. But all these were merely notes, a series of jottings to be used later on in his musical compositions. Besides, he had already produced more than he had been able to put to account, for, as yet, his *Lohengrin* had never been played in Dresden, despite the handsome receipts that his previous operas still continued to bring in. True, the scenery had been ordered, but somehow von Luttichau seemed anything but anxious to put it on. He kept on procrastinating till one day he blurted out that he was not going to do it at all. This was so staggering a blow to Wagner that he nearly sent in his resignation, and he most certainly would have done so had it not been for Minna. The fact of the matter was that the attitude of von

Luttichau reflected with remarkable accuracy the feelings entertained at court, where the republican opinions of the Kapellmeister were held to be a matter of grave scandal. The queen would have it that he had not conducted *Norma* properly and that in *Robert le Diable* his time had been at fault. Richard grew more and more angry. He joined a syndicate consisting of members of the orchestra, spoke at seditious meetings, put forward suggestions for wholesale reforms, and at last had a terrific quarrel with von Luttichau. That, of course, meant the end of all things. The authorities, however, did not want to take action at the moment because of the prevailing unrest, but they left Wagner in no doubt as to what they thought of him by handing over the direction of concerts to Reissiger and ostentatiously decorating him with the Order of Merit.

Amid all these worries and anxieties only one thing came to cheer him, and that was the news that Liszt was putting *Tannhäuser* into rehearsal at Weimar. It was like a star suddenly and swiftly gliding into his artistic life. It gave him courage to endure. And then *The Death of Siegfried* furnished him with a refuge against all these professional pin-pricks. He turned to his work as to a sanctuary whither he might escape from his mortifications and his political anxieties, for the fact was that a strong reactionary movement looked like putting the extinguisher on the democratic buds of last spring. As he had just grounded his faith in a pure, ardent, and guileless conception of humanity, as typified by the youthful Siegfried (representing man in his plentitude, true man) he now turned willy-nilly to seek a way out of all this mortal coil, to seek redemption through death, through self-slaughter. The old flux and reflux of his instincts was showing itself again. On the one hand there was the yearning for a creed, for life; on the other, the refusal of the modern world to make the great adventure of faith rendered self-inflicted death a perfectly sane and natural act, an indispensable means of escape. And for his symbol of humanity he took Jesus, "the expression of that instinct which impels the individual to make war on a loveless collectivity." Such was the theme of another sketch which now came into being side by side with *Siegfried* and which he entitled *Jesus of Nazareth*. "I deliver you from sin by declaring to you the eternal law of the spirit, which is love. So long as your deeds are inspired by love, you will not sin." Such was the gospel of the Wagnerian Christ. Marriage, therefore, is only to be held sacred so far forth as it is a function of love. Where love is not, nor ever has been, or where it has been lost, natural law—and with it the law of God

—ordains that the woman should seek among men for him to whom she is capable of bringing happiness. It is human laws that have brought scandal and sin into the world. Let man live, therefore, according to the law of love, and the terror of death —which is engendered by civilization—will cease to torment the human mind. When we consider the spectacle of falsehood and hypocrisy presented by modern society, death can only be regarded as a benefit and a deliverance, and the artist, in his loneliness and in his powerlessness to cure these ills, cannot but long for his own annihilation.

Thus we see Wagner pursuing that "accord with self," of which we have already made mention, to its most paradoxical yet most logical consequences. For he freely gives expression to both ideas in his work. And, if he did not bring the plans which were fermenting in his brain during the winter of 1848-49 to a fruitful conclusion, it was because the revolution itself interposed to resolve the problem and to give him the certitude for which he sought.

One night, at Roeckel's, he fell in with a new acquaintance, a bearded young man with remarkably large eyes, which, however, were so weak that he was obliged to shade them with his hand from the glare of the lamp. The grim violence of this young man's utterances at once aroused his eager interest. He went by the name of Dr. Schwartz; but everyone knew this was merely a *nom de guerre* that concealed the identity of the most notorious firebrand in political Europe. He was, in fact, none other than Michael Bakounin, the Russian incendiary. He was wanted by the Austrian Government for complicity in the Prague riots, and went about stealthily from one hiding-place to another, awaiting the general conflagration from whose ashes the Republican Federation of Europe was to arise. He was a man of colossal stature, an absolute cosmopolitan and a remarkable linguist. Lounging at full length on Roeckel's sofa, he philosophized at large in the most approved Socratic manner and dumbfounded the company with the revolutionary ferocity of his ideas. "A doctrinaire," said Wagner to himself. Nevertheless, Bakounin held the intellectuals in contempt. What he was out for was action, deeds, not words. Brought up on Rousseau, this ex-officer and aristocrat was so much in love with his fellow-men that he wanted to devour them. "A barbarian reacting to civilization," said Wagner again, "an apostle of red-hot ruin." Bakounin's idea was that, if only the Russian moujiks could be persuaded that setting fire to the castles of the nobility was "a just work and pleasing in the sight of God," all the ills of the modern world would at once be cured. The wholesale destruction of civilization was a theme that made him wild with enthusiasm. Pulling down was far more in his line than building up. His greatest foe, however, was not the Tsar, not the Tyrant, but the smug and pampered philistine of whom, he held, the most perfect type and exemplar was exhibited in the Protestant pastor. Wagner gave him a long account of his *Jesus of Nazareth*, for, like the typical Russian, Bakounin was devoted to music. He declined to read the work, but urged Wagner to portray Christ "as a weakling." With regard to the musical part, he held that the proper thing would be to produce all the variations possible on the single theme, "Kill, fire, burn, slay!" However, another evening later on, Wagner played him his *Flying Dutchman*. Bakounin listened with rapt attention and then exclaimed, "That is a marvellously fine thing!" Then speaking of Beethoven, he said, "Yes, everything will be destroyed; one thing alone will live for ever: the *Ninth Symphony*." So it is not surprising that Wagner's idea of him veered round "from involuntary alarm to irresistible attraction."

Such was the conspirator whose presence in Dresden was fated to put a match to the powder that was only too ready to explode. The dissolution of the Landtag by the reactionary Beust Government gave the revolutionaries their cue. The new Cabinet that took over the reins of government interpreted the signs of the times so well that they mobilized two Prussian divisions on the Saxon border. However, clubs and deputations representing every shade of opinion implored the Government to honour the royal promises and to declare for an empire. They curtly refused. On the 3rd of May Wagner went to a meeting of the Patriots' Union in place of Roeckel, who had had to make himself scarce. The debate was carried on amid general uproar. On his way back from the hall, Wagner had got as far as the post-office when suddenly the tocsin rang out from the tower of St. Anne's. "It was a bright, sunny afternoon; I immediately noticed the same phenomenon which Goethe describes in attempting to give an account of his feelings when he heard the guns at Valmy. The whole square seemed flooded with a yellow brownish light, something like Magdeburg during the eclipse. I was conscious of a great feeling of exhilaration and of a disposition to laugh at what until then I had looked on as a terrible thing." On reaching the Altmarkt he encountered Mme. Schoeder-Devrient, who had just arrived from Berlin, very much upset at the rioting she had seen there and fearful lest she should find the same sort of thing going on in her beloved

Dresden. The Town Council issued a proclamation protesting against the bringing in of foreign troops (meaning the Prussians), and then the trouble began. Some of the popular party attempted to seize the Arsenal, and the troops treated them to a whiff of grapeshot. That was the first bloodshed. A few citizens were killed and more wounded. Wagner saw a municipal guard go by all covered with blood. Great emotion! On every side people began shouting, "To the barricades!" Wagner was borne along by the crowd; he noticed a hunchback rubbing his hands with glee, and the sight made him think of Vansen, the scrivener in Goethe's *Egmont*. The play, with Wagner, was still, as always, "the thing." "Well, it had been a long time coming, this revolution; but here it was at last!"

The insurgents made the Town Hall their headquarters. The king having withdrawn to the fortress of Koenigstein, the rebels sent a deputation to the government. But the government had decamped with the court. So, then, it was civil war. Wagner tore around to the man who printed Roeckel's paper and got him to run off some posters with the words, "Are you with us against the foreign troops?" which were stuck up at the street corners and plastered about the barricades in the hope of influencing the Saxon troops. Wagner himself gave some out to the soldiers on duty at the Opera, heedless of the fact that he might have been shot then and there. All of a sudden, Bakounin, wearing a frock-coat, bursting with rage, a cigar between his teeth, came clambering over the heaps of paving-stones and wooden planks. He swore it was only a comic-opera revolution, mere child's-play, suburban gentlemen, genteel soldiers who said, "Here, sir!" when the captain called their names. There was no blood, no "go" about the thing. Meantime, a five-hours' armistice was agreed upon. A provisional government was formed with Heubner, the Freiberg baillie, a clear-headed, moderate man, at its head. "Taking it all round, the time passed very pleasantly," said Wagner. "Those spring evenings, how delightful they were, with the fair ladies and their cavaliers strolling about the barricaded streets. It gave me, too, a sort of beatific sensation." He went home, his mind running on a new drama, with Achilles for its subject.

On the 4th of May the troops took the offensive and opened fire from the royal palace. Some of the barricades were demolished. However, it was not until the 5th that the Prussians made their entry into the town. The firing grew more intense, and to get a better view of it all Wagner decided to mount the tower of the Church of the Cross. The worst of it was that to get there he had to cross the square which was swept by the fire of the soldiers posted outside the king's palace. Wagner for some extraordinary reason, could not resist the temptation to walk across very slowly. It may have been that just then the idea of death—the ever-present but unseen companion of his art—never came into his mind. As it turned out, "the leaden humming bees" flew clear of the man that marched along so certain of his fate. Up he went to the top of the tower, which was singled out as a special target by the Prussians. A number of other people had also come up to see what they could see, and Richard got involved in a philosophical discussion with a schoolmaster. Blue sky overhead; below, the city running red with human blood; in the distance the Elbe winding away amid fields and orchards gay with blossom; and, just below, the tocsin ringing, ringing to celebrate this solemn springtide feast. It was like being back again in the brave old days of 1813, and, when one of his companions remonstrated with him for risking his life merely to see the show, what more natural than that Wagner should reply, like the Emperor, "The bullet that is going to kill me is not yet made." A tremendously exciting day! As for the night, the artist that he was wouldn't have missed it for worlds—playing the soldier up there, mounting guard, and listening to the fairy tales the stars are ever weaving.

He awoke at early dawn to the song of the nightingale upborne from a garden far below. It was Sunday. How deliciously peaceful it all seemed. A slight mist was abroad through which the strains of the *Marseillaise* came stealing, faint, far-off, yet very clear. The watchers on the tower then descried a long column of armed men winding along the neighbouring road. They were miners from Erzgebirge hastening in to support the republicans of the capital. They had four small guns with them and soon drew up in the space facing the Town Hall. About eleven o'clock, flames began to burst from the old Opera House, where, no very long time since, Wagner had conducted Beethoven's *Ninth Symphony*. In a few seconds the building was a mass of flame. The sight must have rejoiced the heart of Bakounin over yonder in the rebels' headquarters. The tower was then taken over by armed defenders, and Wagner decided to go back home to Friedrichstadt.

He found his rooms full of excited women—Minna, his pretty nieces, Clara and Ottilie Brockhaus, and Frau Roeckel, who was in a state of panic because she had just heard that her husband was back again in Dresden. But the girls and their uncle were so worked up by the noise of the firing, the whole party were

so excited and the day so full of surprises, that this Sunday
went by with all the swing of a festive family gathering. It was
quite true that Roeckel had returned. The very next day he was
seen marching at the head of several hundred students. Bakounin wanted to organize a rising in the rural districts. Wagner
backed up the idea as tending to broaden the basis of the movement, and resolved to leave Dresden with Minna, to establish
his headquarters at Chemnitz at his sister's, Clara Wolfram's.
The whole thing was decided upon and arranged in the space of
a few moments. Richard went off first with Peps, the dog (it
was always a sign that he had come to a turning-point in his
career when he started off on a journey with his dog). "How
gloriously shone the sun that springtide morning when, with
the feeling that it was to be for the last time, I took the path
which I had so often trodden alone. Larks were carolling high
overhead, and others were chirruping in the furrows," while
the guns were thundering in the streets on which Wagner had
turned his back. But no sooner did he arrive at Chemnitz than
he changed his mind and went back again to Dresden. The insurrection had entered upon its last phase, the most tragic. They
were fighting now from house to house, from barricade to barricade, amid uproar and shouting, the smoke of torches, and the
lurid glare of burning buildings. In the Town Hall elderly
bailiff's men in uniform were serving out bread and butter to
the combatants. Heubner, utterly worn out, was still putting up
a fight that every moment was becoming more hopeless. Bakounin, chewing his extinct cigar, proposed that they should blow
up the building if the Germans attempted to storm it. Wagner
started off again for Freiberg to get the reinforcements together
and hand them Heubner's instructions. But while on his way
thither he heard that the rebels were in a very bad way, and
that the provisional government was withdrawing to Erzgebirge. And—yes, good heavens!—here they were coming along
in a smart landau, Heubner, Bakounin, Martin. Some members
of the National Guard in a state of complete exhaustion were
trying to hang on to the axles, to the despair of the driver.
Bakounin was delighted. "The tears of the Philistines," he said,
"are the nectar of the gods." They held a council of war. Heubner and his Russian friend—he hadn't yet quite got hold of his
name, and called him Boukanin—decided to carry on the fight
alone, although Herr Kapellmeister was letting himself go with
a vengeance and shouting nothing but, "War, war, war to the
knife I say!" Amid the general confusion they drew up a proclamation. The disbanded troops came pouring back in the direc-

tion of Freiberg, and Wagner decided to avoid the mob. The Chemnitz diligence chancing to come along just then, he boarded it in order to get to the Wolframs', but, arriving late, he went to the first inn that offered, slept a few hours, and was up again before daybreak next morning. And just as well, too, for Heubner, Bakounin, and Martin had already been arrested, the authorities of Chemnitz having remained loyal to the monarchy. When his brother-in-law told him the news, he was struck dumb with amazement. He saw, as in a flash, the long sequence of perils from which he had escaped, beginning with the time, now so long ago, when the "giant" Degelow was killed the very day before the duel that would probably have been the finish of the *studiosus musicæ*. Well, once again he would have to make himself scarce, and bless the miraculous power that preserved him from all these dangers, though he never knew that power save in a sort of dream.

Hidden from view in the Wolframs' carriage, he got to Weimar and saw Liszt and the Princess von Wittgenstein again. But, even with them, he hardly managed to wake up. It all still seemed like a dream. However, he read through the scenario of his *Jesus of Nazareth* to the devoted pair, and from the silent disapproval with which they listened to the recital he gauged the moral depths to which he had fallen. Nevertheless there was something to comfort him while he was there and that was a rehearsal of *Tannhäuser* under Liszt's conductorship. He was the first musician who had ever thoroughly understood it and brought out all his intentions. So the pleasure that he had experienced on his first visit to Weimar now expanded into full bloom. "Dear Liszt! . . . Marvellous man! . . . This journey has revived and stimulated my artistic instincts to an extraordinary degree. I am now entirely at peace with myself. Hardly a month ago I had not so much as given a thought to what I now realize is the gravest problem of my existence: My profound affection for Liszt makes me feel both inwardly and outwardly the power that is necessary to solve it. It will be our common achievement." He was no longer alone. And it is a new world that opens to a man, when he has rid himself of his loneliness.

Wagner went to see the ruins of Wartburg and meditated on this latest turn in his fortunes as he gazed upon a scene so intimately bound up with his history, a scene which he was only now beholding for the first time, just when he had to leave his country; for it was exile, sole refuge against himself, which now confronted him again. A warrant had been issued for the arrest of Richard Wagner, conductor of the Royal Orchestra,

COSIMA WAGNER

for having been actively concerned in the insurrection at Dresden. His house had been searched and Minna wrote that there was not a moment to be lost. So, from the remote horizons to which he turns his gaze will spring those longings for something afar, those yearnings which henceforth will gradually shape his spiritual home, that harmonious fabric into which he will gather all his passionate desires, all those shapes of love and death which have come to him as in a dream. But before he takes this new farewell he must needs see Minna. However far they had drifted apart in some respects, she still remained his fighting comrade, his companion in times of stress and difficulty. Of course she would upbraid him—he felt that—for mixing himself up in these political affairs, and so losing a position which had been so hard to win, so stubbornly defended, so useful and so comfortable. But if he had to go off again on his wanderings up and down the world, when would they see each other? Liszt having advanced her the necessary money, she hired a post-chaise and joined her husband at Magdala, an agricultural property in the open country, three hours' drive from Weimar. Frau Wagner arrived in the middle of the night. They roused the fugitive from his slumbers. "What?" he exclaimed. "My wife?" Husband and wife greeted each other rather coldly. "Well, you told me to come, and here I am. So be grateful and get on the road again. Me? Oh, I shall go back to Dresden again at once." Nevertheless, she stayed on for forty-eight hours to celebrate Richard's birthday. It was a melancholy business; the atmosphere did not improve. He felt, somehow, what she was thinking about him, felt the bitterness and silent scorn with which she regarded him, she who was for ever being robbed of her peace and quiet. Well, he'd got to make a move. Liszt's idea was that it would be a good thing for him to try his luck in Paris again, and to do so alone. As for Minna, God—and Liszt —would look after her. Possibly she would find a place to suit her at Weimar—a modest retreat for herself and Natalie, on some grand-ducal estate perhaps. As a precautionary measure, the couple separated, Minna going post to Jena, where she was joined by Richard, who had done the journey on foot. They discussed the situation at the house of one of Liszt's friends, and Wagner, armed with a passport of a Professor Widmann, went on his perilous way by the Bavarian coach, making for Switzerland. He arrived at Lindau on Lake Constance without mishap, called down blessings on the gendarmes who passed his papers without a word, and at last set foot on the steamboat with the Helvetian Cross waving in the breeze. In an instant all his troubles vanished. See, there was Rohrschach, the first village in the Swiss Confederation! What a glorious spring sky! He drove post across the pleasant Saint Gall country. Then came the Alps. Ah, what an unutterable sensation of relief! "Nothing can be compared," he cried, "with the feeling of elation which came over me when I realised that I was free. . . . No more need now for concealment or prevarication. I could stand up and tell the world that I, the artist, despised it from the bottom of my heart. For the first time in my life I felt I could stand up and freely face the world, sound in wind and limb, and light of heart, though I knew not where I should lay my head on the morrow, nor of what region I should breathe the air."

Thus he lowers his sword. He forges new bonds with life, he who awhile ago had been so deep "in love with easeful death." All his mouldering, sentimental past he flings from him like a discarded garment. And now, in the peaceful twilight that enfolds him, he renews once more the sacred pact, the pact by which he swears ever to be true to himself, ever to "follow the gleam."

PART THREE

Chapter I

ZURICH—ART AND REVOLUTION

THE question was where was Wagner going to settle down? Now that the poet-musician was free of his professional shackles, released from his oath to the king by the mere fact that a warrant was out against him; now, too, that he was perhaps released—by his wife's own act—from the dead weight that Minna and Natalie had been to him, where should he fix his airy tent? Zurich had its attractions; it was a friendly, cheerful place and Muller lived there, his old friend Muller whom he used to get on with so well at Wurzburg in days gone by. But Zurich hadn't got much of an orchestra or much of an opera. Besides, Liszt had been paving the way in Paris. He had written to Belloni, his former secretary, on Wagner's behalf, and had just given a magnificent, a dazzling account of *Tannhäuser* in the *Journal des Débats*. Wouldn't it be wise to take advantage of these favourable circumstances?

Wagner, therefore, left almost immediately for the modern Babylon, the city he hated, the city laden with the memories of all the sufferings he had there endured; but yet the city of his heart's desire, the ever unconquered city, "a hideous picture," yet one that laid the spell of undying fascination upon the heart. The cholera was abroad there when he arrived, as it had been in Vienna when he went there years ago. Everywhere you could hear the mournful beat of the drum as the troops of the National Guard bore the corpses through the streets. Everywhere you saw bank-messengers carrying bags or portfolios, as if the old plutocracy had got the better of the socialists who had throw them into such a panic, and were trying to regain the confidence of the public by a display of pomp and circumstance. The revolution was as dead as a door nail, the grave had closed on those grand ideals. Madame d'Agoult, bereft of her illusions, wrote thus resignedly to her friend Herwegh: "Humanity is, and always will be, stupid. Socrates will ever drink his hemlock, and Jesus be crucified, to the end of time. Men will always guillotine, hang, or bludgeon their brothers to death—a monotonous story that begins with Cain." Force of habit took Wagner to Schlesinger's music-shop, and there he fell in with Meyerbeer, who jumped to the conclusion that his *protégé* had come back to try his luck in France. Oh dear, no! "But what are you after, then? . . . Do you intend to write scores for the barricades?"

As Belloni was going to spend his holidays at La Ferté-sous-Jouarre, Wagner hired a room in the neighbourhood, at Reuil, in the house of a wine merchant. How were things going to turn out? He must wait and see. He spent his time reading, and writing letters. He wrote to Liszt, to his brother-in-law Avenarius (now back again in Leipzig), and to Minna. His first letter was to Liszt, and ran thus:

"My dear friend, it is to you I am bound to turn when I wish to unburden my heart. . . . Ah, if you could only realize what your friendship means to me. . . . Art here, such as it is, is fallen so low (Meyerbeer), it is so rotten, so decrepit, that it only wants a certain good man with a scythe to finish it off. I don't want to enter upon any sort of philosophical theorizing, but I feel that I must tell you this straight out: on the basis of the counter-revolution art has no longer any chance at all; on the basis of the revolution, the future of art is equally problematic . . . in a word, I'm going tomorrow to write an article for a responsible political paper on the Theatre of the Future, and it will have some stuff in it. This dreadful Paris weighs on me and depresses me. I'm going through exactly what I went through ten years ago. Many and many a time in those days I felt like murder as I contemplated the long foodless days stretching out before me."

To Edmond Avenarius he wrote: "It will soon be four weeks now since I said good-bye to my wife, and I have not had a word from her, from that day to this. I am feeling dreadfully worried. What is happening? Why doesn't she write?"

She did write at last, but it was a long letter full of complaints. Hadn't she always borne with his youthful follies? Hadn't she always stood by him and backed him up when things were bad? And now, when luck had put them into something good at last, he had wantonly sacrificed all the dignity and material security the position offered, by going tearing after some fantastic and utterly worthless political will-o'-the-wisp. No; she had done her level best, but no one in the world would say that she was in duty bound to rush about after him wherever he might take it into his head to go.

Richard was obliged to give her the best of the argument. And, in the long run, it was a good thing he did so. Since Minna began it, since Minna took the initiative by giving him to understand that she was sick of a marriage built on sand—well then, let the wind whirl her away into space. "In my extreme poverty, this complete and definite abandonment brought with it a sense of relief." Liszt said that a spell of rest and change was absolutely indispensable. "No more politics for a bit," he urged; "no more of this socialist claptrap, and no more personal 'hates.' . . . I am instructing Belloni to send you three hundred francs for travelling expenses. I hope Frau Wagner will soon be able to join you again, and before the autumn I will send you on a little more, which will suffice to keep you above water. Your admirable *Lohengrin* score has interested me immensely. All the same I have my doubts as to how the super-ideal tone you've kept up all through will go down with the public. No doubt you think me rather pettifogging, don't you, *cher ami*?" Ah, what a man it was! Well, the needful had come, and so "good-bye Paris and hurrah for Zurich!" Wagner went straight back there, fixed up some lodgings at Muller's, and made acquaintance with some of the distinguished people in the place, among them Jacob Sulzer, the young Chancellor of the canton, who had just taken a brilliant degree in philology. . . . He was therefore the very man to appreciate *Siegfried*. They took to each other tremendously, and musical evenings were got up at the old Chancellerie or at the Café Littéraire on the Weinplatz. Baumgartner, Sulzer, Spyri the barrister, and others, all cultured and broad-minded young people, together with some of the refugees from Saxony or Baden, made up an incomparably charming sodality. To Wagner it seemed like a new life. So exhilarating was his sense of freedom, that all his old faculties for paradoxical expression came back to him, and epigrams simply flowed from his pen. In two weeks he had turned out a brochure to which he gave the rousing title of *Art and Revolution*, and sent it to Wigand, the Leipzig publisher, who declared himself enchanted with it and sent him five pounds right away.

There was nothing so very surprising about that, for in this pamphlet Wagner gives utterance to what was uppermost in the hearts and minds of all the artists of '48, making himself the mouthpiece of their ideals and aspirations. Not only did he believe in the revolution, but he felt himself called upon to guide it into the way of salvation . . . felt himself irresistibly impelled to give an idea of the noble edifice which would one day arise from the ruins of an art that was based on falsehood. It

was not merely a case of verbal fireworks. It was the genuine
endeavour of a temperament to express itself, because it could
not help it and because he was resolved to show that he was a
living and a growing force. And though he was ostensibly setting forth the ideas of a school, he was really voicing his own
personal convictions, talking about himself, vindicating himself.
According to Nietzsche, every philosophy is a sort of intimate
diary, an involuntary confession, a voyage of self-discovery. In
thus writing and composing, Wagner's great aim was, in reality,
to discover fresh syntheses between art and life; between *his*
art and *his* life, so that they might mutually vindicate one another. But the most notable thing in *Art and Revolution* is
Wagner's tacit recognition of the debt which he, as a dramatist,
owed to the Greek conception of Necessity, the conception which
in Greek tragedy linked up all that was noblest in man with
the destiny of the race as a whole. Thus he came to contemn the
Romans as mere war-mongers, bullies, riding rough-shod over
the world, a race whose art culminated in disgust with life and
abhorrence of society, thus paving the way for Christianity
with all its heritage of neurasthenia; for the Christian was
enjoined to endure, without repining, a condition of inhuman
abasement, living a life accursed. The Christian's one demand
was that a man should acknowledge himself a miserable sinner
and renounce every effort to ameliorate a condition from which
the unmerited grace of God could alone deliver him. Thus it
came about that hypocrisy had always been the salient charac-
teristic of Christianity, from the Middle Ages down to our own
times. But nature, eternally and inexhaustibly prolific, had in-
jected new life blood into the veins of the failing world, the
life blood of the Germanic races. Hence arose the struggle
between the Church and the temporal power. The New Spirit
now came into the arena as the adversary of Christianity. A
gulf began to yawn between the reality of life and its fictitious
presentment. It was a new Renaissance. But out of the stern
humiliation which the Church was compelled to undergo
emerged a freer art, which set itself to serve as the handmaid
of the princes and the great ones of the earth, taking as its
gospel, not indeed the virtues of antiquity, but its own inaccu-
rate idea of them. From this ill-assorted union sprang the age
of Louis XIV, which, because of its lack of sincerity and truth,
was fated to come to naught. Art then attached itself to an ally
even more worthless, to industry. "Mercury, the tutelary god
of the merchant, became also the god of rogues and thieves.
. . . Crown him with the aureole of Christian hypocrisy, adorn

his breast with the empty symbols of feudal chivalry, and you will have the god of the modern world, the most holy and most noble god of the Rialto. . . . The real mainspring of modern art is industrialism. Money is its aim, recreation its æsthetic pretext. It has thus become a job, a business. It has fallen from its high estate. No longer, as in the days of the Greeks, is it a religious festival, a philosophy, a welling-up from the depths of the national conscience. The art of the ancients was popular, dramatic, the collective expression of the national spirit. Modern art is individualist, at enmity with the people and revolutionary in its tendencies. But out of that very revolution a new love shall spring up and bring forth as its flower the love of humanity, which shall help us to love ourselves, to rediscover the joy of living. And of that love, which even the Greeks knew not, there shall some day be born the ideal man, perfect in strength and beauty, the man who shall recognize that he, by his very perfection, has fulfilled the one ultimate aim for which he was created. Love of the weak for the weak can but result in a sterile and ineffective indulgence; the love of the weak for the strong, in self-abasement or fear; the love of the strong for the weak, in pity or compassion. Only the love of the strong for the strong is really love, for it is a free gift of ourselves to one who cannot constrain us. In every clime, in every race, men may attain, by the path of freedom, to equal strength; and by strength, to real love; and by real love, to beauty. And beauty, beauty in being, in action, is Art." Utopian dreams, say you? Why? Because the Christian Utopia offers too violent a contrast between its beginning and its culmination. "The Christian idea was morbid, it had engendered a weakening and cessation of human efforts, and offended against the real and healthy nature of man. Art must be released from bondage, reinstated in dignity, rescued from the manufacturer and the exploiter, restored to the theatre which is its plenary and most effective manifestation. The claims of the theatre and the spectacle should be one of the primary considerations of every government, for in the long run its solution will endow the citizen with all his spiritual armoury, enrich him with all the splendours of the imagination." Thus, eighty years after Wagner, speaks Jean Giraudoux. "Let us rear the altar of the future, both in life and in life-giving art, to the two sublimest teachers of mankind, to Jesus who suffered for them, and Apollo who made them the coheirs of his dignity and joy." Such is the note on which *Art and Revolution* comes to an end.

Two or three times ere this we have seemed to catch the clear, ironic notes of Zarathustra amid the trumpet blasts of Siegfried. Here again we hear them, but mingled with the whole Wagnerian orchestra and falling almost harshly on the ear, like a discord unresolved. There is something stridently pagan, something fiercely anti-Christian, in its tone; something, if the truth be told, that is artificial and but little in harmony with this æsthetic profession of faith. The fact is that Wagner was feeling his way through the realms of literature and legend seeking to find himself, for he knew himself but imperfectly as yet. He was waiting in eager expectation for some spark from heaven to fall, to reveal to him the secret of his heart and illumine the path of his future progress. Nothing came . . . save Minna, ready once again to share her life with him; Minna for whom he had longed and called to come to him, whom he had implored Liszt to send to him, "dear, faithful woman that she was." But it was a Minna sadly aged that came, and came in company with all her little household train: her daughter-sister Natalie, Peps the dog, and Papo the parrot. What remained of the Dresden furniture was coming on to Zurich also, thanks to the money that had been supplied by Liszt: the rather worn piano, and the engraving of the Nibelungen by Cornelius in its Gothic frame. The books had all been seized by Henry Brockhaus as a pledge against the 500 thalers formerly advanced by him. Sulzer got lodgings for his friends, and Wagner undertook to conduct a concert for the Musical Society.

And so their married life began again, "cabin'd, cribb'd, confin'd," with the usual daily round of petty vexations and humdrum pleasures, of literary work and philosophic study. For Minna grew no better pleased, ran down her husband's friends, expressed her scorn of Zurich, harped on the good old days at Dresden, and longed to be back again in Paris. Richard buried himself in Feuerbach and wrote a new book, a sequel to the other, which he called *Art and the Future*.

This again was the work of a poet. Wagner did not possess the philosophical apparatus that would have fitted him to take part in a battle of ideas, nor sufficient breadth of culture to provide a sure foundation for his artistic theories. Nevertheless, this essay, free from apriori notions, and conceived under the direct inspiration of what he had read of Feuerbach and Schlegel, is none the less a brilliant and ingenious production. In it Wagner again develops the "why" and "wherefore" of that marvellous efflorescence which goes by the name of Grecian Art, which is, *par excellence*, the art of humanity, the living presentment of a religion. That is the idea upon which his creed is based. Dance, music, poetry are three inseparable sisters whose harmonious conjunction gives art its life and movement. For, since nothing in nature has an independent existence, man's true freedom exists solely in the union of the forces through which he expresses his desires. It is from this convergence of powers that drama, is born. He then proceeds to trace the history of dance, music, and poetry, the successive stages in their evolution, and comes back again to drama, which he calls the culmination of the collective desire for artistic expression. He hastens, however, to disclaim for his idea of drama any connection with the arbitrary and unworthy alliance exhibited by modern opera, in which, each art having reassumed its separate form, "music is bandied about between the dance and the libretto." The redemption of the art of music can only be effected by the fusion of the three constituent elements in one indivisible trinity, one indissoluble union. "Who is it, then, that holds the future in his hands? Without doubt the poet. But who will that be? Most certainly the actor (he who acts). And who, then, will be the actor? Why, necessarily the association of all artists." As for the work represented, that is "a branch of the tree of life, a branch which, having grown unconsciously and involuntarily on this tree, has bloomed and faded in accordance with the laws of life, and then, having become detached from the tree, has been planted anew in the soil of art, there to put forth afresh in new and eternal beauty. Nevertheless, this process must needs come to an end, and it ends with the life of the leader who directs it." Here, then, again we have the glorification of death; not death resulting from chance, but death that is in the necessary order of things: "The glorification of such a death is the most splendid thing that men can celebrate. It is the artistic resurrection of the dead by the living and joyous imitation of his deeds and of his death in the work of dramatic art."

Having, at one breath, written this treatise of universal love swallowed up in the beatitude of death, Wagner made it the theme of a libretto which he entitled *Wieland der Schmidt* and decided to submit it to a Paris theatre. Frau Ritter, the mother of his young friend Karl, having heard of his distress, lent him 500 thalers. It was just what was necessary to provide for Minna for a while and to enable him to undertake this fresh journey to France. But had Wagner any other idea in his mind when he decided thus to set out once more on what he calls the road of destiny? When in after years he was dictating some passages in the annals of his life, he let fall one or two little

hints which make one think that the real motive of his departure
may have been very different from the avowed one. "About this
time," he says, "I received from Bordeaux a letter from the
Mme. Laussot (*née* Taylor) who had come to visit me at
Dresden the year before. In kind and touching words she
assured me of her sincere regard. This was the first symptom
of a new phase in my life, a phase in which I came to see the
outward circumstances of my career becoming increasingly dependent on intimate relationships which, little by little, detached
me from my family." And a little farther on he adds: "It thus
came to pass that early in February (1850) I did definitely set
out for Paris. If, among the complex feelings which then filled
my breast, hope played a part, it had its origin in a sphere of
my inward self very different from that in which lay the hope
ascribed to me, that is, the hope of scoring a success in Paris
as a composer of opera." The sphere of his inward being thus
illumined by a new ray of hope, was Mme. Laussot, as she
calls herself, a young Englishwoman who had come to see him
in his rooms with Karl Ritter and was in fact none other than
the girl who, a year ago, was still bearing the name of Jessie
Taylor. Though so recent a bride, she was far from being a
happy one. Disappointed in a husband who had turned out to
be a fatuous and conceited coxcomb, her thoughts reverted to
the musician she had met the year before, whose longings she
had half-divined, and whose memory was so deeply graven on
her heart. It was, then, not without emotion that she turned to
the artist in whom she deemed she saw one who could broider
so rarely on the warp of sorrow. And so she wrote him a letter.
Perhaps she even came as far as Paris to meet him. At all
events, she invited him to Bordeaux to stay. And Wagner accepted, for it did not seem to him that his third experience of
Parisian life was going to yield him anything more than the
usual crop of disappointments. However, he did see Kietz, who
was still having as much difficulty with his brushes as ever,
still the same openhearted, charming fellow that he always was,
and whose only use for a revolution was that it would enable
him to get rid once for all of his landlord. He also saw Anders,
who still fell asleep over his work at the *Bibliothèque Nationale*
and still cherished the conviction that Wagner would be a great
music-hall success one of these days. And lastly he saw Meyerbeer, whose *Le Prophète* was enjoying a great triumph at the
Opéra; "the dawn of the day of shame and disenchantment
which was to break upon the world." Wagner rose and ostenta-

tiously left his seat before the end of the first act. And then he took coach for Bordeaux.

Eugène Laussot and his wife were expecting him. The man was a well-dressed, vulgar nonentity. Like so many young men in that district, he ran a wine business—E. Laussot et Cie., merchant, 38 Cours du Jardin Public: private address 136 rue Terre-Nègre. It has been asserted that before his marriage he had been the lover of his future mother-in-law. Was it that which made Jessie write to Wagner? Was it that she expected to find in him a purer and a nobler soul, one who would protect her against people who must needs hold her in slight esteem, seeing how cruelly they had deceived her? She was not yet twenty-two, spoke German correctly, having spent a long time in Dresden, played the piano with remarkable technique, was well educated and intelligent. Mrs. Taylor lived close by the young couple. She extended to the newcomer so warm a welcome that he at once felt quite at home in these wealthy surroundings. Whether it was to win Wagner's friendship, or whether it was to please her daughter, she offered to join with Frau Ritter and guarantee him an income of round about 3,000 francs a year. What a relief! Richard was so overjoyed that he wrote to Minna in tones that were almost affectionate about it. However, he soon perceived that between Jessie and himself on the one side, and Mrs. Taylor and Laussot on the other, an impassable barrier was arising—another barricade, the most formidable of all—a barricade of the affections. What sense of mistrust, what secret, unuttered understanding, was it that respectively repelled and attracted these four people, who as yet hardly knew one another? Was it hatred on the one part, and love on the other? From the outset Richard had divined that some outpouring of the heart was in store, some declaration of passionate love. How then could he have failed to hope from a young woman, estranged from her husband, as he himself was estranged from his wife—how could he have failed to hope that by giving herself to him she would give—and take—the inexpressible joy of a sorrow shared in common. Such was Richard's belief. Jessie played him Beethoven's great *Sonata in B*, and he read her the sketch of his *Wieland*, and his poem, *The Death of Siegfried*. Jessie did not hesitate to confess the aversion she felt for her husband, and Laussot went so far as openly to quarrel with his wife in the presence of their guest. Insensibly, without exactly realizing how it came about, the two malcontents became lovers. Almost at once they made up their minds that they would run away, he from his dull-witted *hausfrau,* she from her bullying husband. They would go away, no matter where, but to a country where they would be free to love, to give play to their feelings—in a word, to live. They felt particularly drawn to the East, to Greece and Asia Minor. Maybe they would go into yet more distant lands, to forget and be forgotten. He had written to Minna, and now he wrote to Frau Ritter to tell her all about his love for Jessie, and Jessie's love for him, how sensitive, how delicate her feelings were, since she had understood better than anyone else how he was still drawn to his wife by the memory of the trials and hardships they had shared together.

So as not to give the alarm, Richard left Bordeaux early in April and returned to Paris. There he remained for a few days in a state of great uncertainty and perturbation as to how to deal with the problem which, though settled in principle, he did not quite know how to tackle when it came to giving it practical effect. However, he wrote to Liszt, saying, "I have sundered the last bonds which attached me to a world in which I was doomed infallibly to perish, not only intellectually but physically. As a result of the ceaseless constraint to which my immediate surroundings condemned me, my health has suffered and my nerves have gone to ruin. My great object now will be to get well again. I will let you know from time to time how I am getting on." What did he mean by "constraint"? Who was constraining him? Once again it was the unhappy Minna, who could not understand what had made him leave Paris, or why he had not managed to get one of his works taken on at the Opéra, why nothing turned out as she wished it to do, and now she wrote him a long letter full of unjust upbraidings. She could not have made a more fatal mistake. This time his cup was filled to overflowing. Wagner snatched up his pen. He would see to it that the fresh wound thus clumsily dealt him should at all events be the last. He would have no more of it. Bitterly he went through all his married life, told her how he hated it all, and swore that he meant to have done with it. He had endured enough of this everlasting bickering. It had come to the breaking point, and she would have to fall in with his plan for a separation and realize that it was for her peace and happiness that he had made up his mind to leave her for good. He offered her a share of the money he was to receive, so that at any rate her most urgent necessities should be provided for. . . . "I can see you there in front of me, irreconcilable . . . the things that are nearest my heart you contemn and hate. What form, then, can my love for you take now? Merely the desire to make up to you for the youth you threw away for my sake, for the misery you have endured in my company, and make you happy once again? But can I make you happy by living with you? Impossible." Separation, then, was necessary for them both. A few days later he returned to the charge. "There is something I want to tell you, something which is my special reason for writing you again, for I have an idea that it may soften any pangs you may feel at our separation. . . . I am just about to start for Marseilles, whence I shall take a berth on an English boat for Malta. From there I shall go on to Greece and Asia Minor. For the time being, I am closing the door of the modern world behind me. I loathe it and want to have nothing more to do with what it calls its 'art'. Believe me it is better so, both for you and for me. Adieu, then, Minna, you sorely tried woman."

What had happened then? Had Mrs. Taylor found out her daughter's secret and told Frau Wagner? Or had Jessie got frightened? Impossible to say with any certainty, but, anyhow, in a few days the whole scheme collapsed. Wagner had gone to have a quiet few days at a country inn at Montmorency, when Minna in person turned up in Paris. This was hell and Richard could not screw up the courage to face it. He sent for the trusty Kietz who said he thought he must be the hub on which all the miseries of the world revolved. Richard told him to tell the frantic woman he had left Paris. Then he took coach for Clermont Ferrand and Geneva, went right on to Villeneuve at the far end of the lake, and shut himself up in a room in the Hôtel Byron. There he was joined by Karl Ritter, and there he wrote his preface to *The Death of Siegfried*. There also he received a frenzied letter from Jessie, telling him she had confessed everything to Mrs. Taylor and that Laussot was going about saying he would have his rival's blood. Thus their love-affair, that had only just begun, looked as if it were going to have some awkward complications. Would it survive them? Wagner thought not, for the liaison had been too brief, too furtive, to have taken deep root. It had not yet reached the magic circle in which the death of passion, or the loss of its object becomes the great tragedy of life. But here in this case it was all a mirage, for she had not loved him to the point of doing all and daring all in order to come to him.

All the same, he must let them see that he knew how to play the game. So back he went to Bordeaux, after writing and telling Eugène Laussot that he was utterly at a loss to understand how he could bring himself to restrain his wife by force.

After three days and two nights in the diligence he reached

Bordeaux, took a room at the Hôtel des Quatre Sœurs, and sent
a note to M. Laussot to inform him of his arrival. No answer.
Instead, Wagner was ordered to appear before the Commissioner of Police to have his passport examined. What was his
business? Family matters. Indeed! Well, it was precisely for
the sake of this family's honour that he was requested to leave
at the earliest possible moment. The announcement restored all
his good-humour. M. Laussot had at all events taken all precautions so far as he was concerned. He had left Bordeaux,
and his wife with him. . . . (Wagner did not know his letters
had been intercepted.) He indited an epistle to Jessie and took
it to the house himself. He rang the bell. No one at home. He
went upstairs. Silence. He strode through the vacant rooms and
deposited his missive in the lady's workbasket.

That at least is the tale he told later on. It is a little too
strange to be absolutely true. Perhaps Wagner—and with good
reason—considered it quite natural that Jessie should be treated
as a child. A little reading, a little music, a few rapid love-
passages, and all her longings had been sated. She was a feeble
thing. She was incapable of sacrifice, for against his seventeen
years of conjugal misery she could only put into the scale a
single twelvemonth of humdrum insipidity. Why, take tragi-
cally what, after all, was merely a whim, a caprice, a little trip
that hadn't come off? So Wagner came back again to the Hôtel
Byron, where he kept up his thirty-seventh birthday with the
mother and sisters of his friend Ritter. That generous old lady
was a great believer in his future, and often lent him a helping
hand. After this, Karl and he left for Zermatt and were bored
there. Then they went on for a while to Thoune. It was there
that Karl had an indignant letter from Jessie Laussot, complaining of her lover's conduct, for she was still in complete
ignorance of his journey to Bordeaux. She intended to maintain
silence, so far as he was concerned, for one year. A year! "I'm
not young enough now to live on hopes," he flashed out to Frau
Ritter, who had been trying to console him. "A year! Great
God! Haven't we all been through enough to know what a year
means?"

But this prelude to a blighted passion was not a wasted
experience. It came back to him ere long, as he was writing his
duet for Siegmund and Sieglinde in the *Valkyrie*, when the
portals of desire swing softly open before them and reveal the
perfumed mystery of the sweet spring night.

Chapter II

OPERA AND DRAMA—THE MYTH OF ŒDIPUS

AND now force of habit, the daily round of ordinary life, with its constantly recurring obligations, its succession of little things that have to be done, brings the truant to heel again and bolts and bars the conjugal door upon his frustrated hopes of the larger freedom. Minna had moved during her husband's escapade and taken up her quarters in a modest house on the shore of the Lake of Zurich, which was soon to be christened the "Villa Rienzi," and thanks to his faculty for adapting himself to circumstances—a faculty which so often saved him from himself—he settled down again to work and carry on as usual, still nursing the unconquerable hope that, somehow and some day, his dreams would come true. On the whole he felt it rather a relief that he was not now called upon to take the big fence. Minna asked no questions. The country round was bright and cheerful. Peps resumed his place behind his master's chair, and Papo showed his regard for him by whistling the final march of the *Symphony in C Major*, or a *motif* from the Overture to *Rienzi*, in honour of his return. Alas, the squabbles between Minna and Natalie had broken out afresh (for the girl would not brook being ordered about by one whom she took to be her sister), but after all, he was used to all that; and the news that Liszt was going to put on *Lohengrin* at Weimar gave a rosy complexion to the future. The event was an important one for Wagner and involved a deal of correspondence with his devoted friend. The exile even thought there might be a chance of his getting back to Germany for the occasion, but Liszt made it clear that this was out of the question and took upon himself the entire responsibility for the whole thing—rehearsals and staging—about which Wagner, with his usual eagerness, sent him the most urgent representations. "I will carry out your behests with my most respectful and friendly attention," was the older man's assurance.

The *première* of *Lohengrin* took place on the 28th of August, 1850, and was a considerable success. While it was going on, Wagner, to calm his nerves, made the ascent of the Rigi in company with his wife and Natalie, after which they spent the evening at the Hôtel du Cygne, Lucerne. Alone with his own thoughts, the composer was far away, gazing in spirit at his work as its successive scenes were unfolded on the grand-ducal stage. Thus it was that the most mournful of his works was given in his absence, the work which, more than any other, symbolizes the story of his own life, his own artistic isolation in a world that knew him not. It was not until years later that he actually heard his work. But his young friends were there in his place— Karl Ritter, Hans von Bülow, and some foreigners who had come to Weimar for the celebrations organized by Liszt in honour of Herder, among them being Jules Janin, Gérard de Nerval, and Meyerbeer. Wagner was dithyrambic in his gratitude to Liszt. "My joy at having found you makes me forget that I am banished from Germany. What am I saying? Nay, I almost bless my exile, for I should never have been able to undertake what you have succeeded in doing for me." However, according to Ritter, the performance in some ways might have been better and Wagner wrote off twenty pages to Liszt to expound his theory of dramatic music, and insisting that "every bar ought to have its significance as interpreting the acts or the character of the person represented." But Liszt was not to be discomfited. "Your *Lohengrin*," he wrote, "is a sublime piece of work from beginning to end; time after time it brought tears to my eyes. The whole opera is one indivisible marvel!" He sent on some money out of his own funds, though he pretended that it represented advance royalties, and he wrote a long article on *Lohengrin*, as he had done for *Tannhäuser*. He pointed a prophetic finger at "this new and glorious name which proves that the chain of great men wherewith Weimar adorned herself is not yet broken." This time Wagner was completely won over by his amazing and delightful friend. His heart was touched in that inner sanctuary to which criticism can gain no entrance. And so, when Liszt exclaimed, "And now, what about *Siegfried*?" it acted like a tonic on his spirits, sounding a summons he could not disobey. "All I long for is the happiness of being with you, of being yours, heart and soul, for a while; not merely to say, but to do what it is impossible to explain by letter."

Unfortunately, the time was not yet ripe for starting on the new works which were already beginning to occupy his mind. There were material things to be considered first, particularly the daily-bread question; and as the Zurich theatre offered Wagner the post of making himself responsible for the orchestra, for the concerts, and even for the production of opera, he accepted the offer on condition that he had the assistance of his two young disciples Ritter and von Bülow. When, however, it came to the point, Ritter proved so shy, so raw and so hampered by his short-sightedness, that once, when *Der Freischütz* was being given, Wagner was obliged to take the bâton and conduct it himself. His fire and decision at once brought about the result he had been afraid of; they wanted him to keep on the conductorship at all costs. This would have meant starting Riga, Koenigsberg, and Magdeburg all over again, and that would never do. Then he thought of Hans von Bülow, who, as it happened, had just written him from Constance to tell him that his parents were dead against his taking up music as a profession. Wagner dispatched Karl to see him, armed with a letter in which he explained his views regarding the right every man had to regulate his life according to his moral and spiritual needs. He cried shame on his pusillanimity, laughed at his weakness, and offered him on behalf of the theatre, a salary of 100 francs a month. This, so far as young von Bülow was concerned, was the first of those headstrong, authoritative interventions which always gave Richard such dominion over natures less impulsive, less decisive than his own. And so the young man who went to talk matters over with the emissary of the wan-faced Mariner, the corpse of that same Lohengrin who had made so profound an impression on him, forthwith set out on his way, and having once started, never looked back. They went on foot, through the wind and the rain, trudging it all the way to Zurich, which they reached the following night. "Bülow was hysterical in his professions of gratitude and I immediately realized the heavy responsibility I had incurred towards him and felt greatly pained at his morbid excitement."

It almost looks as if Wagner was forgetting that it was he who had urged him to make the long journey on foot without a penny in his pocket, and that he had little call to be surprised if a certain amount of excitement should be visible in the eyes of a child who had forsaken his family and his work to obey his master's summons. It was a very heavy responsibility. Wagner shouldered it blithely.

The winter was devoted to getting up some high-class orchestral concerts in Zurich and St. Gall. Wagner was quite right; von Bülow at once proved himself a conductor with a sensible ear, conscientious and well worth his salt. But Wagner was hard put to it to prevail on the orchestra to accept so juvenile a Kapellmeister. When he had conducted *The Barber* and *Fra Diavolo*, Bülow was appointed to St. Gall. Then, at his mother's request, and also because he felt drawn to it himself, he joined Liszt at Weimar to study the piano under his tuition. He soon attained a mastery of that instrument, and two years later Liszt was saying, "I look on him no longer as my pupil, but rather as my heir and successor." Once more Wagner found himself single-handed, and to satisfy the requests that came pouring in upon him from all quarters, he undertook several concerts for the Musical Society. Thus he conducted the *Symphony in C Minor* and *The Eroica*, and it was under his auspices that von Bülow made a brilliant début as a pianist, playing a pianoforte arrangement by Liszt of the Overture to *Tannhäuser*. This display of Bülow's talents as a pianist came to Wagner with all the force of a revelation. The boy Hans had departed; the man had come to take his place; a worker with a will of iron, some one on whom you could count as a henchman in your quest of the key to the riddle of art and life.

Now, for Wagner, his own art was still an enigma to him. In *Tannhäuser* and *Lohengrin* he had but sounded the preluding notes. All that he had unfolded of it in his writings, he promised himself later on to clothe in the splendours of music, but, as always, literature came first; and thus, for a space of four or five months, there accumulated on his writing-table an ever-increasing pile of papers, the pages of his most important essay, *Opera and Drama*. No sooner was it finished than he wrote off to Uhlig—it was the 16th of February, 1851—saying:

Mon cher ami,
My dear Friend,
"Here you have my testament; I can die now, and whatever else I may achieve will be a work of supererogation. The last pages of this copy were written by me in a state of mind of which it would be impossible for me to give you, or anyone, a clear account."

What he meant was that Papo, the parrot, was dead. It had been ailing for some time and the day after he had finished his manuscript it was found lying dead on the floor. It was an evil omen. The love which Richard and Minna bore their pets had for many a day been the only bond between them. "Ah, if only I could tell you all that has died for me in this dear creature." It seemed as if every new work was doomed to cost him some heartrending sorrow. Every work that Wagner did was intimately associated with his daily life, with his bursts of anger, with his intermittent kicking against the pricks. Everything he produced has its autobiographical significance. That is why there is always a suggestion of pathos about his works, which—according to what we are ourselves—makes them either so near to us, or so remote.

As in his *Art and the Future*, Wagner begins by tracing the history of opera, and, indeed, of music as a whole, whose frontiers march with those of the drama. If we except Mozart, the opera as we knew it is made for the idle rich and is merely something stolen from the masses for the benefit of the wealthy, and has no other object than to titillate the ear with tunes which are sung today and forgotten tomorrow, and replaced by others just as meaningless; tunes which sound sad when we are merry, and merry when we are sad—but which, withal, we still go on singing. Thus the secret of opera was discovered by Rossini, encouraged by the instrumentalists, the vocalists, and the librettist himself, whose ability lay in the skill with which he could provide situations leading up to what amounted to mere vocal trials of strength. But in the very violence of the effort, opera exhausted its resources and would straightway have died, if the entertainment quality of caricature had not inspired some decadents to pick up pieces here and there from among the ruins. What was now needed was a complete revival of the art of music; it could only grow from its own native roots, and be nourished by its own sap, by gentle contact with nature. Weber had been a gardener of genius. Alas! he also fell into error in trying to make melody the predominant partner in drama. After his death, opera fell into the hands of the triumvirate of the melody-monger, the librettist, and the costumier, whose one united aim it was to keep the barbarians amused, and who even went the length of turning the theatre into a church. The music of metaphysics was brought into being, a jargon in which all the styles are intermingled—historical, hysterical, and neuro-romantic. To this school came one who had no mother-tongue of his own—Meyerbeer the Jew, with ear alert to catch the voices of Rossini's sirens and to unite in one monstrous and mongrel phrase, all the melodies that were floating at large over France and Italy, and bear them off with a resounding crash. In a word, the music of opera is an art no longer, but a mere manifestation of the passing fashion; the artist, a speculator; the poet, the composer's lackey; and the fruit of their association, a counterfeit of the lyric drama.

As regards Lessing and his *"Laocoon,"* Wagner proceeds to
show that it had by no means been the aim of that poet to set
any limits to the scope of dramatic art, which gathers up all the
motifs of the plastic arts at the moment of their highest tension.
On the contrary, a real representation is only possible in a uni-
versalized manifestation of the artistic feeling, since a work of
art is only created by the action of the imagination on reality,
that is to say on the senses. The drama is not, therefore, a
branch of literature as is the epic or the novel. Drama implies
the idea of action, of poetry in action, and it is therefore natural
that it should require music and scenery. Modern drama has a
twofold origin, deriving on the one hand from our historical evolution, the novel; but on the other, foreign, namely the classical
Greek drama. Shakespeare is the outcome of the one; Racine
of the other. Between the two is a vague indeterminate dramatic
literature neither one thing nor the other. But up to the present
it is only the Greek conception of the world that has produced
the work of real dramatic art; and as the subject of this drama
was mythological, it is to mythology we must return, so that the
people may rediscover the god, the hero, and, finally, the man.

Here Wagner devotes some ten pages or so to a profoundly
interesting consideration of the tale of Œdipus. The passage
has a very direct bearing on the work which was then germinating in his mind. For the riddle of the Sphinx, which the man
who unwittingly married his mother thought to resolve, is nothing more or less than the history of man in relation to society,
of man in his pride pitting himself against Destiny. The two
sons of Œdipus and Jocasta, each of whom was to rule over
Thebes in turn, represent, respectively, the state (Eteocles),
"whose mainspring is fear, and aversion for whatever is not in
accordance with tradition." The other (Polyneices), the ardour
of youth, indignation, revolt, the "purely human" of the bad
patriot. In their strife one with the other, these fratricidal foes
were upheld, the one by the practical instinct of the people and
its sense of property, the other by those who loved the heroic,
men imbued with broad sympathies and the spirit of adventure,
who were opposed to a narrow, heartless, and selfish society,
only too quickly petrified in its form of government. As we know,
both brothers fell before the ramparts of the city, and were succeeded by the prudent Creon, their uncle, who pondered long on
this judgment of the gods. He recognized the importance of public opinion, realized that it was based on belief, fear, and the
hatred of new things. The moral conscience of man finding itself

at war with the most powerful interests of society, that conscience drew apart and established itself under the form of religion, while his practical element gave birth to the state. And
morality, which had hitherto been something alive and warm
in the social organism, now became no more than an idea, a desire. As for the state, it contented itself with what was useful.
The only heart that henceforth dwelt therein, a heart of mourning to which humanity had fled for sanctuary, was the heart of
a virgin, and love throve apace therein. Antigone knew naught
of politics. She loved. "She loved Polyneices, her brother, because
he was unhappy." What, then, was the significance of this love,
which was neither sexual, nor maternal, nor filial, nor fraternal?
It was the crowning flower of all these loves. From the ruins of
sexual, filial, and fraternal love, which society had rejected and
the state denied, there came to birth, nourished by the deathless
sap of all these loves, the splendid flower of pure love for humanity. Antigone knew that she must obey the blind necessity
of bringing about her own death, and with this knowledge of
the inscrutable will she was the most perfect of all human beings, she was love in all its power and plenitude. Not a hand was
raised in her favour when she was led forth to die. And yet the
citizens wept at having to condemn her to torture. But law
and order required a human victim, and Antigone's love, more
potent than a curse, brought about the downfall of the state.
Perish, then, the gods who will not heed the cry of sorrow in
man's heart. "Oh, Saint Antigone," cries Wagner yet again,
"unfurl, I beseech thee, thy banner that we may be stricken
down and then redeemed beneath its folds. And still today we
have but faithfully to interpret the myth of Œdipus in its inmost essence, in order to discern therein an intelligible image
of the whole story of mankind, from the beginnings of society
down to the dissolution of the state. The necessity for such dissolution is foreshadowed in the myth. It is for history to bring
it to pass."

Yes, and to begin with, for the artist; the composer; the revolutionary; for Wagner. Even now in this fiery prose we catch
the song of the valkyrie mourning for Siegfried and his faith
in love; we hear the thunder of Wotan's impotent wrath; we see
the vast Valhalla of the old world rocking on its base. Wagner
was ripe now for what he deemed to be the crowning work in
which he would symbolize all his hatred and all his compassion.
He flings down a rapid sketch of the scene with the Nornes
with which the Twilight opens. He traces the outline of Siegfried

the Youth, which is needed to precede, and complete, *The Death of Siegfried*. Notwithstanding that several new friends came into his circle, such as the poets George Herwegh and Gottfried Keller, to whom he naturally read over his essays in literature and æsthetic philosophy, despite other brochures which he wrote in haste to carry off the overflow of his ideas ("A Word to My Friends"; "The Jewish Element in Music") Wagner is haunted by the poetic themes of his great dramatic tetralogy. But money was still lacking, money that would enable him to enjoy those blissful oases of peace and quiet labour in the cloistral solitude of his study. Liszt and his princess, could they not come to the rescue? Without any false pride he wrote begging, imploring them to hear his supplications. "Pressed for money . . . having exhausted all the funds received by me from Weimar on account of *Lohengrin* . . . I am now simply compelled to get money at any price." Liszt does what he can; sends a hundred thalers, two hundred, writes another article. Then the world blossomed forth anew, and likewise the heart. "Again I have found you, you have taken me, heart and soul, filled me with rapture, given me new life, and kindled such a fire within me that I burst into tears; then swiftly recovering myself, I knew there was no joy like the joy of being an artist, the joy of creating. It is quite impossible to describe your influence upon me. All round about I behold the luxuriant springtime, life germinating and overflowing; and, withal, I am conscious of a sorrow so voluptuous and a voluptuousness so mournful, such joy at being man and having a beating heart, even though it knows but sorrow, that I regret that I can only *write* all this to you." This frame of mind inspired him in a flash with the whole of his poem, *The Young Siegfried*, but he was so exhausted when he had finished it that the doctor prescribed a cure at Albisbrunn, a little watering-place about three hours' journey from Zurich. It was at Albisbrunn that he thought out the plan of the *Nibelungen Ring*. The idea had occurred to him as early as 1848, but it was only now, in this time of his literary harvest, that he formed a clear notion of the musical and dramatic shape the work would assume. Just as *Lohengrin* and the *Meistersinger* were conceived at Marienbad, so the Tetralogy was born amid the compresses and needle baths of a little "hydro" in German Switzerland; and forthwith he wrote off to Liszt. "At last I have got a clear idea of my subject. . . . During the autumn of 1848 I began by making a complete sketch of the *Nibelungen* myth, since it belonged to me by virtue of my claims upon it as a poet. A first attempt, made to give one of the essential catastrophes of the principal action to be played as a separate drama on our stage, was *The Death of Siegfried*. After hesitating a long while, I was at last (in the autumn of 1850) on the point of sketching out the musical setting for this play, when the impossibility, now again brought home to me, of staging it anywhere in a satisfactory manner, led me to lay aside the enterprise. As an antidote to this despairing frame of mind, I wrote *Opera and Drama*. But, last spring, I was so much up in the skies after your article on *Lohengrin*, that I quickly and joyfully returned to my task of writing a play, out of love for you. I wrote you about it at the time. However, *The Death of Siegfried* remained impossible for the time being. I saw I should have to pave the way for it with another play, and that is how I came to adopt a plan which I have been cherishing for a long time, a plan which consists in making *The Young Siegfried* the subject of a distinct poem. *The Young Siegfried* itself is merely a fragment. Now I have recently come to the conclusion in my own mind that a work of art, and particularly a drama, cannot produce its full effect unless, in its important moments, the poetical intention is completely revealed to the senses. And since this truth has been arrived at by me, it would be more than usually improper for me to contravene it. It is therefore necessary that I should get a complete idea of my whole myth in its deepest and widest significance and with the greatest possible artistic clearness, in order to be entirely understood. . . . My plan is to have three plays (1) *The Valkyrie*, (2) *The Young Siegfried* (afterwards *Siegfried*), (3) *The Death of Siegfried* (afterwards *The Twilight of the Gods*). To give the whole thing complete, it is necessary that these three dramas should be preceded by a great prologue, *The Theft of the Rhinegold* (later *The Rhinegold*). Where and in what circumstances could such a work be performed? That, for the moment, is not my business; my business is to get it finished, and, provided I keep my health, that will take at least three years. Thanks to a lucky change of fortune in the R[itter] family, who think so much of me, I am easy in my mind and relieved of all financial anxiety, free to devote my time at present, and indeed my whole life, to my artistic labours. And now, my friend, my brother, I give into your hands my poem *Young Siegfried*. . . . You will certainly have more than one shock when you read it. One thing that will strike you will be the great simplicity in the action and the small number of *dramatis personæ*; but picture to yourself the play as coming between *The Valkyrie* and *The Death of Siegfried*, both of which are far more complicated in action: this rustic woodland, with its suggestion of youth, simplicity, and solitude, will, if my intentions are fulfilled, have a novel and beneficent effect."

And this is Liszt's reply:

"Your letter, my most marvellous friend, has greatly delighted me. You have attained, by those amazing paths of yours, to an end which is extraordinarily great. . . . Therefore, apply yourself to your task and labour with a will at a work which will evoke from us the same injunction as was laid by the Chapter of Seville upon the architect who had been chosen to build the Cathedral: 'Build such a fane as, when future generations come to behold it, they shall exclaim the Chapter was mad to undertake a thing so amazing.' And yet that task was accomplished; that Cathedral was built."

That counsel was not lost on Wagner. Yet he let the winter go by and did not set to work until the following spring. "Nature awakes, and I am awaking with her," he wrote on the 25th of March, 1852. By the 4th of April his prologue was written. Early in May he and his wife took up their quarters in a little country inn in the village of Fluntern and overlooking the valley of the Limmatt. In the distance rose the Alps, still swathed in snow. A sense of freshness and peace such as he had seldom experienced, inspired him to work. On the 22nd of May he had reached his fortieth year. A week later, he set his hand to the poem of *The Valkyrie* and finished it within a month. It was a load off his mind, for it was always the case that, whenever he was grappling with a great creative work, a secret fear beset him lest he should die before it was completed. He wrote, as it were, under the menace of death, and the moment he came to the end of his task he hastened to date and sign the final page, "as though the Devil were behind me, to prevent me from finishing." Then, by way of recreation, he went alone and on foot across the Bernese Oberland, thanks to a sum of 100 thalers which Liszt had sent him for the expedition. From Lauterbrunnen he made his way up to Grindelwald, amid the pines and larches. Then, engaging the services of a guide, he ascended the Grimsel, crossed the Faulhorn and Seidelhorn glaciers and the Col de la Formazza whose crags and rocks are limned in everlasting outline in the Tetralogy. And as he had brought with him a bottle of champagne, he drained it on the summit of the Seidelhorn, to the memory of the gods who sleep forgotten in the tomes of the learned, but who, aroused from their slumbers at

Fancy's call, were soon to repeople the earth. Far beneath these lofty solitudes, Italy awaited him like a warm bowl into which he freely glided, feeling that sensation of delight with which men of northern blood ever behold the land which art and beauty have made their home. Domodossola, Baveno, the Borromean Islands, Lugano, soft, wooing climes where Liszt in other days had harkened to the voice of Marie d'Agoult reading aloud the *Divina Commedia*. A young mother singing as she walked with her little one in her arms was a picture that never faded from his memory. And it was not far removed from these regions, on the shore of one of those lakes of green and lilac hue, that Liszt's mistress, nearly sixteen years before, had brought her daughter Cosima into the world. So enchanted was Wagner with the Borromean Islands, that he could hardly believe his eyes and asked himself "if so much loveliness were possible" and to what uses he could put it. He telegraphed to Minna and Herwegh, who came and joined him, together with Franz Wille, a Hamburger of Swiss descent who had settled at Zurich.[1] Finally, he returned home by way of Chamonix and Geneva to find on his table at Zurich a number of letters from the German theatres offering to put on his *Tannhäuser*.

The circumstance marks a further stage in his career, and the beginning of that bitterly-contested, hard-won fame which he owed quite as much to the mistrust of the public and the animosity of the critics, as to the favour and encouragement of his friends and of those who understood his message. And yet, somehow, it brought him no joy to hear of this extension of his interests. Even four performances of *The Flying Dutchman*, which were given at Zurich with wholly unprecedented success, afforded him no lasting satisfaction. He was tired. He was painfully toiling across a moral desert. "My youth is over," he wrote to Uhlig. "I've no longer got life in front of me." One wonders whether it was the work of which he was not yet delivered that was weighing thus heavily upon his spirits. Or was it a fact that his ardour was exhausted? Or was it that he had lost that wager of his, the wager that he would henceforth have nothing to do with the world of his own day, and that he would live his whole life in complete solitude, making no concession to the world without?

[1] The Willes, or rather Vuilles, are natives of La Sagne in the canton of Neuchâtel. At the end of the seventeenth century they settled in Hamburg. Franz Wille returned to Switzerland and resumed his status as a Swiss citizen. His son became a general and was commander-in-chief of the Swiss army during its mobilization from 1914 to 1918. He had seen a lot of Wagner in his young days.

There is no doubt that Wagner was a prey to one of the most painful forms of nervous exhaustion with which a creative artist can be afflicted, *viz.*, a horror of his own times. His hopes of playing a leading part in the revolution had faded away, the grand ideals of 1848 had come to naught; so he shut himself up in a legendary world of his own creation, a legend wherein he tells anew the story of the world; clothing with symbols the doctrine which he needs to enable him to live. But his treasury of ideas would have no living value for him unless he could pass them on to others, unless the procession of spirits, still unincarnate, could force an entry into the actual, living present. The marvellous and the real must needs contract an alliance, establish a new rule of life whereof he, the artist, should wield the sole control. For only thus, it seemed to him, would the man of the coming age discover, between mechanical determinism and the yearnings of the spirit, that harmony which shall set no limits to his aspiration or his hopes. But as long as the work that was to bring that redemption to pass remained in the limbo of the uncreate, all was gloom and vexation of spirit. "With me all is martyrdom, suffering, and unrequited effort." For him, exile was a prison, art a prison. Even friendship, even love, was a prison, since one could never escape from oneself, never really possess the object of one's desire. And yet Liszt, the incomparable Liszt, was writing to him and saying, "The aim of my life is to become worthy of your friendship." Unhappily, that priceless friend was a prisoner, too, fettered to Weimar, to a woman, to his reputation, to the theatre, to the well-worn operas of Berlioz. Did he, then, not see that it was from *life* that one must draw one's strength, and what is the productive value of that same life if it does not urge us to create new forms, themselves life-giving in their turn? "Create, create, and yet again create," is his insistent burden. But, notwithstanding these enthusiasms, Wagner was passing through a phase of absolute and tragic aridity. "Paper is the only link between the world and me." But just as, sometimes, a healthy tree presents all the appearances of death on the very eve of its most passionate blossoming, so we seem to see Wagner stretching forth his sterile arms to heaven. "I am sinking," he says, "ever deeper and deeper into the slough. My life is wretched beyond expression. I simply do not know what it means to enjoy life. So far as I am concerned the pleasures of life, of love, are wholly a matter of the imagination, not of experience. My love, therefore, is wholly mental; a matter of the head, not of the heart; and so I can but live a life of make-believe. I live no longer as a man, but as an artist. The man in me is wholly merged in

the artist." But, deep down within his soul, he felt a raging desire, for the soil of the feelings craves for something other than
the sweat of toil to assuage its thirst. Experience, that is what
he was asking, what he was waiting for. Who are they upon
whose love he can still count? What hearts are they which he
can still call his? Minna's heart was withered beyond recall.
Jessie Laussot seemed to have vanished from the scene. For
three whole years his sister Louise had made no sign. It was
long ago now that he had quarrelled with his brother Alberic,
and all those smug connections of his who would not look at him
because he had been mixed up with that revolutionary business.
So when at length his niece Johanna (who had played Elisabeth
for him at Dresden) sent him her portrait, he was filled with
delight. "Oh, if you only knew," he exclaimed, "how happy we
could make each other simply by giving a sign of our love. My
only need is love. Fame, honours, none of these things fulfil my
craving. Love alone can reconcile me with life. I want some sign
that I am loved, even if it be but from a child."

But the hour for that is not yet come. Love and tenderness for
him were all an affair of books, of philosophy, and bound up
with his faraway comrades, Liszt and Uhlig. All at once he flared
up with a sudden passion for Hafiz, the Persian poet. As in a
dream, the glowing East lay all before him, whispering from its
shady palm-groves all manner of airy, sweet conceits; and there,
far, far above our tortured world, he saw, as in a vision, the
sovereign good for which he longed—peace of the spirit, quiet
for his beating mind. How fain was he to take in his own, that
delicate, bloodless hand which, softly laid upon his brow, would
still the turmoil within him. The *Nibelungen Ring* was finished
at last, as the autumn was drawing to a close, the poem, he says,
"which holds within it all I can and all I have." He hurried away
to read it to his friends. They all collected together at the Willes'
country place at Mariafeld as though for a religious festival.

The "purely human" in opposition to the conventional, love
battling against society; the feelings, the instincts, the senses in
all their primitive necessity; in a word, individual subconscious-
ness as opposed to the constraints of law (that shield of the
pitiless community)—such was the keystone of the majestic
temple of his dreams. A world at war with itself, a world in
which nature, as well as man, has no aim or object other than
itself, no moral code other than that everlasting necessity which
rules the universe,—such is his faith; or rather, let us say, his
lack of faith, his essential atheism. The sole religion which Wagner admits is the cult of humanity. Naturally, then, history is

the record of the struggle waged for power and domination. And that is the main theme of *The Ring*. But in the very midst of this struggle there rises up the man of the heroic age, fair and strong, who, by love and compassion, by purity of heart, nay, even by selfishness, that is to say by truth to himself, makes hallowed his empire. All this is the Wagnerian transposition of the Sophoclean myth of Œdipus. Eteocles becomes Alberic, he renounces love for gold and power, the arch-artificer of evil. Polyneices is Siegfried, the hero pure and guileless; the personification of the people. He is the ideal type and exemplar of what man shall be; while Creon is Wotan, the Wayfarer of Earth and Heaven, the soul vexed and harried by men and gods, torn betwixt heaven and earth, betwixt greed for worldly power and the peremptory promptings of the heart. Wotan is the very centre of the human tragedy. He stands for all that man has achieved up to the present time. Yet the day will come when he will sink down beneath the ruins of Valhalla, yielding place to a newer order.

Wagner was now delivered of that birth with which, for four long years, he had been in painful travail (even as Michelangelo took four years to paint the ceiling of the Sistine Chapel), but he had to a great extent solved his problem, his enigma. He felt in very truth like a man redeemed from death. For if anything can give us the impression of having conquered death, it is the feeling that we have left upon the world an indelible imprint of ourselves. Till now, Wagner had produced but dim and broken fragments of his genius; now he had brought forth into the light of day a rich coördinated thematic scheme, a mighty scaffolding to serve for all the dramas which he dreamed of robing in the glorious vesture of his music. One is inevitably reminded of Buonarroti drawing the cartoons of his Last Judgment on seeing which President de Brosses exclaimed, in ever memorable words "'Tis a welter of anatomies." With Wagner it was a welter of souls, and of souls that were still in Limbo. "We have got to learn to die, to die completely, in the fullest significance of the word," he wrote to Roeckel. "It sets the crown on knowledge." But what about living? He had scarcely thought of that. All-powerful god of a world of his own, he had not yet, like God in the Sistine, laid upon his creatures the awakening Finger of the Spirit.

But the Fates, doubtless in order that Wagner should come to the true knowledge of himself, were now about to chasten him in that school of renunciation whose lessons are necessary to the accomplishment of a work that truly becomes a man. Twice they struck at his heart; first by the hand of death, next by the hand of love. Uhlig, one of the two men whom Richard looked on as brothers, was carried off by tuberculosis. The vast Tetralogy, void as yet of its harmonious riches, was shaken to its foundations. Its architect paced within it as a man might wander in a desolate fane. "I am a wilderness," said he, "I live self-consumed. For me there lies no salvation but in death." But even then the doves of life were winging their way towards the portals of the vast and vacant shrine. Some presage, dimly stirring, made him write even then to Liszt, saying: "I have never been so completely in accord with myself concerning the musical development of my poem. I need now but some living stimulus to bring me to that state of mind in which the *motifs* of my work shall well up in joyful spontaneity."

Well, he was now to have that indispensable stimulus. Already he had come within the orbit of a woman's eyes, in whose light he was to find sweet sustenance for his music and his life.

Chapter III

THE FORGING OF "THE RING"

A friendly invitation is extended to Herr and Frau Wesendonck to lunch with us on Sunday. R.S.V.P.

THE WAGNER FAMILY.

OTTO WESENDONCK, a silk merchant hailing from the Rhineland, was among the most prosperous members of the German colony in Zurich. A comparatively recent arrival in the old industrial city, this compatriot of the Willes' and the Herweghs' was the representative of an important firm in New York and soon became friendly with the Wagners. He had been introduced to them by Marshal von Biberstein, a barrister and political refugee, who had fought at Wagner's side on the barricades at Dresden. Wesendonck was a man of thirty-seven. About four years earlier he had married a pretty girl from Elberfeld named Mathilde Luckmeyer, who was now about twenty-four. They had recently arrived from Germany and were living at the Hôtel Baur au Lac. Both were very musical, went regularly to the concerts, and were particularly impressed by some performances which had just been given under Wagner's direction. Wesendonck was an engaging and hospitable fellow, living in very comfortable circumstances, and Richard soon found himself considerably drawn to him, and, no less so, to his charming and romantic-looking wife. "A sheet of white paper" Wagner called her, adding with a smile, "and I am the man who is going to write upon it." And as he still had a taste for teaching, and she for learning, he amused himself by giving her some lessons in counterpoint and harmony. Of course she must learn to write operas "à la Wagner"; and of course her husband must be brought into it, too, and learn singing. Quite a new idea of music, quite a new philosophy of life, had begun to awaken in Mathilde's mind since this strange little exile of a composer had come into her sphere. She, like him, felt a little bit out of her element among all these

186

business magnates in Zurich. Frau Wagner, whose health was
not of the best, was glad to stay at home. Their rooms were in the
Zeltweg (Maison Escher) and Minna had furnished and arranged them with considerable taste.[1] Herr Wagner, however,
was a man who liked going out and seeing people. And so it came
to pass that, as the days were rather long in the spacious apartments of their large and luxurious hotel, Herr Wagner's visits
brought a little welcome excitement into Frau Wesendonck's
rather colourless existence. He read her his *Poems for Three
Operas*, then his political effusions and his latest essays. And
then, seating himself at the piano, he would play Beethoven's
sonatas to her, or give her an idea of the themes of the symphonies he was working on with the orchestra for the Musical
Society's concerts. Of course she was let into the secret of the
great *Nibelungen* poem which he had had printed to the tune of
thirty copies. He told her all about his idea of producing *The
Ring* in Zurich, and of building an entirely new style of theatre
after the plans of the famous Semper. Meantime, a Wagner
Festival was held in the municipal theatre, the composer conducting in person. It took place on the 18th, 20th, and 22nd of
May, 1853, and was solemnly inaugurated by a public recital of
his *Poems for Three Operas*. Singers and instrumentalists came
in crowds from Germany, where the exile's fame was gaining
ground, although it was enshrouded in that atmosphere of mystery which, though it made him popular in some quarters, had a
very contrary effect in others. It was at these concerts that
Wagner first heard passages from his *Lohengrin* played by an
orchestra. Emilie Heim, a professional singer, who was his
neighbour on the Zeltweg, sang Senta's song from *The Flying
Dutchman* and forthwith became his friend. "All the women
became my friends," he said, "but there was one and one alone
at whose feet I offered the whole festival as a token of my
homage." For some weeks past he had been experiencing a feeling of expectancy, a sensation of something about to happen. It
was too vague, too uncertain to call a hope, and, indeed, he may
not, at this stage, have defined it even to himself. His longing for
love had wrought him up to that pitch of exaltation in which
pleasure becomes almost indistinguishable from pain. His craving for love had become so poignant that his new-found joy in
life, and his old yearning for the bliss of oblivion, were now

---

[1] The house in question, No. 13 Zeltweg, is still in existence. In 1853 it
belonged to Frau Clementine Stockar-Escher, who occupied the ground
floor. She did a portrait of Wagner, which was lithographed by Hanfstangl
of Dresden.

merged in a single flood of passionate desire. "For mankind, a state of indifference is a state of suffering," he wrote in a letter to Liszt. "Today, that suffering is widespread and acute, and it is torturing your friend with countless cruel wounds; but, look you, it is precisely that suffering which brings home to us the divine necessity of love. We bid it come to us and welcome it with a depth and an ardour of which we should have been utterly incapable but for that sorrowful experience. We have thus enlisted a power which man, in his ordinary state, never even guessed at, and that ever-growing power, tending ever more and more to sway the world, will one day make this earth a place which none will wish to leave in search of a better; for man will then be happy; he will live and he will love, and where is he who, knowing love, would wish to bid farewell to life?"

Wagner still seemed to think that the enthusiasm which uplifted him was born of his affection for Liszt. For at last Liszt was coming to Zurich and the spring was already thrilling with the promise of the joy in store. The efforts he had made in organizing his Festival mattered little; still less the money he had spent. What is money, compared with life? One can always borrow. And, this time, he asked Wesendonck to advance him 2,000 thalers against the royalties which were bound to accrue from the Berlin performances of his operas. And Wesendonck produced the funds. Splendid! Enthusiasm! Gratitude! His rooms must be redecorated. He must have new furniture, new carpets! "Richard is very delighted," wrote Minna, adding, "and he is up to his neck in debt again. Well, that's part of his genius, too. He has given me a silk dressing-gown which a queen would be proud to wear."

Liszt came and stayed a week. There never were such demonstrations of affection. And then these two men, so seemingly different, and yet, in their innermost being, united by bonds no tongue could utter, went off together with Herwegh, for a trip on the Lake of Lucerne. All three swore eternal friendship. They talked to one another about their work and urged one another on to further effort. From this time forth Wagner's future operas began seething tumultuously within him. And, as usual when he was busy with anything new, his excitement went on increasing. Now he was longing insatiably for pleasure and enjoyment, now he was a prey to the most profound despair. At length his friend departed and he was alone again. He must needs be off to the Engadine. Mighty fine scenery, but, somehow, the wings of his imagination drooped. It was all grey, sombre, and desolate, and St. George (Herwegh), who was with him on his travels, did not come up to St. Francis (Liszt). Ah, if only he would send him his portrait in a locket! As for writing for Brendel's new musical review, as Liszt wanted him to do, no; he couldn't do it; he had gone off that kind of thing. "When you're working, you don't talk about your work." And now he must away to Italy. He will be able to write and compose there, and take his place as leader of the New School.

But Italy was no better than Switzerland. Nevertheless, at Genoa the city and its buildings stirred the musical soul within him. He was conscious of a great ray of hope. He gave Nietzsche a preliminary idea of his future spiritual itinerary: St. Moritz, Genoa, "meet havens for the harmonious calm of peaceful toil." But Wagner was soon off again. One afternoon at Spezzia, after tossing feverishly upon a sleepless couch all the previous night, he flung himself down on the hard little sofa in his bedroom. Falling into a dreamful doze, he seemed to be floating along on a river. "The murmur of the waters soon began to take on a musical sound; it was the chord of E flat major which rang out and floated on and on in little never-ending arpeggios. After a while the arpeggios assumed a melodic character in which the time was quicker than ever, but still the ringing note of E flat major never varied and its persistence seemed to lend a deep significance to the liquid element in which I lay. Suddenly I felt as if the waves were pouring over me in a rushing torrent. Terror-struck, I awoke with a start and realized at once that the theme of the Rhinegold prelude, which I had been bearing within me for so long without ever being able to give it proper shape and form, had just been revealed to me."

Then he returned to Zurich "to do or die." He did neither; but arranged a visit to Paris with Liszt, who was to join him at Basle. And thither Liszt came with his *amie*, Princess Caroline, and Marie, the princess's daughter. Wagner read them his *Siegfried*, and the ladies were so taken with it that they wanted to hear the *Nibelungen* right through. And so, when they arrived at the princess's hotel, they shut themselves up in a room for hours till they had got to the very end of the heroic work. And then and not till then did Paris resume her sway; and the two friends went forth to revive the memories for each of them so diverse, that attached them to a city so deeply graven on the fate of both. For Wagner, it was the city of almost ludicrous penury and spiritual enfranchisement, the city that spoke to him of the third act of *Rienzi*, of *The Flying Dutchman*, of Lehrs and Kietz and the *Ninth Symphony*, and next of Jessie Laussot and the hopes he had entertained of her, of his game of hide and seek with Minna. And now what new sensation lay in store for him in this city of surprises, this chosen realm which Meyerbeer held in fee, Meyerbeer whose name was yet again triumphantly emblazoned on the posters at the Opéra? *Robert le Diable.* . . .

And then—wonders never cease—he ran into the Wesendoncks. But he hardly seemed to take them in at all, and Mathilde's fair visage faded forthwith into limbo. And then came the Marin-Chevillard quartet. It made almost as deep an impression on him as had the *Ninth Symphony* at the Conservatoire long ago. "It was not till I went to Paris," he said, recalling his memories in after years, "that I really got to know the *Quartet in C sharp Minor*. Then, and not till then, did I really grasp its melodic significance." Franz's great friend, Mme. Kalergis-Nesselrode, a very beautiful woman and a pupil of Chopin's, invited Wagner to dinner. But for all her swan-like beauty and conversational charm—for she talked admirably on all manner of subjects—he did not enjoy himself and felt tired and worried all the time, with never so much as a gleam of real pleasure to relieve his boredom. He was eating his heart out. He saw quite clearly that they thought him unsociable and morose, and yet, when he was in the mood, he could be the gayest of the gay, putting even the wittiest talkers in the shade. But there was no point of contact between this brilliant company and this demon-haunted man. "Your wound will never be staunched," said Liszt.

One evening Liszt took his friend and Princess Caroline to see his children at No. 6 rue Casimir-Périer, two young girls, Blandine and Cosima, aged eighteen and sixteen, respectively, and Daniel, a boy of fourteen. They were living very quietly ι nder the governance of an elderly lady who was very distinctly (ιe of the "old school." It was eight years since their father had en them and there was tremendous excitement on both sides. Lιszt, a great connoisseur where women were concerned, was delighted to find he had two such charming girls for daughters. They had been exceedingly well brought up by this governess of theirs, Mme. Patersi, and their mother, the Comtesse d'Agoult, had maintained a distant but highly intelligent control over their education. More than that, they were great favourites with their grandmother, the aged Mme. Liszt, who had lived in Paris ever since the time, now so long ago, when her son used to teach the piano to the young ladies of the aristocracy. A musical evening was arranged. Berlioz was invited and Wagner read *The Death of Siegfried* from the last act of *The Twilight of the Gods*. All he noticed about the girls was that they were terribly shy and that they kept their eyes glued to the floor the whole time. He soon forgot that little picture, but the younger girl, Cosima, must have carried with her to her dying day the memory of that evening when her father's friend, with his hair just turning grey, first dawned upon her view.

At the end of the month Wagner returned to Zurich. Things at home were about as favourable as they well could be for composition: pressing debts, most complicated contracts for the sale of his operas which he was trying to negotiate with Haertel, the publisher, all kinds of worries and bothers, his nervous trouble, and five and a half fallow years during which nothing creative had been done. And then suddenly came a sort of migration of his whole soul to the realms of music. In less than three months the whole of *The Rhinegold* was mapped out, as well as the majority of the *motifs* that form the framework of the Tetralogy. "*The Rhinegold* is finished; but so am I," he said in a letter to Liszt on the 15th of January, 1854. That, however, was not true. His momentary fit of depression was all due to an indifferent performance of *Lohengrin* at Leipzig. Wagner always attached immense moral importance to the manner in which his works were performed, any shortcomings in scenery and staging being regarded by him as prejudicial not only to himself, but to the cause of art. "I see in it the humiliating punishment for the crime I perpetrated against myself and my conscience in going back on my resolution and consenting to my opera's being performed. Dishonour, humiliation," and so on, "for a life I hate, a life I curse." And now for money again! He must get hold of 4,000 thalers somehow or another. Ah, Liszt, of course! Liszt, his *creator*! He'll let him have it. He's bound to understand. "It was in a state of frenzy and desperation that I held on through thick and thin and got the work done. What a tangle I've got into over this cursed money business! I swear no one else ever composed in circumstances like these. I should think my music would frighten people out of their lives. It's a medley of horrors and triumphs." And all the time he is thus down in the depths of despair they were giving "Wagner Nights" in Boston, and the theatres in Germany were raking in the money wholesale from his works. And all the time he, their composer, was in the direst distress. Never mind. He would keep on. His *Nibelungen* anchored him to life; they and they alone. How he wished now the authorities would grant him an amnesty and let him go back to Germany so that he could conduct his works. "Where am I to get energy, real will power? There's only one thing for me to do and that is create." And create he does, working like a madman. He must needs have an amanuensis to make fair copies of his drafts as he scribbles them out, for his writing is getting quite impossible. A secretary! A fine luxury that for a man who hasn't got a penny to his name! Can't he get hold of a Mæcenas somewhere or other? Some crack-brained enthusiast? If he could only find some one to supply the cash, he could bring to pass the finest and the likeliest of all his dreams; he could build a Wagner theatre, play *Lohengrin, The Rhinegold,* and *The Valkyrie* in it. And then he could set fire to it and fling the scores into the flames.

While all this fever was devouring his vitals, life in Zurich went on pretty much as usual. He had to tear himself away from his writing in order to direct concerts, entertain the usual friends, fight things out with Hulsen, the Intendant of Theatres in Berlin, who couldn't make head or tail of all the things which Wagner and Liszt said would positively have to be done in connection with *Tannhäuser* and *Lohengrin.* Then he had to go and keep Minna company—Minna who was undergoing treatment at Seelisberg for her heart trouble, find money for her journey to Saxony, where she saw their old friend Roeckel, now undergoing his fifth term of imprisonment.

And then he got back again to his writing-desk and his piano. On the 28th of June he started on *The Valkyrie,* and before August was out Act I was finished. The fair Mathilde Wesendonck gave him a gold pen for a present. ("I must have a thousand thalers. Anyone who lends it me shall have a bill payable in three months—absolutely square and aboveboard.") What a fool's paradise was Fame! What a lying jade was Hope—hope, the flattering unction you lay to your own soul. He had been making a scrupulously careful copy of *The Rhinegold,* which he finished on the 26th of September. By way of offering himself a little relaxation, he picked up a book which Herwegh had strongly urged him to buy and which had been lying about for some time on his table. No sooner did he begin to read it than it took him completely captive. He glanced at the end; then back again he went to the beginning. He was amazed, transported, completely won. There, in those pages, clearly and logically set forth, he found what he had been driving at all his life long, about pain, personality, the tragic element in life, in *his* life. And quickly he took up his golden pen. "My dear Franz, while struggling slowly and painfully along with my music, I have been turning my whole literary attention to a man that has fallen into my solitary life like a gift from the gods. The man I mean is Arthur Schopenhauer; the greatest philosopher since Kant and the first man to pursue Kant's ideas to their logical conclusion, as he himself says. . . . His governing idea, the final renunciation of the will to live, is a terrible thing to contemplate, but it is the only way to salvation. It was not new to me, of course, and no one could understand it unless it had already quickened as a living idea within him. However, this man is the first to make me see it clearly. When I think of the storms that have swept my heart, when I think how—in spite of myself—it still clung to the hope that things would all be well, even now, sometimes, when the winds arise again and swell to a hurricane, there is but one thing that calms me, one thing that brings sleep to my restless pillow, and that is the sincere, the fervent longing for death. Complete oblivion, utter annihilation, no thoughts, no dreams, that is the supreme, the sole deliverance."

It was only to be expected that a heart so bitter would find in the great philosopher of pain a friend to his art and a grim consoler for himself. From this time forth Schopenhauer was a prop to whom Wagner continually looked for support. It was pessimism he preached, but it was a beneficent pessimism. His idea of the omnipotent will—the universal generator for ever consenting to die in order to create itself anew, the unending alternation of life and death, death and life proceeding one from another in a cycle that never stops—all this shed a powerful light upon his own nature. Since all living beings were but parcels of the one source of energy and had but one uniform mode of action; since they were merely distinguished one from another by the potency of their dreams, their illusions, the individual must sooner or later come to recognize in the universal suffering nothing more than the image of his own suffering, and, thus enlightened, it will behove him to resolve on his own course of action. Then (if he is wise) he will reject existence as an evil, an error. He will abolish his own will to live by killing his own desires. The normal, everyday man gratifies his desires, reproduces his species, and disappears. But the man of finer clay, be he genius or saint, fights against the will to live and ceases to be its slave. By this means he attains to the passive, that is to say to the æsthetic, contemplation of the world, the artist within him looks on and interprets. What then does he see? Suffering. What does he feel? Pity. In their *naïveté*, the saints of Christendom asked only that, when released from the flesh, they should be born again to some higher life, free from the bonds of nature. But the East aimed at something higher than this when the Brahmins of India rewarded the soul with the paradise of nonexistence. True, they accepted the myth of the world's creation by God, but far from looking upon that as a benefit, they represent it as a sin on the part of Brahma, which he expiates in his successive reincarnations. He will only reach Nirvana through an incessant migration in which, by a constant process of purification and regeneration, his spirit will gradually attain to the perfect bliss of uninterrupted oblivion.

Acceptance of death, charity, compassion—such were the cardinal points of the philosophy which Wagner derived from Schopenhauer. And did it not square with what he himself had adumbrated when he assigned to intuitive knowledge a place above the results of reason; with what he asserted in his book, *Art's Work in the Future*, in which he lays it down that all life derives from necessity, that no true art is ever the result of caprice or hazard, but the fruit of instinct ripened and brought to perfection in the forcing-frames of talent. His great poem affords clear proof of this, since it reveals principles of whose range and scope he himself was not fully aware. Those words came into his mind, words he had written as if at the very dictation of the philosopher of Frankfort: "Real consciousness is the recognition of our own unconsciousness." But it was not only his philosophy which captured Wagner's heart; there was something more potently seductive still, and that was his theory of music. For Schopenhauer, music was the universal language, the voice of things, the most delicate mode of expression for all our emotions. Music, therefore, is, in a sense, our surest means of escape from the world of phenomena, since it describes and represents not only human life, but life itself, its most secret stirrings, its dreams, all those bright and elusive gleams that flash like lightning athwart the soul. He sees now, suddenly, into the dark places and hidden recesses of his *Nibelungen Ring*, sees how even its secondary mechanism, the wheels within its wheels, were yet arranged in accordance with the dictates of an ineluctable necessity. "I never really understood my Wotan until then." He had thought to build a work inspired by optimism and revolutionary aspirations; and it turned out that, despite himself, it was a work of pessimism, sounding the eternal notes of sadness, which was conceived and brought to birth by his other, his subconscious, nature. *The Ring* was no fable, no allegory, but a living reality. Nevertheless this very pessimism was capable of inspiring action, of engendering a faith. Therefore it was that he hailed it with all the longing in his soul, hailed it—that hope of the world vouchsafed to man to hallow and to justify his dominion over the universe; and its name is Love. That is the measure to which human heroism will henceforth march—that is the resounding rhythm of Wagner's heroic world. And since, with him, inspiration invariably outstrips experience, he now awaits the coming of Love, even as he had waited for fame, for the revolution, for Liszt and sorrow and Schopenhauer—knowing they would surely come at last. And since come they did, to prove his presage true, he needs must limn upon his fresco yet one vision more, the last crowningly pathetic scene, of his great synthesis of heaven and earth. Even before it had laid its finger on his heart, Love issued from his being's hidden depths, as the central figure of his triptych. On one side Siegfried typifies eternal youth, on the other Wotan stands resigned to death; and in the centre shines the twofold countenance of Tristan and Isolde.

In the same letter in which he tells Liszt about his discovery of Schopenhauer he says: "As in my whole life I have never really known what love is, I design to raise to this, the fairest and noblest of all our dreams, a fane wherein love may find an everlasting home. In my own mind I have sketched out a *Tristan and Isolde*, simple in its musical idea, but full of intensest life; and in the folds of the dark banner that casts its shadow over the final scene I shall enshroud myself for the tomb."

Yet once again the fates obeyed. The woman for whom he longed so sorely, for whom he would have cast aside his art, was no myth; she did indeed exist. He had not beheld her, had not realized her all at once. Slowly and softly she had stolen into his life like a subtle perfume, like a good and gentle habit. There was nothing in the nature of a plot between them; nothing strained or tragic; scarcely even any sense of surprise. There was no apparent change in the long succession of days. The husband was as kind and generous as ever; a real friend. Minna, ailing and moody, grew more and more out of touch with her husband's eager, questing spirit. She went to Germany for a change, and tried various cures for her health; while every evening, Richard, scarcely knowing whither his feet were wandering, bent his steps towards the Hôtel Baur au Lac. In her *salon* Mathilde would be awaiting him, "the Twilight Man," as she had come to call him, who would come with varying moods according to the fortunes of the day. If he were merry, he would talk and jest; if he were weary, he would take his ease; if his heart were laden to overflowing with music, he would unburden it at the piano. Once he offered for her acceptance the prelude to *The Valkyrie* which he had inscribed with three letters as a mark of his regard: G[esegnet] S[ei] M[athilde]. Blessed be Mathilde! Another day he gave her a *Sonate d'Album* which he had written expressly for her. He laboured now no longer like a man alone in the world. His work was an offering. It had an aim, a hidden life. And all those pages and pages of newly created music which, till now, had wasted their sweetness on the desert air, were henceforth steeped in significance, rich in implications. On the 27th of December, 1854, the music of *The Valkyrie* was finished. "Brünnhilde sleeps . . . but I, alas, am still awake." A few days later the treasurer of the London Philharmonic came to see him, having been sent on a special mission to Zurich to enquire of Wagner whether he would undertake to conduct the eight big spring concerts of that old-established association. Wagner accepted the invitation. Since Germany had no need of him, why should he not bring out his new things in England? He started off alone, found comfortable rooms in Portland Terrace, and then proceeded to face the inevitable difficulties with which twenty years of battling with the die-hards of the past had made him only too thoroughly familiar. The Philharmonic people were perfectly agreeable to his having seven Beethoven symphonies, a few samples from *Lohengrin*, and the prelude to *Tannhäuser*, but they absolutely insisted that Mendelssohn, Spohr, Cherubini, Onslow, and—Oh, crowning humiliation!— Marschner and Meyerbeer should have a place on the program. Well, he had to bow to the inevitable. The orchestra was a slave to old-fashioned ideas. The members were tickled rather than angry at the biting remarks of this fussy Kapellmeister. They did not take him seriously. All they were used to was "mezzo-forte," "Piano" and "fortissimo" were quite beyond their stars, and the *finales* they always took at the gallop. It was the same in London as in Paris and Berlin and in every theatre in the world. So Wagner gave up all idea of ever seeing his works properly performed. "The things which I create," he wrote to Liszt, "will never see the light. If I die without having had my works performed, I bequeath them all to you, and if you die without having been able to have them worthily interpreted, commit them to the flames. Let that be a pact between us." Fortunately he made a happy discovery in this orchestra, a young first-violin called Sainton, who came from Toulouse. He took a violent fancy to Wagner and communicated his enthusiasm to the orchestra. Thanks to him, things underwent a considerable change; the rehearsals were now conscientiously performed, and, before long, these excellent mechanics found there was a greatness of soul in Beethoven and a wonderful temperament in Wagner, the existence of which they had never suspected. Though the first concert went down well with the public, the critics were frankly hostile. (It may have been because Davidson, the most influential of them, could not forgive him for what he had said about the Jews). The second, which included the *Choral Symphony*, was a revelation. The only point on which any fault was found with Wagner was that he had conducted the *Symphony* from memory. That was not treating great music with the seriousness it deserved—so, at least, the papers said. Wagner was for throwing up his job and departing forthwith. They besought him to stay, and stay he did. Thenceforward he conducted the greater classics with a score open in front of him. But he quite forgot to turn the pages, and such members of the audience as were furnished with opera-glasses observed with horror that the music was upside down. Nevertheless, the *Tannhäuser* Overture was such a success that Queen Victoria and Prince Albert requested that it might be repeated at the succeeding concert, on which occasion both offered their congratulations to the composer. If those four months in London were terribly uncomfortable for Wagner, he read some things which filled him with delight, among them two Hindu legends, Sawitri, "which is divine," and Usinar, "which is my whole religion." Moreover, he made some new friends, whom he kept all through his life, and he rediscovered an old one, a *confrère* with whom he had been long acquainted. The first of these new-found friends, Klindworth, a quondam pupil of Liszt's, was a visiting music-teacher and gained a meagre livelihood "in the arid wilderness of English life." As Wagner, who had been keeping strenuously at work in his bedroom, had just finished the orchestration of the first act of *The Valkyrie*, he decided to take a couple of days off, and invited his friend's young pupil to dine with him. After the repast, Klindworth seated himself at the piano and attacked his master's latest work, the *Sonata in B Minor*, the most dazzling expression in music of Liszt's sunny personality. Now, all the Wagner-to-be, the Wagner of the future, lay in those high-sounding pages, filled—as are those of the *Faust Symphony*—with phono-æsthetic innovations pregnant with the harmonies of *Tristan* and *Goetterdaemmerung*. Straightway Wagner wrote off to Liszt: "My very dear Franz, I have felt you very close to me. The sonata is beautiful beyond expression, grand, gracious, profound, noble, sublime as you are yourself. It stirred me to the very depths of my being, and all my London vexations vanished at a stroke."

Another friend-to-be who, during these London concerts, listened with fervour to the author of *Art and Revolution* was a young girl. Malwida von Meysenbug—such was her name—though belonging to the lesser German nobility—her father had been a petty Minister in a petty German court—had had her sympathies aroused by the humanitarian and socialistic movement of 1848. She had attached herself to the young communists of Hamburg, had been head of a "Rationalist" school, was acquainted with Mazzini and Louis Blanc, and was now lavishing all her care and energies on the children of the Russian revolutionary Alexander de Herzen, who, like so many other political outlaws, had made his home in London. Malwida professed a lofty idealism, championed the cause of female emancipation, and cultivated the acquaintance of men of distinction. Some mutual friends invited her to dinner to meet Wagner. But Wagner was not in a communicative mood and talked of nothing and nobody but Schopenhauer. However, the young woman was not abashed, and doubted not that one day she would convince him of the value of her friendship. And convince him she did, bringing him to realize the sincerity of a friendship that was destined to endure as long as life should last. As for the *confrère*, that was Berlioz. He had come over to conduct for the New Philharmonic, a rival society. The two composers derived no small pleasure from the little dinners which the invaluable Sainton organized for their entertainment. Yet, though they got on well together, it can scarcely be said that they understood each other. "We went on and drank punch at Wagner's after the last concert," says Berlioz. "He hugs me furiously, saying that he had had no end of prejudices about me. He weeps and stamps his feet. . . . He has a free style of conducting. . . . But his conversation and ideas are very engaging" (no mention, it will be noted, is made of his music). "There is for me something very attractive about Wagner. His ardour, his warm-heartedness, are superb, and I confess that, even in his most outrageous moods, he rather carries me away." Wagner, on his side, informed Liszt that he had taken quite a fresh liking to Berlioz. "Meeting him like this has made me conceive a deep regard for my new friend; he has come out in quite a new light. We each recognize in the other a companion in misfortune, though it seemed to me that I had had better luck than Berlioz." There was no doubt about that; he was better off than poor Berlioz, who had married a second time and married badly, who was misunderstood, lonely, and poorer even than Wagner. "I saw the weariness and despair in the man's heart, and I was seized with a profound pity that so great an artist, and a man so far above his rivals, should find himself in such a plight." So much has been said about Wagner's alleged jealousy of Berlioz, that it is as well to give currency to the facts of the case. Let it be added that for months he kept asking both Liszt and Berlioz himself to send him the latter's scores, and it was not his fault if he did not get them. At the last of these eight concerts, the public accorded Wagner an enthusiastic expression of their gratitude. The whole orchestra stood up to applaud. The people in the front row stretched out their hands and Wagner pressed them warmly. That was the only time, during all these four months of untiring labour, that any emotion had been displayed. He was not sorry, in fact he was overjoyed, when he had finished what he called his martyrdom and was free to go home to Zurich, to the summer, to his manuscripts, and to enjoy some benefit from his "English music," as he called the modest peculium he had amassed from that source. And modest indeed it was. No matter. "Everyone knows he is not on this earth to make money, but to create." But to do so in peace, must he not be furnished with money? He never felt more conscious of his strength. His strife with the world was like one head butting against another. The harder of the two would win, as he said in a letter to Otto Wesendonck. "You, my dear friend, have interposed your good nature between them, doubtless to soften the blows. Mind you don't go and draw some of them on yourself in the process."

But there was a cloud that completely overshadowed the joy of this homecoming. Peps, who has been his ever-faithful companion since the *Rienzi* days, died in his arms. A terrible blow, this, and plain proof that the world, as Schopenhauer says, is nothing more or less than a stage for the emotions. The summer was bad; the autumn no better. He went to Seelisberg for the waters there, for an attack of eczema, brought on by his London worries, was now added to his nervous trouble. Nevertheless, he carried on manfully with his orchestration of *The Valkyrie*, "the most tragic work he had ever conceived," and at last, by the 3rd of October, he was able to send Liszt the first two acts fully completed. And that friend really must come soon and sing and play them over with him. But no Liszt arrives. The princess and her protracted divorce proceedings, the theatre, the Grand-Duke of Weimar, keep him chained to the spot and the best he can do is to write. "Marvellous! You are truly a godlike man: an admirable, colossal work, with its horns marking the rhythm in D. I thrilled with emotion as I read it." And in January of the next year (1856), he telegraphed from Berlin: "Yesterday, *Tannhäuser*. Excellent performance. Staging and scenery splendid. Absolute success. Congratulations." Johanna Wagner sang Elisabeth and, according to Liszt, sang admirably. This, at any rate, made up for a good deal and promised a little something on

account of royalties. But as they were not immediately forthcoming, and as a fresh course of treatment for this cursed
eczema had become indispensable, to whom was he to turn for
help if not to Liszt? "Living is very dear here and I cannot
manage to make the two ends meet, with the resources I've got.
If it were not for my wife I would provide you with a curious
sight; I'd go and beg from door to door, and glory in it." What
should he do? Float a limited liability benevolent association?
Mortgage the Tetralogy? But isn't the simplest and safest way
out of the difficulty still Liszt? And Liszt knows that as well as
he. Though his *Symphonic Poems* don't bring him in a halfpenny
in royalties, though all his surplus funds go in providing for his
mother and his children in Paris, he promises to send on a thousand francs. And Wagner accepts, because love accepts all
things. He accepts because he is unhappy, tormented by the
imperious desire to get back again into some German capital
(Berlin, Weimar, Leipzig, Munich, no matter where) so that he
may make his works live, justify his long withdrawal from the
scene, redeem his position, obtain an amnesty. He would pay
back all he borrowed in twofold measure. "But a proper performance, just one, of my *Lohengrin* is the one stimulus needed,
the only one that will preserve me from irrevocable shipwreck.
. . . Pardon, I only implore all this in my capacity as an artist."
But the king was not of a forgiving nature; the longed-for favour was not forthcoming, and Liszt's thousand francs were
spent on a course of treatment at Mornex, a place not far from
Geneva, on Mont Salève.

Away up in this lonely Savoy retreat to which chance had led
him he at last drank in the joys of real silence. What a blessing
after the din of the three pianos and the flute that made life a
hell at Zurich. He was treated at a hydropathic establishment,
the principal of which, Dr. Vaillant of Paris, subjected him to
a strict diet from which he derived immediate benefit. There
were very few foreigners there, and the country was lovely. He
lived in a summer house with a balcony from which he could gaze
upon Mont Blanc and the Savoy Alps that stretched in an unbroken chain before him. He had the place all to himself save
on Sunday mornings, when he handed it over to a Genevese
pastor, who, as he was pleased to put it, conducted his service
in a place "inhabited by a wicked member of my species." There
was even a second-rate piano there for him to play upon, and
on it he drummed out the *Symphonic Poems* of Liszt, which he
said were "so fine, so incomparable, that it would be a long time
before the critics would be able to place them." Then he read

Walter Scott, on Schopenhauer's recommendation. He also roughed out some verses, *Tristan*, and a new poem, *The Conquerors* . . . "The saint of saints, the most complete deliverance; but I cannot tell you about it yet." What he was alluding to was the great Asiatic idea, the story of Cakyamouni, of Ananda, his disciple, and Tschandala, his bride, which he had just come across in Burnouf's *History of Indian Buddhism*.

In a few weeks, Wagner's eczema, obstinate though it was, had yielded to the treatment of that astonishing Frenchman, Dr. Vaillant. Those who have suffered from the scourge will gauge the measure of his joy.

"Listen, Franz. I've just had a sublime idea: you absolutely must get me an Erard Grand." Nor was that all. He must now have a house, and a garden far removed from all manner of noise. The longing for these things had become a passion with him. Why couldn't Haertel, the publisher, buy his two new articles so that he might at least acquire his plot of land?

While waiting for a reply on this momentous matter, Wagner returned to Zurich and flung himself with a light-hearted zest, such as he had never before experienced, into the composition of his *Siegfried*. All would have been going on swimmingly had not a fresh torment been added to the pianos and the flute. A tinsmith had opened a workshop just opposite his windows, and the noise was as though some one were hammering on his very brain. Richard was for giving up in despair and flinging away his pen and paper, when his exasperation suggested a musical *motif*—Siegfried's anger with Mime, the cunning blacksmith. Forthwith, he sat him down at his piano and worked out the theme, sang it and burst out into fits of laughter. Once more a paroxysm of tortured nerves had plunged him into a kind of creative trance. "Strange; it was only when composing, that the real significance of my poem was brought home to me and its secrets laid bare."

But in the autumn, Liszt and the Princess von Wittgenstein came to pay him a long visit, and the labours, thus ardently begun, were temporarily suspended. Wagner heard Liszt play his *Dante Symphony* and two of his *Symphonic Poems* (*Orpheus* and *The Preludes*) and the experience marks a decisive stage in his musical evolution. "Since then, my ideas of harmony have been very different," he wrote long afterwards to von Bülow. After their departure, he returned to his task, and by February, 1857 the first act of *Siegfried* was entirely set to music.

It was now, after this long succession of restless months, that a great change took place in the tenor of the exile's life. Haertel had refused to buy the *Nibelungen*—unplayable, unsingable, and condemned to death in advance! Thus the last hope of finding some little sanctuary where he might possess his soul in peace was fast disappearing from his mind, when Wesendonck intervened to change the course of his existence. He had purchased, a few months previously, in the outlying district of Enge, a fine piece of ground on a hill overlooking the lake, and on it he had built a handsome residence in the Italian style. He was busy with his plans for laying out the property, when he learnt that a plot of ground next adjoining his own had been acquired by a doctor, who proposed to build a lunatic asylum upon it. Such undesirable neighbours must be kept away at all costs. Wesendonck therefore bought in, at considerable expense, the little house, which was separated by a byroad from his own, and offered it to Wagner for life, at an annual rental of 800 francs.

Wagner happened to be busy composing at the piano when this letter was handed to him. He had come to the scene where Siegfried snatches the sword out of Mime's hands in order to plunge it into the fire himself.

> My father's steel shall do my bidding,
> I myself will forge the blade.

What a sudden glow lit up his spirit when, at the very moment of this interruption he was humming under his breath Notung's triumphal song.

> Lo, the blade is forged.
> Forge, O hammer, forge a doughty blade.
> Blow, ye bellows, make the furnace glow.

"Shall I tell you how I felt today when I heard the unexpected tidings? A deep, deep peace came down upon my heart. To the very depths of my being I was invaded by a grateful warmth, unmarred by any trouble; only a great, bright glow. I beheld the world transformed before my gaze, then solemn tears welled up and splintered the picture into a thousand wondrous fragments. Never, my friend, have I lived through such a moment. My feet no more shall stumble. I know whither I am going, where is my abiding-place, where I shall labour, where I shall find my strength and my repose." How should he fail to divine, veiled yet half-revealed by the missive that trembled in his hand, the countenance, the very eyes of Mathilde? She who for so many months had dwelt within his thoughts stood there as in the flesh before him. Fearlessly she enters now into his life. The "blank page" whereon he had designed to write, was it not now, and only now, that the writing had begun—and was it not she her-self who proffered him the pen? . . . Ah, what youthful ardour, what strength, was in him yet, despite his blanching hair! What tender grace, what sweetly stubborn resolution in one who even now was but a girl—Mathilde! Forty-four and twenty-eight! Well, what of that! He and she had all to learn, and from each other they would learn it. On the morrow the world would begin for them anew! And life, on the wings of love, would have risen from its tomb.

It was Good Friday in the year 1857. Wagner climbed the hill until he stood before the little habitation which had been in part rebuilt at Wesendonck's expense and which he called "The Sanctuary." It was a clear bright morning, and the pure, crystal-line air seemed to be ringing a carillon of fairy bells far and wide out over the world. A few days longer and all would be ready for the moving-in. On this, the anniversary of Christ's death upon the Cross, Wagner would fain look kindly on the world, the world now born for him anew. As he stood before his haven, he heard a voice within him, a voice from far horizons, from distances beyond belief, a voice from the land of Lohen-grin, the City of the Holy Grail whose mystic story he had read long years ago in the summer forests of Bohemia. And the voice spoke to him, saying, "Thou shalt bear no arms the day thy Saviour died upon the Cross." That heaven was empty, he could not doubt. In poetry alone he deemed that love and truth find their divine expression. And the only divinities that he confesses now are three and they still walk the earth: Schopen-hauer, Liszt, and Mathilde! But since this day it behooves us to lay aside our arms in the presence of the Crucified, let His wounds at least convey one lesson to mankind and tell them, not indeed of vain, illusive hopes, but of the gracious miracle of pity.

And on that same Good Friday, while yet the primroses were hoar with rime, Wagner with swift, inspired strokes dashed in the outlines of his *Parsifal*.

◆◆◆◆◆◆◆◆◆◆◆◆◆◆◆◆◆◆◆◆◆◆◆◆◆◆◆◆◆

Chapter IV

THE HILL OF HAPPINESS

BETWEEN the four ill-fated souls who were now dwelling on the Hill of Happiness the secret was well kept. Here, amid surroundings that called to mind some Old World mezzotint, no overt sign betrayed the drama that was moving to its climax in the hidden chambers of the heart. A great artist is at work at an open window that frames a view of the Aberli countryside. In the room beneath, his wife listens anxiously as from time to time he paces to and fro. She spies upon his every movement, tries to divine his lightest thought or act and find a key to its significance. What is he doing? What is he writing? What new means has he now devised to complete the ruin of their dolorous past and smother it amid the roses whereof he weaves for "That Other" his poison-laden bouquets? For many a day now she has realized what manner of leaven was working out of sight. This was not the first time her heart had been tormented with misgiving. Already there had been Mme. Schroeder-Devrient, Frau Pollert, Frau Heim, Jessie Laussot, ambitious actresses or unscrupulous women, all bent on robbing her of her own. But this time the fates had gone to work more subtly than any human agency.

In the well-appointed house on the other side of the way sits a young woman waiting for the hour when her friend shall come to read her a further chapter of their story. Her brows are knit and resolute, and the words she had uttered just now to her husband—cold, calm, convincing words—still seemed to linger on the air. And Otto—today, as now for many and many a day, had departed for the scene of his work with a little poniard planted in his bosom by his wife's own hand, and driven every day a little deeper in, though it was never permitted him to display his wound to the world. He must endure in silence, so that no shadow should come to mar the calm of him whose whole existence was but an endless burden of pain. There was nothing craven in this loving, truthful soul; but, far from that, a dire sincerity and that ineffable ruthlessness that prefers the sword of truth to the cataplasms of compassion. Mathilde had a stronger will by far than Richard, who little guessed the puissance of her womanly instincts. If the last twenty years of his existence had been one long dalliance with death, it should be her pride and glory to set his heart and mind atune again with life. For the peace of his sad heart—so that he may fulfil his task—let the suffering fall on her and on her husband, but let not the poet ever guess the pangs that rend them, nor divine, beneath the glow of passion or the smile of friendship, the tears that pay the price of his repose. Thus, with tenderness and resolution on the one part, with jealousy stifled and silenced on the other, they fondly think to bring to pass a state of things not too unlike to happiness.

At first all seemed to prosper well. Minna found distraction in the pleasures of the garden. The Wesendoncks were absorbed in the arrangement of their costly house, in setting in order their gallery of pictures. And Wagner got through the second act of *Siegfried*. But suddenly new troubles arose in addition to the old, and it became too clear that, despite the charm and sunny beauty of their new abode, the threatened trouble which up to now had been concealed between the two establishments was soon to blaze forth into open war. Minna, tortured by suspicion, never laid aside her arms, and prosecuted with more untiring energy than ever her old campaign of pin-pricks and fault-finding. Otto defended his home with all the skill of a practised diplomat, and beneath the mask of easy nonchalance which he displayed to the world, no one could guess the line that he would take. Mathilde had resigned herself body and soul to the Wandering Mariner, "the man who can find salvation if he meets a woman who shall remain true to him till death." She was Senta, Elisabeth, Elsa, pure love, mystical love, and human love. She was Isolde, the sovereign inspiration, who looks through love and all the pleasures of the senses, to the death beyond, and longs for its repose. Even now Wagner laid aside his *Siegfried*—under the lindens of the second act. "I have ripped Siegfried from my heart and have put him under lock and key like some one that one buries alive. There he will stay shut up, and no one shall see him, since I am obliged to part from him myself. I must work some neat little miracle, so that people may believe in me." But the miracle did not turn out to be the one needed in order to reassure the publishers and revive the confidence he had lacked and lost since the days of *Rienzi*. The miracle was *Tristan*, whereof he stood in need to put the coping-stone upon his work, whence should arise, when seven more years had passed, that mighty scion, the fruit of tranquillity following on the storms of passion; to wit, the third act of *Siegfried*. So, then, he loves and he creates. He creates because he loves. Never before had the well-spring of inspiration reached such heights as now. If he had to endure all day the naggings of his peevish spouse, the joy with which he started forth at eventide to greet his "Muse" was thereby made the sweeter. In the little drawing-room that had now become their kingdom, they clasped each other in a fond embrace. Then Richard would take the manuscript of *Tristan* from his pocket and they would read it over together. One by one, Mathilde gave him the five poems she had composed and which he set forthwith to music. *The Angel; Dreams; Sorrows; Immobility; In the Greenhouse.*[1] What cares he for visits and visiting, for society, for friends, all fleeting shadows in the world's Great Shadow Show? Nothing could interrupt their converse. "A solemn silence" enwraps that summer of 1857, in which Wagner began and ended the poem of *Tristan*. Nevertheless, in the pretty guest-chamber above his study he put up, one after another, Edward Devrient, manager of the theatre at Karlsruhe; Richard Pohl; Robert Franz, the composer; and one day Hans von Bülow, who had just married the youngest daughter of Liszt and the Comtesse d'Agoult, wrote to say he was coming. The couple were on their honeymoon. He was just paying a flying visit to Geneva and Berne, and then coming straight on to Zurich. And so, while Wagner was in the very midst of *Tristan*, and when the twofold drama which he was enacting with his art and his destiny was drawing to a climax, Bülow, whom he had not seen for ages, was hastening with eager joy to show off his bride to his master—his bride, a tall young woman of twenty summers, with features that betokened a lively energy, the living image of the beloved St. Francis, her father. She, too, was fated to become the exile's friend; she too was fated to acknowledge the magic thraldom of his genius. So it came to pass that, at this hour of poignancy and pathos, chance brought together in a single group, upon the fair Green Hill, the girl who had been wedded but a fortnight, his own Isolde, and Minna, the minion of misfortune. But for the first time in his existence, Richard was living neither in the past nor in the future. Only the present counted now, those pregnant hours in which his poem, enacted in real life, scene by scene, was uttered by the lips of Mathilde, as together they plumbed the secrets of a passion for which they

[1] Two of these pieces form the first ideas for *Tristan* (*Dreams*, Act II and *In the Greenhouse*, introduction to Act III).

knew the day of reckoning would surely come, when they would have to pay with tears the price of all their bliss. What matter! After such joys as those and the oblivion they bring, why not the sleep of death? "It is through death that we testify to our solidarity with the living," he had said long ago in his *Jesus of Nazareth*. Death, self-inflicted, was the destined end towards which all his actions lured him. Love is but the last supreme expression of his longing for Nirvana. The passion of Tristan and Isolde—their own—is then the deliverance for which *The Flying Dutchman* had so passionately yearned.

Hans had arrived ill, with an attack of rheumatic fever. When they had been for some days in the Hôtel du Corbeau, Richard went round and brought them both back to his cottage, installing them in the turret-room just above his own. He would hasten away to the Wesendoncks, and, returning, take Cosima for a walk, delighted to find in her such a lively intelligence, such poise, and, notwithstanding a certain timidity which she found it hard to overcome and which occasionally amounted almost to coldness, such strength of mind and all her mother's French grace and charm, mingled though it was with something of the sensitive mobility of Liszt. As soon as Hans was well again, they sat him down at the piano and, with a mastery beyond compare, he played through *The Rhinegold*, *The Valkyrie* and the rough draft of *Siegfried*. And every week, to his select and eager audience Wagner read aloud a new act of *Tristan*. "On the 18th of September," he wrote when, a little late in the day, he was chronicling events for Mathilde, "I finished the poem and brought you the last act. You came with me to the chair by the sofa and pressed me to your bosom, murmuring, 'Now is my joy complete; I have no more to ask.' On that day and at that hour I was born again. Till then my life had been but a preparation, and after it began my posthumous existence. In that one ecstatic moment all my present was summed up. You know how I took it; no tumult, no storm, no wild, tempestuous bliss; but sedately, sweetly stirred to my very depths, gazing calmly on the infinite before me. The world I had left ever farther and farther behind me, and I was consumed with sorrow. My whole being had become a negation. My very creations spoke to me of anguish, longing, symbols of an insatiable desire to find something to oppose to this negation, to this nostalgia, to this renouncement. I was as a man wandering forth in search of a kindred soul. In that supreme moment my longings were fulfilled. A woman, tender, timid, and trembling, cast herself bravely into a sea of sorrow to give me that one adorable moment, to tell me that she loved me. Thus you gave yourself to death that I might live, and I was granted life to suffer and to die with you."

The 18th of September . . . Mathilde . . . "The Sanctuary" . . . Cosima . . . *Tristan* . . . Divorce . . . Death. . . . Such were the wild eddying shapes that whirled through his brain, inspiring him with such a longing to create, that no sooner had the Bülows departed than in a paroxysm of creative ardour he flung himself into the composition of the work that was gnawing at his vitals. To that task he devoted every morning. In the afternoon he went for a long walk in the neighbouring woods with Fips, a dog which Mathilde had given him. In the evening would come a visit to the Wesendoncks or the Wesendoncks would come to them. Scene with Minna! Explanations! Reconciliation! Fresh disputes! Poor soul, it was thus she thought to regain her captive's love, while all he thought about, of course, was how he might make good his escape, once and for all. Yet he hesitated all the same, rent in sunder by that terrible pity which was, with him, an article of faith. "I must make up my mind. And yet, whatever I do, I must inflict pain, and the choice is so cruel that I must have my only friend to advise me, the only friend that God has given me. Hoping to find the solution that will entail the least suffering, I am thinking of going to Paris." Liszt, however, did not intervene. He himself was too much preoccupied. The Princess Caroline's divorce, his work at the theatre, and some other sentimental complications were a sore trial to him. So Wagner hides his head in the sand. By Christmas he had got through a rough draft of the music for the first act of *Tristan*. His wife, however, was becoming ever more and more of a burden to him and relations with Otto Wesendonck were growing increasingly strained. He must have some breathing-space, a little time to reflect; he must find some money and, somehow or another, get out of the *impasse* he was in. Suddenly, in January, 1858, he made up his mind and started for Paris.

Berlioz, who was then at work on *The Trojans*, gave him an eager welcome. He spent one whole evening reading his libretto to his visitor. Wagner found his diction dry and affected and thought it boded no good to the music. He even hoped that he would not meet Berlioz again, "because it would be impossible to illude myself and the other people in such a manner as to keep him in good tune with himself and me." He next called on Emile Ollivier, the barrister, who had recently married Blandine Liszt, Cosima's elder sister. It was a very good thing he did so, for his new friend at once undertook to safeguard his interests in the matter of the royalty dispute. Ollivier's wife was a charming blonde, to whom he felt greatly drawn, the attraction, it appears, being thoroughly reciprocal. In a letter to Bülow he describes her as "profound and calm." Then came another present from Liszt, and the whole Liszt family vie with each other in showering kindnesses on this restless, petulant traveller who seems like a man devoured by some inward flame. Paris itself is all smiles for him this time. People are beginning to talk about this German composer and his operas. Some say they mark a revolution in music. At Hérold's he came across the score of *Tannhäuser*, and Mme. Erard made him a present of a piano, a splendid instrument. At last the dream he dreamed at Mornex had come to pass. Paris was a finer city than he thought. But then, how could he go on staying away from his mistress? Surely he could not suffer the preluding strains of his *Tristan* duet to be drowned in this Parisian hurly-burly. Therefore, he hastened back to "The Sanctuary" to begin, as he imagined, the second act of his tragedy. In point of fact, it was the third and final act of his own life-drama that was about to be unfolded. It was that "Death in Love," so long implored, so often sung, that now awaited him.

"Either part for ever, or for ever be united." People write like that and talk like that; but is such a thing really possible in practice? Mathilde and Richard thought it was possible, the thought, in this case, being father to the wish. But when they came face to face with each other once more, they could not help seeing that it was as impossible to renounce their bliss as it would have been to ensure it by breaking some one else upon the wheel. Now, to cross the Rubicon, to dare all, would be to kill Minna. To give each other up would be to die themselves. Was there no middle course between these two extremes? Could they so sublimate their love that while dwelling so close to each other yet so sundered, they might, despite the world, remain wedded, heart to heart, in a silent, unincarnate union? To achieve that, the flame of all desire would have to be extinguished. But what human lovers would agree, without a struggle, to renounce their surest joys? Richard could not bring himself to relinquish a passion that was yet so young, a passion on which his whole future seemed to depend. As for Mathilde, the twilight of each day and the joys it brought sufficed for her. But Minna had a watchful eye for these love passages so carefully hidden from her sight, and resolved that the lovers should not have things all their own way. She spied the goings and comings between house and house. It was not jealousy, she swore, that inspired her vigilance

—not jealousy, but she hated meanness and deceit, and what she did she did in order to keep up appearances. But the storm was brewing and swiftly gathering to a head. At last it broke. On the 7th of April she noticed that her husband was very excited and restless. Every time the bell rang he came out of his room with a big bundle of papers in his hand. It was the complete sketch of the last act of *Tristan* which he wanted to be taken across to the Wesendoncks'. Doubtless he was expecting some one to come and fetch them. No one came and at last he gave them to his domestic. This was the moment Minna, downstairs behind the curtain of her room, had been waiting for. She called to the man to come back, told him she would take the papers over herself, opened the parcel and took out the letter which she knew full well she would find in it. It was the unhappy letter of a man who was himself unhappy, jealous (of Professor de Sanctis then staying at Zurich and a friend of the Wesendoncks'), all trembling with impatience, breathing tenderness and so profoundly sincere, so truly impassioned! Minna read it through with frigid rage, perhaps a little disappointed.

"Oh no, no! it is not de Sanctis I hate, it's myself for always being so weak. The state of my nerves and the resultant irritation—can that be my excuse? The day before yesterday, at noon an angel came and blessed me. . . . It did me so much good, made me so happy, that when evening came I felt a burning desire to go and see certain friends in order to make them partakers of my joy. . . . de Sanctis was with you. . . . I waited in vain. . . . Happy man, he kept her to himself away from me. . . . Why does she make such a fuss of these pedants? They are terrible bores. . . . I felt in that mood all night. When morning came, I became sensible again and managed to send a heartfelt prayer to my angel . . . and that prayer is love, all love. How my spirit rejoices in that love! Thence comes my salvation. The day dawned and brought bad weather. The joy of seeing you was denied me; I made no progress with my work. And so the whole day went by in a struggle between ill-humour and the longing for you. And every time I felt that I must see you, our appalling pedant interposed—he who had stolen you from me. . . . I had to tell you, I couldn't help myself. . . . But as soon as ever I see your eyes, I can say no more. All that I could say seems to lose its value—listen, all becomes so indisputably true for me. I am so sure of myself when those adorable, sacred eyes fall upon me and I plunge into their depths, that it is no longer a question of subject and object; both become one; all is harmony, infinite and profound. Ah, that is peace, and in that peace

RICHARD WAGNER AND HIS FAMILY IN 1882

is the highest life, ideal life. Mad is he who would essay to gain peace, or to grasp the world, from without. Blind fool, he has not seen your eyes nor found his soul within them. . . . Even to you I can speak only of myself, explain myself, when I see you not. . . . Today I will come into your garden as soon as I see you. I shall hope to find you alone for a moment. Take all my soul by way of morning greeting."

Minna thrust this letter into her pocket, crossed the sunken road, and went to seek out Mathilde. "If I were a common woman," said she, "I should show this letter to your husband." She did not know that Otto was aware of all, that his wife had never kept him in the dark about her feelings. Most important of all, she did not know that he loved his wife with so generous a love that he understood and made excuses for her, doubtless awaiting the hour when the spell should be at an end and the erring one come back to him. Moreover, if he knew the story of Isolde's passion, there might well be a doubt in his mind as to the actual intimacy of her relations with this bankrupt, bohemian Tristan, who, after all, was but an intruder on his territory. Mathilde did not take the affront calmly. She politely showed her neighbour to the door, and then unfolded the affair to Wesendonck. Meeting them in the afternoon, just as they were driving out of their gates in their carriage, Wagner noticed that they looked rather worried and at the same time he thought he detected a little smile of satisfaction playing about Wesendonck's lips. Minna, on her side, displayed a like contentment. He questioned her and then the "explanation" followed—a torrent of angry words, each knowing they had been betrayed and trying to look ahead and to see what would be the aftermath of this painful scene, how far the consequences of this outbreak would extend. Wagner declared that they would not be light. Minna would have to give up the cottage and make the best of things elsewhere. Meanwhile she would have to go away at once for a rest cure, which the state of her heart and the disordered condition of her nerves imperatively demanded. Minna willingly bowed to this decision, for she knew that the battle was won. If she had to pay dear for the victory, well, it could not be helped. Her pride was saved and, with a woman, that means honour. It was not Richard she had been out to conquer, but Mathilde. She could quit the scene now, for the charm was broken, and broken that magic circle within whose bounds the lovers had given free play to their dreams, without a thought for any save themselves. She had aimed true and Mathilde deeply resented the outbreak. Not only had she been flouted by this little underbred *bourgeoise*, but she felt annoyed that Wagner had not been authoritative or frank enough to spare her such an affront. Otto saw his opportunity and took his wife away for a month to Piedmont. But just before they started, the Erard grand arrived at "The Sanctuary." It brought a welcome respite when the crisis was at its height. Wagner had it installed in his room and played it at the open window, and Mathilde, leaning over the balcony of the billiard-room, caught from afar the famous chords as they stole into her lover's mind—the chords of the Night Scene from the second act of *Tristan*. Mathilde bore away in her heart the memory of that wondrous music, *The Song of the Swan*, for it was thus that Wagner christened the ebony piano which wept the last tears of his expiring love. Minna went off at once to Brestenberg for treatment, and her condition became so alarming that Wagner might any day have had news of her death. He stopped behind, all alone, on the Green Hill, and, going for long walks, endeavoured to find rest for his soul in the silence of the radiant summer weather amid whose golden splendours, the neighbouring house, with its closed shutters, looked like a deserted Tuscan palace. The bird-haunted pleasance was filled with flowers and statues—Dianas and Jupiters—brought from Italy for its adornment. Was it meet that he should quit so soon those regions where he had only just come to realize the bitter-sweet delights of existence? Would she forgive him? He went to take counsel of Mme. Wille, his confidante and Mathilde's. Delicately and with a good grace that lady undertook to do what in her lay. Yes, Mathilde forgave him, because she loved him. One day a letter came to tell him so. His joy was profound, grave. It seemed that she was effacing from her heart every sorrowing trace of self. But if he found himself overcome by this fidelity in the face of despair, the certainty of being loved came fraught for him with unexpected power, the only power which could help him to transpose his feelings into that mystical world which it was his aim henceforth to attain—the power of renunciation.

"My child," he wrote on the 6th of July to Mathilde, "I know of but one cure, and that can only come from the very depths of my heart and not from any external circumstance, and its name is Peace. Peace to my heart-hunger, peace to my desires, the noble and meritorious conquest of self. To live for others—the only consolation we can offer ourselves. You see now in all its entirety this decisive disposition of my mind. It extends over my whole attitude towards life, over my future, over all that is dearest to me, and therefore over you, who are dearest to me of

all. . . . I shall not come to you often, and henceforth you will
only see me when I am sure of being able to shew you a countenance that is calm and cheerful. Awhile since, I used to seek
you in order to unburden to you my sufferings and my sorrows.
That must be so no more. If you do not see me for a long time,
pray for me in silence. For you will know that I am suffering.
But if I come back, be sure that I shall come back bearing new
gifts to you both, and such, perhaps, as it is vouchsafed to me
alone to bestow, to me who have so grievously and so wilfully
suffered. Probably, nay, certainly, the time will soon come—at
the beginning of this winter indeed—when I shall take my leave
of Zurich. . . . My child, these last few months have whitened
not a little the hair about my brows. There is a voice within me
that cries out in desperation for repose, the repose for which
my Wandering Mariner voiced his longing many a year ago.
That longing has naught to do with the joys of fleshly love. It
breathes from the home within, the haven of the heart. A dearly
loved and faithful woman can alone procure it for me. Let us
then dedicate ourselves to that sweet end which will appease
and fulfil all our desires. Let us die to ourselves, blessed, transfigured, with the smile of courage on our lips; so that none shall
be vanquished, if the victory remains with us."

Was that a last farewell? By no means. They loved each other
too dearly to separate like that. Nevertheless, facts had to be
faced, and it was evident that the concrete and practical element
in their liaison would now, for a long time to come, be out of
the question. Otto would have to be calmed, and so would Minna.
That peace which he desired so ardently for himself would have
to be restored to those into whose lives he had brought such deep
anxiety. Therefore he must needs set out anew upon the path of
exile, must needs become once more the hapless wanderer fated
never to meet the woman capable of giving up all she had to
throw in her lot with him and set him free from bondage.
"Wherever he goes," Mathilde says, "he sows the seeds of revolt." It was for that she had loved him; it was because of that
that he must flee. Even for Minna his going would spell deliverance. Writing to Liszt, Richard told him how grave was the
heart-affection with which his wife was troubled. "The situation," the famous egoist went on, "imposes new duties upon me
which compel me to relegate my own troubles to the background." Meanwhile some visitors arrived and created a temporary diversion: Tichatschek and Neumann the singers; and
Tausig the amazing pianist, with whom Wagner was delighted.
He was a delicate youth of about sixteen, as wild as a schoolboy

and as wise as an old man, and he went about everlastingly smoking enormous cigars. His skill as a pianist was astounding and he let himself go with rapturous delight on the new Erard. They persuaded him to read Schopenhauer, and he made a wonderful arrangement for the piano of the first two acts of *Siegfried*. Minna also returned; not cured, but a great deal better in her general health. Then shortly afterwards the Bülows reappeared, with the Comtesse d'Agoult, who, to use her own words, had come to Zurich, "to make acquaintance with the great." How like she was to Liszt, her sometime lover! Siegmund and Sieglinde. . . . Klindworth arrived from London. They sang *The Valkyrie* and *The Rhinegold*. However, though he was the centre of attraction and they were all very eager and very interested, there was a feeling of constraint and tension because of the agitation and nervous strain plainly legible in the faces of Wagner and his wife. Amid all this musical excitement, the dénouement of the crisis was approaching.

On her return from Brestenberg, Minna found occasion for creating fresh trouble. The incident was both painful and comic and the effects of it were destined to become apparent as soon as the migratory guests had taken their departure. They left one after another, the Bülows being the last to go. Hans was in tears, and Cosima maintained a gloomy silence. And then the play began. Minna was fool enough to imagine that what she had done had put the extinguisher once for all on her husband's amorous adventure, and that things would now go on calmly, as before; the rose a little drooping, perhaps, but disencumbered of its thorn. Well, it happened that their man-of-all-work had celebrated her home-coming, as Swiss people do, by putting up a floral arch outside the front door, in full view of the Wesendoncks' house. Now Minna wanted the decoration to be kept where it was as a symbol of her triumph. Mathilde naturally regarded this as an affront, and, this time, insisted that her rival should quit the house. Minna refused. Richard endeavoured to make her go and, as she was the weaker party, she had to give in. So that was the end of "The Sanctuary," and whatever bonds had kept the establishment together till then, snapped asunder in the crash.

"The woman is furious, beside herself," wrote Frau Wagner to a woman friend, "so jealous that she cannot bear me to be here. Richard, forsooth, must stay on alone. That he cannot do. He's got two hearts; one of them bewitched. The other clings to me, but purely out of habit, that's all. Since this woman won't have it that I should live with my husband, and as he's weak enough to give way to her, I've made up my mind to go and live at Dresden, Berlin, and Weimar till God or Richard, one or the other, calls me to his side. I am going to sell up the furniture and make arrangements for the move. Richard will go first, I don't know where yet, possibly to Italy. I'm not saying a word to him about all this business, and to outward appearance we get on well together. He gets upset sometimes, but not about me. Whereas all *my* sufferings are on his account. I hate this world, and all the troubles men bring upon themselves through their own weakness." One cannot help being sorry for her. Yet it was all her own doing. And, after all, wasn't she a little forgetful of her own affairs with Schwabe and Dietrich and her goings-on in Berlin and Hamburg? No doubt she thought the suffering she had endured, and the hardships she and Richard had been through since then, had atoned for all that. But who imagines it is possible to resuscitate a dead love, no matter what the price you pay? As for Wagner, he was weak, of course. People always say a man is weak when he is in love and cannot make up his mind whether to forego his new attachment or to break with the old one. In Minna's eyes his duty was plain. It was, of course, to come back to her. But Wagner found his feelings no less imperious. It was her selfishness pitted against his. Perhaps the lover would have ousted the husband but that pity and the memories of twenty years made the forces equal. Minna would not yield an inch. Nor would Wagner. Finally, they decided to separate— on terms. She would leave him free so far as the future was concerned; he would give up living near Mathilde. So he and she, each hugging his and her special sorrow, went their separate ways. "I could not have felt more bitter anguish if I had laid him in the grave," said Minna. "To say good-bye like this was so hard, because I felt somehow that it was going to be for ever. Only once did Richard shed a tear, and that was when he was in the train. Till then he had not had a thought, nor a glance, not a vestige of feeling for me. When I went with him across the garden, he walked beside me as if he did not know that I was there, his eyes fixed on the Wesendoncks' house across the way, totally indifferent to my sorrow until I took him by the hand, saying, softly, 'Richard, come, look at me then.' I could not get rid of the thought that I should never see him again in this world. And yet, if he wrote me and asked me to come back to him now, I could not do it. I assure you I could not. A year, perhaps years, will have to go by before I shall be able to do that."

And Wagner, who had at once begun to keep a diary for Mathilde, opened with one of those chants of death which, for him were ever the songs of love. From Geneva, four days after his departure, he wrote, "My last night at 'The Sanctuary' I went to bed at eleven. I had to be up and away by five next morning. Before I closed my eyes, the thought came to me,—and, oh, how clear!—as it always came to me there before I fell asleep, that in that very room, some day, I should come to die. It was there that I pictured myself lying as you came to me for the last time, and openly, in sight of all, you raised my head in your arms to receive my soul in one last kiss. That death was the sweetest of all the dreams I ever dreamed. It took shape and developed in that room. The landing door was shut; you passed in beneath the curtain of my study; you folded me in your arms and I died with my eyes resting upon you. . . . And now? Is all possibility of my dying thus denied me? Sick at heart, like an outcast, I turned away from the house where I had been imprisoned with a spirit of which I could not rid me, save in flight. Where, then, will it now be that I shall die? With these thoughts in my mind I fell asleep. A strange touch woke me from this troubled dream and I distinctly felt a kiss upon my brow, followed by a gentle sigh. It was so real that I trembled and looked all round about me. Everything was quiet. I lit a candle. It was nearly one o'clock, the time when spirits are wont to fade away. Had some phantom been mounting guard beside me? Were you, at that time, awake or asleep? What were you thinking of then? I could not close my eyes again that night. Long I lay and tossed upon my bed. At last I rose, dressed, and strapped the last of my travelling-bags, then, pacing up and down the room or casting myself from time to time upon the sofa, I anxiously waited for the morning. Morning came, but more tardily than ever before, during any of my long and sleepless nights last summer. At length the rose of dawn appeared behind the mountains. I cast once more a long and lingering look in your direction. O God, I did not shed a single tear! But it seemed to me as though the hair about my temples was turning white. So I had taken my last leave of you! I went downstairs calmly, quite master of myself. My wife gave me some tea. It all seemed dreadful and forlorn. She came with me across the garden. The morning was radiantly fine. I did not look back. When it came to the last goodbye, my wife broke down, weeping and moaning. But my eyes were dry. Once more I pleaded with her to be kind and generous, to seek some Christian consolation. But the old, bitter anger flared up in her anew. Nothing can cure her. Nevertheless, I could not try to make the unhappy creature suffer. She has made her bed and she must lie on it. I was terribly grave, and bitter, and sad; but I could not weep. At last I started, and behold I felt a new man; I breathed again. I was going forth into the wilderness, but a wilderness which is home for me, a wilderness in which I have the right to draw in the love of you with every breath I take. . . . No doubt we shall forget all this and the sorrow will fade away. There will remain for us only a very lofty thought, the consciousness that a miracle has been wrought for us, such a miracle as nature works but once in many generations; such an one, maybe, as she has never worked so triumphantly before. Let us have done with grieving. Who so happy as we? With whom should we change lots?"

In Zurich, the following appeared in the papers:

"Furniture for sale; a great bargain. Owner going abroad."

On reaching Geneva, Wagner had a leather case specially made to hold the letters which he expected to receive from Mathilde. It was understood that he should keep a diary for her and, further, that he should correspond with Elisa Wille. He ran across Karl Ritter again. They had had a quarrel, and had not seen each other for some time, a circumstance that had had rather an adverse effect on his finances during these last few trying months. No sooner did they make it up again than they decided to go off to Venice together and spend the autumn and winter there. They felt as though a long holiday, a healing, restful holiday, was opening out before them.

A few days later the train arrived on the railway jetty and the travellers saw the city a flame of fire beneath the setting sun and they flung their hats through the carriage window to show their joy, and walked bareheaded into Venice. A gondola came up to take the new arrivals to the Piazzetta. The gondola was painted black and its awning was half-drawn. Wagner crept in beneath the sombre hangings and was deeply impressed.

Chapter V

THE DEATH OF ISOLDE

EXTRACTS from the Diary kept by Wagner for Mathilde Wesendonck:

3rd September, 1858. What buoys me up, what remains steadfast in me, is the joy of being loved by you. . . . Venice, the Grand Canal, the Piazzetta, St. Mark's Square—a world that is no more. Everything grows objective like a work of art. I have got rooms on the Grand Canal in a vast palace where for the time being I am alone.[1] Vast and splendid rooms through which I wander at will. The sort of place I live in has always had an important bearing on the workmanship and the material side of my work, so I am taking care that my surroundings shall harmonize with my taste. I have written straightaway to tell them to send on the Erard. It will sound splendid in the lofty rooms of my palace here. The strange silence of the Canal suits me marvellously. I never quit my abode until five, to go and have something to eat. Then comes a stroll in the public gardens and a short spell on the Piazza San Marco, a most theatrical sort of place where the alien throng about me merely distracts my imagination. About nine I go back in a gondola and find my lamp already burning. I get through a little reading, and then, bed. . . . This solitude, which is all I need . . . and which is so pleasant here . . . encourages me to hope. Yes, I hope I shall get well for you. Keeping my health for you means devoting myself to my art. To bring you consolation through my art—such is my task; it accords with my nature, my destiny, my will, and my love. In this manner I am still yours. And you also, you will get well for me. Here I shall finish *Tristan*, let the world rail as it will. And I shall come back again with him to you, to bring you peace and happiness once more. That is the prospect that lies before me as the fairest and the most hallowed of my hopes. Heroic Tristan, heroic Isolde! Lend me, my good angel, lend me your aid! Herein pour the blood of your wounds; your wounds shall be healed. You shall be made whole again. It is from here that the world shall hearken to the triumphant agony of the sublimest love, to the laments of the most dolorous delight.

7th September. I have heard from Frau Wille today. This is the

[1] In 1858 the Palazzo Giustiniani was the property of an Austrian who let part of it as lodgings. Since 1876 it had been in the ownership of Count Brandolini.

first news I have had of you. So, then, you are calm, resigned, and still determined to hold to your renouncement? Kinsfolk—children—duty. How strangely these words fell upon my spirit, in the grave ethereal and almost hallowed mood in which I found myself. When I thought of you, never did kinsfolk, children or duty come into my mind. All I knew was that you loved me, and that whatever is lofty and noble in this world is consecrate to suffering and sorrow. Then, on a sudden, I picture you in your splendid house, I hear your voice, and see before me all those to whom we must throughout our lives remain a riddle, those who are strangers yet, withal, our kith and kin, but who, shaken with vague alarms, withhold from us the very thing that makes us one. And it makes me wroth to think that I must tell you that to those who know you not, and understand you not at all, yet ask all things of you, it is your duty to yield yourself in sacrifice. I cannot bear to see and hear such things, if I am worthily to accomplish my task on earth. Nowhere but in the profoundest depths of my inmost soul shall I find the strength I need; for all things in the world without fill me with bitterness and paralyze my resolution. You hope, you say, to see me for a few hours in Rome this winter? I am fearful lest that could not be. To see you, and then to let you go again, to abandon you to the complacent satisfaction of another—have I already come to that? No, a thousand times no! And so you would not have me write?

13th September. I was so sad, I could not even find a heart to write anything in this diary. And then, today, there came your letter, your letter to Frau Wille! That you loved me, I knew already. You are, as always, grave and thoughtful and kind. . . . I understand you, even when I think you are at fault. But something too much of this! I shall write to Frau Wille soon; yet even in my letters to her I shall keep a hold upon myself. O God, it is all so difficult, and only by self-restraint can the loftiest soul rise to its greatest heights. Yes, all is well; all will be well. Our love is wingèd now and material obstacles do but enrich, etherealize and ennoble it, bringing us ever nearer to its core and essence, rendering us ever more and more indifferent to whatsoever in it is contingent and subsidiary. Yes, my kindest, purest, tenderest one, we shall conquer—the day is already ours.

16th September. Tristan will cost me many an effort yet; but once my task is done, I feel that a strangely significant epoch of my life will then be closed and that I may turn my gaze on you and on the world, with a spirit renewed, calm, clear, and profoundly conscious of itself. That is why I long so ardently to set to work again.

23rd September. Thus, though our lips are mute, we tell each other things that words cannot express.

29th September. This evening, when the sun had set, I took a gondola and went towards the Lido to greet the moon. The strife betwixt the day and night is always a wondrous thing to behold when the skies are clear. . . . I turned my eyes towards the region where you dwell, where you, too, were gazing at the moon, and I searched the heavens for the comet. It had no terrors for me, for nothing henceforth can make me fear, since now I have no hope, no future. . . . Am I, too, a sort of comet? Am I, too, a harbinger of ill? Is all that has happened, my fault? We came back again along the deserted Canal, palaces on either hand. No sound save the dipping of the oar. The moon flung far and wide enormous shadows. Once more I stood before my sombre palace. An immense hall and vast rooms untenanted save by me. I picked up a book and read in it awhile. Then I fell a-thinking. All was still. Suddenly I heard a sound of music on the Canal and presently there came in sight a gondola lit up with multicoloured lamps and filled with singers and minstrels. Other gondolas, thronged with listeners, drew near to hear, and all down the length of the Canal the group went on, gliding so softly it scarcely seemed to move. Lovely voices rang out in song, the musicians accompanying them not without some skill upon their instruments. Every note was clearly audible. At last they turned a corner and, passing behind the walls, disappeared from view. But long after they were seen no more their music, artless as the voice of nature herself, and sounding the lovelier by contrast with the silence of the night, still stole upon my ear. At length all again was silent. The last echoes melted away into the moonlight, whose gentle rays seemed to enmesh and hold suspended some fairyland of music grown visible to the eye. . . . On the table in front of me is a little portrait. It is a likeness of my father (Geyer), which I did not have an opportunity of showing you when it came. It reveals a noble countenance, gentle, suffering and reflective, which touches me to the heart. It has become very precious to me. If anyone came in and looked over my shoulder, he would doubtless take it for the likeness of a woman with whom I was in love. But no. Of her I have no picture. But I bear her soul in my heart.

3rd October. My child, Buddha, the adorable Buddha, was well advised to send art into exile. Who could tell that better than I, since it is art that brings me all my torments and makes my heart the home of unending contradictions? If that wondrous gift, that mighty power of the creative fancy, was not in me, I could follow the clear knowledge and the promptings of my heart; I should become a saint. And as a saint I should have the right to say to you, come, abandon all that holds you back; break the bonds of nature; at that price I will reveal to you the way of redemption. We should be free; we should be Ananda and Sawitri, the disciples of Buddha. But it is not thus with me. For that knowledge, that clear intuition, is for ever making a poet of me, an artist. The moment it unveils itself, it becomes an image to my eyes, an image instinct with life and soul, but still an image which enraptures me. I must needs examine it ever closer and closer, and ever more intensely, so that I may take accurate note of it, develop it, and animate it till I have made it mine, a thing of my own creation. That I may not founder, I turn my gaze towards you. And the more I cry to you, "Help me! Stand by me!" the more you elude me, while something makes answer to me, saying, "In this world where thou takest upon thee such anguish in order that thou mayest give reality to the airy phantoms of thy dreams, in this world, she shall not be thine."

9th October. I have begun to work. At what? I had only the pencil jottings of our *Lieder*, some of them scarcely begun and so indistinct I was afraid, and no wonder, of forgetting them altogether. So I began playing them in order to call them back to mind. Then I noted them down with care. That was the first thing I did. Now my wings have been tried. I have never done anything better than these *Lieder* and few things as good.

12th October. I am now going back to *Tristan* so that it may speak of you to me in the deep harmonies of silence. For the moment, this solitude, the absolute seclusion in which I am living, brings comfort to my soul. It enables me to collect my grievously scattered forces. For some time now I have been enjoying the blessing of quiet sleep, a boon that has never before been mine. May I give its fruits to all of you! I shall profit by it till my marvellous work has prospered and attained completion. Then, and not till, then, shall I see with what manner of countenance the world will look upon me.

24th November. There is no doubt I have never been so clear about myself as I am now, and so, nearly all my bitterness has gone. Whoever knows with a certainty like mine that he has no more to seek or expect, but only to give of what he has, that man, in truth, is at peace with the world. For his aversion to it arose from the fact that he was seeking in it something it could not yield him. And how does one attain to this miraculous power to give? Only by demanding nothing for oneself. Whoso realizes to the full how unique, how unfathomable is the boon to which his heart aspires, is immune from all earthly contingencies, and understands that whatsoever he cannot give, the world may lawfully withhold from him.

1st to 8th December. These last few days I have been steadily going through the major work of friend Schopenhauer, and, this time, he has led me on in the most extraordinary way to enlarge on his system and test the soundness of its foundations. The thing of primary importance is this: to prove that you can attain to a complete satisfaction of the will by love, not by love in the abstract, but by sexual love iself, the love born of the mutual attraction of man and woman, a road which no philosopher, not even Schopenhauer has recognized as being the way of salvation. This line of thought becomes more engrossing to me every day, because it involves data which I alone can furnish, there never having been a man as yet who was, at one and the same time, poet and musician in the sense that I myself unite those rôles; never a man capable of bringing to bear upon these inward motions of the spirit such insight as has been vouchsafed to me and me alone.

Since yesterday, I have been working again on *Tristan*. I have reached the second act, but what music it is becoming! I could work at it all the rest of my days. Oh, it will be beautiful and profound. The most ravishing miracles adapt themselves in it so subtly to the mind. I have never done anything like it and my whole soul blossoms forth in this music. I wish people wouldn't talk to me about finishing it. I wish to live in it for ever and ever, and with me. . . .

Extracts from letters:

20th December, 1858. Up to my eyes in philosophy again. I have arrived at some important results which supplement my friend Schopenhauer's conclusions. But I prefer turning these things over in my mind to putting them down on paper. On the other hand, poetical ideas suggest themselves readily and in large numbers. *Parsifal* has been much in my thoughts. An idea strange beyond all others, the idea of a weird, spirit-haunted woman (the Messenger of the Grail) is becoming increasingly vivid in my mind and holds me spellbound. If I could only succeed in giving form to such a poem, it would be something profoundly original. I wonder how much longer I should need to live if I were to put all my plans into execution.

19th January, 1859. Thank you, dear, for the beautiful fairy tale.

Its style is limpid and, like all that comes from you, seems to be ever invested with a symbolic character. Yesterday your message reached me at the hour, nay at the very moment, of my most crying need. I was seated at my piano. The old pen of gold was spinning its last web over the second act of *Tristan* and, after prolonged hesitation, was telling the fleeting bliss of my pair of lovers when first they were reunited. When thus I give myself with tranquil mind to the enjoyment of my own works—as happens when I undertake their orchestration—I often find myself absorbed in endless thoughts which involuntarily awaken in me the consciousness—so foreign to the world at large—of what it is to be an artist and a poet. What is wondrous in it, I plainly recognize, is that—contrary to the ordinary conceptions of the man in the street—while the latter exclusively bases his ideas on the data of experience, the views of the poet apprehend of their own authority that which gives experience its true significance, its real value. . . . This observation seems to me particularly striking and susceptible of verification in my own special case. My poetic conceptions have invariably preceded my practical experiences, so much so that I am forced to consider my moral development as entirely conditioned and guided by them. *The Flying Dutchman, Tannhäuser, Lohengrin, The Nibelungen, Wotan,* were all in my head before they passed into the sphere of actual experience. But the extraordinary and strange position in which I now find myself in regard to *Tristan* you will have no difficulty in divining. I frankly aver that never did an idea enter so directly into the realms of experience, although it would be intelligible only to the initiate. The question as to how far idea and experience are reciprocally interactive is, to begin with, so complex and delicate a matter that a superficial investigation would only give an incomplete and wholly distorted view of it. Now, therefore, when Sawitri and *Parsifal* fill my mind with the prophetic consciousness of things to come, and are striving to indue a poetic form; now when I am bending in dreamful tranquillity over my *Tristan,* who can harbour any doubts as to the miracle whereof I am the theatre and which withdraws one so utterly from the world, when that world already deems me almost wholly overcome? You divine my meaning: you know—and you alone. . . .

According to the law of the admirable and perfect Buddha, the penitent sinner must confess his sins aloud in the presence of the whole community. Only so can he be delivered from them. You know how I too involuntarily became a Buddhist. Even the rule of mendicity have I carried out in accordance with the Buddhist precepts. Now I mean to read my destiny through and through, not because I would go against it, but in order that I may face it without illusion. Germany I renounce calmly and dispassionately. I have made no plans as yet about my future, except that I shall finish *Tristan.* I shall see if I can complete the sketch of Act III while I am here. I shall certainly undertake the instrumentation in Switzerland, probably not far from you, at Lucerne, where I was very comfortable last summer. Next winter I shall most likely spend in Paris. . . . No doubt future generations will be astonished that I—I of all people—was obliged to make a business deal of my work. But there it is and there is no altering it. And I do not change much; I still have my little weaknesses. I like to be comfortably housed, I like carpets and beautiful furniture, and when I am at home it pleases me to attire myself in silks and velvets.

Finally on the 25th March, he writes from Milan:

Well then, I have said good-bye to my dreamful Venice in your name and now I am as though in a new world, all round me the noise of the streets, dust and grit, and Venice seems like a fairy tale. One day you shall hear the dream which I turned into music there. But a night or two before I left, I had a vision which I will tell you about, although it was too beautiful to be put into words. . . . A pair of doves came smoothly gliding over the mountain tops. I had sent them to you to tell you of my approaching return. Two doves; why two? That I do not know. They were flying side by side. When you described them, you suddenly rose up into the sky to meet them, holding a large laurel wreath in your hand. You pursued them, you frolicked with them, and at last you caught them. Suddenly a dazzling ray of light fell on you, such as you see piercing the clouds after the storm, and the ray was so bright that it awakened me. . . . May Saints Antony and Stephen and all the saints of heaven give you their blessing. I shall not say good-bye, because I am coming so close to you. So take my greeting. Tomorrow I cross the Alps.

Seven months, then, had come and gone since Wagner arrived in the City of a Hundred Silences, seven months in which he had suffered grievously, and worked, and again and again called down curses upon life, ere he composed the loveliest *canzoni* ever dedicated to death. For if his diary and his letters are eloquent of the ever-bleeding wound the parting had inflicted on him, the sweet peace of Venice, the silence of Isolde and the hard yet helpful discipline of acquiring new habits had slowly and surely wrought their healing influence upon the wounded Tristan. As in the last act of his drama, his gaze had long been fixed on the horizon, day after day, week after week, with a hope against hope that tidings would come, tidings that should tell him the long absence was over at last and that Isolde was coming to him through storm and tempest. And if this dream did not come to pass, at least he might tell himself for sure, that she would erelong recall him, that she would write, that he would return to "The Sanctuary" once more, that she could never do without him, and that, from the ruins of their dead passion would spring the mystical ivy of unincarnate love. That was the "victory" that shone like a jewel on every page he wrote. But Mathilde had not come, nor had she written, and the tidings he received through Frau Wille, so meagre and so cautious—how could they have failed at last to convince him that the heart of his beloved had sought the safe and slumberous haven of dutiful resignation? Mathilde had found refuge in the shelter reared around her by her husband, her children, and her duties—all those things that had echoed so strangely in Richard's inward ear. She had embraced the doom assigned. And Wagner too, perhaps. But renounced her, he surely had not. When a man truly loves, he never brings himself to cast away such a passion as that, even though it be at last naught but a bitter memory, a poignant sorrow. And insensibly, that sorrow had become as precious as his love. It mingled with his very being, inspired those cheating hopes whereof he had deemed himself cured, but which kept alive that wistful yearning which he needed, not merely to live, but to create. Here, then, it was that on the warp of feeling he wove the woof of thought; here that Isolde came in place of Mathilde; here that life and death, for a moment interlocked, went their separate ways, leaving behind, as the fruit of their embrace, the wondrous offspring of genius. When he was composing the first act of *Tristan*, Wagner had sped forth on the wings of a hope that coloured all his future. When, alone in the solitude of Venice, he came to compose the second, he realized, on a sudden, how hopeless was his dream of love, and poured forth all his pent-up passion into his music. His whole heart welled forth into his piano. And in thus toiling at his deliverance, he was never truer to himself. For if it had seemed to him at one time that in love man's longing for oblivion found its most exalted expression, Wagner had now reached the certainty that in death alone lay its crowning accomplishment. Yet once again, intuition had been beforehand with experience. And to Wagner we owe the most glorious, the most passionate, commentary on the pessimism of Schopenhauer. The music of *Tristan* is one long lament, one ceaseless cry of love and anguish. Wagner had no need to look about him for the form in which to cast it; from the Prelude onwards it gushes forth as the blood flows from the wound. Its whole musical theme is a motive in four chromatic tones seeking its resolution in a triumphant harmony. But from its very structure, the problem, like the problem of love, admits of no resolution; and this it is, this impossibility of resolution, that supplies the key to the whole drama. The unattainable in music is here the interpreter—the inspired interpreter—of the unattainable in life. So, to solve his enigma, Wagner composed, as an antidote to the Prelude, the famous Postlude erroneously called, "The Death of Isolde," in which these two opposing infinitudes are merged and mingled in one. But Isolde's death is not its burden, but the "Death of Love." As Wagner expressly stated in his subsequent programs, it was the death of a longing unrequited, unappeased, followed by physical death, which he denoted a redemption. What fate has held asunder in life, it saved and made one in death. The gateway of immortal union is now flung wide. Isolde, dying upon the corpse of Tristan, will come at last to the sublime fulfilment of her desire and, free of every earthly trammel, will abide with him in union everlasting in the realms of illimitable space.

Such was to be the theme of Act III, which Wagner wanted to go and write at Lucerne. For he had exhausted Venice. He had gone there to seek refuge, like Tristan at Kareol. There he dwelt alone with his sorrow and gradually came to lose his faith in happiness. As at Zurich, as in Paris and everywhere he went, he was at once penurious and princely. His money had gone on medicaments and decorations; new red damask hangings for the great hall of the Palazzo Giustiniani which echoed to the waves of his passionate music; and ointment for a boil on his leg which it took him weeks to cure. His watch had gone to the pawnbrokers, and likewise a gold *bonbonnière* presented to him long ago by the Princess von Wittgenstein. Some meagre royalties from Vienna for some performances of *Lohengrin* came and floated him off the rocks for a while. But that was only a temporary relief. The King of Saxony still refused to entertain the idea of an amnesty, and Wagner was lucky to be tolerated at Vienna, where he might have been a good deal less comfortable but for the influence exerted on his behalf by Signor Crespi, a high police official and a great lover of Wagner's music. However, neither Weimar, nor Karlsruhe, nor Munich seemed to care anything about *Tristan.* Then again Richard had fallen out with Liszt. His worries, his disappointments, his poverty had inspired him to write his friend a letter ironically twitting him with his "good luck," as he called it. And Liszt, with whom things had recently not been running very smoothly, either in love or in business, was, for the first time in his life, annoyed with Wagner. But such a friendship as theirs could not long remain under a cloud. His last remaining funds for 1858 went on a telegram to Liszt; then, to pledge his health with Ritter and the friends of Venice, he launched out on a bottle of champagne. Shortly afterwards Franz sent him his *Dante Symphony,* thus inscribed, "Even as Virgil was Dante's guide, so have you led me on through the mysterious realms of music so abounding in life. From the bottom of my heart I cry, 'Thou art my Master, and my Author,' and to you I dedicate this work. Accept this homage from a friend whose affection will never falter.—F. L."

Of a certainty, Venice had yielded up her whole secret to Wagner. She had no more to give. He clothed her in music, as he clothed his love. Working, one sleepless night at his *Tristan,* he was leaning over the balustrade of his palace, listening for the cry of the gondoliers as they hailed one another on the Canal, in the stillness of the night, "and I recognised the ancient lilt which Tasso in his day had adopted for his verse, and which is certainly as old as the canals of Venice and its people. . . . And on yet another evening, all the poetry of that ancient folk-tune came home to my heart. I was coming back very late in a gondola along the dark canals. Suddenly the moon rose, shedding its beam on the palaces and lighting up my gondolier as he deftly handled his huge oar at the stern of my barque. Forthwith he uttered a loud cry that sounded almost like the wail of an animal. It was a long moan rising in crescendo to a prolonged 'Oh' and ending with the exclamation, 'Venezia!' I was stirred to my depths, and the sensation remained with me till I had finished the second act of *Tristan*. Perhaps it was that which suggested the plaintive, lingering notes of the shepherd's horn at the beginning of Act III."

So Wagner came back to Switzerland and settled down at Lucerne, at the Hotel Schweizerhof, where he rejoined his friend "Swan" *i.e.*, his Erard grand. He had rugs nailed against the windows of his rooms to deaden the sound of the neighbouring pianos. He started on the third act. There were days when his heart was absolutely sterile; others when the music welled forth in a quenchless spring, and he wrote Mathilde, saying, "It has become quite evident to me that I shall never discover anything new. This great efflorescence has implanted in me riches so great that it suffices me now to draw upon them for all the blossoms I require. . . . *Tristan* is becoming something overwhelming! That last act. . . . I am afraid they will forbid my opera, unless some shoddy performances make a thorough hash of it. That's the only thing to do to bring it through alive, for if it were perfectly rendered, the people would go mad."

However, the great event to which Wagner had so long been looking forward at length took place. At last he saw Mathilde again. Otto Wesendonck invited him to come, thinking thus to put an end to the tales which the charitable gossips of Zurich had been industriously disseminating. Thus plainly to prove that they were friends was surely the best way of stamping out all these rumours. Wagner hurried off, mounted the Green Hill, and the lovers who for eight long months had not so much as set eyes on each other now stood face to face. "It was a sad meeting, but wholly without embarrassment," he wrote later—much later —on. "It was like a dream within a dream. Nothing seemed real to me." But those who delay too long to bring to pass some imagined reality which they have long pondered on and moulded to their dreams—how should they not be cruelly disappointed, when that reality appears before them, not arrayed in the romantic vesture of their cheating dream, but in the plain, prosaic garb of everyday, when their future is only discernible to the threadbare warp of the past. No enviable experience, such a meeting. It was all very well for Wagner to exclaim just afterwards, "We could only bear to meet again because no separation had ever been really possible." Before long his changed world inspired him with a different tale: "Present, we see each other no more; only when absent one from the other do we at length behold ourselves."

They still loved each other, but only the soul of their love had survived the long-drawn trial of silence. The physical part was dead, smothered out of existence, and Mathilde henceforth was what Liszt happily denoted "the ambassadress of the Ideal." She, with her gift of insight, knew that their love could only live on at the cost of her refusal—and that, doubtless, was to be the price of Tristan's ransom. Wagner found her with her husband at her side and compassed about by her son and daughter, and still wearing mourning for a child that had died some months before. Her sombre presence helped him to regain his calm. He now could write without constraint to the woman who had ceased to rack his heart, but, rather, fortified his convalescence.

Work was easy to him now, nay, a thing of joy. Every morning he went for a ride on horseback, made plans for a lengthy sojourn in Paris, and at last, on the 9th of August, put the final touch on his mighty 'score. The long task was over. He telegraphed the news to Liszt. But now, without repose or respite, he must needs take steps to turn into cash this precious reliquary of his suffering. Who, on such a pledge, would advance the 10,000 francs he needed to keep himself and Minna, and to pay for the projected stay in Paris. "Dear Friend," he wrote on the 28th of August to Wesendonck, "can we not fix up a business arrangement together?" Wesendonck? And why not? Would it not be an absolutely convincing proof that there was no ill-will between them? All the same, it would scarcely do to make *Tristan* the subject of the deal. One can understand that. It should be the *Nibelungen Ring*, unfinished though it was. Since he had no heirs, it did not matter to him if he gave up all his rights in the Tetralogy to Otto, keeping only for himself the percentages payable by the theatres as and when the operas were performed. "If you agree to my proposal, I will have a regular deed of sale drawn up on the lines of the draft enclosed herewith. In exchange for my copyright, I should stipulate for a payment of three hundred louis d'or—*i.e.,* six thousand francs. On this basis there would now be due from you twelve thousand for *The Rhinegold* and *The Valkyrie,* the two works already finished." And Wesendonck agreed. For the entire Tetralogy he advanced twenty-four thousand francs. No doubt he considered that this bargain offered him a sufficient guarantee that his rival, now under a fresh and heavy obligation to him, would be absolutely at his mercy. This business man was no mean diplomat, and if some have called him a dupe, he really proved himself the possessor of a keen psychological insight. Mathilde would never have forgiven him for cold-shouldering the man who had opened her eyes to the tragedy of life, the man whose life-story she knew would ever be interwoven with her own. And Otto knew her well enough to feel sure that magnanimity towards the vanquished would be his best weapon. Moreover, he could not, in a way, help liking this man, this artist whom he had watched for so many years now, battling with the world and paying for each defeat with a new creation. The pride of this bankrupt, so confident in the future, filled him with amazement and admiration. Mathilde and posterity would one day pay the husband for his apparent credulity. As for Wagner, he wrote, a few weeks later, to Hans von Bülow: "I have spent four days with the Wesendoncks at Zurich. The husband is most devoted, and in truth one must admire him. We have established relations of a very fine and very rare order, which show what a really serious nature can rise to, even when other gifts are absent. Here, then, is a husband who is at once the sincerest friend to me and to his wife, whose affections, however, he has had completely to forego. I take credit to myself for the development of this situation. I have been guided throughout solely by the desire to stand by this poor woman. Well, extraordinary as it is, the thing has come to pass. Several visits have been exchanged between Lucerne and Zurich. I have always stayed at their house and I have done so to help this loyal-hearted woman to bear her difficult life, while the husband was genuinely glad to see me a visitor at his house. That is a good piece of work and I defy anyone to imitate me."

It would indeed be no light task; and not the least singular thing about it is that he should have written such a letter to von Bülow, of all people. But the latter never dreamt that Wagner would one day make him play the part of Wesendonck. "Why prepare me such a hell as this, from which no heaven can redeem me?" groaned King Mark when he beheld Tristan and Isolde locked in each other's arms. Now that Tristan had disengaged the embrace of two arms too weak to hold him, now that he had passed through his "Death of Love," he was becoming once more the Wanderer, the Mariner launched in the pursuit of an unattainable peace. "One day, however, he may gain deliverance, if he finds on earth a woman who shall be faithful to him even unto death." Of that loyalty, Mathilde had not been capable. Did there really exist the Senta of the ancient ballad, ready to sacrifice all for the repose of the eternally Unappeased? Would it be Paris that would give him that repose, that so hostile, yet always fascinating, city? At that time everything was devoted to the honour and glory of the "Latin Sisters," France and Italy, united against the ancient Austrian foe. The victories of Magenta and Solferino had just been celebrated. On the 15th of September Wagner arrived more rich and more lonely than he had ever been before. "Here am I once more in the 'Inferno,' with the 'Paradiso' far behind," he wrote to Otto. "But happily I am firm enough now to keep a firm foothold on the green field which serves as the vestibule to Hell."

Chapter VI

"TANNHÄUSER" IN PARIS—THE DEATH OF TRISTAN

IN THE year 1859 Wagner little suspected that he, or rather his music, had a following in Paris. Nor is that surprising, since not a single one of his operas had been produced there. He knew little of France, and still less of the French people. What was more important still, he had never encountered, in Paris, any of those great popular outbursts of enthusiasm, nor—save in the case of a few compatriots by this time scattered far and wide— had he experienced any of those enduring friendships which awaken an artist's affection for the clime in which the best and most abiding of his gifts had come to their flowering-time. Nevertheless, though he knew it not, the light of his genius had reached, as it were secretly and without observation, the seemingly frivolous capital of the French Empire. "Seemingly," we say, for, in reality, Paris was the only city in the world where art was looked on as other than a pastime, appealing as it did to the native virtues of the race and so firing their imagination as to bring the inward speculations of the mind to flower and fructify in strong and passionate fulfilment. Wagner deemed he had come to Paris for no other purpose than to hear a good orchestra now and again and to establish regular relations with the main organizations, the chief "going concerns," of the musical art. The real truth of the matter was something very remote from that. "People flock to the great centres," says Paul Valéry, "to get on, to triumph, to better themselves; to have a good time and devour their substance; to merge their lives and change their natures and, in a word, to gamble, to expose themselves to the greatest possible number of chances for good or ill. . . . Every big city is a vast gambling-establishment." When, therefore, the Venetian dream had melted into thin air, Wagner felt that he must forthwith play for heavy stakes at the biggest table in the most brilliant of all casinos, and by bringing off a *coup*, regain his self-esteem. He had a taste for running risks and was never afraid of losing. His gambling instinct prompted him, this time, to call up all his reserves and put them on the unlikeliest, the most speculative, card on which he could possibly have staked his fortunes. The thing had come off before, when he had risked his mother's annuity in a Leipzig gambling-hell. It would come off again.

And Paris was agog for his coming. Not the crowds, nor the professionals, nor the little fashionable cliques on the lookout for something strange to lionize; but a few artists and poets and good fellows; modest, quiet-living folk, whose sober convictions are more important for a man in the long run than anything the serried ranks of prejudice or the organs of blatant publicity can do to make or mar him. On his return from a tour in Germany, Théophile Gautier had spoken with enthusiasm about *Tannhäuser* in the *Moniteur*. Baudelaire had the music played over to him on the piano. Champfleury, the novelist and painter, exhibited such a grasp of it that Wagner himself confessed that he never had known any pen save Liszt's produce such pertinent observations on his style. One day, when he went to see about getting his furniture through the customs, he was respectfully approached by a young employee who eagerly put himself at his disposal, informed him that he was acquainted with all his works and that he had, hung up on the wall over his piano, a medallion portrait of the man whom he hailed as "master." The name of this admirer was Edmond Roche. Wagner made a note of his name and address. Two women also were eagerly awaiting his arrival—Malwida von Meysenbug and Blandine Ollivier. Finally, there were some others whom he did not know, such as Léon Leroy a teacher of music, and Dr. Gasperini. The latter called on him immediately after his arrival. He had found Wagner in a purple velvet dressing-gown, on his head a beret to match—magnificent, but a little eccentric. The two men hit it off marvellously well, and Gasperini and the composer immediately sallied forth in search of a house that should be at once commodious and quiet. Their choice lighted on a little residence with a small garden in front, No. 16 rue Newton, between the Avenue d'Iéna and the Avenue Josephine in the new district of the Champs-Elysées. The house had a charm about it, but was sadly out of repair. Octave Feuillet, the novelist, had just vacated it. There were a number of little things that required seeing to at once, and the owner, who insisted on a three years' lease, was asking 4,000 francs a year for it. But what mattered that, seeing that he would be staying in Paris most

likely for the rest of his life? And—notwithstanding his arrangement with Wesendonck—he had just pocketed 10,000 francs
which his new publisher, Schott, had sent him from Mainz in
respect of his *Rhinegold*. So Wagner installed himself on a scale
of unprecedented magnificence with what was left of the furniture at "The Sanctuary"—the green sofa, the large writing-
table—and at once started getting the text of his *Tannhäuser*
translated into French. Royer, the tenor at the Opéra had the
job to begin with; but he betrayed a lack of perseverance in his
task. Wagner then remembered Edmond Roche, the Customs
House enthusiast; but as his German was not good enough, Ru-
dolph Lindau, the song-writer—in whom Wagner thought he
had discovered "a genius"—was put on to assist him. So great,
alas! was his ignorance of French, as well as of German, that
it became necessary to get Charles Nuitter to begin the whole
thing over again. Meanwhile, Wagner had been going from M.
Carvalho's offices at the Lyric Theatre, to M. Royer's at the
Grand Opera, no longer, as twenty years before, as a candidate
for the chorus, but as one parleying on equal terms. Carvalho, it
seems, was really alarmed when he heard this man in his strange
accoutrements banging out chords on his piano and yelling at
the top of his voice fragments of some work or other in which it
seemed that the mystical element was battling for supremacy
over resounding military marches. . . .

However, nothing was decided. *Tannhäuser*, which everyone
discussed, and nobody knew anything about, was going to be
very difficult to stage. There were no singers equal to such parts.
Wagner grew worried and nerve-racked. He knocked off work,
and saw with alarm that, while his money was dwindling, his
expenses were increasing, for he had never lived on such a scale.
As if all this wasn't enough, he now learnt that Karlsruhe would
not take *Tristan* because they considered it unplayable. And he
had been counting on that to put him in funds. The money he
had got from Wesendonk and Schott was melting away. Wagner's thoughts began to revert to Mathilde, to the Swiss mountains, to the peace and quiet of his beloved "Sanctuary." He
couldn't help confiding to Otto that he would like to cut the
whole business and get back to Switzerland. "Let me be free to
go on creating the works I conceived there, in that wondrous and
peaceful Switzerland . . . miraculous works I should never have
thought of elsewhere."

And then, one day, back came Minna from Dresden. Minna!
So the eternal separation had lasted just fifteen months! But
this also was a matter of minor importance, now that the "Death

of Love" was accomplished. And he owed some consolation to the worn-out companion of the old days. "You must manage the house and look after the cash; everything shall be as you say; but you mustn't do any work yourself; you must have help." So in addition to his valet and the cook, he engaged a nurse-companion for his wife. Thus they began again on the old "friendly" basis and, as formerly at "The Sanctuary," Richard had one floor to himself, and Minna another. The drawing-room they shared in common, but it was forever swarming with people whom the poor woman avoided, either because she couldn't make them out, or because she was scared by them. But Wagner himself was in his element among this motley crowd. He started holding Wednesday receptions—his *"mercredis"*—which were frequented by such people as the Olliviers, Baudelaire, Malwida, Champfleury, Gounod, Nuitter, Countess Kalergis, Berlioz, Frédéric Villot, curator of the Louvre, Gustave Doré, who made a sketch of Wagner conducting an orchestra of spectres, Jules Ferry, and Baron Erlanger.

With all these people about her, Minna was always jealous and always ineffective. Her husband was friendly, attentive, even, but he studiously avoided anything approaching intimacy. He never confided in her, and she never asked any questions. She laid down the law to the three domestics, with whom she was often at loggerheads, ordered the meals, and went out for walks alone or with Kietz, who was now back again in Paris, and she looked back with regretful longing on the old days in the rue du Helder and the rue Jacob. That was their *real* Paris, the Paris of *Rienzi*, of the *Faust* Overture and *The Flying Dutchman*, the Paris of dear old Kietz, of Lehrs, Anders, and Robber, the City of Hunger and Hope. Whereas the Paris of the *Barrière de l'Etoile*, however much it might become Richard's City of Glory, could never be more than a travesty of those old, happy days. She loathed all these well-dressed strangers, these *dilettanti*, and above all this Blandine Ollivier in whom she instinctively scented a rival, and who (like that other at "The Sanctuary") would come in at any time of the day, go straight up to the "master's" rooms, and never so much as trouble to have herself announced to the "master's" wife. An impertinent, self-confident little thing, like her sister Cosima, who, if all reports were true, had already been giving von Bülow some food for painful reflection. These two "advanced" young things were very unlike their delightful grandmother, old Madame Liszt, who had now become her confidante. Never mind. Whatever happened, Minna was determined to hold her own; she would not be vanquished!

"Not I!" she wrote to one of her women friends, "I wouldn't hand over my Richard to anyone." In order to get the Parisians tuned up to hearing *Tannhäuser*, Wagner decided to get up three concerts by way of introduction, and for that purpose he hired the "Salle Ventadour," at that time the home of Italian opera. Von Bülow hastened to the scene to support his master and, under his direction, excerpts from *The Flying Dutchman, Tannhäuser, Lohengrin,* and *Tristan* were copied out. But even at this early stage the rehearsals were anything but plain sailing. Wagner insisted on strict discipline and the musicians said that they would be hanged if they were going to stand that sort of Prussian bullying. In order to bring them round he had to invite the whole lot to luncheon. On the 25th of January, 1860, the first of the three concerts took place. The house was packed with people, among whom were Meyerbeer, Gounod, Ernest Royer, the aged Auber, and Marshal Magnan representing the court. But Wagner had omitted to invite the press. . . . The audience were enthusiastic—they started to cheer during the March from *Tannhäuser*—and the newspapers were of course ironic or spiteful. "Wagner is a great musician," said the *Menestrel*, "but his tendencies are deplorable. Fifty years of such music and music would cease to be." "Music without melody [that was the usual complaint]; all formulas and diagrams" (*Messager du Théâtre*), "A revolutionary," said another, "a musical Marat." As for the celebrated Fétis, he made this entry shortly afterwards in his *Biographie universelle des Musiciens*: "To-day curiosity is satisfied and indifference has taken its place. The music which was to be the music of the future, is already the music of the past." Nevertheless, the Parisians, according to Bülow, showed more intelligence, courtesy, and artistic feeling in their attitude towards Wagner, than the Berliners. For the second and third concerts hardly any seats were booked, and they hurriedly filled the place with paper. But although the hostility of the press landed him in a loss that worked out at 11,000 francs, and although Berlioz made himself rather unpleasant in the *Débats* about the music of his quondam friend, it was quite evident that a dead set was being made against him, a circumstance that provoked a popular revulsion in his favour. People did not really understand the artist in him as yet, but they dimly divined him. How should they have realized straightaway that his art was transitional, a stepping-stone to something new, especially in a program made up of fragments? "That art," he said, in a letter to Mathilde Wesendonck, "is wholly dependent on life, but my particular task is precisely to create, by the necessary transition and preparation, the state of mind requisite for its reception." Who was there capable of understanding these gradations? A few artists, perhaps, but certainly not the public. To Wagner, as for so many foreigners, France was not a land of poets, but an arena for rhetoricians and grammarians to display their prowess. The French language was too definite, too impatient of the vague undercurrents of the instincts, and Music, that *sesame* of the inexpressible, was the only means of finding a way to French hearts. But was Wagner's music going to work this miracle? Great was his surprise to receive from Champfleury a brochure taking up the cudgels on his behalf. It was still greater when Baudelaire sent him a couple of those spontaneous and incisive letters which compensate an artist for all his mortifications. Shortly after this, the beautiful Mme. Kalergis, hearing of his financial quandary, sent him, in the most natural manner in the world, through Malwida, the sum of 10,000 francs, observing that people who looked after Wagner stood to gain a great deal more from him than he from them.

Besides these, there were others who gradually rallied to the cause of the mishandled musician, among them Princess Pauline von Metternich-Sandor, wife of the Austrian ambassador; Count Albert de Pourtalès,[1] at that time Prussian ambassador in Paris, and Count Hatzfeld, his attaché. These were supporters and worth having, for they were all in particularly good odour with the Empress Eugénie. So Wagner was talked of at the Palais des Tuileries, and M. Royer, director of the Grand Opéra, received orders that *Tannhäuser* was to be performed in the theatre of the Imperial Academy of Music. Fould, the Minister at the Palais, was apparently anything but pleased, but Napoleon III, who had given his word to the Princess Pauline, stuck to his guns. Wagner was taken to interview Count Bacciochi, His Majesty's Chamberlain, who asked him what his story was about. "Ah," exclaimed he, "it's all right, then. You don't bring in the Pope? I was told that you brought the Holy Father on the stage and that, you know, would never have done. We know now, monsieur, that you are richly endowed with genius; the Emperor has commanded a performance of your opera."

All this, coming so suddenly, seemed like a dream. But wasn't there some mistake? Well, there was. The very first interview he had with him, M. Alphonse Royer requested Wagner to intro-

---

[1] Albert de Pourtalès was descended from a French Huguenot family who had gone into exile on the Revocation of the Edict of Nantes at the beginning of the eighteenth century. At the present day the family numbers three branches—French, Swiss and German.

duce a ballet into his second act. The thing was preposterous. Wagner offered to withdraw entirely. In his inmost mind he was not now so keen on this performance. He saw that they were bound to make a terrible mess of it. Up to this point he had regarded it simply as a matter of prestige. He now realized that his instincts had not misled him and that things would come to a deadlock, it being Royer's desire to please the public, and Wagner's to please the Muses. The director insisted. The essential thing was to placate the group who were at once the most faithful and the most exacting of the Opera's supporters, namely the members of the Jockey Club, who wanted to see their mistresses dance. . . . Wagner thought it over. Perhaps he could extend the Venusberg scene in Act I. "No good at all," said Royer, "the Jockeys never turn up in the theatre till they're well on with the second act." Wagner wouldn't allow any further tampering with his work. However, he at last took back his score and rearranged it, composing a Bacchic Song to which Nuitter adapted a new dialogue between Venus and Tannhäuser, with the final result that Royer accepted it in that form. Moreover, Royer was a good-natured, obliging man, and he had received definite instructions to do everything he could to meet the composer's requirements. Never—except at Dresden, when he was making his début—had he been so completely and intelligently obeyed and understood. For the rôle of Tannhäuser they gave him Niemann from the Theatre Royal, Hamburg, who was engaged at the fabulous rate of 6,000 francs a month for a whole year. The celebrated Mme. Tedesco was to be the Venus, and young Marie Sax, Elisabeth. Although he came off nothing like so well as his interpreters (Wagner was to get 500 francs for each performance, of which he was to pay his translators fifty per cent of the first twenty), he lived in a state of perpetual amazement at the turn things were taking, and a sudden sensation of pleasure, of consciousness that he was being made much of and of a consequent kindliness to all the world came over him. Never had any musical work been so much talked of as his *Tannhäuser*, and he might well boast of being as famous in 1860 as he had been obscure twenty years before. He had, therefore, no grudge against Babylon, nor even against Berlioz, his ill-starred, embittered rival, who had now married again and married badly, and who had not received from his Emperor a tithe of the support and encouragement which was being lavished in such unlooked for profusion on a mere stranger. So, when Berlioz published an article on *Fidelio*, he wrote him a letter out of the fulness of his heart to say how it had delighted him, how he agreed with and admired it. He even addressed him as *"cher maître,"* a thing he had never done before. Wagner has so often been accused of injustice towards the most illustrious of his French colleagues (and later on he afforded plenty of grounds for the accusation) that we feel in duty bound to draw attention to some remarks he made to Liszt. "The fact that I wrote in those terms to the great man so dogged by misfortune, has brought a strange warmth to my heart. Berlioz's article has made it clear to me, once again, how lonely are the unfortunate, and that he too is tender and sensitive. A richly gifted man can only find an understanding friend in a man of similar endowments, and I have come to the conclusion that we—that is to say you, he, and I—make up a self-contained, exclusive triad, because we are all three alike. But we must take care not to tell him that; he puts his back up the moment one talks to him about it. My friend, so dear, so kind, unique among all others, when am I going to see you again?"

The work went along merrily. They said *Tannhäuser* was going to be a regular battle, a second *Hernani*. Wagner, all tuned up for the coming fight, did marvels in the development of his Venusberg, where, in the necessary adjustment of the music to the words, the absence of the tonic accent in French, the even stress laid on every syllable, gave the passage a totally different sound-value. It was a truly happy time. The composer was seen on horseback in the Bois de Boulogne (but only once, for on his second outing the animal took fright in the Place de l'Etoile, and began to rear, and the cavalier thought it wise to take it back to the stables). After that he was seen every morning taking a long walk with his dog Fips. He wrote his *Letter on Music* to M. Frederic Villot, which figures by way of preface in the French edition of his *Four Operatic Poems*. Before long the rehearsals at the Academy of Music came on to add to his mental tension. "Never before," he confided to Liszt, "have I had placed at my disposal the material requisite for a really outstanding performance. All I hope is that some day a German prince will do as much for my new compositions. My works have gained so many whole-hearted admirers that, on the strength of what they have said, the Emperor has decided to give orders on a truly imperial scale, and I have an absolutely free hand. . . . I am sure to have the best singers there are and my opera is being staged with more zeal and attention to detail than I ever experienced in Germany." The *chef de chant* was excellent, a model of conscientiousness. The scenery—by Desplechin, who, long ago, had done the scenery for *Rienzi*—was quite to his taste. Everything was first-rate except Louis Dietsch, the conductor, the identical person who, in 1840, had been mentioned as a candidate to supply the music to *The Flying Dutchman*, instead of Wagner. In this department, the old, the everlasting, squabbles between creator and interpreter broke out afresh, for, needless to say, Dietsch thought himself a much better conductor than Wagner. To begin with, Wagner treated him like a machine. But he soon got so exasperated at the shortcomings of this regimental-band sergeant that he went for him furiously. They were continually quarrelling, and on one occasion Dietsch was observed to be beating one time with his bâton, while Wagner, seated on the stage, was beating quite another with his hands and feet. That sort of thing was not calculated to make things easier for the performers. Wagner asked that Dietsch might be superseded, and offered to do the conducting himself. But as the rules of the Opéra did not permit a composer to conduct his own works, that was of no avail. The Emperor was asked to intervene, but he said he could not go against the regulations. By way of compensation Wagner was allowed to have as many rehearsals as he wanted. Then other troubles cropped up, to show him that his evil star was still above the horizon. The cutting of a new avenue in connection with Baron Haussmann's reconstruction scheme, involved the condemnation of part of the rue Newton, and Wagner's house was shortly due to be demolished. His lease, which had stipulated for a considerable payment in advance, therefore fell in, as by *force majeure*, but the landlord refused to refund a single farthing. Reluctantly, therefore, he saddled himself with a lawsuit, had to interview advocates, law-court officials, and so on, and finally moved to No. 3 rue d'Aumale, a dismal house not far from the Opéra. All these worries brought on a chill. A few days later his temperature went up and Gasperini diagnosed typhoid, with a possibility of meningitis in the offing. *Tannhäuser* had to be postponed till the Greek Kalends.

For several days he was delirious, tended with devotion by Minna and this providential doctor. It was touch and go, but at last his constitution pulled him through. He was still barely convalescent when he went back to the theatre, where, of course, the rehearsals had been completely hung up. His prestige, however, had not waned during these weeks of absence. On the contrary, it had increased, as the growing hostility of the official and professional world clearly demonstrated. Berlioz, Meyerbeer, and the *Débats* were openly ranged against him. Even Count Walewski, the successor of Fould, would have it that there

must be this ballet in the second act, the idea which M. Royer
had had on the brain. Wagner would not give way; but he was
no longer under any illusion; it was clear now that the thing
was bound to miss fire. He wanted to withdraw his work, but the
authorities at the Opéra would not return it, as they had sunk
too much money in it. So there it was. Neither Paris nor Germany
nor Switzerland had the least idea of his requirements. Well,
that merely proved that artists have no country, or rather they
carry their country about with them. "Mark my words," he
wrote to Liszt, "we have not got a country of our own. If I am
German, I carry my Germany about inside me. . . ." And to
Mathilde he exclaimed: "*Heimatlos* . . . neither town nor village nor country. All is strange to me, and the only country
towards which I turn my gaze with infinite desire is Nirvana."

At the Café Tortoni, France, Germany, and Italy sometimes
sat down side by side in the persons of Mm. Auber, Wagner, and
Rossini. Old Rossini was modest, and liked to discuss theatrical
matters seriously. He gave Wagner the impression of being a
survivor of an age to which he had perhaps done less than justice, since it bred men to whom the honour of art was a trust
they faithfully observed. Rossini lamented that he had not gone
in for a career in Germany, saying, "I had some facility, and
I might have done something." Auber, when Wagner tried to
say something nice to him about his *Circassienne*, replied with
a laugh, "Oh, let the farces take care of themselves," and then he
eagerly inquired how *Tannhäuser* was progressing. "Ah, so there
will be something to look at? Then it will be a success right
enough; no fear about that," and he rubbed his hands with glee.

At last the great night arrived. The long-expected *première*
took place after no fewer than a hundred and sixty-four rehearsals, which had already become legendary. The performances
were no less so. "Wherever he goes," Mathilde Wesendonck used
to say, "Wagner brings life with him." She sometimes added,
"and revolution." That was never more true of anything than
of these famous nights when there were mingled together in
what Baudelaire calls "one of those solemn crises of art, one of
those *mêlées* in which critics, artists, and public merge their
passions in one welter of confusion," a great creator, a few enthusiasts, lately fallen beneath the spell of the demiurge of the
Venusberg, a public on the tenterhooks of excited expectancy, a
band of critics animated by a blatant and preconcerted hostility,
and a handful of imbeciles such as are only too easily got together whenever it is a case of "ragging" a foreigner who inter-
feres with their established customs.

All went well during the first scene of Act I. Indeed, the vast audience seemed inclined to greet certain passages with marked approval. When, however, the curtain went up on the next scene, which disclosed the Wartburg dominating the valley, some dissentient murmurs became audible. Wagner looked nervously out of the managerial box, thinking the disturbance betokened the arrival of the Emperor and the court. Nothing of the sort. At this point, the opposition had arranged for a concerted outburst of laughter. Certain critics (Wagner believed Meyerbeer had brought them), the leader of the *claque* and his acolytes, whose services Wagner had made it a point of honour to decline, gave the signal for some well-organized explosions of laughter which, from then onwards, punctuated the rest of the performance. There was laughter at the famous oboe *ritournelle*, laughter at the *Pilgrims' Chorus*. The Princess von Metternich leaned out over the rail of her box and broke her fan in a gesture of annoyance, and the audience, exasperated at these too obviously premeditated interruptions, seemed for a moment disposed to rally to the author's support. . . . There was nearly a free fight. . . . During the second act calm was restored. But when Niemann came on again in Act III a loud voice shouted, "Another pilgrim," and the whole audience, strung up with excitement, burst into a roar of laughter. That was ruin, absolute and irretrievable, the more terrible for being so utterly stupid. However glorious this reverse may seem to us, now that sixty years have passed, at the time it spelt ridicule and nothing else. "One would almost have needed not to be a Frenchman, to have kept from laughing," said a journalist next day.

What one did need to have was courage, courage to keep the second performance on the bills. Nevertheless, it took place on the following evening, the 18th of March, the great subscribers' day. As on the previous occasion, the first act was loudly applauded, especially the final septet. The composer and the artists were beginning to think the conspirators had been routed, when, during the second act, a broadside of hisses burst suddenly forth. M. Royer turned to Wagner with a look of resignation on his face and said: "That means the Jockeys are here. It's all up." And it was the fact that the gentlemen of the most aristocratic club in France had arranged this manifestation in order to prove their attachment to the traditional ballet and their displeasure at being deprived of it, as well as to display their taste for the music that commanded their preference. True, there were some protests; a few people shouted, "Outside with those Jockeys"; but the Emperor himself did not venture to rebuke these "lions," who belonged, nearly all of them, to the Imperial household. In spite of these squalls, the performance went on. Niemann was singing his grand solo in the third act, when he was interrupted by catcalls. Snatching off his pilgrim's hat, he flung it, over the heads of the orchestra, at the people in the stalls, as he might have flung his gauntlet, and, bowing low towards the royal box uttered some words that were drowned in the uproar. For a moment there was complete silence. Then the storm broke out again more fiercely than ever, because the artists and the musicians had the effrontery to carry on. Whereupon Niemann began deliberately singing out of tune. Bülow wept with mortification. Kietz, who had been vociferously reviling the doughty band of hissers, had by this time lost his voice; Minna was shaking all over with fright. Wagner alone seemed imperturbable. But one can readily imagine the hatred that would certainly be fermenting in the bosom of a man subjected to such treatment. He demanded that the third performance should be the last and that it should be held on a Sunday, a non-subscription day. But of the three battles, this last was fated to be the fiercest. The Jockeys turned up in force, armed this time with little silver whistles on which the words "For *Tannhäuser*" had been specially engraved. The composer's friends and supporters came in a body; the combat was fiercer, the interruptions more vehement than ever. Mademoiselle Sax and Morelli (Wolfram) sometimes had to wait ten minutes before they could establish contact. Wagner stopped at home, drinking tea and smoking his pipe. He definitely withdrew his opera as from the next day. "The real tragedy for me," he wrote, "is that my boldest enterprises are at the same time my bread and butter."

These three scandals cost the Opéra 250,000 francs. Wagner received his percentage and duly paid Roche, the customs official, his share. The whole year had been taken up in preparation for this Parisian début and when everything had been accounted for, it brought him in the sum of 750 francs. But he had no regrets. In spite of all it was, together with *Rienzi*, his most instructive, his most amazing, victory. "God grant me such a failure!" exclaimed Gounod. Berlioz said nothing. His silence was eloquent. And Jules Janin, Erlanger, Catulle Mendès, and Prince Edmond de Polignac were proud to declare themselves friends of this victim of public opinion. He was elected to the committee of a large and fashionable club, a rival of the Jockey Club. It became the thing to give an international status to a revolutionary whose æsthetic and philosophical ideas, and above all his reverses, would bring him to the top tomorrow, for it is only our defeats that enlarge our frontiers. Some enthusiasts went so far as to suggest starting a Wagner theatre; and if Germany never betrayed such overt hostility as he had recently met with, yet never had his art been greeted with such genuine and lasting fervour as had been his lot in Paris.

Three weeks after this envied defeat, Baudelaire published his pamphlet on *Tannhäuser* in Paris, predicting that the day would come when Wagner would be fully avenged for the insult that had been offered him. "People who imagine they have got rid of Wagner are crowing much too soon, we must tell them. . . . They don't know much about the swing of the pendulum in human affairs, or of the ebb and flow of popular passion. Today the reaction has set in; it began the very day that Spite, having entered into an alliance with Folly, Red Tape, and Envy, did its best to bury the work." It was a fact. The reaction started at once. It has been going on for sixty years. A handsome revenge. In 1931 we find an eminent composer and critic delivering himself as follows in giving an account of the week's music in Paris: "Wagner on Saturday, Wagner on Sunday . . . that's going it strong. Alas, I am bringing no charge against the musicians of the Association. People must live. Up to now, what one could always rely on selling was something to eat or drink. Now we shall have to add *Tristan* and the Tetralogy to the list. That is how time brings its revenges. It is also a corollary of the improvement that has taken place in the public taste. The time will no doubt come when what sets the teeth of many people on edge today will slip down the throats of their descendants like barley water."

Wagner quitted Paris with indifference. "One becomes all-powerful when one can treat the world as a joke" (letter to Mathilde). The fact is that he belonged to a time when today was nothing and tomorrow all in all. His confidence in his creative powers was too firmly established for him to be conscious of any misgiving about himself. Among his admirers he could count poets and ambassadors' wives, and fame has no significance of any positive value unless one is loved. Never had Wagner been less sociable, never more individual, more solitary, than he was now; no one could offer a more striking contrast to the revolutionary of 1849 than the derided composer of 1861; no one was less like Rienzi, tribune and mystic, than the Tristan of Venice who had breathed his last over the lifeless remains of his dead love; no one a greater foe to Eteocles than his brother Polyneices. The myth was being fulfilled. Wagner had been

Alberic, the man who desired greatly and longed for power. He had been Siegfried, the Youth of the World, Poetry, and Revolution. Until on the very threshold of his maturity his heart was spotless and cruel, his heart on which, when the appointed hour should strike, Isolde was to inflict an incurable wound. He was now worthy to become Wotan. Now that he had been the incarnate medium of all the possibilities that fall to the lot of youth, he had gained the right to assess them at their proper value, to laugh at them, and, knowing well what he was doing, to choose the rôle of that tragic god who, to a happiness that failed to achieve his ideal perfection, preferred the destruction of the Valhalla that had been reared to accommodate his unattainable desire. It was then the Traveller—the name with which Wotan disguises himself in the Tetralogy—that now set forth upon the road. Thanks to the intervention of Metternich, Pourtalès, and Hatzfeld, he was enabled to dispose of his establishment in the rue d'Aumale and he therefore started for Vienna, where he witnessed a performance of his *Lohengrin*. The whole house— orchestra, singers, and audience—gave him such a rousing reception that he was moved even to tears. It was the first time since *Rienzi* that he had tasted glory. He rose in his box and with a bow remarked: "I have just heard my work for the first time. . . . What am I to say? Let me bear my burden with humility; aid me to accomplish my artist's ideals. That you can do by preserving your regard for me." He grew to love Vienna, because Vienna was kind to him. Here and everywhere and throughout his whole career the public were on his side. His foes were the critics, the professional coteries who deemed that they had the exclusive prerogative of laying down the law on all matters appertaining to the arts. Still Wagner's works were well known, especially in the concert-room, where Johann Strauss—"Blue Danube" Strauss—had played the overtures and sundry excerpts from *Tannhäuser* and *Lohengrin* long before the operas as a whole had been performed, with a success by far more brilliant than in any other city.[1] It seemed that Vienna

---

[1] Johann Strauss and his brother, Eduard Strauss (sons of the Strauss whom Wagner had heard as a child), laboured loyally to popularize Wagner in Vienna throughout a period of several years, and they merit the gratitude of all Wagnerians. When Wagner decided to repeat one of his Vienna concerts, Eduard, who had a promenade concert fixed for the same evening, decided to cancel it so that not a single member of his audience should Wagner lack. Wagner, for his part, was one of Strauss's warmest admirers. One night, at a dinner, he invited the company to drink "to all our classics, from Mozart to Strauss."—(Ernest Newman, *Fact and Fiction about Wagner*, 1931.)

was, of all cities, the one where he was best understood and where the means of staging his works seemed to offer some chances of success. He, therefore, decided to stay on there for some little time, for he now made up his mind that it was useless to attempt to settle down permanently anywhere, and that it was better to remain a *sans patrie*, calling no country his own. He went back to Paris to put his belongings together, and there learnt a surprising and important piece of news. Thanks to the efforts of Albert de Pourtalès, a Prussian passport was granted him, which once more gave him access to Germany. For ten long years he had been waiting and hoping for this amnesty, but now when it had come at last, his joy seemed somewhat flat, as occasionally happens with hopes too long deferred. He sent Minna on to Dresden and himself made a stay of three weeks with the Pourtalès. A drawing-room was put at his disposal, a quiet apartment overlooking the garden, in which was a pool with three Australian swans. In this peaceful chamber his Erard was installed—his own particular Swan—and here he composed his *Black Swans*, which he dedicated to his hostess. "I am looked on as one of the family," he wrote to Malwida von Meysenbug. "I am enjoying a momentary sense of well-being because of the delightful quiet of this house. . . . To be alone, absolutely alone, that, when all is said and done, is the one thing I long for. I am extraordinarily tired. Two good years have been utterly wasted. Still, what Art has lost, it may be that Life has gained."

At last, after twelve years of exile, he found himself back in Germany again. His first visit was to Liszt at Weimar, where a National Musical Festival was in progress. Franz was in the theatre when Wagner made his appearance. He ceased the rehearsal he was conducting. Then followed a complete silence. The door opened and the composer whom Paris had greeted with hisses came in to be hailed by an assembly of artists who for ten years past had looked on him as the foremost composer in the Germany of his day. The two friends stood locked in a long embrace and gave full rein to their emotions. Liszt was living alone at Altenburg (for a year past Princess von Wittgenstein had been in Rome, awaiting her divorce). The old house in which they had lived so happily together, and which had recently been like the abode of the dead, with poor St. Francis on the eve of a nervous breakdown, suddenly came to life again. Twelve guests had been invited for the festival, among them the Olliviers, Bülow, Tausig, and Cornelius. Wagner made the thirteenth. Was that a bad omen? Liszt was superstitious—but Wagner would have it that it was a sign of good luck. For sometime past now the friendship between Marsyas and Apollo had been suffering an eclipse. His jealous princess was the cause of that. She was afraid the flute-player would have too much influence over the feminine temperament of her divinity, and over his work, too, and she had, therefore, done her utmost to keep them apart. "Liszt has become very communicative," Wagner had recently confided to Mathilde. "They've taken advantage of his weakness to keep him in a horrible state of subjection. . . . But he loves me still, because he is loyal and magnanimous." Now it was a union of souls; they were again united, and Wagner once more made a triumphal entry into his friend's heart, a heart ever fated to fall under the spell of the magic flute.

Franz then left for Rome, where he expected to be married, and Richard returned to Vienna. The Olliviers invited him to go round with them by way of Reichenhall, near Salzburg, so that they might all go and take a glance at Cosima von Bülow who was there undergoing a sour-milk cure. The friendship that had sprung up in Paris between Wagner and Blandine had by no means cooled off and the expedition was fully the light-hearted affair they had hoped it would prove to be. The two sisters talked over all their affairs and Blandine related how Wagner, before leaving Paris, had made her a present of his writing-table. A few days later they said good-bye. Blandine and Cosima never saw each other again, for Mme. Ollivier died shortly afterwards at her husband's place at St. Tropez. Just as they were about to part, a silence seemed to fall upon the three of them, a silence which hinted that there, in that little far-away village, it was Heaven's will they should spend awhile in silent communion with their souls ere they entered upon the fresh turning in the path of destiny which, though it lay right before them, was yet hidden from their sight. They looked at one another in silence, and in the eyes of Cosima Wagner beheld a question, one of those mute interrogations that leave behind them a memory more durable than speech.

At Vienna that look still haunted him. Four months he lived there, a restless, purposeless existence, making little advance in the tasks he had proposed to himself. Solitude weighed on him more heavily than ever. "I feel more and more that I am nearing the end of my earthly journey," he wrote to Mathilde. "I have no object in life now. . . . Nothing gets hold of me these days. . . . I have no more faith in anything. There is no way to my heart save for those who mingle their tears with mine." Seeing how near he was to a nervous breakdown, the Wesendoncks invited him to join them at Venice. Towards the middle of November, Richard went, and again beheld his Isolde amid the scenes where, three years before, he had so unavailingly desired her.

"Frightful weeks," he wrote to her soon afterwards . . . "the horrible end of things; I am through with it at last. . . . Now, and not until now, am I completely resigned." What that meant was that for once King Mark had triumphed over Tristan. A single hour was enough for Wagner to realize this, to feel in every fibre of his being that the bonds which had still been linking him to Mathilde were broken at last. She was happy—a crushing thing for a lover to discover. . . . At all events, she seemed to have forgotten, and the most agonizing proof of that physical severance she now revealed to her lover—in the following spring she was expecting again to become a mother. . . .

There and then, on the very instant he wanted to tear himself away. Mathilde kept him back. She alone could soothe the pain which she knew obsessed him like an agonizing dream. If *Tristan* marked the grave wherein their love lay dead, Richard should plant beside it the deathless flower of their twofold recollections. Why, she suggested, should he not resume the *Meistersinger* of which, long ago, he had let her have a sketch? The idea came to Wagner like a saving grace. It was the only way for him to make his peace with the world. *Die or create!* Such was his device. How thoroughly she knew him! And so, despite the wrench which he knew full well was final, he blessed her through his tears, she who consented to survive him in order that he might fulfil the destiny for which she had moulded him. Wagner, in a letter to Frau Wille, thus records his feelings: "She was and will remain my first and only love. She was the culminating point of my life. The years of anguish, the beautiful, love-burdened years, lived beneath the enchanted shadow of her presence, in her ever-glowing hold upon my heart—this sums up all the sweetness of my days."

Venice then should be their burial-ground. There, Isolde had been the first to die—in Tristan's heart. And now Tristan's hour had come and in the soul of his beloved he too lay dying. Thus was fulfilled the presage that had flashed across his spirit after his flight from "The Sanctuary," when, with head uncovered, as though in honour of the dead, he set foot in that dark gondola draped as for a funeral.

Chapter VII

THE WORLD MY TRIBUTARY

DID you ever chance to see, in some seaport or other, a man just home again after many years abroad? Do you remember how, still hardly believing his eyes, he strode up the familiar street, looking lovingly at the houses he knew so well, staring at the shop windows, eagerly gazing about him and presenting such an air of childlike curiosity that the passers-by cannot forbear a smile. Back from his lonely life, back from the everlasting sun and magical mirage of his tropical abode, he soon adjusts his vision to the old familiar sights and takes on the *blasé* expression of those who have never been tempted to set sail in search of the Islands of Desire. Something like this is the man who has lived through the excursions and alarms of a passionate love affair. Awakened awhile ago, from his long trance, he knows not whither to bend his steps. Nothing in particular attracts him now, yet everything affords him something to look at, dreams have vanished, but mediocrity, that solid basis of the world's morality, is there to take their place. And so he reaches out like the rest, to grasp the substance of things, to claim his share, and forgets that he was ever a poet.

Wagner has come back again into the world and wave of men. He has said adieu to Mathilde, the *Nibelungen* and *Tristan*, those régions where he blazed the trail. To forget, and to work— this is what he had made up his mind to do. Everything was endurable now, since happiness had ceased to be his goal. His inward life should be art and artistry, a hymn chanted to the things that are not, across the world of the things that are. He went back to Paris, to the Hôtel Voltaire on the quays, where, over against the Louvre and the Tuileries, he shut himself up to write the book in which he celebrates the craftsmen of Nuremberg. And once again the stream comes flowing forth as though the ancient wound, opened anew but a day or two since, was destined to furnish an inexhaustible spring of fresh blood. Now

as ever it was from a time of stress and difficulty that he drew
his liveliest and most original inspiration. Beneficent weeks were
these, weeks that made him whole again. Tremendous work,
walks, and talks with the *concierge* and the waiters, such, he
writes to Malwida, "were my four happiest weeks, the only time
I really lived." In these friendless days, some of the loveliest
he had ever spent, reaction inspired him with the airiest and
serenest of his works. Never did any poem give him such joy in
the writing as the *Meistersinger*, that procession of Gothic
tableaux, born of the impact of his fancy upon the French classic
mode. It was when passing through the galleries of the Palais
Royal on his way to dine at the Taverne Anglaise that the
melody of Hans Sachs's couplets on the Reformation came into
his mind. That character haunted him; he was dear to his heart.
He is the Wotan of the *Meistersinger*, the poet of bourgeois
life, the man of ripe experience whose passions were at rest and
who could look back without bitterness upon the past. Hans
Sachs was the philosophic hero in whom Wagner portrayed himself. He is "the peace which renunciation brings to the heart."
Love henceforth is naught to him and, tendering him a last regret and bidding him as it were farewell, Hans Sachs recalls for
Eva and Walter, the couple he takes under his wing, the sorrowful tale of Tristan and Isolde.

> My son
> Of Tristan and Isolde
> The story sad I know,
> The fortunes of King Mark. . . .

Doubtless Wagner, who was now close on the fifties, seriously
deemed that the days of *Tristan* were past, and held, like the
cobbler of Nuremberg, that "the seduction of eternal youth
would henceforth bloom no more save in the poet's laurel crown."
As for King Mark—that should never be his rôle.

His work finished, he proposed to take it to his aforetime
hostess of the Garden of the Black Swans, who had recently lost
her husband. Despite her bereavement, Mme. de Pourtalès made
him welcome, and on the very evening of his arrival he read the
whole thing through to her. Thus, says Wagner in his memoirs,
"she was the first person who heard the finished poem, and the
impression it made on us was sufficiently lively to make us burst
out laughing again and again."

Wagner had now nothing further to keep him in Paris, and
he began to look out for some sequestered spot where, amid
entirely new surroundings, he could work at his music undis-

turbed. Settling down with Minna in Dresden was hopeless. Richard sent her subsidies out of the money he made or the money he borrowed, and he wrote her regularly, reminding her, when occasion offered, that he had done his level best to rub along with her and "keep the home together." Alas! things had come to such a pass that even an armistice was out of the question. Every time they had come together she had promised not to rake up the past and never to mention the name of Mathilde, so that silence on either side should be the proof—a melancholy one indeed—of their self-control. That was her promise, but she never kept it. Jealousy, with her, had become a disease which poisoned her whole system. A chance allusion, a mere word, even a date, was enough to bring on an attack of hysteria. Poor soul, she was past curing, and she knew it, and so she resigned herself to separation—without divorce. She had celebrated her silver wedding all alone. "The twenty-fifth anniversary of our wedding day," she wrote to a friend, "my husband sent me for a present a gold bracelet and a year's leave. 'In a year,' that is what he said, 'we will meet if we can, at Munich, or somewhere on the Rhine.' . . . If I could blot out those twenty-five years from my life, perhaps I might get my spirits back again. I shall be here until next April. Where my wanderings will take me after that, the gods alone know. And that's what we owe to the Tristans." Tristan indeed. To be alone and to work—to forget—freedom from care and what he called "a naïve and indefectible morality," those were the notes of Wagner's present state of mind. He now took it into his head to go and pitch his camp near Mainz, in the neighbourhood of his new publisher, Schott, who had agreed to let him have his advances on the *Meistersinger* and the Tetralogy (25,000 francs) within a few months. Besides that he was fond of the Rhine, and the spring of 1862 seemed rich with promise; particularly as the King of Saxony and his advisers had come to the conclusion, after twelve years' investigation, that Wagner was hardly to be looked on as a political firebrand.

The majestic calm of the great river, the country, the walks, the silence in his heart, the tranquil activity of nature, how good it all seemed to him. He settled down at Biebrich, in the villa of an architect who rented three rooms, overlooking the Rhine, and once more "undid his corded bales," his furniture, his carpets, and his books. The Schotts made him welcome and gave some parties in his honour. He read his *Meistersinger*. It was much admired. They lauded him to the skies. Really there were some very nice people among these prosperous bourgeois, quite a little

world of enthusiasts, agreeable women, charming young girls.
One of them, it seemed, had known some one who had known
Schopenhauer. How very interesting! At one of these "evenings"
at the Schotts' Wagner was put next to a Mathilde Maier, a
pretty girl of twenty-nine, with easy natural manners, who immediately took his fancy. Before many days were out they were
fast friends.

Mathilde Maier was the elder daughter of a notary's widow.
She lived at Mainz with her mother, a brother and sister both
younger than herself, and two aunts. There was something in
Wagner's melancholy air that attracted her. And he, divining
a kindred spirit and one to be trusted, warmly responded. He
became a visitor to the family, and liked to stay and gossip, and
conceived a great liking for the young woman who bore a name
to him so dear. "Ah, child, I shall soon be fifty now. At my age
a man has but one sole need, and that is what my Flying Dutchman needed—calm after storm." That had nothing in common
with his way of life on the Green Hill, and yet in this free and
open exchange there was a charm that reached his heart. This
simple, in some ways almost too simple, girl, brought rest to his
soul. On her side the new Mathilde admired him desperately and
was entirely wrapt up in trying to serve him. But there were no
demands about it all, no sentimental complications, no King
Mark. She possessed one great art to perfection, the art of
silence. It was exactly what he needed for the atmosphere which
was to bathe old Nuremberg in its gracious charm. Things
couldn't have happened better. And so when he awoke on the
22nd of May, his birthday, to receive a present of some fine rose-
trees from Mathilde, small wonder he exclaimed, "Since this
morning I have realized that the *Meistersinger* is to be my
masterpiece." However, in spite of the sedulous transplanting,
his heart had left behind a root or two in the old soil. For, less
than a month later Wagner was making his first declaration to
Mathilde. Already he addressed her with the familiar "thee"
and "thou." Already he could not get on without her. "All that
gives richness to the human soul makes you worthy to be loved.
And I love you in your whole being, your sweet, your firm yet
pliant nature. You are so diverse, yet always so sure and so true,
that I would not merely have this piece or that of you to make
them mine. So you will be all in all to me, even though it be never
granted me to possess you. For me you will be a last well-spring
of the noblest purity. And if I find in you the woman in whom I
can bring my development to perfection, you will not regret
falling in with me on your path. Let us trust our star, our

destiny. Join with me in working at that which is ours, our inward life. Only the vulgar are happy; one way alone leads the noble to salvation, the way of sorrow." All unwittingly he uses the phrases he had used long since. Does it ever occur to him that he had written almost those selfsame words before? The soul had received its lasting imprint, and the heart, stained at its source, tinged all his blood with the same passionate hues. Mathilde Maier, however, struggled with the energy of youth against the sombre fatalism of the Wandering Mariner. She was not cast in the tragic mould. For her the sap of youth was stronger, not indeed than love, but than the lure of death. And it was precisely that which Wagner divined in her, precisely that which attached him to one so richly endowed with sane, sound sense. She gave him back just what he needed to fortify his powers and revive his energies just when they seemed doomed to fade away. But this Eva in love with her Hans Sachs was not the only woman that watched over the welfare of the poet. First of all there was Minna. Her husband continued to write her letters of enormous length, seeking to pacify his irritable spouse, to make her feel that he cherished, with feelings of affection, the memory of their common past. He went out of his way to play on her feelings, and gave her the impression that he had need of her. So one fine morning along she came from Dresden. Wagner was not in the least put out; she would be able to help him arrange the furniture. Moreover, Minna was looking better and seemed anxious to make herself agreeable. What about living together again? Couldn't it be done, if she behaved properly and did not nag and storm? Her husband enveloped her in an atmosphere of affectionate solicitude and they spent a happy evening together. It was the only one, for, by a remarkable coincidence, the very day after her unexpected arrival the postman handed in, under Minna's very eyes, a letter from Mathilde Wesendonck of whom Richard had been without tidings for several weeks. And the day after that came a little box with some Christmas presents which had been sent in error to Vienna and had remained there ever since. You would have thought the whole thing had been prearranged. The unhappy Minna could not contain herself. She broke out into a violent fit of hysterical weeping. She went through all over again, and seriatim, the whole catalogue of her grievances in terms that Wagner could not admit. Ah, terrible yet sorrow-laden Minna! Richard himself was moved to pity for her. Yet he, her husband, with nerves sensitively alert to anything harsh or grating, to the cries of animals in pain, to the tortures of cut flowers (he could not look at a rose unless it were growing in the soil), when it was his tortured wife that was in question stopped up his ears and became once more inexorable. Henceforth nothing could cure their mutual hatred. If it is intolerable to be reproached for a living passion which is tearing your very vitals, how much more cruel is it to be called on to defend that which is merely a memory and nothing more. No peace was possible between them now. Each had devoured the happiness of the other. They looked at each other face to face aghast, for in that brief and violent outbreak they read all the pent-up horrors that the future held in store. "Ten days' hell." That is how Wagner described it to Cornelius. And yet the young musician, Weisheimer, with whom the composer was on friendly terms, observed how attentive he was to his wife, going out of his way to order from the hotel hard by the things she liked best to eat. Weisheimer went for walks with them and listened to a reading of the *Meistersinger*. Wagner had donned one of his celebrated velvet dressing-gowns for the occasion. He had been through the list of the characters, told her the various parts they enacted, and was describing the scenery—where this was and where that—when she flung a piece of bread full in his face, crying, "Yes, and here's the audience!" Wagner started up, pushed away his papers. "For heaven's sake," he said to Weisheimer, "stop here the night!" If he had been alone with her, perhaps he would have struck her. She went back to Dresden. "It's a certainty I cannot live with my wife any longer. . . . My heart bleeds, but I know I must show no weakness, for our only chance lies in firmness and sincerity. . . . My wife will manage. . . . I'll make things look all right. A divorce is and always will be an impossible thing for me. It is too late, and I loathe the heartlessness of the proceedings. My wife will take the furniture and settle herself in Dresden. She will keep a room for me in the house. Maybe I shall go and stay with her for a week or two now and then. I'm quite certain that any faltering on my part would only prolong the agony for us both. O God! here am I beginning to shed tears. And then, I begin to dream. Suppose I were to find some friendly feminine being who would give me a kindly welcome. But no; all that is over and done with now. And so it seems my wife will be avenged for all her suffering."

He penned that last sentence a little prematurely, for the friendly feminine being for whom he longed was almost at hand. But was it quite certain it was going to be Mathilde the Second? For summer had come and, with it other visitors had arrived, too, and the solitudes of "Biebernest," undisturbed these last few months save by the white flutter of a young girl's skirt, were now peopled by the most elegant of feminine toilets. Two of these ladies were of particular importance; one was Frau Schnorr of Carolsfeld; the other, the Baroness von Bülow. They had come with their husbands to spend part of the holidays in Wagner's neighbourhood. The Schnorrs were artists who had already attained celebrity at the Karlsruhe Theatre; Tichatschek had told Wagner what an exceptional voice the man had, and he was still quite young. Unfortunately, an untimely tendency to obesity had made him more of a Hercules than a Tristan, and because of this defect Wagner had kept on putting off hearing him. One day, however, he went incognito to Karlsruhe, where his *Lohengrin* was being performed. As soon as he saw this "legendary hero" advancing upstage, Wagner was dumbfounded. When he saw and heard this miraculous singer who understood the work so thoroughly, he asked no longer, "What manner of man is he?" but exclaimed with conviction, "'Tis he in truth!" And now Schnorr and his wife were his guests and so were the beloved Hans von Bülow and his enigmatic Cosima. Enigmatic is the word; for Cosima's likes and dislikes were different from anyone else's in the wide world. She thought the Rhine scenery boring, stupid, with a sort of English stupidity, stupid as ivy-clad ruins. She did not care for Wiesbaden; the people that crowded the Casino made her sick—all those mountebanks and Jews, a corrupt herd who didn't so much as know what honour meant. The only pleasure she got in this land of rogues and thieves was Wagner's music, sung of an evening by the Schnorrs and accompanied by Hans or the Master himself on the piano. Her idea of Schnorr was that he was more of a musician than a tenor, and more of an artist than a musician. He set himself to study the part of Tristan. A tragic and nerve-rending delight. But what moved the young woman still more than that was the poem of the *Meistersinger*, so gay yet so profound, a truly Shakespearean work in which—she saw it at once—the real greatness is summed up in the autumnal splendour of Hans Sachs. She was angry with Wagner for that. The man dominated her. Yet not so much as he dominated Bülow, whose nervous irritability seemed to grow more and more disquieting under his master's influence. Why does he let himself be subjugated, hypnotized, enslaved like this? In five days he copies out the 145 quarto pages of the *Meistersinger*. He has lost all interest in his own work; doesn't trouble to correct the proofs of his *Lieder*, feels quite insignificant in the presence of The Other, and talks about writing a Suicide Symphony. "I wish," he said, "that the hour of

the last long sleep had come. . . . I have lost all consciousness of
my personality, all joy in life." What task can a man undertake
whose only asset is an ineffective piety? And all that sort of
thing made Cosima suffer. She blamed her husband even more
than she blamed Wagner. Wagner was at all events himself, cynical and as hard as a diamond. One evening he began to talk
about his future plans: *The Conquerors* (an appropriate title and
no mistake!) ; *Parsifal*, which was to be his last work, his testament. And Bülow, standing in a window recess, murmured *sotto
voce* to Weisheimer, "Mark my words, he'll do what he says; and
this *Parsifal* he talks about, he'll write it." They went on an excursion, climbing the Drachenfels, always hanging on the word
of "The Joyless Man" whose gaiety had something strident about
it that gripped your very vitals. He sang, too, when Hans was at
the piano; he sang *Siegmund*, and the two first acts of *Siegfried*
(the only ones that were finished), himself taking the part of
Mime. It was horrible, terrifying, marvellous. One day Willich,
the painter, arrived from Rome; the Wesendoncks had sent him
to paint Wagner's portrait. Wherefore came the spirit of Isolde
thus to revisit the land of the gods of the Tetralogy? All this was
a new burden. However, Wagner dutifully consented to sit, and,
as of old at "The Sanctuary," got some one to read aloud to him.
Only, this time, instead of Mathilde, the reader was the young
Baroness von Bülow. And now again, again, and again, when
chance seemed to be playing a part so obviously preconcerted,
Wagner received from his lithographer the *Five Poems* composed during that pathetic summer on the Green Hill, and an
evening was arranged at Schott's to try them over. The memories that would keep rising anew from the ashes of the past
hung heavily on the heart of her who seemed to be yet another
of those under the spell of the Venusberg. She questioned her
inner self. Was she happy? Why had she married so young? Was
it not first and foremost to please her father? Her early girlhood
in Paris, fenced in by the studies ordained by her mother and
her governesses, was a pleasant enough memory. They saw few
people; went often to the museums. Those prudent ladies were
strict disciplinarians. And then, one fine day, after years of
absence, their father had come back, bringing with him the
friend of his heart, the very one to whose music they had been
listening that evening, as to music from beyond the tomb. . . .
Did it not seem that even then, all those ten years ago, he was the
stranger, he who owns nor home nor country, who comes and sits
himself down in silence at the door of your heart like the ghost
in the legend he had sung just now? Then the amazon at Weimar,

the dark lady of Wittgenstein, enveloped in the smoke of her cigars and all on fire with the literature of mysticism, insisted on having her lover's children. She would uproot those Parisiennes, transplant them, put them to board with Frau von Bülow, and transform them into young ladies of Berlin. And so their father's favourite pupil became their pianoforte teacher. Cosima took to music instinctively. The young teacher admired her, adored her. Perhaps he divined that she, too, like Liszt, had a genius for love. For loving Hans! After a concert (it was the 19th of October, 1856—how well she remembered the date) in which he was conducting the Overture to *Tannhäuser*, the audience began to hiss and Hans went off in a faint. Then, out of pity, and because she alone that night had shared his pain, she had become engaged . . . and a few months later she was married. How overjoyed her father was! But the Comtesse d'Agoult, her mother, made no secret of her misgiving. She was an adept in psychology and she knew her daughter. And although in the end she gave her consent to a marriage which seemed so eminently desirable, she was none the less aware of its perils. Six years earlier, in a letter to her friend, Emma Herwegh, the poet's wife, she had said: "Cosima is a child of genius, very like her father. Her force of imagination will take her far from the common paths. She has a demon, a spirit, within her, and she knows it and she will resolutely make any sacrifice that demon may require. Circumstances have pitched her into a marriage which I am very much afraid will bring happiness to nobody." But of this not very optimistic prophecy Cosima knew nothing in July, 1862, when the image of the man she secretly called her master suddenly became so vivid. We may be sure that she searched her heart, and with anguish, for the "demon within" was not going to score so easy a victory over her as over the general run of lovesick women. Her proud spirit was not made for happiness. As her mother had divined, she had a genius for the crowning tribute love can demand, a genius for sacrifice; but it was not merely the sacrifice of herself; it was the sacrifice of others, too, the bitter immolation of all one holds honourable and binding on the heart. It was not for nothing that she had called her elder daughter Senta, after her who was faithless to her promise but true to her destiny.

No hint of all this hidden struggle passed her lips. Cosima was vowed to silence, and neither Hans nor Richard had any notion of it all. When, after two months at Biebrich, the Bülows returned to Berlin, Wagner, in his letters to his wife, did not so much as mention their name. "The Schnorrs have come," he said, "and the Dustmanns, etc." The "etc." included Cosima, Mathilde Maier, and a new female admirer who, at this period of ferment and agitation, had just appeared on the Rhineland horizon, an actress whom he had met in the theatre at Frankfort: Frederica Mayer. Two Mathildes in his life and two demoiselles Mayer. . . . Such was the will of Fate. And each one brought him something different: one, passion; the second, steady devotion; and the third—the third was Venus of the market place. Frederica was the sister of that Frau Dustmann who came to Biebrich because Wagner was going to get her to play the part of Isolde in the future performances at Berlin. She was an agreeable girl, whom he had seen and applauded in a play of Calderon's. She had friends at Mainz and took advantage of the fact to come and pay a visit to the composer in his retreat, and take part in the festivities he was getting up in the neighbourhood in honour of his band of artists. The unfortunate part about it was that she had a regular "protector" in the person of M. de Guarta, the manager of the theatre at Frankfort; and if he was not dangerous in the amorous sense of the word, he was unquestionably jealous. The problem was to elude his vigilance and plot an escape. A thing on which Frederica had long set her heart. She and Richard, therefore, decided to run away to Vienna together, in the autumn.

However, that was not destined to be a very lasting affair, for if Wagner was in one of those moods when he must have distraction at all costs, what he really desired was to come to anchor. Repose, quiet, work, such were the *leit-motifs* of all his letters. And well they might be, since he had glimpsed a haven for which he had searched in vain since the early stages of his tempestuous voyage. At the moment when he might seem to have sunk to his nadir, in that almost desperate hour in which the dejected artist is for giving up the struggle because he is weary of himself and of others, and sick of his own ideas, when he grows uncertain whether what he thought was good in him had, after all, any real value, and whether his whole work was not vitiated by some fundamental intellectual error, even then, at that dark hour, there rose up one who was predestined to save him, him and his work, from irremediable disaster.

Wagner was seated in the old concert-room of the Gewandhaus at Leipzig, where he had not been since the Mendelssohn days. His young friend Weisheimer was giving a concert to which he had promised his support. It seemed that a whole host of forgotten faces had come back to the place, gathered together as if for the funeral of some member of the family. There was Brendel, the champion of the pen for the musicians of the future; Alexander Ritter, the brother of Richard's Venice friend; Francisca Wagner, his brother Albert's daughter; Ottilie, his sister; the Brockhauses, looking very much aged; Richard Pohl, a faithful henchman; the old counsellor Kustner, sometime intendant of the Theatre Royal, Berlin; and finally Bülow on the platform playing, as formerly at Zurich, a new piece by Liszt. But when the night of the concert itself arrived, it seemed to Wagner that he was as one "rapt above earth" and all he beheld in the whole assembly, whose gaze was turned towards him (he was the real ghost come back from another world) was a pale visage enveloped in a mourning veil. Cosima had lost her sister Blandine. She had arrived from Paris, where she had left her grandmother Liszt seriously ill. For her, as for Wagner, time marked a halt that evening. The past was on the other side of that black crêpe. Here at this point starts a present, wholly new and uncharted, yet even now laden with insoluble problems. "What we felt was so grave, so profound, that the mere joy of seeing each other again sufficed to make us forget the painful times that lay before us." Both were invaded by a sort of panic; and yet, by what a fullness of heart! . . . And yet again Wagner perceived, in a revealing flash, that to make the port for which his heart so longed, he had still to round the cape of storm and tempest. This last setting sail for the Islands of the Blest, takes place under a lowering sky. What manœuvres and what hardships it will cost him ere he reaches them! Nevertheless, it rests with him. He can refuse to sail. His age suggests, nay threatens, such a refusal. Is he not twenty-five years older than his friend's daughter? But neither Cosima nor he could abjure their destiny. It might all be mystery and silence between them, but they knew from that moment onwards that they belonged to each other. Both heard the admirable Bülow on the piano. Possibly Wagner may have recalled the days when the young man came to see him in the heart of the Saxon countryside when he was composing *Lohengrin*, and to lay before him the assurance of his fealty and love. "Bending over the tiller, the pale Mariner keeps his unending watch." And today, even as then, does he not say to Senta, "The dark fire that burns within me, shall I call it love? Alas! no; it is the restless longing for deliverance." They laughed a little over some of the crudities in Weisheimer's work. Then the orchestra played the Overture to the *Meistersinger* followed by the Prelude to *Tristan*. But enough! This time again 'twas but a fortuitous medley of his finest melodies—and the living had nothing to fear from the dead.

From Leipzig Wagner went to Dresden, to see one of his life's companions, one whom he had not asked to the Gewandhaus—Minna! She came to the station to meet him and took him back to her new abode. On the threshold lay a little mat on which the lonely wife had embroidered the word "Welcome." Here he found all the beautiful furniture that had been theirs in Paris—the red silk curtains, a bedroom specially fitted up for him, and a study in which the great bureau of the old days was waiting to greet him. Minna had bought it back through the agency of Frau Ritter, to whom she still owed a considerable amount of money on it. To break the ice, Minna had invited her sister-in-law, Clara Wolfram, to come and stay. Two days went by pretty satisfactorily. There were visits to the Brockhauses, to Dr. Pusinelli, and to the Ministers to whom Wagner was anxious to express his thanks for the amnesty which had been granted him. They explored the old city in which every face was strange, from the glove merchant's to the soloist's in the orchestra. One evening, to please his wife, he read his *Meistersinger* aloud to a group of friends, the *Meistersinger* which she had so unhappily interrupted during her ill-fated visit to Biebrich. Thanks to an unexpected gift of money from the Grand Duchess of Weimar, he was able to supply her with enough money to carry her through the coming winter. He then decided he must be off again at once. This came as a great blow to Minna. But what was Richard to do with a woman who was virtually dying? The least little shock might cause an extension of the trouble that weighed so grievously upon her heart. Silently she saw him back to the station, the pretty Minna of Magdeburg of whom he had once been so jealous—the pampered and faithless Minna with whom he had served his apprenticeship of sorrow, Minna the wife who had bravely borne so many years of hardship, and, finally, Minna the adversary, the stranger. And he stood and gazed at the forlorn little figure standing there on the platform and watched her as she swiftly disappeared from sight. Husband and wife, who had worn away their love grating so harshly one against the other, were still to exchange a few letters, but they saw each other no more.

That winter Richard spent in Vienna, where he had arrived with Frederica Mayer, an easy-going, docile woman, but delicate in health. Their liaison, which was a good deal talked about, was very distasteful to Frau Dustmann, Frederica's sister. It was mortifying because it was Frau Dustmann who was to take the part of Isolde when Tristan was performed at the Théâtre de la Porte de Carinthia. The position having rapidly become untenable, Frederica resolved to go and make a long stay in Italy, to get her health in order and to try and forget the man to whom she had become so deeply attached. Wagner was therefore free again. But hostility and ill-fortune were in the air that year in Vienna. Ander, the tenor, was continually falling ill and was unable to get up his part. And Frau Dustmann had by no means got over her displeasure. Meantime, to tide him over his difficulties, he had to give three concerts. They were a stupendous success, but, alas! so heavy had been the expenses, they brought in no money. However, the young Empress Elisabeth had been present. Standing up in her box, she had united her applause to an ovation accorded him by the wildly enthusiastic audience. Brahms, the new composer, was also there, but he remained unmoved and laughed at Weisheimer, who clapped so hard that he split his white kid gloves. Wagner was recalled twenty-three times (Weisheimer kept count), and then he hadn't enough to pay his hotel bill. This was evidently the time to order champagne on credit. "What I lack is a country, a home. I don't mean an earthly one, but a home in some one's heart. I shall be fifty in May. I cannot marry so long as my wife lives, and a divorce now, seeing how ill she is, would be her death blow. So you see I'm drifting on to the rocks. I long for a feminine presence, for some one who would make up her mind through thick and thin to be what a woman could and should be, if I am to go on living. . . . I must have some one I love about me even if it be only a child. Then I tell myself some day I shall find a woman who will love me like that. Such, you see, are the thoughts a desperate man is turning over in his mind for Christmas and the New Year. God knows what you will say to it all." Mathilde came to the conclusion that the step was beyond her powers, that it was too much to ask, seeing the kindnesses her family had already lavished on this demi-semi-widower whom she at once admired and feared. Wagner knew it, and he did not insist. But the longing to settle down, the longing for a home, for rest and repose became so importunate as almost to make him ill. This everlasting lack of security—that was the real tragedy of his existence, and if he extended inviting hands to every woman he met, it was only because he thought their quiet skill would enable them to arrange and set in order a home, a sanctuary in whose peace his brain could free itself from the ideas that burdened it, a haven where the household would be carried on without noise and without money troubles; where his meals would be decently served, and where his clothes and his dressing-gowns should be hung in orderly array.

March found him at St. Petersburg and Moscow, where he had been asked to direct some concerts. This time the trip was not only a triumph such as he had never dreamt of, but it was a financial success as well. Seven thousand thalers to the good! Never before had Wagner taken in anything like such a sum on a single tour. Some of it he sent to Minna. With the rest he decided to set up house. Possibly he would have a place somewhere on the Rhine. That was the old, old plan that was always cropping up. Detailed letters about it went off to Mathilde Maier. "I have decided to buy an estate. . . . Have a look round for a place on the river . . . something fairly big with plenty of trees." The young woman became his steward and the custodian of that Rhinegold which shone like Alberic's treasure. He bombarded her with his requests and requirements. He felt himself a man of substance because the people showered their plaudits on him. He would go back now to the land flowing with milk and honey where the Grand Duchess Helen had taken him under her wing and presented him with a magnificent diamond. But it was at Moscow, too, that he first felt a strange sensation in his chest. . . . Was he going to die just when the prize was within his grasp? It was nothing, nothing at all. Only a false alarm, a thing of no importance. A few days later he returned to Vienna, where Tausig had found him a comfortable house out in the Penzing direction. Wagner at once gave up the Rhineland plan, for he was anxious to furnish as he really wished to furnish while he had the money to do so. And in spite of that wave of emotion that came over him in the Gewandhaus, he still clung to the idea of getting his lady steward to join him, so greatly did he dread being alone. "Yes, I tell you, when I thought of a place on the Rhine it was not to have you, but to be something to you. You don't know, as I do, what it means to be alone. It has made me absolutely ill. . . . *Mon enfant,* instead of dividing us, we are destined to be united for ever. I love you deeply. Away with pride. Give over weeping. You are mine. The rest will settle itself." Yet it was Cosima he wanted. But there was something so dispiriting in the emptiness of his new abode that he felt he must fill it at all costs. He needed some one there, that was all. And as Mathilde could not make up her mind to ride rough-shod over her family's bourgeois prejudices, he did the next best thing and engaged the services of a comely chambermaid, a cheerful and obliging Viennese. She helped him to get the villa in order, and at last Wagner was able to fancy himself well settled in a home of his own. He also engaged a valet, a married man whose wife would do the cooking. And this time he went in for furnishing with a vengeance, indulging his fancies to the top of his bent. The dining-room was hung with a dark brown paper embellished with rosebuds; the big drawing-room was plain lilac with red and gold stripes at each corner. For the music-room he chose serge curtains adorned with Persian designs; sofa and easy chairs to match. For his bedroom a mauve paper with green stripes of a velvety finish, and violet bed-curtains. Every door had its portière, and twenty-four silk dressing-gowns hung in his wardrobe. "I am still waiting," he told his upholsterer "(1) for the two brown armchairs for the music-room, (2) for the furniture to go in the corner at the back of the sofa, (3) for the two easy chairs of purple silk for the green bedroom, (4) for the large purple silk armchair, (5) for the seat upholstered in red velvet, (6) for the large mirror, (7) the purple velvet carpets and the mahogany cupboard, (8) for all the curtains for the green room, (9) for the woollen blinds for the study," etc., etc. This mighty battle of the colours filled him with glee and set his imagination ablaze. He was as excited as a young bridegroom. When he had to absent himself in order to direct some concert or other, he gave his pretty housekeeper detailed instructions against his return. Everything had to be up to the mark, in apple-pie order, comfortable and cosy. "My study must be tidy and agreeably scented. Always buy the best quality. I like a pleasant perfume about the place. . . . Yes, yes; be pretty and nice. I want to have a good time of it for a bit." But the money soon evaporated in this hothouse, and it soon became evident that they were not going to do *Tristan* in Vienna. After seventy-seven rehearsals, the Kaernthner Thor Theatre finally gave it up because the score was absolutely unplayable. Esser himself, a remarkable conductor and a man of the highest professional principles, one of the best men Wagner ever had, declared *Tristan* to be "ridiculously difficult" and, though he acknowledged that the public were mad about Wagner's music, he confessed that he did not share their enthusiasm. It had been the same story over and over again for the past twenty years: an ever-growing and ever-widening popularity with the public, but unmistakable hostility among the managers and in administrative quarters. Moreover Schott, sick of being perpetually bombarded for money by a man whose ideas might or might not bear fruit in the future, refused to pay out any more. There was only one thing for it, and that was to give some concerts at Budapest and Prague. But the financial result fell far short of his expectations. The situation was becoming rapidly acute. Indeed, he had never been through such a crisis. He had recourse to borrowing. He signed promissory notes. In his distress he took up his pen and wrote appealingly for help. And the first name to come into his mind was Mathilde—Mathilde Wesendonck. "I have no luck, and a little luck a man must needs have if he is to go on thinking that he still belongs to the world. . . . I have had enough of life. . . . But one doesn't die easily when one's hour is not yet come. . . . I have no longer any desire. I cannot call my soul my own. A profound and agonizing anxiety holds my inner life in bondage. The present is denied me, and I see no future in store. No glimmer of confidence or faith. Believe me, it gives me a strange feeling to think that not even you know my works. What then is my inner self? What are these works of mine? Apart from me (who alone understand them) they would exist for no one. Yes, it is when I look at it like that that I hold my *self*, my *ego*, of paramount importance; for my ego, too, exists for me alone. The world has no knowledge, no appreciation, save of the virtuoso. Well, penury has forced me to become one. When I am conducting an orchestra this power over men is vouchsafed me. Thinking over the best way to make use of my time, it seems to me that I had better go touring about, giving concerts. Perhaps things will turn out well and I shall find a haven (yet another) to call my own. But absolute solitude I can no longer endure; and I cannot rest content with only an old sporting dog, a present from my landlord to keep me company. The only pleasant thing left me, the only thing which enables me to relax my mental tension, is the memory of the past. But of that I must not, cannot speak."

Such was the attitude of resignation, the growing nerveless-ness of this Wotan of the Broken Spear, and the woman who was at once his beloved one and the child of his spirit—Isolde and Brünnhilde in one—answered his letter in words that thrilled with the emotion of those bygone days. "My whole being," said she, "is uplifted at the thought of sharing your sorrows with you. . . . He should be a proud man who has the right to lend you his aid. My heart bleeds as I learn of your 'triumphs,' and overflows with bitterness when they are spoken of as matters for congratulation. I feel then how little people know you, how ill they understand you. . . . My heart is continually longing to call you back to Switzerland, but that heart is selfish and its voice must stay unheeded. Could any other home be found for you there save the one of old? From that one my tears till now have banished all intruders; but I doubt whether they can still do so in the future."

So, then, that memory too would disappear, and over all would sweep the waters of oblivion. The hostile powers were hot on the scent of this artist seeking some lair in which to earth himself and die. He had cast up his accounts. His debts amounted to 30,000 crowns, which was the more disquieting seeing that in Austria debtors were still liable to imprisonment. Any day he might be seized and flung into gaol, he, of all composers in the Europe of his day, the most illustrious, and the most necessitous. Then began the final double in the chase, the one before the kill. He goes to Prague and on from Prague to Karlsruhe. There he sees Mathilde Maier and Mme. Kalergis, his benefactress who had now become Mme. de Moukhanoff (and the funny thing was that her young husband wrote him in these surprising terms: "Dear Sir, I love you.") From Karlsruhe on again to Zurich, where he hoped to find the reinforcements he so sorely needed. But Otto was only just recovering from a serious illness and Mathilde could do nothing. The meeting was a sad one and left them both with the impression that those recent letters that had passed between them would also be the last. From Zurich he returned to Mainz to press his suit with Schott. Schott refused point-blank. From Mainz he decided to go on to Loewenberg, where the Prince Hohenzollern-Hechingen had his abode. He was a friend of Liszt's and favourably disposed towards the new school of musicians. He went by way of Berlin and paid a flying visit to the von Bülows. Hans invited him to come to a concert at which he was conducting that same evening, and for which his preparations left him not a moment to spare. But Cosima was expecting the fugitive, for she knew at a glance that the refuge the poor wayworn wanderer so ardently desired awaited him neither in Switzerland nor in Silesia nor anywhere else in the wide world save in her own heart. They went for a drive together, passing through the Tiergarten without exchanging a word. But there was now no need of speech between them. Their eyes confessed the secret which, for months past, they had been hiding in their hearts. They knew the fullness of their joy and took on themselves, without a second thought, the burden of sorrow that lay in store for them. Not the world, nor any one in it, should now prevent them from coming together. What cared he for the concert, and Hans, and the supper that followed, and the sleepless nights spent in the Bülows' flat. The nightmare of solitude was at length dispelled, like some chronic malady suddenly healed by a miracle. Had the Mariner's long-sought deliverance come at last? Had he found that home for which his heart had yearned so sorely? Even if he glimpsed, even now, the tragedy to come, his soul at all events was saved.

Back again in Vienna for the last time, Wagner spent a few more months vegetating, while his financial position went from bad to worse. *Tristan* at the Kaernthner Thor was now nothing more than a fairy tale. He was compelled to sell the Grand Duchess Helena's diamond, the gold snuff-box presented to him by the Moscow musicians, and even his Black Swan, the famous Erard. A project for a concert tour in Russia was suddenly cancelled, as out of the question. His friend Cornelius, Standhartner, Tausig, and Prince Lichtenstein strongly advised him to disappear. There was barely time to get a few things together and to liquidate his effects, just retaining a few of the most valuable remnants of all that luxury which once had been a newspaper sensation. On the afternoon of the 24th he took train for Switzerland, once more passing through Munich on Good Friday. The city was in mourning for King Maximilian, whose death had occurred a fortnight earlier. His son, as yet a stripling, had just succeeded him on the throne. Looking in at a shop window, Wagner saw a portrait of the young man, who, clad in his royal ermine, looked like a prince out of a fairy tale. What had the fates in store for him? The artist was conscious of a strange emotion as he contemplated the grave beauty of the solitary youth who seemed as though he were looking at him with a question in his eyes—at him, the sorcerer, dogged everlastingly by evil fortune. Wagner laughed a bitter, ironic laugh, and wrote a humorous epitaph for his own grave.

Arriving next day at Mariafeld, he went to see the Willes. Elisa Wille was all alone, her husband being away in Constantinople. But she invited Wagner to stay in some quarters close to the house, where he had often been put up in the old Zeltweg days. His hostess was kindness itself and did everything she could for the comfort of her unexpected and ailing guest: Fires were lit in all his rooms, and the Wesendoncks, being apprised of his arrival, sent along their own piano. But he was in no mood to work. He went out for walks by himself or else sat on the terrace enveloped in his cloak, his velvet cap on his head, looking like some patrician out of a picture by Albrecht Dürer. Sometimes he would go in and keep Frau Wille company in her drawing-room, where, seating himself near the window, he would discourse of his young days, of his vanished dreams, of the works he had composed, and even of his wife, whose solitude, so like his own, weighed heavily on his mind. "Things might have been all right between us, but she never realized that a man like me cannot live with his wings in bonds. What knew she of the divine rights of passion which I proclaimed in the flames of *The Valkyrie*?" Some letters came for him, and a little money from his French royalties. Sometimes he would read the whole day through—Jean Paul, Walter Scott, George Sand, and a novel by his hostess. One day, when Frau Wille was talking to him about the future, he broke out excitedly, striding up and down the room: "The future? But who will stage the work which I alone —with my demons to help me—know how to produce? I am not like other men. I am all nerves. I must have beauty, colour, light. The world ought to give me the things I need. I cannot live on a miserable organist's pittance like your master Bach. Am I making a wildly extravagant demand when I ask for those crumbs of luxury which I need, I who am writing works that will bring such happiness to thousands upon thousands of my fellow men?"

One morning he seemed to have recovered his calm. They noticed he was reading his Schopenhauer again; and he smiled as he remembered how, long ago, the philosopher had sent him this message: "Thank your friend Wagner for me for sending me his *Nibelungen*; but he'd better hang up his music. I, Schopenhauer, am going to stick to Rossini and Mozart."

One night Wagner dreamed that he was King Lear and that he was driving the daughters of his spirit over the wide heath. One evening he sat down at the piano and played some passages from *Tristan*. "The ancients," he said, "put an inverted torch into the hands of Eros as though the genius of death." At length the postman brought him a packet of letters that seemed to trouble him. He said he must be gone. And with his usual abruptness he gave out that he would go next day. Going up to Frau Wille, he said, "Friend, you know neither the extent of my troubles nor the depth of the distress that awaits me." However, his departure was marked by a sort of calm dispatch, as of a man busy with some secret preoccupation, and the Willes watched the steamboat as it faded from their sight, bearing with it the old vagabond of the empty pockets and the high-sounding speech.

This was what his letters had told him: All the furniture he had in Vienna had been sold up to go towards paying off his debts. Tausig, who had gone security for the balance, was unable to return to Austria. His sister, Louisa Brockhaus, had given him the cue to try for the post of conductor at Darmstadt. Schott agreed to make him a further small advance, and, lastly, the Wesendoncks had decided to make him an allowance of 100 francs a month. And what Wagner was flying from now was the humiliation of it all, this new and lamentable loss of self-respect. He was flying from his memories and, more than that, he was flying from Franz Wille, who had returned from the East and had regarded him with a jealous and suspicious eye. Never yet, it seemed to him, had he fallen so low as now. He decided to make an end of it.

On the 29th of April he was at Stuttgart, where he occupied a room at the Hotel Marquardt near the theatre. He telegraphed to young Weisheimer to come to him there. Weisheimer arrived next day and found Wagner a broken man. They took counsel together. "I'm finished," he said. "I can't go on any longer. I must disappear, no matter where." That night they went together to a performance of *Don Juan* under the direction of his friend Eckert. Wagner wanted to get hold of the latter to ask him to put him on to some place in the suburbs where he could bury himself and finish off the first act of his *Meistersinger* before putting an end to his life. On the 3rd of May the move was decided upon, and Wagner was packing his bag at the hotel in company with Weisheimer, when the waiter brought him up a visiting card on which he read: "von Pfistermeister, private secretary to H. M. the King of Bavaria." Should he accept it? What new trouble was this? Something wrong with his passport? Some liability he had overlooked? What *could* it be? He kept fingering the enigmatic piece of cardboard and was still hesitating, when the visitor sent word that he came from the king himself and that his message was urgent.

The stranger was shown up. He had, he said, come from Vienna, where he had been looking for Wagner in vain. He had then proceeded to Mariafeld and had altogether been three weeks on the road. He next presented Wagner with a photograph of his royal master, a diamond set in a ring, and a letter. "The words were few, but they reached my heart." Cosima had saved his soul, and now, lo! his prince of the shop window was about to save his life. Wagner sank weeping into an armchair. The Mariner was saved and the vessel with the black sails that had roamed the seas for so many years might sink now and go to the bottom with all her spectral crew. Lunching with Eckert that same day, they learnt by telegram that Meyerbeer was dead.

PART FOUR

Chapter I

HAMLET OF BAVARIA AND THE
REVOLUTION IN MUNICH

WHEN, in his boyhood days, the Musician of the Future was paying court to the gracious Shadows of the Past, what time the music within him was naïvely weaving echoes faintly caught from the poet of the viewless countenance, he little thought the day would come when, having conceived a dream world of his own, he would encounter one who should help him bring it into being, a veritable prince out of Shakespeare, born the same year as Tannhäuser, a prince whose brilliant and too brief career would flame, meteorlike, in the Bavarian sky just long enough for a king to pass from throne to study, there to complete his pilgrimage alone, and finally to seek a tragic death in the waters of a romantic lake.

The world is full of Hamlets in hot pursuit of their respective ghosts. What is rarer is to find one with a civil-list at his command, a heritage of regal power, one who, Narcissus-like, is enamoured of his own image and has seen the prince he fain would be mirrored in the story of the knightly Lohengrin. Ludwig was not yet twenty when he girt his brows with the ancestral crown. His father's austere shade yet filled his mind with awe; his grandfather, as he knew, had bartered his throne for the kisses of a dancing girl named Lola Montez. He himself was deep in Feuerbach and Edgar Allan Poe. He had beheld upon the stage the grottoes of the Venusberg, and had thrilled with enchantment at the sight. He had eagerly devoured Wagner's writings and pondered long and deeply on the appeal to which he gave utterance in the preface to his *Nibelungen*, "Will ever a prince be found," the musician had cried, "who shall make it possible for my work to be performed?" One month after the obsequies of King Maximilian, Ludwig dispatched Herr von Pfistermeister to seek out the poet, for he had resolved to make him the minister of a reign dedicated to beauty and stately architecture. On being brought back to Munich, the captive of his own wizardry, the artist, just saved from self-inflicted death, found himself for the first time face to face with the young king. It was the meeting of Wotan and Siegfried on the symbolic heights of a dying world. But in this palace the rôles were reversed. The master, for the nonce, was not Siegfried, charmer of birds, vanquisher of gods and monsters; it was the restless Mariner, the love-seeking Wanderer, Tristan, worn and weary, fleeing from his creditors, he whose present task it was to show that the old gods were dying, yielding place to mortals, to men immersed in the life and action of the world. Thus, from the very first, though they knew it not, a misunderstanding was fated to arise between the young idealist and the old campaigner, who hungered and thirsted so sorely after pleasure. For the revolutionary of '48 had merely changed his camp. His soul, his temperament, remained what they had ever been. He was still, it is true, the hierophant of Death, but, like all who truly desire it, it was not to be till he had drained Life to the very lees. And then, what meaning are we to attach to these metaphors of "Victory" and "Defeat"? Antique forms which we of today cloak in the more living words of "Will" or "Failure." Wagner's demand is to be believed in, to be loved, and now, though late, to

> . . . stretch a hand thro' time to catch
> The far-off interest of tears.

He bowed low over the royal hand, the hand of a king on whom, even at this early hour, hung the shadow of inherited disease, the disease of illusion. Ludwig pressed him to his bosom. "Though you knew it not," he said, "you have been the solitary source of all my joy, and, from my tenderest childhood, my veriest master, my tutor and my friend, a friend that, like none other, has spoken to my heart. . . . Be sure that, to the utmost of my power, I will make up to you for all that you have suffered in the past. All sordid cares I will for ever banish from your mind. The peace for which you yearn I will bestow on you, so that, untrammelled, you may develop your marvellous genius. Now that I have donned the royal purple, the time has come for me to mitigate the trials of your life." Wagner cried aloud his joy, his amazement, to his friends. "The unbelievable has come to pass. A king has been sent to me from heaven; through him I live, and am become myself; he is my country and my joy." (To Mme. de Moukhanoff-Kalergis.) "He understands me like my own soul. . . . You have no idea how magical is his look. . . . He is alas so fair, so full of spirituality, that I tremble lest I should behold his life dissolve like some celestial dream." (To Frau Wille.) "I believe that if he came to die, I should die the moment after." (To Bülow.) Already, at the very well-spring of his joy, comes the fear lest death should bring it to an untimely end. And yet, a few weeks later we find him lamenting his lost solitude. However, the king straightway gave him quarters in the villa of Count Pellet on the Lake of Starnberg, a quarter of an hour from his own abode. And every day he went to see him, or requested his presence at the castle. The disciple, whose upbringing had been devoid of tenderness, listened with fervour to the wonder-worker of the feelings, the lord of the supernatural realm of the spirit. Baseness or cupidity he saw or divined among his court officials; no matter; he washed himself clean of it all in the society of this paternal, this brilliantly gifted, Lohengrin whom he had had the good fortune to welcome to his kingdom. And Wagner, though in this enchanted world his slightest wish was law, yet lamented the incurable ill that had given him access thereunto. His debts were paid. He had a house in Munich given him as a present; theatre, orchestra, management, all were at his beck and call, but his *salons*, like his life, were empty. In spite of the royal miracle, he breaks out into loud lament. "My solitude," he cries, "is terrible. To keep in favour with this young monarch I have to continue on the loftiest heights." Peace was his now, his powers were immense, yet it gave him small delight to wield them; things somehow seemed to have lost their charm. It was all very well for his sovereign to make him the object of a kind of quasi-mystical adoration; it touched him, it flattered him, and he was grateful, but it brought no easement of the ancient fever. In Ludwig's court Wagner felt himself indeed an object of worship, an idol, but, oh, how cold beneath his godlike trappings! Since he had lost his Isolde, the solitary gleam of that sweet pain whereof a man must die to live again upon a higher plane, had visited him in the Gewandhaus, and on the cushions of a landau, side by side with Cosima. In her it is that lies his last, his only hope of calling forth his crowning music. And so away he wrote to Hans von Bülow, imploring him to give up vegetating in Berlin, and come. "It would be a fine thing if you could settle here for good as pianist to my young King. For we have resolved to create for ourselves a world apart." Then he sketched out a program of what they might do: 1865, *Tristan*, the *Meistersinger*; 1866, *Tannhäuser*, *Lohengrin*; 1867-68, a full performance of the *Ring*; 1869-70, *The Conquerors*; 1871-72, *Parsifal*; 1873, glorious death and redemption of the plighted one. He wrote to Bülow on the 1st of

June, on the 5th, and again on the 9th. "I invite you with your wife, children, and nurse, to come and make my house your summer quarters, for as long as you can manage. . . . Hans, you will find me in comfortable circumstances, my mode of life is completely changed, but . . . my home is desolate. Come and bring some life into it, at least for a while, I beseech you from the bottom of my heart. Remember it is the most important phase in my life on which I am about to enter. . . . An immense garden, boating excursions on the lake, rambles among the mountains. . . . Perhaps you will come and bring Papa Franz [Liszt]. And you, my little Hans, you'll be completely set up in health again; you will stay on as long as possible (perhaps for good). Really, my dear ones, you alone are wanting to complete my happiness."

Cosima was the first to arrive. She came with her children at the end of June. Her husband could not make up his mind. Munich scared him, and, still more, Wagner. He was afraid it would be as it was at Biebrich all over again; afraid he would be crushed, annihilated. He came, notwithstanding, a moth dazzled by the light. And then, a little later, after he had gone away again, he had a letter from Wagner containing these enigmatic reflections: "I am worried about Cosima's health. Everything about her is out of the ordinary and unusual. She is entitled to freedom, in the highest sense of the word. She is at once childlike and profound. The laws of her being lead her always and exclusively upwards. Nor can anyone help her, except herself. She belongs to a special type of humanity which we must learn to know through her. You will later on have leisure to meditate on this subject and nobly take your place beside her. That thought consoles me."

What this means is that Wagner's life had returned once more to the tragic mode. He was once again the Man of Destiny. Now, when ripening years and happier fortunes were bringing him repose and peace, he threw everything into the melting-pot again. The Traveller refused to go ashore. He went about and once more put out to sea. Already he was for quitting the royal haven to set forth anew upon his wanderings, along the only ways that led him to himself. The death he seeks had naught to do with laurel wreaths, with academic honours and gratified ambitions. No; it was the death of the pilgrim who comes back from Rome condemned by the Pope, but pardoned of God. It was not the Venusberg he sought, but Elisabeth. And Cosima consented, at the cost of her own peace, to redeem this helmless soul. She had pondered it seriously, and counted well the cost. She

realized now that she did not love Bülow, that she never had felt
for him more than a sort of pity, a desire to mother him. His
moody disposition, his nervous irritability, his biting tongue, his
outbursts of rage, disquieted, nay, even scared her sometimes.
She knew his failings, his uncertain temper; she knew his keen
critical insight and his astounding lack of creative power. His
ideas were lofty, his brain was keen, but he had a tortured heart
and none of the moving simplicity of genius. The very consciousness of his virtues and defects made him dictatorial and bitter.
For some months, now, she had been summing him up and noting
the divergences between them, till at last she was face to face
with the terrible certainty that her marriage had been an error.
Cosima Liszt had now arrived at the parting of the ways. She
had to choose her path. She made her choice. It was the path
of tragic suffering. It was the old human dilemma over again.
Either make up your mind to sacrifice yourself on the altar of
domestic duty, in order to keep the home together, or take the
risk that offers, hurry on the break-up of a home that is now a
home no longer, and, with another, set sail to seek the Happy
Isles. She had counted the cost, she realized what it meant; the
public censure, the separation from her children. The insecurity
of the future, the difference in age and religion, and, above all,
the blow it would be to Hans and its reaction on herself—she
had taken it all into account, and of all the arguments she called
into play against herself, it was the last-named that pained her
the most. For though everyone of us is imbued with the idea
that he has an inalienable right to be happy, that it is as lawful
and imperious as any social duty that may be laid upon him, as
great or greater than any moral obligation, nevertheless memory
remains and one cannot banish from the mind the recollections
of old habits, old ties, old affections. The lure of the future, of
the life ahead, is great; so also is that of the past, of the life
that has been lived, of the years that lie behind. Cosima, however, was one of those people whose soul can find no air to
breathe save in clearness and light. The worst crime, in her regard, was wilfully to play at hoodman-blind with one's affection.
Whatever doubt or confusion her hesitations implied disappeared immediately, as in the light of a summer's dawn, the
moment she saw Wagner again. She saw plainly that she herself had not even begun to live. That Richard had a wife, as she
a husband, did but make their trials equal. When she left Berlin
to seek coolness and repose at Starnberg during that scorching
summer, she had scarcely dared to think that all her doubts and
troubles would so swiftly vanish when she set eyes on him again;

on him, "the glorious one," as her father called him. To look upon some one with passionate admiration, that is what her life had lacked till now, and now her heart was overflowing with gratitude. "A new birth, a redemption, a merging of all that was useless and evil in my nature in a single outpouring of my soul towards love, made me vow that by death, by the most sacred of renouncements, or by giving myself wholly and completely, I would justify the love that was coming to fulfilment within me." Thus she wrote later on in her *journal intime*: "When the gods had thus decided, I cried aloud to the friend in his joyless solitude, my friend of friends, the guardian of my soul, to the friend who revealed to me all that is noble and true: 'I am coming to you and I mean to look for my noblest my most sacred happiness in helping you to bear the burden of your life.'" And then to her friend, Maria von Buch, the future Countess von Schleinitz, she says: "I have been here [Starnberg] three days, and it seems an age already. . . . At last my spirit has come down to its rest."

Thus Wagner entered upon that decisive phase of which he has made mention and which straightway suggested the first musical theme of a Starnberg Idyll, which, later on, was given another name. For with this new love, against which it never for a moment occurred to him to struggle, his creative spirit returned. His fighting spirit also; as well as his love of luxury, his appetite for life, and, be it added, his powers of persuasion, since Bülow agreed to leave Berlin and settle down in Munich, to support his master. Even his literary productiveness returned, and he composed a treatise *On Art and Religion*, dedicated to King Ludwig II, as a manifesto for his reign. He entered into possession of the house in Munich of which His Majesty had made him a present, No. 21, Briennerstrasse, quite close to the Propylæa. Standing in the midst of a fine garden planted with walnut trees, the house, in which he wished to dwell till he was carried to the grave, was spacious and convenient. With the help of Cosima, who took up her quarters in the Luitpoldstrasse, Wagner settled himself in. Close relations were established between the king and these friends of the "Well-beloved." Von Bülow was appointed court pianist, and shortly afterwards, conductor at the Theatre Royal, and Wagner became a naturalized Bavarian.

By the end of November, His Majesty had made up his mind to build a great theatre on modern lines, in order that the *Nibelungen Ring* might be worthily presented. On December 4th, *The Flying Dutchman* was performed under Wagner's personal direction; the very work which, twenty-five years before, the Intendant at Munich had pronounced unsuitable for Germany. The house was packed but undemonstrative. Munich was a capital notoriously averse to foreigners, and it looked as though there were already some warring influences at work, some people favouring the young king with his grandiose delusions and his plebeian favourite; others silent and anxious, filled with mistrust concerning this *Eminence grise*, this power behind the throne, who wielded so strong an influence over the heart and purse-strings of the sovereign. They did not forget that he was a revolutionary, and he himself made no secret of the fact that he was a Protestant—that is to say, a free-thinker. Sensational items of news were being whispered abroad. It was said that Semper, the architect, another revolutionary of 1848, had arrived in Munich to submit plans for a model theatre that was to cost a ruinous figure; others said that Wagner was drawing huge sums from the civil-list funds; others again gave out that a vast amount of public money had been spent in paying off his debts. Then the newspapers came out with some rather spiteful comments on these highly engrossing topics. Envy, too, was stirred into activity. Musicians, conductors, minor poets were all incensed at the intrusion of this little scribbler who wrote his own librettos, published philosophical treatises, and prated about reforms. Who was he, this futurist musician, this "down-and-outer" whose path was strewn with failures, this enemy of Mendelssohn and the Israelites?

Politics also came into his world. One party was for making use of Wagner to obtain Ludwig II's support to a scheme for founding a new Rhineland and Westphalian kingdom, which should include a portion of Belgium under the sceptre of the princely House of Tour and Taxis; a sort of kingdom of Burgundy. In exchange for his support, Bavaria was to be promised some additional territory. . . . The Jesuits had charge of the affair, which was financed by an agricultural credit-bank, with ramifications extending even into Austria. The conduct of the pourparlers was entrusted to a retired diplomat who was none other than old Klindworth, a relation of the pianist's and father of the charming Agnes Street, who, a few years since, had been a loving pupil of Liszt's. Thus do the lines stretched by sentiment and friendship over the length and breadth of political Europe cross and intermingle. Wagner declined to be drawn in, although the secretariat of the Cabinet and founder's shares in the future bank were dangled before his eyes. Whereupon followed fresh enmities, and, shortly afterwards, open attacks in the papers. For Wagner had a foe in very high quarters, in the government itself, no less a person in fact, than the President of the Council, von Pfordten.

Meanwhile, in February, 1865, *Tannhäuser* was performed, and as the king did not show himself in his box, it was immediately given out that Wagner's day was over. "Dull people, who talk in that fashion," said the king in a letter he wrote him. "They have not, and cannot have, any idea of our love. They do not know that you are, have been, and ever will be all in all to me until my dying day; that I loved you before ever I set eyes on you." All the same, February saw the beginning of an open war against the composer. They raked up all his Dresden past, accused him of extravagance, criticized his luxurious establishment, and blamed His Majesty for his weakness in pandering to such a prodigal. Even old Ludwig I, who could tell them something about wine and women, took sides against the man who, after an eighteen years' interval, succeeded, as court favourite, the dazzling Lola Montez. No matter. Wagner had the king and Cosima on his side; he wanted no one else. With all the energy at his command he was preparing the way for the official inauguration of the New Art. It should mark an epoch in the history of art, should the projected performance of *Tristan*, on which composer, scene-painters, theatre staff, and the king himself were all at work. Frau von Bülow was indefatigable, despite the fact that she was again in an interesting condition. She acted as the master's secretary, set herself to collect materials for a Wagner book to contain all the major articles that had been published concerning Wagner's works; she answered his letters for him and even went the length of replacing him in his correspondence with the king. It was a queer sort of relationship that thus sprang up between the lonely prince and this young woman who suddenly interposed herself, like a screen, in front of the heart in which he deemed that he alone had the right to dwell. Ludwig, not being of suspicious nature, guessed nothing, and the art which Cosima possessed in a supreme degree was that of tempering firmness with geniality in her diplomatic activities. This combination of the *suaviter in modo* with the *fortiter in re* she had inherited, with all the intellectual graces, from her father, with her mother's clear-headedness thrown in. She won, and she retained, the confidence of the king. Her popularity in the *salons* of Munich was no less marked, and often availed to smother over annoyances occasioned by Bülow's offhandedness, and made up for the little wounds to people's pride which Wagner dealt all round about him without being in the least aware that he had done so.

LUDWIG II, KING OF BAVARIA

But the time was at last drawing nigh when *Tristan* was to be brought into the light of day, *Tristan* whose begetter had been transporting him about the world for six years, vainly endeavouring to animate him with the breath of life. And seeing that for more than half a century now Wagner's life had always been punctuated at important junctures by signs and portents, these weeks of rehearsals, so trying and so magnificent, which Wagner calls the greatest epoch of his life, could hardly have passed without some such distinction. Nor did they. This was the sign vouchsafed:

On the 12th of April, in the morning, and two hours before the first orchestral rehearsal, Cosima gave birth to a daughter. And that daughter was christened Isolde, a name that tells, clearly enough, that she who bore it was the child of one of Love's most glorious deceits; one of the most heroic also; one of the most ineffaceable. Perhaps it is not given to any man to realize the strength of purpose that a woman needs to sustain such a part with dignity, never suffering her lips to make avowal of a fault whereof she sees nothing but the sweetness and the glamour. Cosima was too strong to be seduced by happiness. The tribute she paid that day to the man she loved has lent a touch of rugged grandeur to her life. It did not sunder her from Bülow. On the contrary. If from now onwards she ceased to belong to the man who had given her her name and her first two daughters, this Isolde of a day had opened her mother's heart not only to joy, but to a comradeship of suffering whereof she had scarcely deemed herself capable, and if, for more than fifty years, she was fated to carry her head unbowed before the world, her bosom was rent with the hidden agony of it. She was exorcised, and Wagner, too. For now, and not until now, did the other Isolde fade into "the passèd world."

Against the background of domestic events the rehearsals of *Tristan* stand out arrestingly. And *Tristan* was now as much of a political battle as the grand offensive of the musicians of the future. Various incidents, some comic, some painful, marked the course of these rehearsals, incidents embittered by the gall of Hans von Bülow's venomous comments. He is said to have referred to the audience-to-be as "a pack of dirty swine." Away with him! The orchestra swore they would go on strike. They had to be pacified and brought back to duty. Fortunately, Schnorr von Carolsfeld filled Wagner with a preterhuman emotion that made him impervious to all these vexations. That man was one in a million and there was no need, with him, for compliments and excuses. Just a word or two, a few stage directions, and the most esoteric, the most mystical significance of his rôle was an open book to him. In due course the dress rehearsal came on; and for that Wagner's enemies had been carefully laying a mine which they now proceeded to explode. They had dug up an old promissory note which Wagner had signed five years before to cover the expenses of his Paris concerts. It had never been paid. They now brought an action against him and demanded that he should be flung into prison as a defaulter. Of course the king at once paid the money, begging his friend to forgive the wretched people, for "they knew not what they did." That crisis averted, Frau Schnorr was taken ill and the performance had to be postponed, though every seat in the house had been sold and the city was filled with friends who had come from more or less everywhere—London, Paris, Frankfort, Dresden—to see it. The only absentees were Minna, Mathilde Wesendonck and Liszt; Minna because she was seriously ill, Liszt because he had just entered into the ecclesiastical state and had had minor orders conferred upon him at the Vatican, and Mathilde because to see the drama of her life publicly exhibited on the stage would have been more than she could bear. Wagner invited her specially; she did not come, and he was filled with bitterness at her refusal. He deemed it "petty." He did not see that it was the most delicate testimony she could give him now of the love she bore him. But he wanted her to be a witness of his revenge for the wound inflicted on his pride. An artist rarely has any compunction about a thing like that. To write that work he had dipped his pen into his life's blood, he had hallowed it with his agony, carved and moulded it till it had become as it were the picture of himself, and now it had passed from him like a child brought forth in an agony of sweat. At last the pangs were over, and with pride he displayed his offspring to the world. And so it came to pass that it was not only on the stage of the Munich Theatre Royal that, on that 10th of June, 1865, the famous *première* took place. Many a heart wore out in solitude the hours of that impressive night, in which the genius of Wagner broke out in the soul-stirring cry of a love unattainable, or in the crashing thunder of some moral catastrophe. Never did Wagner show himself so consummate a wonder-worker as in this music in which, like an Indian fakir, he charmed from the soil of his sorrows the roses of passionate delight intertwined with the wintry leaves of his dread of life.

As the enchanted music stole into those hearts so deeply stirred, the tragedy was depicted on the face of each of them. In his box, gazing dreamily into space, the king sat alone, the sweetness of his love for the poet-musician sweeping over him like a torrent. "My only one, my all! Creator of my bliss! Oh, day of all delight! *Tristan*. . . . Born for thee, and by thee chosen, my vocation, it is there!" The thoughts of Ludwig I, the old ex-king, went back to Lola Montez and the delicious torments she forced him to endure. Side by side, Wagner and Cosima listened to that evocation of a love long dead, a love that from that time forth seemed interwoven with their own. Bülow conducted. Another King Mark, he, on whom Tristan had cast his dominating spell. Schnorr, excelling himself, sang what was fated to be his last rôle, setting up a model, for all time, of how the work should be performed. And in the crowd that thronged the theatre, how many were there who were fated to fall in the following summer, in the swift campaign in which victorious Prussia was to wrest three cantons from Bavaria, shattering King Ludwig's childlike belief in the sanctity of his crown? The first performance of *Tristan* marked the end of one epoch and the birth of another, and Wagner himself might well have betrayed his limitations. Success is always a risk, in art no less than in love. Fortunately for him, Wagner was blissfully unconscious of this, for he had had no experience of success. For twenty years he had eaten the bread of failure and defeat. When he came on the stage it was with his interpreters around him, and on his pale face naught was legible save weariness and disquietude. Not here the victor of *Rienzi*, crowned with the facile laurels of a night; not here the victim of that mob of clubmen. He stood as a man bereft of self, a man that had no more to give, who knew that his last word was said. The difficulty overcome counted for nothing, for the struggle had been unnoticed by the public. Officially the day was won, but *Tristan*, in spite of all, had not got across the footlights and Wagner felt that night that his art, his thought, belonged to him and only to him, in all his loneliness. The "country" of which he had so often dreamed, he would never find. . . .

Four nights in succession the applause rang out, yet Wagner had arrived at such a pitch of nervous exhaustion, of self-mistrust, that he forbade all future performances. He desired that *Tristan* should never be given again. The association between creator and interpreter had been too perfect that time ever again to be repeated. Such, at any rate, was the pretext he invoked to account for the mental anguish which paralyzed him.

A young French student, Edouard Schuré, wrote to him to express his admiration and afterwards paid him a visit.

"Your letter gave me extraordinary pleasure," said Wagner. "I showed it to the king and said, 'You see that all is not lost.' "

"Then you are not satisfied?"

"Satisfied? . . . Yes, when I have got *my* theatre. Then perhaps I shall be understood. For the moment I am tired."

One remembers the last words of Isolde, "To melt into air, amid the waves of mist, amid the sounding billows of the ethereal heights, to melt into the universal breath of the absolute, drowned, engulfed. O perfect oblivion! O bliss unutterable!" But Wagner had assigned himself a new task. *My* theatre! That parish remote from the world which he fain would seek, to build therein his temple, his dwelling-place and his tomb—that, henceforth, is the home whither all his thoughts return. Even now he feels that it will not, cannot, be Munich. Thus it was that the very brilliance of these triumphant nights, hurried things on to their appointed end.

The king returned to his Castle of Berg, riding on the engine of his special train, to calm his nerves. By His Majesty's command, there was to be a specimen audition of all his friend's works in the famous rococo room of the castle theatre, the following fortnight. Schnorr took part in it and Wagner himself conducted. Hidden from view in the shadow of his box, the king sat and listened to the last message of the incomparable Tristan, on whom Death had already laid his finger. A week later he fell dead. "The Master's evil eye," the whisper went round. And indeed Wagner interpreted this taking off as one of the most terrible of omens. "Every man has a demon of his own," he said to Schuré. "Mine is of a terrible, a monstrous nature. When it roams at large about me, disaster is in the air. The only time I was ever on the sea, there was nearly a shipwreck. If I went to America, I am sure the Atlantic would greet me with a cyclone. The world of men has treated me the same and, strangely enough, I always come through. But you might think that Fate, unable to crush me, wreaks its vengeance on those who love me. When a real man, a man who is strong with his own strength, gives himself to me unreservedly, I always know the Fates will vent their fury on him. But enough! When you are at war with destiny, you must not look behind, but in front of you." The king himself could bring him no balm. "This night will end in everlasting radiance," he said in a letter to Wagner. "Light and Truth alone can triumph. Such will be your work. Courage then, have done with grieving. A dazzling victory!" Too late. For despite his efforts to grasp the sceptre, Hamlet is the slave of words. His words were splendid—but nothing came of them. The time had gone by when Wagner could be saved by words. The Poloniuses were plotting against their prince, and they had sworn to be the undoing of Horatio.

"We will never part," said Ludwig II, when sending an invitation to Wagner to join him in his mountain home. Thither the musician went, sailed on the lake in the royal yacht, went for solitary drives with his "Parsifal" in a calash drawn by six horses, and made yet further plans for the future. But in his heart he put no faith in them. His power, he knew full well, had no moorings save in the imagination of a builder of castles in Spain. But the power of the Pfordtens and the Pfistermeisters was based on the law, on the money-bags, and on popular credulity. "Of a truth," wrote Wagner yet again, in a letter to Elisa Wille, "I am no longer alive. It is all a miracle and a dream. If it were not so, the pain would be mortal." But there was work to be done, to wit this *Parsifal*, of which he had just made a first rough sketch. Then Semper arrived from Zurich and together they drew the plans for the theatre of the *Nibelungen* on the quays of the Isar, facing the royal palace, to which it would be linked by a new avenue and a magnificent bridge. In addition to the theatre, a new conservatoire was to be erected. A newspaper for art and artists was also to be set on foot. Ludwig was in the seventh heaven and gave himself three years to transform these dreams into granite. "I will, I will," he cried. Weak words and vain. Of all these sumptuous designs, that might have made Munich the musical capital of the world, nothing afterwards remained but a water-colour painting in Wagner's drawing-room.

But this time the politicians meant business. The cards were dealt. Pfistermeister, the ex-privy councillor, was at the head of a conservative cabal who were representing Wagner as a public danger, not only as regards expenditure, but as regards ideas. Von der Pfordten was an Ultramontanist who had contrived to evict, one after another, all the members of the old governing body and to replace them by reactionaries whose monarchical propensities were particularly gratifying to the king with all his leanings towards absolutism. Needless to say the newcomers were radically opposed to what they held to be the dangerous ascendancy of the artists. "If princes were better acquainted with their duty," said Pfordten, "Wagner's music would be everywhere forbidden."

However, the papers continued to speak out. But, although they criticized the Cabinet, they all united to deplore the back-stairs influence of "a certain personage." Had he not recently contrived to secure a grant of 40,000 gulden from the royal funds? Obviously the moment was propitious for fomenting public discontent with Wagner. And thenceforth an adroitly manipulated press made common cause against the composer. It was alleged that he designed to tamper with the Constitution, that he bragged openly about introducing dangerous innovations, and that he was laying sacrilegious hands on the time-honoured rights of the Kings and Commons of Bavaria. Wagner became Lolus, masculine form of Lola (Montez). There was much talk about the coming carnival, which this time would obey not the crack of a woman's hunting-crop, but the bâton of an orchestral conductor. It was not merely the music of the future that was the interesting thing, but the politics of the future. Wagner wanted to do away with the army. "This 'musicaster'-in-ordinary, who was once at the head of a band of incendiaries and assassins and tried to blow up the royal palace at Dresden, now means to sunder the King from his loyal subjects, to isolate him, and to incite an insurrectionary party to give practical effect to his treasonable doctrines." The King was brought to book for his weakness, his blind prodigality. So great was the effect of this campaign that the public, ever easily impressible, took alarm and began asking whether the Wagnerian virus were not a gangrene which, sooner or later, would invade the whole social organism. There would have to be a surgical operation. An article in which Wagner defended himself and denounced the real agitators brought the rage of officialdom to white heat.

However, for the time being Ludwig stands his ground. "O my beloved one," he writes, "all things are made difficult for us. The thoughts of you are my lasting support. I will never abandon my only one, were the feeling against him even greater than it is. We will be faithful to one another always." But this faltering Majesty was stiffly hedged about by his government and his family. His greatuncle, Prince Charles, the Queen Mother, Herr von Pfistermeister, President von der Pfordten, the Counsellor Lutz, all gave alarming accounts of the situation at home. They insisted that the throne was in danger and that the popular petitions made it clear that calmness would never be restored until Wagner was dismissed. On the 6th of December the Cabinet unanimously declared to His Majesty that he would have to choose between the affection and welfare of his people and the friendship of a man who had incurred the hatred and contempt of all the upright and healthy elements in the kingdom.

That night a great struggle took place in Ludwig's mind. He somehow divined that his fate was trembling in the balance. He must either play the King and establish his greatness, or consent to be for ever side-tracked. Would he be loyal to his friend that night, or weakly throw him over? Next morning Wagner received a letter couched as follows: "My very dear friend. In spite of the pain it gives me to do so, I must ask you to conform to the request made to you yesterday by my secretary. Believe me, I was *compelled* to do this. My love for you will always remain, and for my part I conjure you always to retain your friendship for me. In the fulness of conscience I can say to you: 'I am worthy of you.' Who can separate us? I know that you realize all I feel, that you understand how deeply I am grieved. I could not do otherwise; be well assured of that; and never doubt the loyalty of your best friend. It won't be for always. Till death, your Ludwig."

There are no farewells betwixt lovers, so the saying goes. And similarly there are no valid answers to certain sorts of letters. To begin with, Wagner thought about standing on his dignity. The king replied that he would see to that and safeguard their "ideal." Words, words, words! But it was precisely words that this handsome young prince pursued in his realm among the clouds.

On the 10th of December, as soon as it was light, Wagner departed, none with him save his old dog, Pohl. Eighteen months previously, when he arrived in Munich, he thought to settle there for the rest of his life—as he had always thought before, everywhere he went. Once more the Wanderer had the whole world before him, in which to tempt his fortune. He accepted his fate without regret. Hardly had the train begun to move than the outlaw began to breathe the blithe air of freedom. Glory, playing the celebrity, had clearly no place in his plan of campaign, and the veteran rejoiced to savour on his lips the bitter tonic of misfortune.

And now he once again beholds his beloved Switzerland, the Lake of Geneva, Vevey, and the Pension Beau-Rivage. Erelong he resumes his interrupted labours on the *Meistersinger*. "I look on myself as saved. . . . My hopes are in my work. . . . Complete isolation in a strange land, to live cut off from everybody—that is what I absolutely must have if I'm to come back to life." Thus he wrote before long to Mathilde Maier. To Cosima he says: "I've got to be deaf and blind for a time. . . . Nature in me is dead. You understand what I mean, and my consolation I hope will be that my appeasement will be complete. O Heaven grant that all experience be fallacious, all knowledge vain, and that only our love shall abide, strong and true." His thoughts also strayed to the young king who had given what he could give of his love, but had not had the strength to assert his rights. Wagner believed in him still, and pitied him, but put no more reliance on the strength of a hand that was altogether too heavily laden with rings.

So Wagner was back again in Geneva, where he had taken refuge after bidding farewell to Mathilde Wesendonck. He took a delightful little place in the country called "Les Artichauts" ("The Artichokes"), unpacked his case of manuscripts and drew forth the unfinished orchestral score of the first two acts of *Siegfried*, and likewise of the *Meistersinger*. An upholsterer was called in, and Wagner, for the twentieth time, set to work again, decorating, driving in nails, hanging curtains and portières. As of old, he devoted his mornings to work and went for long walks in the afternoons. But a most untimely outbreak of fire in his study, just after it had all been arranged, drove him forth in midwinter from his new abode and he set himself to find a place where the climate would be milder. From Geneva he went to Lyons, Avignon, and, finally, Toulon.

At the end of January in the new year, 1866, he was at the Grand Hôtel Marseilles when a telegram which had been following him about for two days was put into his hands. It came from Dresden, was signed by Dr. Pusinelli, and briefly announced the death of Minna. She had died suddenly of heart disease. It was too late now for Richard to be at the funeral.

Thus husband and wife, who had dwelt so long asunder, were quite alone when the hour of final separation sounded. For a time Wagner was stunned by the shock. It was years now since they had seen each other, months since he had so much as answered any of her letters. This silent exit set the final seal upon the past. The last frail breath of the unhappy woman, did it have any sort of effect on the husband who survived her, powerful yet disarmed? "Oh, she is to be envied," he wrote to Pusinelli, "for she has quitted the struggle without suffering. Peace, peace to the tortured heart of that unhappy woman." Fixedly he looked on the half-open door of the future, the lock of which had just been forced.

Chapter II

TRIBSCHEN IDYLL

"WAGNER'S wife is dead, and so is his dog, Pohl. A fine article could be written on his heartlessness, since he was not present at the funeral," said Bülow to Ritter. He meant Minna's funeral, for Wagner was very solicitous about the dead body of his old dog, and had a grave dug for him in the garden at "Les Artichauts," overlooking the lake. Shortly afterwards Russ, the Newfoundland, filled the place of the departed. And now, in the semi-solitude of Geneva, the first act of the *Meistersinger* was brought to a conclusion. Cosima came and joined Wagner, and the two set about discovering some sequestered place of retreat.

From now onwards, the secret love passages exchanged at Munich assumed the form of an open liaison. Neither one nor the other thought it worth while any more to study appearances, now that the Bavarian catastrophe had forced their hands. And since Minna, by thus vanishing from the scene, had left one part of the field clear, it remained to bring Ludwig II and von Bülow gradually to recognize the inevitable.

After a deal of searching about in Switzerland, the longed-for hermitage was at last discovered, quite near Lucerne on the shores of the Lake of the Four Cantons at the farthest extremity of a peninsula. It was an estate that had long been in the possession of the Am-Rhyn family. It was approached by a drive leading out of the highroad and terminating at the house itself, which was hidden behind a group of trees. In front, the lake curved gently in to the right and left, enclosing a grassy lawn planted with poplars, which was encircled by a pathway on a level with the water. The building, though simple in character, was a worthy example of the Lucerne style of architecture. It dated from the eighteenth century and commanded a view of the Rigi and the Pilatus. It was built on a terrace which, in turn, was flanked by two poplar trees. The entresol and the two upper stories consisted, each, of five bedrooms, in addition to the dining-

283

room and drawing-room. There was an abundance of air and space, and though somewhat ancient and out of repair, the whole place was full of charm. A high-pitched tiled roof, the stabling and offices, and a coach-house, completed the picture. But what was most important of all, a park of several acres, which secured the place against intrusion, made of Tribschen a retreat whose attractiveness it would have been difficult to surpass.

It was Easter Monday in the year 1866 when they took up their quarters there, just nine years after the beginning of Wagner's sojourn at "The Sanctuary." The weather was fine. The same April sunshine was warming the fruit trees now in blossom. It was a region of peace, of airy lightness, of music, and even the cow-bells seemed so sweet sounding and harmonious that he would not have exchanged them for the bells of all the churches in Rome. "No one," he said, "will turn me out of this."

A one year's agreement was forthwith signed and moving operations were put in hand at Munich, much to King Ludwig's despair, who saw the dearest friendship of his life thus slipping away from him. But the young monarch remained faithful to him all the same, and, as he had given his sacred word, subsidized Wagner on a generous scale out of the royal funds. Cosima wrote to His Majesty respecting the composer's affairs, and her husband's as well. For she had naturally decided to leave Munich, and wanted Hans to do so, too. Why, they were commonly dubbed (especially since relations between Bavaria and Bismarck had become so acutely strained) "the Prussian spies!" She, then, would settle herself in with Wagner at Tribschen, while Bülow would put up for the time being at Basle. "In Germany there's no place for our art," she declared. And in Bavaria not even the king's own friends were safe from molestation.

Thus, for each of these three began a strange part-ownership existence. Ludwig II, now more lonely than ever, an object of base suspicions, hedged around by plots, compelled to submit to the daily, dull, official round, incapable of making any resolution on his own responsibility, either avoided or ignored the exigencies of public business, which he called "official twaddle." Inspired with a belief in the sacredness of his mission, this young man, who was at once intelligent, weak-willed, and autocratic, sought relief from his duties as a monarch, in his reveries of art and beauty. He took refuge in the Isle of Roses from the importunities of his ministers, and busied himself drawing plans of castles in imitation of Versailles. In his eyes, Bismarck's declaration of war against Bavaria was not so much a disaster as a gross affront, and when, after just a month of fighting the

Prussians were everywhere victorious, Ludwig II immured himself in his Castle of Berg and professed his desire to abdicate. Such a swift and unlooked-for defeat, though it failed to cow his spirit, was a severe blow to his *amour-propre*. The fact that Bavaria had, in consequence, to relinquish a portion of Franconia was merely looked on by him as an incident detrimental to his prestige. Never did he feel the need of Wagner's friendship so keenly as during those weeks of defeat and humiliation. And Wagner did not fail him. It was the exile of Tribschen who inspired the king with courage to go on reigning.

"Praise be to God," wrote Ludwig II to Wagner, "Bavaria will retain her independence. Otherwise, if we had to submit to a Prussian hegemony, it would be good-bye so far as I am concerned, for I would never consent to be an impotent simulacrum of a king." And to Frau von Bülow he wrote: "I feel that I must write and tell you that it is altogether impossible for me to live any longer apart from the man who is all in all to me. I cannot bear it. We were made for one another; the Fates intended it; that, I see more plainly every day I live. But, dear friend, it is impossible for him to be here with me. I assure you that people misunderstand me and will go on doing so to the end of the chapter. It is no use hoping for anything here. As long as I am king, I cannot have him with me; the stars are against us. But things cannot continue like this—they cannot, for I simply could not go on living. Without him I am lonely and forlorn. We shall have to be united again for ever. The world does not understand us. What does that matter to us? My dear friend, I implore you to break it to him that I have made up my mind to relinquish the crown. Ask him to have pity on me, and not to insist that I should go on bearing these hellish torments. It is my sacred mission ever to be near him as a loyal and loving friend, and never to leave him. Tell him, I implore you, what I say. Show him that our plans can succeed; tell him that I shall die if I am called upon to live without him. Love works miracles. I could be of greater use to him this way than I could by remaining king. My brother is now of age. I will pass on the crown to him."

What answer could Cosima give to such a tale of passionate hope and black despair? What answer could Wagner give? Both he and she had arrived at a grave turning-point in their careers. They might easily have been tempted to wreak their revenge on Munich, to snatch this neurotic prince away from following a career of which none could, with any certainty, predict the issue, and thus make him a partaker of their exile. This time it would not have been a woman only that the Wanderer would have drawn within the vortex of his fate, but a king and, peradventure, a whole dynasty. That Wagner refused to do. Cosima took up the pen and, in the name of both of them, sought, without demolishing his hopes, to comfort and encourage the unhappy man. "You appear to me just as much a martyr to the crown as is your Friend to his Art. But it seems to me that the cross wherewith you are laden, is precisely your sovereignty's most lofty and most sacred dignity. How should I not understand you, my very dear friend. . . . But—but—in these troubled times, when all belief is debased to the level of filthy lucre, I have still retained my faith in the Divine Right of Kings. For me that has been an article of my creed. Yes, I have believed in you and you alone as the true king. The Friend will write to you. He is, of course, much calmer than I. He seemed prepared for what I told him. His strong spirit is not, like mine, a prey to anxiety and misgiving. He surveys the future with steady eye, and to him it is given to rebuild the art of the future, on the ruins of the present." All this meant "You must go on reigning." Ludwig resigned himself to the inevitable. But what Wagner and Cosima did not say was that they had now come to look on Bismarck as the saviour of Germany, as the strong man who would some day bring about the unification, under one ruler, of all the Germanic peoples. After the Prussians had been victorious over the Austrians at Sadowa, Bülow, who at the time was staying with his wife at Tribschen, exclaimed, "We three, Wagner included, say, 'Long live Bismarck and down with Austria!' Bismarck, in my eyes, is the Revolution as I want it to be, as it contents my heart." It seemed as though the hour had come at last for far-reaching reforms, for the New Age to arise, the hour that these patriotic idealists had been waiting for since 1848. They had outgrown the idea of a narrow Bavarian nationalism, confined to the valleys where Parsifal was dreaming of building his city dedicated to the Holy Grail of friendship. Deep in the seclusion of his Lucerne retreat, Wagner was striving to bring to birth the New Order, the Brotherhood of Man. To Bismarck the task of building the Empire; to Wagner the moulding of the New Art, an art so full of life and blitheness, the art of the *Meistersinger*.

Wagner devoted all his energy to the prosecution of his task, while the von Bülows were busy settling themselves permanently beneath his roof. To them and their two children was assigned all the upper part of the house, Wagner retaining the ground floor for himself. On the surface, all seemed calm and peaceful, but beneath that delusive semblance of tranquillity there was a

strong undercurrent of strain, irritability, and that acute nervous tension which usually made itself manifest when Wagner
was engaged on one of his great works. Hans was aware now
of all that was going on between his wife and Wagner. He had
accidentally discovered a letter which Wagner had sent her while
she was still at Munich. He knew all about the plans they had
formed for throwing in their lot together. He beheld their affection for each other growing and growing beneath his very
eyes. He saw how every walk they took, every sunset they admired, every page they conned together, and all the music that
winged its airy way through the wide-flung windows of Richard's study, seemed to lay his wife ever more deeply beneath the
spell of the enchanter. Von Bülow was like one fascinated by
the divine serpent. It never entered his head to turn and flee.
He listened, he marvelled, and he hated. Yet he would have given
all that he was, all his art, all his sorrow so only that that wondrous charm might grow more perfect still.

A few weeks earlier, Wagner had sent him a pressing invitation, couched in exactly the same terms as the one he had received when first they came to Munich. Hans knew that he, too,
was indispensable to the life of his tormentor. "Come! I ask you
in all sincerity, in deep and genuine friendship. If you but
hearken to my prayer, you will play a great, nay an unparalleled,
part in my development, in prospering my work, in which all my
future activity is bound up. Do exactly as you wish; be perfectly
free to come and go as you will, but henceforth, look on my house
as your house, my home as your home. . . . Hans, will you
grant my prayer? Yes, assuredly you will, for you know that I
love you and, save for my extraordinary relations with the
young king that well might dizzy and amaze, nothing, nothing,
absolutely nothing, binds me to life but you and yours." That
was true; but what von Bülow knew even more thoroughly was
that it had come to this, that Wagner could neither live nor work
now without Cosima. The moment had now arrived for Bülow
to decide whether he would claim his wife for his own or
whether he would let her go, in order that the work of "The
Other" should be brought to its glorious fulfilment, even though
his own happiness were to be the price. But the decision was
difficult—too difficult, and as yet he could not make up his mind.
In principle, he agreed to a separation, but he stipulated that
there should be no divorce for two years, and that during those
two years Cosima should go and live with her father in Rome.
He was hoping against hope that some miracle would happen.
Even now he could not bring himself to believe in any actual

infidelity. On the contrary, he felt constrained to take up the cudgels on Wagner's behalf against the base campaign of slander that had been launched in the Bavarian press. They had begun to harp on his debts again, to refer to his liaison. "Frau Hans," some of the papers gave out, "is the homing pigeon that links up Munich and Tribschen." Bülow sent his seconds to more than one editor, but no meetings took place, and Hans was reduced to defending his honour in a letter addressed to the *Volksbote*. King Ludwig was dumbfounded. "I cannot and will not believe," he said, "that the relations between Wagner and Frau von Bülow exceed the bounds of lawful friendship. Such a thing would be appalling." He further went bail for her fidelity, in an official letter addressed to von Bülow. But the journalists would have their say. Even Frau Schnorr, the singer's widow, put in her spoke, and the woman that Wagner had always looked on as a friend showed herself venomous, vindictive, and disgruntled, the reason being that Wagner had not asked her to marry him, now that he too was unattached. The poor crack-brained creature was devoted to spiritualism and announced that the ghost of her late husband commanded her to marry Wagner, while the medium of these seances—Isidora von Reuter—was to become the wife of Ludwig II. However, both these semi-lunatics were removed from Munich shortly afterwards and, as von der Pfordten, whose fall had been brought about by the 1866 defeat, had been replaced by Prince Hohenlohe, the anti-Wagner campaign became somewhat less bitter. Bülow sent in his resignation to the king and took up his winter quarters at Basle. Cosima divided her time between Basle, Tribschen, and Munich.

In spite of these disturbing events, the *Meistersinger* continued to progress. During the day, Wagner busied himself with the instrumentation of the first two acts, and at night he dictated his autobiography to Cosima. The undertaking was a delicate one, for, resolved though he was "to out with everything," he was bound to have some sort of regard for the feelings of people who, in whatever capacity, had played a part in his life. Still more important than that, he had to reckon with the retrospective jealousies of his fair amanuensis. That lady has been much criticized since not only for having hindered Wagner from expressing himself freely, but for having, in many cases, distorted the truth, by glossing over or entirely suppressing a number of passages. But how could it have been otherwise? The only sincere confessions are those a man makes to himself, if indeed there be any such, for, after all, the most constant piece of play-acting a man indulges in is the comedy he plays to himself. The most important thing of all is that we should explain away, to our own satisfaction, the various indefensible things that deface our lives. Our apparent frankness is, generally speaking, nothing more than dissembled pride. But the man who draws for one he loves the portrait he desires to bequeath to posterity, is infinitely more likely to limn it with strokes at once so indulgent and so flattering that everything ugly, petty, or unworthy—even though he make no secret of it— will be explained away by some hidden disability, some inherited tendency or some moral error whose vicious character is swallowed up in the effulgence of his ultimate renown. Nay, more; he prides himself on his very imperfections, because they furnish forth the portrait with shadows and half-tones that add to its interest. But this was not how it appeared to Cosima. When she gave herself to Wagner, she was not content merely to enter into the brilliant orbit of his genius; she took upon herself a mission; she set about constructing a firm foundation designed to explain the stormy past of a man who, she deemed, deserved to find, in the evening of his days, the noblest conclusion to his long and restless life. What she aimed at doing was to bring him, yet living, into the country of the gods, his own true home. That is her excuse. For it is unhappily true that Cosima cut a great many things out of Wagner's original manuscript, and that she afterwards burnt a number of documents which, though important, would have toned down and perhaps impaired the marble she had so patiently chiselled. All this is regrettable. Still, one must understand her desperate anxiety to justify him to the world, for her own apologia was to some extent his. Her own story was becoming part and parcel of Wagner's. It was not now the story of a life she was trying to tell, but a legend which had been told her and which she forthwith hedged about with the most zealous care. It was a fairy tale dedicated to posterity.

"We hear and see nothing of what is now going on in the world," she noted down for Ludwig II's benefit. "About midday, he tells me how he has been getting on with his work during the morning. In the afternoon he goes out for a walk across the fields, and I go to meet him. Then he spends an hour with the children, who are thriving here. In the evening he tells me the story of his life and all its difficulties, and the narrative always concludes with a hymn in praise of Parsifal. We hear only the sound of the bells as the herds come down from the uplands into our sunny meadows, where they gaze after us with their great big eyes. In the *salon* are the pictures of *Tannhäuser, The Rhinegold*, the busts of the Protector of the house and of his *protégé*. On the mantelpiece stands the 'Clock of the Minnesingers,' your first Christmas present, which Loge has moved in here. On the opposite side, between the two doors, is the portrait in oils (a present from the king), and underneath it all the different things he has had presented to him in the course of his career—silver cups, crowns, statues of Tannhäuser and Lohengrin. The piano is between the two windows; and above it hang the medallion-portraits of Liszt and von Bülow. The little room alongside the *salon* has been turned into a library. Upstairs is the study. Today Beckmesser has been set to music, following the incredibly beautiful scene between Walther and Sachs. When he sang me the passage he had just composed to the words: 'they were exacting masters, and their minds were oppressed with weariness and the struggle for existence,' we both began to weep."

And so even his Olympus Wagner peopled with his melancholy dreams. Nevertheless, he was now tasting, and that for the first time in his life, something like happiness. He had got his work to do; his house had people in it; he passed his word to the king that he would resume the *Nibelungen*, which he had not touched for years, as soon as the *Meistersingers* was completed. But his health had declined; the heart attacks had become more frequent; he was an old man before his time and he was continually wondering whether he would ever have time to finish what he considered was the greatest of his works.

Meanwhile the king was urging him to return to Munich. His grief seemed inconsolable. Nevertheless, completely solitary as his days now were, he suddenly became betrothed to the Princess Sophie, the Empress of Austria's younger sister. Wagner and Cosima at once sent their congratulations; and the king wrote back to Frau von Bülow, saying: "I was greatly touched at your letter. I am sure that you and the Friend will like to take an early opportunity of making the acquaintance of my dear *fiancée*. My love for her is deep and loyal, but the Great Friend will never cease to be dear to me beyond all others. This year will be a healing year." The unhappy man thought that this gracious Ophelia would set him free, not only from the love he bore his vanished Lohengrin, but from other obsessions besides. The last of his race, the poor tortured soul saw his brother's reason growing more and more beclouded, the family eccentricities becoming more and more pronounced, and he had long been aware of his own defects, whereof he was soon to have so disquieting a proof. In marriage, then, he thought he saw both a possible means of salvation and the necessary subordination of himself, his tastes, his Greek and Wagnerian ideals, to the exigencies of his royal state. The Princess Sophie would be his angel of salvation, but he recoiled from the notion that she would also be his wife. Richard Wagner would ever be, was bound to be, the purest well-spring of love of which his heart was capable. "You know," he said confidingly to Sophie, "you know what sort of destiny is mine. I wrote you not long ago from Berg on the subject of my mission in this world. You know that I have not many years to live, that I shall quit this earth when the horror is accomplished, when my star shines no more, when he shall have ceased to live, he whom I love so faithfully. Yes, then my life, too, will be extinguished, since to live on will be impossible for me."

That was a very melancholy utterance for a man who had just become engaged. The implication of these words did not long escape the princess, nor did they delude the king thus at war with his own nature. Less than a month after his official betrothal, he said to Sophie, "Of all women in the world, you are the one I love the best . . . but the god of my life, as you know, is Richard Wagner." During the autumn of that same year the engagement was broken off, and Ludwig II returned once more to his solitude and his castles, to play his part of the Doomed King.

And it came to pass that the loneliness in which he dwelt was even sadder than he had imagined it. Wagner was a traitor. The king was now no longer unaware of the bonds which attached Richard to the daughter of Liszt, and the secrecy with which the truth had been withheld from him made his beloved's crime all the more horrible in his sight. His thoughts reverted to von Bülow. He pitied him, he hated him, for not having been able to defend himself more capably, little thinking that, writing from Basle, von Bülow was even then delivering himself in this strain, "For six months now, I've been living alone, as a bachelor, with no family, no house, no home. All my belongings are at Munich, where I shall go on paying rent up to the end of April. Long live King Ludwig II, who is responsible for all this sorrow!" Poor Bülow, however, hurried off to Tribschen, where, on the 17th of February, 1867, his wife was delivered of her fourth daughter (the second by Wagner), who was called Eva after the heroine of the *Meistersinger*. Three weeks later, the final touches were put to the musical part of the mighty score. The author of it wanted to give it as a wedding present to his patron, and he thought of having it performed, in all its glory, at Munich on the day of the royal marriage.

Wagner was the only one who was contented. Cosima and her husband, henceforth completely disunited, nevertheless found themselves together beneath the roof of the "Glorious One."

But husband and wife could reproach each other as much as they would over the ruins of their shattered home; Wagner was in the seventh heaven because he had finished his opera. He could hardly be said to be living any more among the sons of men. He dwelt in his music, in generations to come, in that unknown future wherein artists extend their lives from season to season, surviving in their spiritual posterity. For in hearts that are growing old there occur certain "transmutations of values," and if Wagner no longer betrayed his one time yearning for death, it was because his joy in life was to some extent exhausted. The repose, on whose name he had so often called, for which he had yearned so ardently and which he now at length possessed, he would not employ to brood upon his sorrows, but rather to complete the work in hand.

Thus his first return to Munich was but a wearisome peregrination amid the vanities of worldly things. He saw Ludwig II once more, but a change had come over the relations between Richard and his disciple, and heart spoke to heart no longer. These fifteen months of absence, the peacefulness of Tribschen, Wagner's attachment—now openly avowed—to Cosima, Ludwig's political pusillanimity, his betrothal, and, finally, the new, post-Sadowa Germany that was emerging from the welter of diplomacy and threatening with its imperialism the ancient feudal monarchy of Bavaria and its exclusively nationalist ideals, were so many hidden barriers between the youthful ruler of a "passèd world" and the old musician of a dawning era. The only durable bond between them was Wagner's music. Therefore it was that Ludwig flung all the love and energy that remained to him into the task of organizing a revival of *Lohengrin* and *Tannhäuser* and the first performance of the *Meistersinger*. He founded the Conservatory of Music, which had been on the *tapis* for two years, prevailed on Bülow to withdraw his resignation, and appointed him director of this new academy.

But these various things did not go through without all manner of complications, moral and domestic. The Bülows took up their quarters again, for the time being, in Munich. The strangest part of these decidedly new-fashioned arrangements that now existed between the four actors in this bloodless drama was that Cosima now became the confidante of the king. Her cleverness and insight had enabled her to grasp, far better than Wagner himself, the feminine and stormy temperament of the moody king, how sensible to flattery he was, how weak and how completely he had identified himself with the characters of Lohengrin and Parsifal. Ludwig sent her gifts of flowers and pictures, and showered all manner of attentions on her, while she employed her utmost skill in maintaining him in a state of (Wagnerian) grace and in furnishing him day by day with proofs of her own fidelity, and Richard's, to the Protector that hovered on high above those ravening wolves, his subjects.

It was no enemy that Ludwig II saw in this young woman whose ethereal devotion was consecrated to the mystic Lohengrin, and to the artist's intellectual welfare, but an ally, an ambassadress between his heart and Wagner's. "Whoso has enjoyed his intimacy," she wrote, in a letter to the king, "whose spirit is inextricably mingled with his, feels naught but indifference for the rest of the world. I cannot think or say anything without asking myself what he would say about it, or recalling something he has already said. I confide these things to you, to you alone, for you alone understand them without the need of words." She tells him all about her daily life, keeps him informed of everything that is going on at the theatre and in town, about the difficulties of staging, about the orchestra, what her husband is working at, and Wagner, the things her children say, and so on. And Ludwig is grateful for it all. He who had once seen in her a hated rival was now overwhelming her with gratitude. Thanks to her, to her counsel, to her interest in public affairs, the burden of the crown seemed to have grown lighter. Cosima even succeeded in reconciling him to his people. For Ludwig had not forgiven his subjects for the way they had behaved over the "Wagnerian Revolution" and still less, perhaps, was he disposed to condone the hostile attitude they had displayed towards himself when, on the declaration of war with Prussia, they had publicly greeted him with hisses. But Cosima had a way of passing so soothing and delicate a hand over all these wounds! With a very different brand of tact from the Queen Mother's, she contrived to bestow on this builder of dreams the thing he lacked the sorest, namely, confidence in himself and his undertakings. Ludwig's horizon grew perceptibly brighter as he read these letters filled with expressions of gratitude and trust, of little things slipped in to fortify his *amour-propre*. And paradoxical as it may seem, Frau von Bülow was called on more than once to smooth over misunderstandings that would occasionally set the king against his beloved Richard. The Tichatschek incident was a case in point. Wagner had given his old friend the part of Lohengrin. But when the king saw him at the dress rehearsal and beheld, not the young and brilliant hero of his dreams, but a thickset sexagenarian, a veritable "knight of the rueful countenance," as he straightway christened him, he commanded that some one else should take the part. Wagner, all enthusiasm for the voice of the one-time Rienzi, refused to obey. The king persisting in his veto, Wagner, without a moment's hesitation, took the road to Trib-schen. It was a most disturbing interference with the course of affairs. But all those long months of slighted affection, and his unhappy engagement, had changed the timid disciple into an irritable fanatic, an impatient and captious fault-finder. Once the initial fit of rage was over, message upon message was sent to recall the offended *maestro*. He came back. But the atmos-phere of passionate enthusiasm was never quite restored. It was on Cosima that the task devolved of chasing away the shadows from the royal brow and putting things right with her husband, of bringing together two friends who had ceased to understand each other. "I most urgently beg you," wrote the king, "to do your best to prevail on him to come back at once. Oh, if he only realised the pain his departure causes me. If you knew what good every one of your letters does me! Any permanent separa-tion between me, you, and him could never be. The world would forsake its orbit ere such a thing could come to pass. It is nearly two in the morning and those heavenly harmonies are all about me still. I cannot tell you how the end [of *Lohengrin*] moved me. To hear one of his works is bliss so great that there is no other happiness on this earth to compare with it."

But the love-affairs of Wagner and Cosima were going to cost them dear, and, despite their efforts to preserve intact the affec-tions of Ludwig, von Bülow, and Liszt, they were fated to a large extent to lose touch with all of them, though they were the very three whom they would have given the world to keep.

The illustrious abbé did, as a matter of fact, arrive just then, to spend a few days in Munich with "Cosette." He was not in the dark concerning his daughter's liaison with his dearest friend, but however easy-going he might be—and oblivious of his own past—Liszt could not bear the idea of her abandoning her husband and her children. Bülow was not only his dearest pupil and his son-in-law; he was his spiritual heir. It caused the great and simple-hearted virtuoso an extraordinary pang to think that his daughter was betraying her Christian duties and making herself an object of scandal to the world. He therefore resolved to go and see Wagner at Lucerne, and get him to agree to the one and only honourable course of action. In order to prepare himself for this difficult step, Liszt went to six-o'clock Mass every morning; and then from the farthest recesses of a box witnessed the performance of *Tannhäuser*. "House packed, general enthusiasm," he wrote to the Princess von Wittgenstein, who was then in Rome. "After the first act, His Majesty brought a magnificent bouquet and handed it to his *fiancée*, who was present at the performance. The marriage has been announced for the end of November. But His Majesty's matrimonial ardours appear very temperate, and some people think it may be put off again, and that *sine die*." A fortnight later, this disastrous engagement was in fact broken off. Ludwig was free; no one's prisoner but his own. As for Liszt, he set his face towards Tribschen.

It was three years since the two friends had seen each other. Wagner was alone. Liszt found him aged and wrinkled, but scintillating with genius. They shut themselves up in the study, where Franz had made up his mind to demand what he felt was impossible, but what, for the sake of Hans, he hoped he would obtain. But what reasoning, what arguments ever convinced a lover against his will? Open on the piano was the manuscript of the *Meistersinger*, and Liszt, as a matter of course, took his seat at the keyboard. Very soon, in the lovely autumn afternoon, the chords of the Overture were echoing through the red-fruited orchard. Liszt read on with his customary sureness of vision, his incomparable power of divination. And Wagner sang. . . . All that they had been going to say to each other had completely vanished, swallowed up in the music. No other explanation was possible between them. That day, the inexpressible had been expressed.

"I have seen Napoleon at St. Helena," said Liszt, when he got back to his daughter's at Munich. He passed no judgment; he pronounced no blame. Only, a little while afterwards, he wrote to his friend Agnes Street as follows: "Things that are regarded as right and proper in ordinary life are only binding upon ordinary people. Wagner has bigger things in his head than that. He creates masterpieces, mountains hewn out of diamond." That was the excuse he found in his heart. But for himself God's love was the only love for which he craved henceforth. And if Liszt, in spite of all, still took his stand by Wagner, the silence was deep that fell, like a curtain, between them.

Ludwig II had recovered his peace of mind. "You may imagine," he said in confidence to Cosima again, "with what terror

I beheld the approach of the day fixed for a marriage which could never have brought me happiness. My one desire is to be free. She can start life again—and so can I. What would have become of our plans if this unhappy union had been brought to pass; if anguish of heart, sorrow, mortification had driven me to desperation? Where should I have found the enthusiasm for carrying on our ideal? No School of Music would have been built, no Festival Theatre. For me the *Meistersinger* would not have existed, nor *Parsifal*, nor the *Nibelungen*. I should have wandered about, the mere ghost of my real self, and death, for me, would have been a boon to long for. But now, everything, everything will be accomplished. Need I tell you how happy the recent performance of *Lohengrin* has made me feel? Thence it was I derived the strength to burst asunder the heavy bonds that held me. That divine work always indues me with miraculous strength." He went so far as to confess that he would have killed himself rather than consent to a marriage which he loathed. But the famous Festival Theatre was never built. The energy he deemed was his again he employed on ensuring that the *Meistersinger* should make its début and that was all. His thoughts then went wandering away to his castles. With him, poor deluded neophyte, not even his hatred of women and his contempt for his subjects ever took firm root. He merely devoted himself to the most banal displays of his regal state, and plunged into reckless expenditure, compared with which Semper and all his plans would have been moderation itself. Finding the door of the future shut against him, he turned his gaze towards the past. The thing that Wagner had most strenuously fought against, namely imitative art, Ludwig II now made his æsthetic ideal. Wagner gave place to Louis XIV, King of France, and architecture took the place of music. He himself wrote a monumental poem in which he sought to take his revenge for the wrongs that Fate had inflicted upon him as a lover. And the castles of Linderhof, Neuschwanstein, Chiemsee, and Falkenstein became his uncompleted Tetralogy, the sombre and magnificent memorials of his shattered dreams.

It was at Tribschen, with a wintry lake and snow-clad mountains before him, that Wagner brought to a close the orchestration of the *Meistersinger*. This tremendous work, conceived in 1855, begun at Biebrich, laid aside, resumed again at Vienna, and again forgotten during the whole of the Munich days, had been worked upon without intermission and brought to a conclusion during the last sixteen months. Now he must needs go down into the world again and fulfil the king's behest. Yet it

was not without a wrench that Wagner resolved to bid farewell
to his Lucerne abode. For one thing, he was tired. The pains in
the pit of his stomach had begun to trouble him again. However,
Cosima was awaiting his arrival. Richard and Hans! A heavy
burden, but she was young and strong, and she could bear it. So
Wagner started off, and reaching Munich by Christmas, took
up his quarters with the Bülows, and forthwith they set to work.

Wagner saw the king again; persuaded him to appoint Baron
von Perfall intendant of theatres in place of the existing holder
of that office and—Lachner having resigned his post as conductor—Bülow was commissioned to take entire charge of the
Meistersinger. That was just what Hans desired. Despite his
shattered health and his harassed nerves, work seemed to offer
him the only refuge, the only means of forgetting his domestic
trials. And now that he had his master and rival dwelling beneath his very roof, the racked and tortured soul flung himself
more completely than ever into the service of his tormentor.
They chose the singers between them, Fraulein Mallinger and
Frau Diez, Messrs. Vogl, Betz, Schlosser, Holzel, Nachbaur
(later the king's first favourite). They set young Hans Richter
to train the chorus and to tone down one or two of the soloists;
while, from the vantage ground of her *salon*, Cosima ably performed the indispensable task of keeping things sweet with
Ludwig II till the day arrived when, after many months of
strenuous work, the curtain once more arose on the *grande
première* of a work by Richard Wagner.

It was on the 21st of June, 1867, that this great event occurred.
Not merely did it blazon forth the universal glory of the composer, but proclaimed the newest development of his musical and
political doctrines, the metamorphosis whereby the revolutionary
had been transformed into the imperialist. For the first time, the
standard of a national German art floated triumphantly over
the Opera. Wagner had carefully prepared the ground by a series
of articles in the *Suddeutsche Presse*. These he brought together
in a brochure he entitled *Deutsche Kunst und deutsche Politik*.

As he had often done in his previous pamphlets, he introduced
his subject by comparing French art, which was wholly imitative, fettered by rules, and directed solely at achieving perfection of form, with the popular, undisciplined but wholly free
and profoundly poetic art of Germany. All honour to Winckelmann and Lessing, who brought to light the divine Hellenes,
their artistic ancestors, and revealed to the Germans the pure
ideal of human beauty as contrasted with the French theory of
civilization. And honour to Goethe, who succeeded in wedding

Helen and Faust! Honour to Schiller, who bestowed on the newly-risen spirit the name of "Young Germany." It was the German Youth that rescued Europe from Napoleon's yoke. After their victory over Napoleon, Napoleon that necessary corollary of Louis XIV, the Young German discarded the formal garb of France for the ancient German habiliments. He was a steady, clean-living fellow, religious, yet free from clericalism, and a great lover of dramatic poetry. But he did not immediately realize that in the theatre there dwells the germ and marrow of all national development, not alone in the domain of poetry, but in that of morality. And that because, if the theatre is not in the hands of the Great Enchanters, it relapses into those of the Furies of Futility, of the lewd and vulgar gnomes of fatuous diversion, all under the control of retired and wealthy bureaucrats. The theatre is an institution infinitely powerful for good or ill. Now, the basis of all theatrical art is pantomime, which is merely an imitation of nature. That is what realism is, mere aping, a necessary thing, no doubt, but low down in the scale. But the poet's duty is to interpret this realism, to reproduce its essential qualities, to isolate its character, and gradually, by means of this elimination, he will approximate to such a present-ment of his subject as will correspond with our notion of the ideal. Wagner then proceeds to an analysis of the French char-acter, that mixture of ape and tiger (as Voltaire has it) who, with the lapse of time, had become so perfect a comedian, that all Europe was ambitious to copy him. Germany wore herself out in the attempt. Germany had failed to take account of the fact that in Paris, owing to its size, there was always a fresh public to draw upon, and that a single play might be given a hundred or even two hundred nights in succession. But in the little German towns ten or fifteen performances would exhaust the box-office possibilities. The necessity of providing, night after night, for the entertainment of one and the same public created a problem of first-rate importance, to which the only solution was to in-flate the repertory with an appalling quantity of plays drawn from every period and every nationality. Such an expedient was both costly and unsatisfactory. Recourse was therefore had to the subscription system, and to royal patronage. But then some wanted one thing, and some another. The result was chaos, and the Hoftheater became "the Pantheon of Modern Art." From that, to making a play out of any sort of book or poem, no matter what, was but a single step, and the step was taken. And now there remained no other resource save to set it all to music. Another step—which they took at a bound! *Faust* was sung;

Schiller's *William Tell* was retranslated from the French and set to music by Rossini. As a reaction against these blasphemous proceedings, there was nothing for it but to turn again to the Young German, and to get hold of him as soon as he was old enough to go to school. And who was to have that task? Church or State? Under our modern social conditions the State seems to be usurping more and more the rôle of the Church, which appears to be resigning all its influence over the intellectual life of the people. And of this abandonment, the effect has become pretty rapidly manifest; for the lack of reverence resulting therefrom is part and parcel of the basic insincerity, the canker, which is at the root of our contemporary art. The State stands for nothing, and recognizes nothing, but what is "useful." "For that reason it rejects, with the most logical determination, whatever cannot establish a claim to being of immediate practical utility." The State's urgent and absolute duty was then to bring about its own regeneration, to rise from its merely utilitarian level to something that would satisfy the loftier aspirations of the people and offer it an education truly humanitarian and idealistic. Such an aim could not be attained save with the monarch's approving help. Supported by a wholly unselfish, chivalrous, and independent aristocracy, whose sole ambition it should be to serve the State, the king stands for the predominance of the moral over the merely practical law. He is the sacred depositary of two prerogatives essentially appertaining to the crown; mercy and beauty. Now, had not the time come for a king (the King of Bavaria above all) to facilitate the formation of a real German style? "And by that we mean the whole-hearted alliance between the art of the theatre and the typical work of a real German poet." Commercial considerations, as between public and stage, would here be completely done away with. Actuated no longer by a mere desire to be amused after the day's work was over, but inspired by the need for self-communion after the pleasures of a festival held at long intervals, the audience would pass into a special temple of art, which would be opened solely and exclusively for these rare and exceptional performances, there, in the noblest and most exalted spirit possible, to seek release from the cares of life.

Such, then, was the nature of the program that was designed to occupy the audience, on that night of the 21st of June, 1867. Ludwig II was deeply impressed. No one could doubt now that, one day or other, Wagner would come to build that "Temple of Art" which the development of his music logically required. *Tristan* had been a paroxysm, a sort of apotheosis, of the sorrows of man; whereas the *Meistersinger* was as it were a restful and refreshing glade opening out through the leafy landscape of German music. In this work, Wagner revealed an unknown facet of his genius. Reaching over the cruel experience of his Venice days, he joined hands again with his youthful past. He even recalled the memory of his journey from Bayreuth to Nuremberg, in the days when he was hurrying about from place to place in search of actors for the Magdeburg Theatre. And if, in spite of all, the vision of Mathilde Wesendonck would persist in mingling with this present task of his, it was wholly a vision of tenderness, support, and consolation. Long ago he had experienced that salutary influence; as long ago as 1861, on his return from Venice, when Isolde had bidden him seek, in work, an effective antidote against the philtre of desire. He had obeyed. And behold, he was whole again! And that is why the *Meistersinger* has that note of cheerful gravity, that serenity, that amplitude, which led Bülow to say that it would last as long as the German language itself should last. Of all Wagner's operas it is the only one which is not dedicated to death, but to life, the sort of life he liked and understood best, the plain, honest, unpretentious life of the craftsman, kindly, human life, firmly planted on the solid earth. Let us praise, too, the simplicity, the sober happiness, the mellow resignation of the dream of life as dreamed by this lonely voyager "through strange seas of thought," for whom at last the harbour was stretching out its arms.

A rare moment was this in the life of Richard Wagner. Cosima was not yet his wife, and he was about to lose King Ludwig. But he had won a hard fight, a fight which, for thirty years, he had been waging against himself. His musical problem was now resolved; his intellectual aim determined; that may be summed up as an imperial federation of the Germanic nations under the ægis of his art. Such, in truth, is the doctrine proclaimed by Hans Sachs at the end of his great appeal to the people of Nuremberg.

> Honour your German masters!
> You will enlist the aid of kindly spirits
> And if you forward them in their tasks,
> Even though the Holy Roman Empire
> Should fly away in smoke,
> There would yet remain to us
> The Holy Art of Germany.

The Wagner of '48 is dead. The Wagner of '70 has just been born. Mathilde's lover has yielded place to the future husband of Cosima. And the artist, now quite alone, who sits beside the king in the royal box, is neither the Flying Dutchman, nor Tristan, but a Wotan revisiting the earth to sing again the old romantic song of his faith in man, and—not without a touch of irony—to laugh at the rules, the laws, and the prejudices which separate routine from genius. The essential theme of the *Meistersinger* "gives utterance to the sad lament of the man who, though resigned to his fate, yet presents to the world a countenance instinct with cheerfulness and energy," as Wagner himself expressed it. It is the lesson of the god of Valhalla disguised as a cobbler. He is not rich like Pogner, or of noble blood like Walther; he can boast no asset save his honest, poet's heart.

Otto Wesendonck had come to Munich for the great event; but Mathilde did not accompany him. Bülow had never known such a triumph, but he was a broken man. That delicate spiritual pollen which rests upon the soul as the bloom upon the rose, so long as no cankering worm eats its way within, had vanished and left no trace for Wagner and von Bülow. And Liszt? Liszt had not quitted Rome. The very day on which the performance took place, he heard Mass in the Sistine Chapel, after which he played on his Bechstein for the Holy Father's delectation; and Pius IX rewarded him with a box of cigars!

Wagner set out alone for Tribschen when the performances were over. And Cosima received the following from the king: "I look on the hours spent with the beloved friend, the great and immortal master, during the first performances of his admirable work, as among the loveliest of my life." That was the last letter written by Ludwig II to his ambassadress. A few days later she went to join Wagner for good. The king and his "beloved" were to meet again after many years had passed; Wagner and von Bülow, never.

◆◆◆◆◆◆◆◆◆◆◆◆◆◆◆◆◆◆◆◆◆◆◆◆◆◆◆◆◆◆

Chapter III

THE MARTYRDOM OF HAPPINESS—
NIETZSCHE, FISHER OF MEN

VON BÜLOW knew that the time would come when he would have to separate from Cosima. His pride rose up against Wagner, though he recognized how great a man he was. Nevertheless, his animosity increased. He knew his wife would not flinch when it came to the point. He knew her too well to hope for that. Could he "do away with" his rival? For a little while he thought seriously of attempting the thing, and went in for some revolver practice. But he soon put aside such a childish idea. Scarcely had the curtain rung down for the last time on the *Meistersinger* than Cosima departed. She said good-bye to Hans, leaving behind her the two elder girls, and, bruised and broken as she was, yet all but free, she fled for refuge to the man who was awaiting her.

Wagner took her straightaway to Italy, where they spent some weeks in travelling. A new chapter of life was opening for them, and at the head of it they were fain to write no words but these: "Tribschen, Peace, Love, Work," the old, old blason of o'erwearied hearts, for Cosima was scarcely less foredone than Wagner. She was thirty-one and a half; he, fifty-five. Yet she felt older than this young-hearted veteran, who had been tossed about too rudely on the sea of life to grow old in mind or body. Nevertheless, Cosima felt very sure that her strength, her calm, her love were indispensable to Wagner, and that without them he would risk irreparable disaster. Therefore she took up the burden and became—as one of her intimates later on declared—the martyr of happiness. To her scrupulous and sensitive soul, the problem presented itself in many guises: there was the moral problem (Hans) ; the maternal problem (would they let her have her daughters?) ; the parental problem (Liszt's disapproval) ; the religious problem (she was a Catholic and Wagner a Protestant). The social aspect of it was the only one which did not trouble her at all. But, little by little, Wagner applied the salve, a soothing philosophic salve, to all her troubles and perplexities. And soon their love of solitude, their mutual sympathy and understanding, made up for all that they had lost. "I am always so much overwhelmed by his kindness to me, that, seeing how great I know he is, I feel like bursting into tears." So runs an entry in her diary under date of the 1st of January, 1869.

It was with a very genuine enthusiasm that she flung herself into her new duties, not only the material ones—the ordering of the household affairs—but the intellectual ones as well: letter-writing, negotiations with theatres and publishers, and, in particular, the autobiography which Wagner went on dictating to her. It was not without repressed emotion that she wrote the story of Richard and Mathilde. It is true that Wagner treated the events of 1858 with an assumption of airiness, and glossed them over in a way we can only now describe as regrettable, yet they struck pretty heavily at the heart of the woman who was now recording them and who had dared the thing from which Mathilde had recoiled. All these occupations filled her with pride and a sense of gratitude. Furthermore, she found that she was again pregnant. "In my womb the uncreate is stirring. My blessing be upon him! May his spirit be clear and kindly as this starry night, profound and peaceful as this lake. May the day come when he will think of his mother with love, of his mother who, with love, brought him into the world." Was this not Sieglinde's awakening amid the mountains of the Valkyrie, learning that she is to give birth to Siegfried, the fruit of her pain and the hero of the Young World. Count Eckart du Moulin, in his recent biography of Cosima, has rightly drawn attention to that. Indeed, in the record of all these domestic events, it is not "to consider too curiously," to read in them a living commentary on the Tetralogy.

The sweetness of love rested like a benison upon this period of their lives, especially for Wagner, who now, for the first time, pursued his labours with a mind entirely at rest. But, though she did not let it be seen, Cosima's heart was troubled, troubled because of her children; because of Hans, because of Wagner, of whom she still persisted in deeming herself unworthy.

At dawn, on the 6th of June, 1869, a Sunday, little Siegfried, Wagner's only son, was brought into the world. At the very moment of his birth the sun shone out above the Rigi. The bells of the churches in Lucerne began to ring, and Wagner's face was wet with tears. With his own hand he noted down these things in Cosima's diary, and then, resuming his work on the third act of *Siegfried*, the theme for which he had been searching came into his mind—"Blessèd be the womb that bare thee!"

This new bond between the two lovers was destined inevitably to bring on the divorce. At last Bülow realized that there was no alternative but to make up his mind to the sacrifice expected of him, and he gave up trying to save his face, as, for the last three years; he had been attempting to do. He asked the King's leave to relinquish his conductorship, and resigned his position as director of the School of Music which Wagner and he had founded. He would not, and could not, go on living in Munich. After some hesitation, Ludwig II agreed that he was right. Then the forsaken husband took up his pen and wrote a generous letter in reply to that which Cosima had written to him, asking him to set her free:

"I am grateful to you for taking the first step, and will not seek about for any reason to deplore it. I feel too much suffering of my own causing, not to refrain, at all costs, from laying the slightest blame on you. I take all the reproach upon myself, and to that position I shall firmly adhere in the discussions that are bound to take place, on this matter, with my mother and your father. I repaid you very ill for the attachment you showed me during our life together. I poisoned your life, and I can but feel grateful to you for the foresight which enabled you to find the necessary substitute when you could no longer put up with things as they were. But, to speak quite truly, the one, solitary spar to which I could cling in my shipwreck has been taken from me, now that you have gone. Your heart, your love, your patience, your prudence, your sympathy, your encouragement, your counsel, but above all your presence, your look, your words, all, all made up the rock, the very basis of my life. The loss of all these precious things—whose worth I learned not till I was bereft of them—is the undoing of me both as man and artist, and shows me I am bankrupt. Do not imagine that any hint of irony lies hid in this lament, or that I am endeavouring to hurt you; but I am suffering so greatly that I may be forgiven for uttering this cry, though I neither blame nor seek to blame any other than myself. You have seen well to devote your life, the treasures of your heart and mind, to one who is in every respect a great man, and, far from blaming you for what you have done, I grant that you are right from every point of view. I swear to you, the one consoling thought which now and then steals across my darkened spirit, and soothes my anguish, is that Cosima, at least, is happy."

But the strangest thing of all is that von Bülow's hatred appeared, in the first place, to be aimed at *Tristan*, which seemed a thing fraught with disaster for the human heart. One passage (suppressed) in his letter made the charge in so many words. Nevertheless, Bülow was to conduct many and many a performance of *Tristan* in the days to come. Nay, once he went so far as to exclaim, as he was coming away from the theatre after one of them, "Must not everything be forgiven the man who wrote a work like that?" But he was one of those who gloat over their troubles and live in them. If he showed that he knew how to play the game with regard to Cosima and Wagner, once, at all events, the bitterness of his soul bursts out in a letter he wrote to the Comtesse de Charnace, his wife's half-sister, an elder daughter of the Comtesse d'Agoult, explaining his attitude in the matter. We shall see, as we read, that Bülow wished it to be included in the schedule of his sufferings as a justification of his conduct:

You have had the kindness, madame,[1] to bestow gratifying praises on the spirit of equity and unselfish accommodation which I have manifested in a very difficult situation. I cannot but fear that you will be disposed to deprive me of your very precious approval by reason of the latest step I have been compelled to take, a step which in your eyes may appear gravely illogical. It is almost as painful to me to explain my action as to leave that explanation for time to unfold. Believe me, madame, I have done all that it was humanly possible to do to avoid a public scandal. For more than three years I took it upon me to live a life of ceaseless torture. You cannot form an idea of the corroding cares to which I was incessantly a prey. When, at long last, it came to the point, I sacrificed my artistic and my material position. There was only one other thing I could sacrifice, and that was my life, and I confess that that would have been the simplest way to settle the difficulty, to sever the inextricable knot. But from that I *did* recoil. Can that be imputed to me as a crime? Perhaps I should not have shrunk even from that, if only I had seen in him, in the man who is as sublime in his works as he is incomparably abject in his conduct, the least indication of a loyal impulse, the most transient sign of desire to act in an honourable and upright manner. Well, I shall bring no charge, and lay no blame, for fear lest I should impair the one thing that remains to me, and that is the consciousness of having behaved less guiltily towards him than he has behaved towards me. But the accusation that I have just set forth, and of which twenty years of close relationship have afforded me more than sufficient proofs, it was necessary to bring forward in order to free another person from blame, one who, in times gone by, bore so close and sisterly a resemblance to you, madame, not only in her high intellectual gifts, but in the loyalty, the openness, and the elevation of her character. When your half-sister is free (perhaps we shall have to wait a year from now for judgment to be pronounced), when she has legalized, so far as the world is concerned, her association with her lover, she will be herself again, nor any longer be compelled to prevaricate from morning till night. Now, what is there

[1] The original letter is in French.

illogical in my desire for a separation for which I was at first inclined not to seek a legal basis? Last November I asked her something that might almost have seemed indelicate, as to why she wanted to get away so quickly (I had vainly implored her to wait for Liszt, who was due to arrive in January). C. had no compunction in swearing a lie. That it was a lie I learned a few months ago, through the newspapers, who, without any beating about the bush, made public the good fortune which had befallen the *maestro*, whose mistress (so they openly referred to her) had at last presented him with a son, baptized in the name of Siegfried, a happy omen for the approaching completion of his opera. With this magnificent flourish was the copingstone set on the edifice of my cuckoldom. I could not get away from Munich, but the hell I've had to put up with during the latter part of my office there, no one can imagine. I was everlastingly in contact with crowds of musicians, professors, pupils; and, what with the publicity in the press, who did not mince matters in what they said about me (after I had conducted the last performance of *Tristan*, the paper with the biggest circulation commended me for the pains I had bestowed on the opera of my wife's "friend"), two things were open to me, either to be regarded as the most pitiable fool imaginable, as being unaware of what was plain to everyone but me, or to be taxed with the infamy of having entered into the most disgraceful bargain as favourite of a favourite of the King. At the same time, and before I had made a move in the matter, the newspapers announced that my divorce was imminent. I never spared myself in my efforts to arrange the divorce with the least possible amount of scandal, and the minimum of friction. But I cannot alter the law of Prussia. "By mutual consent"? Impossible to put that in. The only thing is to put down "desertion."

I am afraid I have been far too wordy in this explanation of mine. Still I hope it will serve to prevent you from judging me unfairly. That would be the only thing that could grieve me now. Time, they say, heals many ills—but even time has its limitations, and I am too deeply covered with shame to look for any mitigation from that quarter. I feel that I am an exile from my own musical fatherland, an exile from all civilized countries—I shall endeavour to drag out the remainder of my poor life in the obscure position of a teacher of the pianoforte. The only thing that upholds me now is the satisfaction of having made up here below for my sins. I do not expect a reply from you, madame, nor shall I write to you again, but, encouraged by your offer of sympathy and friendship, I beg that you will do me the favour of not bringing too severe a judgment to bear on your most humble servant

HANS VON BÜLOW.

15th of September, 1869.

Hans was not at fault. It took just a year to get the divorce through. This period of waiting, Wagner devoted to finishing *Siegfried*. But although he had chosen Tribschen as an inviolable hermitage where he would be safe from worldly interference, some new faces appeared there that were fated to play an important part in his life.

(On Whit-Monday, in the year 1869, a young German of twenty-five presented himself at the front door at Tribschen and asked to see the master. It was Friedrich Nietzsche, professor of philology at Basle University. He had called a few days earlier, but Wagner, being at work, would not be interrupted, and the only impression the young man carried away with him of his first visit was a few chords struck repeatedly on the piano, giving the effect of a complaint, a wearied yet persistent interrogation. (Nietzsche afterwards identified them as the passage in the third act of *Siegfried* in which Brünnhilde cries: "He has wounded me, he who awakened me.") He returned, however, this time in answer to an invitation, and could not have arrived at a worse moment, for the very next night Frau von Bülow was delivered of her son. Nevertheless, the young *savant* was hospitably received by Wagner, who had met him the previous winter at his sister's, Louisa Brockhaus's, and knew that he was passionately fond of his music.

Nothing could have been more momentous, one might almost say more dramatic, than the meeting of these two men, the one on the threshold, the other almost at the end, of his intellectual life. And yet they had both arrived at the point of junction where two generations still understand one another, ere yet the later one disowns the earlier and turns its back upon it. The fame which the older man had at length achieved, after a life-long struggle, seemed to him, despite the contempt with which he affected to regard it, to be the radiance of dawn. To the younger man it was as the fading glow of twilight. Wagner was living in his past, Nietzsche in his future. Wagner had expressed himself; he had given form to a symbolism in which his contemporaries recognized their faded ideals of 1848, next the resignation which succeeded them, and lastly the enchantments of a pessimism full of compassion for the human race. Nietzsche was a new fighter who was as yet unconquered, and whose strategy was as yet wholly offensive. He was intact. He had neither published, nor in any way revealed, the ideas that were labouring within him. He had not even selected his adversary. He only knew that he was endowed with a formidable might, that he would put it at the service of the mind, and that he would employ it one day to make visible, and then to destroy, "the calamities, public, latent, and elusive," that corrode the happiness of mankind. Wagner and Nietzsche had come face to face like dwellers on two different planets who, having discovered one another by means of the telescope, had contrived to meet together to compliment each other on their separate labours, never suspecting that one of them was fated to perish through the science of the other. And at the same time they resembled a father and son influenced by a common heredity and filled with that bashful, family timidity which makes them devote themselves to each other, baffle, combat, and help each other, without ever perceiving that they divined one another too accurately ever to come to an understanding.

Wagner, however, was not so old but that he knew how to make effective use of his magnetism, his convincing voice and even of his humour, which was ever at the service of his active intellect. He at once cast his spell over the short-sighted, shy professor, who could hardly summon up courage to show how pleased he was to have fallen in, on Swiss soil, with so stimulating a compatriot, whose society was a welcome change after that of his colleagues and pupils in Basle. The two men became great friends, and Nietzsche, on his return home, spoke of Wagner to his friend Erwin Rohde in the following terms: "Wagner is in reality everything we had hoped for: a great, a rich, and generous mind, an energetic temperament, a man of bewitching charm." Almost every Saturday Nietzsche set out on the road to Tribschen, where he spent the night and the Sunday following. They discussed Schopenhauer, the Greeks, and Wagner's writings. The young professor was completely won over. For him Wagner was the perfect example of what Schopenhauer calls by the name of genius. "His idealism is so great, his humanity so profound and so moving, his attitude towards life so grave and so sublime, that I feel, when I am in his presence, as though I were beside a god." Nietzsche ever found something new in his inexhaustible nature. He opened his heart to his fiery teaching. His life had been a studious one and he had been somewhat thrown in upon himself, but now it was nourished and transfigured. Nor were these high emotions all the tale. There was the gracious charm with which Frau von Bülow adorned their intercourse. That she should be daring enough to live openly with the man she loved, discarding any sort of hypocritical subterfuge, at first rather surprised the professor of philology, whose father was a pastor. But he admired courage wherever he encountered it, and Cosima struck him as beautiful, high-spirited, and worthy of a shining destiny. Love, thus proclaimed, carries with it a hint of tragedy which makes it akin to death, as Wagner had just exemplified in the third act of *Siegfried*. In regard to the kiss bestowed by the hero upon Brünnhilde, he explains, "The kiss of love is the first sensation of death, the cessation of the individuality. That is why Siegfried, in bestowing it, is filled with fear." A pregnant utterance. But Nietzsche was still too much of a neophyte, still too inexperienced, to discuss the truth or falsity of such a statement. Quite the reverse, he had something very different from a discussion in his head; he aimed at proving Wagner right on all points of his teaching. He dimly felt that his intellectual suppleness and the wide extent of his knowledge were capable of furnishing a solid basis to the Wagnerian ideas. He immediately began to try and establish, for the great myth of the Tetralogy, a sturdy genealogical tree that should link it up directly with the traditions of the Æschylean theatre.

The artistic atmosphere which now enfolded him was a rare stimulus to his own mental processes. "My Italy," said he, speaking of Tribschen. "My Greece," he should rather have said, since it was Greek art and the Greek drama that formed the subject of their conversations. "It is not only the great Æschylus whom you should seek at Tribschen," said Cosima in a letter, "but *your* Homer." For Nietzsche was preparing a course of lectures for his Basle students on Homer the Man. He read them over to his new friends, who at once realized their importance. And even now he was pondering on his *Birth of Tragedy, apart from the Genius of Music*.

Nor was Wagner slow to realize the important effect which the arrival of this exceptional reinforcement was going to have on the history of his life and art. His keen vision had enabled him to see that Ludwig II's royal sway had come to an end on the day that sentimental prince made it clear that he could not put the claims of the mind on an equality with the dictates of the heart, that is to say on the day when frustrated love bore down with it, in its fall, the vision of Parsifal Triumphant. And now the poor disciple wrapt in his useless purple was replaced by this new fisher of souls armed with a science universal, and Wagner was dazzled at the sight. Here indeed was the man he needed, the eleventh-hour craftsman, the apostle of a new gospel, the gospel of the New Art, of that German *Kultur*, imperial and popular, the gospel he himself had announced in *Siegfried* and the *Meistersinger*. Nietzsche was an example of the finer and more thoughtful kind of German youth, who would urge on the spiritual revolution of the morrow in accordance with the Tables of the Law drawn up by Schopenhauer and revised by Richard Wagner. A wonderful fulfilment of his destiny, since even in this secluded corner of the Canton of Lucerne the spirit of fire—that Loge, invisible yet omnipresent —broke out from between the stones of his wilderness to set fire to a crumbling world. How could he have guessed that a day would come when this attentive listener, with his delicate taste for music, this youthful proclaimer of his doctrine, would deny him, even as St. Peter denied his Master before Caiaphas. How should he know that this other architect of human happiness had wrought, when he was no more than twelve years old, another and a strange Trinity: "God the Father, God the Son, and God the Devil," for this, he tells us, was the beginning of his philosophy.

In Nietzsche, Wagner only saw a messenger from a purer and a better world, a man who trusted himself and a man worthy of trust. He asked him to arrange for his autobiography to be printed at Basle. He wanted it to be a surprise for Cosima and a few chosen friends at Christmas. The manuscript could only be delivered chapter by chapter, and there were to be twelve copies in all.[1]

Nietzsche's services were also enlisted by Cosima for the purchase of Christmas presents for Richard and the children. He inclines a patient ear to Wagner's complaints about the performance of *The Rhinegold* which the king insisted on having played at Munich, against his express desire. For the king had now taken the bit between his teeth. He adhered to his decision, apparently wishing thus to convince himself that he was free to do as he liked. He had acquired all the rights in the Tetralogy (having purchased them from Wesendonck), and it was to be given piecemeal, to suit the royal pleasure. Wagner regarded the experiment as premature, and felt that it would have a detrimental effect on his work as a whole. He therefore refused to support it. But Ludwig would have his own way. The performances were to be conducted by Richter. All this made it clearer than ever to Wagner that he would have to go back to his old plan and build himself a theatre of his own.

As good luck would have it, fresh guests arrived in the course of this summer and took his mind off all these worries. The visitors, this time, were French people, who had come all the way from Paris on purpose to see him. There was Catulle Mendès and his wife, *née* Judith Gautier (Théophile's daughter), and a friend of theirs, Villiers de l'Isle Adam, the writer. Judith Gautier-Mendès was not an absolute stranger to Wagner. She had heard his works performed at the Concerts Pasdeloup in Paris, and had sent him a number of articles she had written praising him up to the skies. He, in his turn, had written to her,

[1] It is now established that the narrative began, "I am the son of Ludwig Geyer," a sentence which was suppressed when, twenty-eight years after Wagner's death, *My Life* was published. Of the twelve copies, all but one— that in the Burrell collection—have disappeared.

and now behold her wafted across the lake from Lucerne, in a sailing-boat. Judith was fair of face. Mendès, and especially Villiers, were full of quaint conceits. They talked brilliantly and without any sort of stiffness, and Frau von Bülow at once felt delightfully at home with them. Wagner showed them all over his house and garden, displaying his pictures and the collection of rare butterflies he had brought with him from Paris. They got on wonderfully well together, notwithstanding that Villiers's elliptical mode of speech—scintillating though it was with sparks and flashes—was occasionally quite incomprehensible. Before long, Wagner sat down at the piano and played through some passages from *Siegfried*, "recited and [according to Judith] sang with incomparable gusto and power, and with such perfect expression that you would have thought the drama was being enacted before your eyes." These agreeable strangers prolonged their stay beyond the week. It seemed as though an attachment were already springing up between them. Judith was particularly enthusiastic. Yet once again the master's fascination had brought a woman's soul beneath his spell. "Wagner caught me today on the threshold of his study, that holy of holies which I did not dare to enter. I was peering in at the piano, the sheets of paper scattered all about, with the ink still wet on them, and I felt impressed to the last degree at the sight of all those human details of what to me was so evidently superhuman. Suddenly—it nearly took my breath away—I heard his laugh, a foot or two away, the laugh of the man whom I seemed to descry down the aisles of time, side by side with Homer, Æschylus, and Shakespeare, a man whom I should certainly have ranked among the greatest.

" 'What an enthusiast you are!' he exclaimed. 'You mustn't let it go too far, though, it's bad for the health.'

"He spoke as in jest, but the tender look in his eyes told me plainly enough what his laughter dissembled."

Judith Gautier's account reflected her enthusiasm, and there is no doubt Wagner was somewhat excited by it. On one occasion he climbed to the top of a fir tree; another day, he scaled the front of the house and, by clinging on to the projections and mouldings, managed to reach the first-floor balcony. He was still the acrobat of fifty years ago, Geyer's "Cossack." "Whatever you do," said Cosima, "don't look as if you thought it wonderful, or there's no knowing where he will stop." However, a cloud of unhappiness hung upon the fair face of Frau von Bülow. Once, when they had a few moments to themselves, she confided in Judith that the cause of her sadness was Liszt's opposition to her divorce. A few days later Judith was at Munich, visiting Frau von Schleinitz, the wife of a Prussian Minister and a close friend of Cosima's, when a priest, with clean-shaven face, piercing eyes, and bushy eyebrows, was shown into the room. It was Liszt. All the women present rushed forward and almost fell on their knees before the autumnal majesty of this erstwhile King of Love and Music. Liszt was with Madame de Moukhanoff-Kalergis, the friend of Chopin's, Musset's, and Wagner's.

"Have you seen Cosima?" he asked, hurriedly, the moment he was introduced to Judith. "Please say nothing against your daughter," was her reply. "I side with her completely, and I will not have it that she is in any way to blame. Who would not gladly yield to the prestige and fascination of genius?"

"I agree with you, absolutely," answered Liszt, under his breath, "but I must not say so. My cloth imposes certain views upon me which I cannot openly repudiate. I know the power of these attractions of the heart too well, to judge them harshly. If, for appearance's sake, I am compelled to keep silent, no one longs more ardently than I for the legal settlement of this painful affair. I can do nothing to hasten it. As for hindering it in any shape or form, such an idea has never entered my head."

All these people had come to Munich for the first performance of *The Rhinegold*, which had been put on by order of the king, but against the wishes of the author, who knew how inadequate, puerile, and ridiculous the stage arrangements were. But the king insisted that it should be played, come what might. He had spent 60,000 florins on the scenery, and he had made up his mind to hear the music he loved.

Hans Richter, a young man of twenty-eight, and an admirable conductor, who had just been appointed to the Theatre Royal in succession to von Bülow, sided with his master and sent in his resignation. Betz refused to sing and Wagner secretly hurried from Tribschen to look into matters. He was not allowed to see the king. Perfall—though he owed his post as Intendant to Wagner—came out as his implacable foe. But the artists, every one of them, were for Wagner. They received threatening letters because the performance was postponed. Even the Mendès and Villiers were bombarded with anonymous and insulting missives. "You're the people who have prevented the theatre folk from carrying out the king's orders. You're the hirelings of a traitor, and traitors yourselves." The authorities implored Wagner to go away, for fear of fresh trouble. He went. And *The Rhinegold* was performed with whatever conductor and whatever Wotan they could lay hands on, for Ludwig II would have it so, in order that no one in his kingdom should henceforth tax him with weakness. None of Wagner's friends were there, not even Liszt, who thus missed *The Rhinegold*, the *Meistersinger*, and *Tristan*. But Franz was determined to keep the promise he had made to Judith. He therefore went *incognito* to Tribschen, spent a night there, and the cloud which had so long been lowering upon this strange assortment of friends dispersed in tears.

The last few months had been highly eventful ones, and everyone was feeling the nervous strain. "Thank Heaven, Wagner's health is good," wrote Cosima to Judith, "but yesterday I found him sitting in his armchair weeping; I didn't ask him what he was weeping for; I knew too well. . . ." Another time, talking of von Bülow, she made this confession to her new friend: "I have been in such a terribly desperate state of remorse that all night long I kept asking myself whether it was not criminal of me to go on living, whether the situation did not require the sacrifice of a life, and whether it did not behoove me to fulfil that sacrifice. In the morning, when the master came to greet me, I flung myself into his arms, and for the first time in my life let him see all the heaped-up misery of my heart." However, calmness again prevailed. Wagner went on with his work, and Cosima waited for the divorce to cut the Gordian Knot. "The master goes on with his work; *Siegfried* grows apace, both on paper and in his cradle, and all the rest goes well. Only, your friend, my dear Judith, now and again heaves a sigh as the notion steals into her mind that all this well-being is as it were the crystallization of her tears. . . . Guess how we've been spending the last few evenings, the Master and I! Playing Haydn's symphonies for four hands, and—would you believe it? —playing them with infinite zest. We chose the twelve English symphonies which Haydn wrote after Mozart's death, the workmanship of which is a marvel of care and delicacy."

Ottilie Brockhaus, the Orientalist's wife, also came to see her brother. She was beginning to realise that he was making a stir in the world. She admired the furniture. "The sister," says Cosima, "said it was no wonder I stuck to my guns, seeing what nice furniture I had got. The Master, in a state of consternation, kept on telling me he had not seen her for twenty-five years. Then, in a fit of desperation, he ordered the boat and took them back where they had come from, for good and all, it appears, for I have not seen them since. As a set-off against this, we have had a visit from a young philologist whom I am sorry I had not an opportunity of introducing to you, for he is distinctly one of us

—kindly, intelligent, and whimsical. He went quite pale as he listened to the third act of *Siegfried*, which the Master has just sent off to the King."

The young philologist was Nietzsche. Thus came into being the intellectual sodality of Tribschen, admiration of Wagner being the common bond that united them. But if on the one side all this enthusiasm was perfectly blameless, it was less so on the other. For this the responsibility must be laid at the door of the fascination always exercised by Wagner over the female heart, which was further reinforced by the conditions of loneliness in which he lived. No, Judith had not been wrong. She had rightly recognized something more than platonic regard in the "tender" glance of this connoisseur of life and form. Artist, creator, philosopher, yes, but when a man of fifty-six goes playing the gymnast to show how strong and lissome he is, it is surely because he wants to be admired as a man. And Wagner was, terrifically, a man. That is really his distinctive note. The finest homage he could pay to death was this determination to drink life to the lees. It never left him, and one thing he never grew out of, the love of showing-off. Wagner loved being loved. It was then that his energies were at their height. "I know I'm getting old," he said, about this time, "and yet my life is only just beginning."

To love him as Cosima, Judith, and Nietzsche loved him, that was well and good; but not as Ludwig II loved him—for his own exclusive pleasure. For this rage for things theatrical on the part of the king was nothing but pride, jealousy, and revengefulness. This and nothing else it was that led him to give orders, after *The Rhinegold* reverse, that they were to perform *The Valkyrie*. Again the author attempted to oppose it, and again Ludwig insisted on having his way, finding fault with the Secretary of his Cabinet, Counsellor von Dufflipp, for taking Wagner's part. Why didn't he come back to Munich? Was it for the king to put up with the consequences of his self-imposed exile; of his wilful temperament? Wagner shrugged his shoulders, sat down again to the instrumentation of the third act of *Siegfried*, and began *The Twilight of the Gods*. After all, had he not found a magnificent compensation in Nietzsche?

Nietzsche was ever the unfailing guest at Tribschen, where he would arrive at any time of day, where he even had his own "sanctum," his "thinking-room," his *pensoir*. Cosima read over the sketch of *Parsifal* to him and the master talked to him about the philosophy of music, and discussed Nietzsche's recent essays on *The Greek Music-Drama* and *Socrates and Tragedy*. "Richard

Wagner gave me a most thrilling account of the destiny he believes to be in store for me. It is all very heart-searching." What
this meant was that he thought the doctrines of *Opera and
Drama* were rather confused. Even at this stage he feels himself called upon to revise them, to link them up, by fresh
formulas, to the Hellenic tradition as, in the light of Schopenhauer, he had come to conceive it, a conception far removed from
the high and dry university tradition. The great misunderstanding which later on produced such a gulf between Nietzsche and
Wagner was in being in their earliest letters. But if the pupil
was already on the *qui vive* and anxious, the master never
detected a hint of the discord. He kept urging Nietzsche to attack
the *magnum opus*, the future book in which he looked to find the
justification of all his theories and the apotheosis of his musical
philosophy. "Perhaps you could relieve me of a good half of my
mission, and, in the process, discover your own in its entirety.
. . . Explain to us then what philology does for us and help me
to inaugurate the great Renaissance in which Plato will join
hands with Homer and in which Homer, enriched with Platonic
ideas, will become, in truth, Homer the Great." But though
speeches such as that might well have struck alarm into
Nietzsche's breast, the atmosphere of Tribschen was too exhilarating for his youthful enthusiasm to suffer a decline. "It
vastly enriches one's life to get to know a genius like that at
close quarters. So far as I am concerned, all that is best and
finest is bound up with the names of Wagner and Schopenhauer, and I am proud and happy to find myself in agreement,
in that respect, with my best friends."

The fact is he never was more happy. With Cosima, "the only
highly gifted woman he had ever known," in that peaceful
garden with those snowy uplands before his eyes, Nietzsche felt
his knowledge expanding and shaping itself into an entirely
new whole. He takes stock of his ideas; he discerns the secret
of music, of music as a whole, of all philosophy. He perceives
that "tragedy is born of the genius of music," a maxim with
which he was soon to preface his first book. He dwells upon the
inscrutable enigmas of Brünnhilde, Wotan, Empedocles, and
Ariadne, the heroes of Greek and Wagnerian mythology. And
he longs for the glorious distinction of explaining them by an
entirely new philosophy of art, namely the Dionysiac conception
of the world. Wagner was to be the spiritual godfather of the
work, seeing that he alone acknowledged that "the existence of
the world can only be justified as an æsthetic phenomenon."

But if there was, intellectually speaking, no one to whom

Wagner felt himself more closely drawn than Nietzsche, he only became the more uncomfortably aware how, owing to the conduct of Ludwig II, the cleavage between his music and the public was growing more formidable than ever. All along he had suffered by reason of the mistaken interpretation of his work. This time, in the case of *The Valkyrie*, it threatened to be disastrous. This was why the idea, which he had long entertained, of building a theatre for himself came into his mind again more forcibly than ever. Cosima agreed with him and wanted to set to work.

On the 5th of March of the following year, 1870 (she notes the date), there came to her lips a certain name, the name of a little village to which reference is made in the autobiography. When he was a young man of twenty-two Wagner had been there and seen the sunlight flooding down upon its Old World, sleeping palaces, and the name of that village was Bayreuth. She turned up the name in her gazetteer, and this was what she read: "A small town in Upper Franconia, formerly the capital of the margraves of Bayreuth-Ansbach. . . . Castle of historic interest. . . . *Hermitage*. . . . Magnificent theatre in the rococo style." Why shouldn't the Festival Theatre be built at Bayreuth? It was what Wagner had dreamed long ago. It would also be the final, the crowning fulfilment of his work. Twilight? He did have a vague presentiment of something of the sort, now that he was composing the fourth part of his Tetralogy, the last instalment of his myth. But Death, who was always leaning head in hand at his piano, would wait till the work was done.

On the 22nd of May Wagner celebrated his fifty-seventh birthday. Cosima hired an orchestra of forty-five musicians from Lucerne, befittingly to commemorate the solemn occasion. Liszt sent a telegram: "In good and evil days, indissolubly thine." And King Ludwig II, visited by a sudden inspiration, presented Wagner with Grane, the very steed of the Valkyrie. . . . Nevertheless, Cosima was sad, torn with anxiety, beset with apprehensions. Her thoughts turned to von Bülow, who had now taken up his quarters in Florence. How lonely he must be! She has a choking sensation in her throat. She hurries away to her room to hide her tears. And, mindful of her youth, she puts down in her diary the following phrase of Madame de Staël's, which had come into her mind: "Those days when the weather was so fine, and I was so unhappy."

Early in July her divorce was pronounced. Hans even let her have the children. She was now free to marry Richard. It was at this precise juncture that there began to be talk in the newspapers about the possibility of a war with France. On the 19th war was declared, and it was Emile Ollivier, her brother-in-law, president of the Imperial French Government, who ascended the tribune of the Palais Bourbon, to proclaim the news to the nation.

On the 25th of August, after the amazing victories gained by the German armies at Froeschwiller and Forbach, one week before Sedan, and in the Protestant Church, Lucerne, Wagner was married to Cosima Liszt. He addressed a patriotic poem to Ludwig II of Bavaria and a letter to his mother-in-law, the Comtesse d'Agoult. His wife wrote to Mathilde Wesendonck; and a few days later Isolde sent to Cosima a bunch of edelweiss.

Chapter IV

"THE TWILIGHT OF THE GODS" AND
THE DAWN OF BAYREUTH

Two days after the surrender of the French Emperor, little Siegfried was baptized at Tribschen, in the middle of a thunderstorm. Their old friends, the Willes, had run over from Zurich. To Judith, Wagner wrote as follows: "It looks as if thunder and lightning were going to play a big part in the life of this redoubtable child. But I love these portents from the sky, though those earthly ones which have robbed us of the pleasure of your company displease me mightily." The guns were sounding in 1813 when Richard was born and Napoleon I was defeated. Again, the guns were sounding in 1870 when Siegfried was baptized and Napoleon III was overthrown. It seemed as though the annals of the Wagners were destined to be linked with German victories. It was not to be wondered at, therefore, that the strains of a Cantata to the Armies were heard at Tribschen, or that Wagner, the aforetime revolutionary and internationalist, had now become a militant imperialist. "Those earthly portents which displeased him so mightily" was but a *façon de parler* designed to let his Parisian friends down lightly, for during these early months of national enthusiasm over the triumph of a cause which lay so close to his heart he was as much carried away as a soldier of victory could well be. Moreover, he held that he himself had had a hand in bringing about the triumph. Still, he had retained a certain sense of irony and his little comedy, *A Capitulation*, has no more importance than a caricature for the *Kladerradatsch* (the German *Charivari*). The wit was rather heavy-handed and it gave considerable offence in France. There was no need to be so angry. Wagner himself confessed, later on, that he had done it with the sole purpose of showing what a contrast there was between French wit, with its lightness and originality, and the lumbering clumsiness exhibited by the Germans whenever they try to embark on such flights of fancy. Whatever importance we may attach to that not very convincing explanation, he gave evidence of greater generosity when he wrote, almost at the same time, his *Souvenirs sur Auber*.

Be that as it may, one cannot be seriously angry with Wagner for displaying this lapse of taste when his country was taking so formidable a revenge for the starvation he had endured in 1840 and the insult to his *Tannhäuser* in 1861. Deep down in his heart these things had always rankled, and his anger with Paris was all the more bitter because Paris had been the seat of all his hopes. It was like being jealous of a woman who has withheld her love from you and bestowed it on some worthless rival. But her coquetry, her refusals, nay, her very cruelties, prevent us from forgetting her. And in the end we forgive her her fickleness, for, with all her bourgeois tradition, she has a warm heart. Wagner, in 1870, had not lost his love of Paris, and Paris had scarcely begun to conceive a liking for Wagner. "You remember what you went through during the siege," he said, writing shortly afterwards to Judith. "It's horrible. Let us always avoid quarrelling about those things; they're not worth the powder that was wasted on them." And to Cosima he remarked that the only fitting attitude to maintain in regard to such events was silence. Silence, indeed, was advisable since some of his dearest friends were strangely divided in their sentiments regarding the new state of affairs in Europe. Liszt, for example, an inveterate and unalterable Parisian, one of whose sons-in-law was called Emile Ollivier and the other Richard Wagner—Liszt remained staunch for France and Napoleon. Ludwig II, despite that his hand had been forced by Bismarck in the matter of the convocation of the German princes when the Empire was proclaimed, did not put in an appearance at Versailles, but sent his brother instead, for he was afraid that the triumph of the new régime would cost Bavaria her independence. Nietzsche himself, the herald of the New Age, took up a very enigmatic position. He had gone off with the troops as a hospital attendant. He went all through the siege of Metz and contracted dysentery and diphtheria in the process. Back again in Basle he expressed himself thus in regard to the situation: "The course civilization is taking causes me the gravest anxiety. Provided we don't pay too dearly for the nation's astounding success in a domain where, for my part at least, I don't intend to endure any sacrifice: I look on present-day Prussia as a power highly dangerous to civilization. Let us be philosophical enough to keep our heads in the midst of the general excitement."

Christmas however found him at Tribschen with Wagner, who had just published an essay on Beethoven, "a revelation of the spirit in which we shall live henceforth."

The fact was that there was something in this intellectual music which recalled certain Dionysian touches from his own lyre, that had little enough to do with the piping of Marsyas, and the young professor was gifted with too fine an ear not to detect them. But what matter? The other music was so beautiful, so convincing! And how fervently did Nietzsche listen to the master's latest work, *The Idyll of Tribschen* (Siegfried Idyll), played for the first time that very Christmas morning, which was also Cosima's birthday! Wagner stationed an orchestra on the staircase of his house and it was to the appealing strains of this symphony, conducted by Hans Richter, that his wife awoke. What exuberant strength it showed, and what a fine piece of stage-management on the part of the old enchanter! Nietzsche was profoundly sensible of it all; and these days made an epoch in his life as being those in which "the Glorious One" truly underwent the influence of the man who afterwards called himself his successor. It was the sole occasion too on which Nietzsche spoke of a mission of the German race, a mission founded on courage, and not, as heretofore, on the vain and perishable graces of Franco-Jewish civilization. However, the effects of this Wagnerian anti-Semitism did not long endure. Nietzsche soon uprooted every trace of it, and took arms against the Christianizing element, the dawning mysticism, betrayed by his master, in a word, against the whole ethical idea of *Parsifal*. They had come to the parting of the ways. Nietzsche, for the sake of his health, made a journey—his first—southwards, as far as Lugano, and when he came back, brought with him a rough copy of his completed work. He went over to Tribschen to read it to his friends. They were disappointed. Neither Richard nor Cosima could recognize that theory of tragedy from which, in classic panoply arrayed, the Wagnerian opera was to arise. The philosopher returned to Basle to revise his manuscript and in a few weeks brought into being the wonderful book which is known as *The Birth of Tragedy*. Meanwhile, on the 5th of April, Wagner put the finishing touches to the orchestration of *Siegfried*, and then set out for Bayreuth.

"Bayreuth, a small town in Upper Franconia, formerly the capital of the margraves of Bayreuth-Ansbach. . . . Magnificent theatre in rococo style. . . ."

For a hundred years, that rococo palace had been wrapt in slumber. It was long now since the little margravine, own sister to that great King Frederick II, had ceased to receive in royal state the homage of those noble lords, her vassals, in their silks and golden trappings. No more did she busy herself with her painting, or bid her minstrels play, her ballerinas dance. No more did she squander the substance of her faithful lieges. She slumbered like her palace of stucco and marble, like the rustic Hermitage which she had built at the gates of her capital to serve as a sort of Masonic Lodge within whose sheltering walls *les dames galantes* of her court might keep their tryst secure from prying eyes; and by her command, it was adorned with rose-coloured quartz, mother of pearl and dainty shells and softly murmuring fountains. And now, for many a day, all round about the palace of this fair, dead butterfly the town had stolen with muted tread, lapsed in the silence of a city discrowned. Year after year had come and gone, and no Prince Charming had ever drawn nigh to disturb the calm of her repose. And then, at last, as the eighteenth century was drawing to its close, there came a poet thither who styled himself Jean Paul, those being, in truth, but his own two Christian names. There, for twenty years, he wrote his books and charmed the ear and won the heart of Germany, telling her of all the marvels of her forests, the quaint comicalities of her little courts, of the beauties of Italy, of the reality of things invisible. And on his death, a public statue was erected to his memory, and then, for half a century more, the town resumed its slumbers.

But one morning—it was the 18th of April, 1871—the seneschal of the palace was startled by a lusty ringing of the bell. Hastening to answer the summons, his eyes lighted on the figure of a man below the middle height, whose age appeared to be in the neighbourhood of sixty. His features, which were well defined, were fringed by a pair of grey whiskers. His brow was furrowed, and a deep line traversed his nose just where it left the forehead. He spoke with an air of authority, asked to be shown the park, made enquiries regarding a wooded site which adjoined it, and declared that the place pleased him so well that he, too, would build himself a house there. Then he hailed a fiacre, drove all about the town, north, south, east and west, and finally informed the burgomaster that he had chosen a site on the summit of a hill commanding a view of the city, and that there he intended to build his theatre. He leaned firmly on the arm of his young wife, looking before him with unfaltering gaze, firm in the assurance that King Ludwig and the whole of modern Germany would second him in an undertaking which should set the crown upon his life's work.

He was still the Musician of the Future, the Philosopher of the New Age. Once more he was fain to cast off the trammels of the past. Some days earlier he had returned her love-letters to Mathilde Wesendonck. Now he was making ready to bid a last farewell to Tribschen and Switzerland, thereafter to make his home at Bayreuth. He was for taking it all unto himself, the houses with their flower-decked balconies, and those antique, aristocratic-looking streets, where all those many spirits that obeyed his spell were one day soon to congregate. All should be brought to pass, even as he had willed, and to the Wandering Mariner should come at length the saving ransom of a faithful heart.

He took Cosima to Leipzig, to show her the House of the Red and White Lion where he had been born, fifty-eight years before. From there, they went on to Dresden, Dresden where his *Rienzi* had first seen the light and where Minna had looked her last upon it. They saw once more the friends of other days, and, in the evening, went for a stroll round the Opera House. The sconces were ablaze with lights. The theatre was packed from floor to ceiling. The music smote the ear in gusts, with a sort of subterranean, unreal effect. It was the music of the *Meistersinger*. Thus did Wagner behold his name flinging a wider and ever wider shadow athwart the world.

In Berlin there were *fêtes* in his honour. A concert, organized by the Countess von Schleinitz, took place in the presence of the Emperor and Empress, making magnificent amends for the hisses that had greeted *The Flying Dutchman*. Next, Wagner paid a visit to Bismarck. But the two great men of Germany did not succeed in finding any particularly close bond of sympathy. "They looked long at one another," notes Cosima, in her diary. But Wagner thought it inadvisable to ask the Chancellor for any financial assistance for his Bayreuth scheme. The fact, no doubt, was that their spheres were too wide apart; moreover, it is likely enough that the Prussian giant who had just put Europe on a firm basis of fact and reality, looked a little askance at the little revolutionary, about whose reputation there still clung a hint, a savour, of the burnt-out idealism of '48.

Wagner had doubtless too much independence about him to hit it off very well with princes and rulers. And now, King Ludwig II gave him to understand that he totally disapproved of the Bayreuth scheme. But Wagner would not budge an inch, and the enterprise was advertised in a large number of German towns through the medium of the various Wagner societies. The aim was to get together somewhere about a million marks in the shape of founders' shares, at 900 marks apiece. Ludwig repented of his opposition and subscribed to the tune of 75,000 marks. Other groups soon joined in. The conscript fathers of Bayreuth, fired with enthusiasm for a plan that looked like rousing their city from its long trance, offered to make a free gift of the site for the Festival Theatre. Abbé Liszt, infinitely poorer now than his illustrious son-in-law, drew on the little sum he had laid by in the Franciscan treasury for the 2,700 marks he needed in order to take up three founders' shares. Good news was pouring in on all sides, when suddenly came the tidings that Tausig was dead, Tausig the amazing pianist, and president of the Berlin branch of the "Friends of Wagner." He was barely thirty, and the news came as a great shock to Wagner. It did indeed seem as though, for every step forward on his road, "Fate"—as he said to Schuré at the time of Schnorr's death—"was to rob him of a friend."

However, Wagner did not flinch, and never abandoned hope. The number of *Vereine* increased by leaps and bounds. *Lohengrin* was being played with a success beyond all expectation at the Teatro Communale, Bologna. And, most important of all, the end of his task was in sight. Amid the peaceful surroundings of Tribschen, he continued working at *The Twilight of the Gods*, encompassed about by Cosima's adoring love. Yet she, on her side, was consumed with anxiety about the future and stood in constant need of solace and encouragement. "A noble sentiment is immortal because it takes from life its instability," was a thing he used to say to her; "it has nothing to do with yesterday, today or tomorrow. Hell begins with arithmetic." Nevertheless, he was preaching a serenity which he did not possess. Real peace of mind was for ever eluding him. "I curse this music which thus puts me beside myself and never suffers me to enjoy the good that fortune brings me. Here is my own son who is passing by me as in a dream. The *Nibelungen* ought to have been finished long ago. It is sheer madness. Or else one ought to be like Beethoven, and revert to the savage state. It is not true, as you all will have it, that music is my natural element. My vocation was to pursue my cultural development and to make the most of life." Would it not be true, then, to say that the trend of his life was in constant opposition to his deeper nature? For inwardly, the idea of leaving Tribschen where he had spent more than six years of peace and contentment, filled him with dread. And Cosima still more. Highly strung and intensely sensitive as she was, she knew perfectly well that her husband looked to her to make the most painful sacrifice a woman could be called on to make: to immolate her own individual happiness on the altar of Wagnerian glory. She continued to look after the administrative side with admirable precision and ability, seeing to the running of the various theatrical enterprises, the Wagner societies, attending to the details connected with the publication of his works, literary and musical, conducting the correspondence with Feustel (the banker) and Adolf Gross, new Bayreuth friends who had taken in hand the weighty business of the Festival Theatre; caring for the children, managing the house, replying to questioners, and satisfying the curious. But if in public she bore no traces of fatigue from the performance of these onerous duties, it was different when she was alone. Then a kind of physical depression weighed her down, so that she had to open her diary, where, under the outward flourishes of admiration and gratitude, she hid the anguish she felt in her heart, when, seeking the man she loved, she found no more than a celebrity. The woman who has been taxed with having no thought for anything but fame and glory, had all the jealous apprehensiveness of a young girl. Tears would come at any moment, and in those notes in her diary that reflect the secret workings of her heart she set down the incurable sorrow that was hers because she had not been his Isolde. Sometimes she would come rushing into Richard's room and, taking both his hands in hers, ask him, "Do you love me?" And he would reply, "If I had not found you I should never have written another note of music." And then she would go back again to her pen. "It is on these days of merrymaking that one feels how sad a thing life is. When I try to tell him how I love him, I feel how completely powerless I am. Only in death's last embrace shall I be able to tell him that." So Cosima was to be what Wagner had willed that Senta should be, and would fulfil her mission to the very end.

The winter—the last winter at Tribschen—went by tranquilly enough, beneath a somewhat sombre sky, what time the marvellous *Twilight* grew to maturity, culminating in the funeral march of *Siegfried*. Nietzsche had sent them his *Birth of Tragedy*, which had been published on the 2nd of January, 1872. "On every page," he said in a letter to Wagner, "you will see I have tried to thank you for all you have given me. . . . I feel with pride that I am marked with a sign and that my name will evermore be joined with yours." Wagner's reply was prompt: "I have never read anything finer than your book." And Cosima, "How beautiful and how profound it is! How

THE CASTLE AT BAYREUTH

LOWER GROTTO OF THE CASTLE

profound and how daring! Who will repay you for it! That is
what I should feel so anxious about, did I not know that in the
conception of the work itself you have found the highest reward. In this book you have called forth spirits whom I had
thought obedient to our Master alone. . . . I have read it like
a poem which should give us light on the deepest problems, and
I cannot put it aside, any more than the Master, for it gives
an answer to all the mute, instinctive questions of my soul."
Every day Wagner reread a page of it before settling down to
work on the third act of *The Twilight*. Nevertheless it was a
book for the few, for everybody and nobody, as Nietzsche said
later on of his *Zarathustra*. Above all it was a book for the
people of the future, whose minds had been formed by Wagner's
music. Such at least was what its author held in all good faith,
when he tuned *his* thoughts to the music of the Tribschen
Wizard, and the fair landscape animated by the softly gliding
figure of the graceful Cosima. As Professor Andler remarks:
"For Wagner, Naxos was wherever Cosima was. And wherever
Wagner was, there was the spirit of Dionysus." But this friendship's honeymoon was about to draw to an end and the house
at Tribschen to close for ever.

As early as January, Wagner had interrupted his labours
and had set out on his journey to Berlin and Bayreuth, where
his business was to fix on a definite site for the theatre as well
as for the house which he had resolved to build to shelter his
declining days. He then returned to Tribschen and sent out
invitations to the shareholders to take part in the ceremony of
laying the foundation stone of the building. The date was fixed
for Whitsuntide of the current year (1872), although the subscriptions were still far short of the million required. But great
hopes were placed on King Ludwig and the *Vereine*, particularly those in Berlin, Vienna, and Mannheim. When it was
made clear that the king was immovable and would not give
another penny, they thought about getting up a public lottery.
Then Ludwig said he intended having *Siegfried* put on in
Munich, regardless of the fact that the composer wished him
to do nothing of the kind. Wagner for a moment felt inclined
to let the whole thing go hang, and to make his home in Italy.
. . . Or should he accept the proposals made him by Darmstadt, Baden-Baden, and even far-off Chicago? Cosima had all
she could do to smooth him down and bring back her galley-
slave to drag his chain of glory. What a piece of irony! There
was happiness, heading away to sea like a barque on the tran-

quil waters of a bay. At last the old prisoner gave in. He went
back to his chains.

On the 22nd of April he bade adieu to Lucerne, to that little
poplar-fringed nook of ground, the home of liberty and dreams.
Then he set out for Bayreuth. His wife and children were to
join him a few days later. And Cosima wrote thus to Judith:
"One last word from Tribschen, my dear Judith, Tribschen
which we are quitting with full hearts, and I, at least, with an
anxious one. We could not leave without sending you our re-
membrances and our love. Wagner has finished the pencil draft
of Act III of *The Twilight*. He has not been working as much
as we had hoped, for he has been unwell, and very much put
about. I don't know when he will find time to get back to work, because there are no end of things to be done, negotiations, jour-
neys. . . . On the 12th of May a concert at Vienna; on the 22nd
the *Ninth Symphony* at Bayreuth and laying the foundation
stone of our theatre."

Nietzsche came to say good-bye to Cosima after Wagner had
gone. It was the last Saturday in April. There were trunks and
packing-cases not yet closed down, all over the house, which
was now almost quite empty. The air, the very clouds, seemed
heavy with sadness. The servants were in tears. The big Newfoundland would not touch his food. The piano was still in its
place; Nietzsche sat down at the keyboard, and began to im-
provise so movingly that Cosima was completely taken aback.
She did not know that Nietzsche possessed this gift, and that
he was able thus to give expression to the pure affection that
linked his soul with those who had entered so deeply into his
life. Did she divine in it some deeper implication? Did she guess
the hidden significance of that wordless avowal? How should
she have failed to realize that he was making her his Ariadne
and that this Naxos of their dreams, which, that day, was
collapsing in ruin, would rise again, sixteen years later, when
the lips of Nietzsche were unsealed in the garrulity of madness
at Turin. He had to depart abruptly, to hide his emotion. And
Cosima, in her diary, wrote these words: "What fate is awaiting us? Where is our destined home?"

On the 19th of May, Whitsunday, the guests poured into
Bayreuth from the four quarters of the globe, wafted by all
the winds of heaven. The old city was robed in all its best.
On every hand people pointed out to one another celebrities of
one kind and another, singers, conductors, great ladies of the
Berlin court (the Countesses von Schleinitz and Doenhoff), Malwida von Meysenbug, Madame de Moukhanoff-Kalergis, young

Professor Nietzsche, all friends of the master's and founders of the theatre which would soon be rising on the summit of the sacred hill. But Wagner's thoughts were running on the absent ones, alas! eternally the same, on Mathilde Wesendonck, and Franz Liszt; to whom, this time, were added Hans von Bülow and King Ludwig II. Thus the most intimate of his friends, those who were nearest him in heart and mind, were by some malign and secret irony debarred from joining in the consecration of his life's work. Nevertheless, Bülow had forgiven him. And twice at least he made proof of it, like the generous fellow he was, giving two concerts, at Mannheim and at Munich, in aid of the Bayreuth theatre. Liszt was at Weimar. There, for some years now, his old mode of life had been resumed. The Grand Duke had installed his old friend in a little house standing in the flower garden where he reigned over a whole concourse of adoring pupils. His dark princess had stayed on in Rome, a voluntary anchoress, closeted the livelong day with her theological manuscripts. But since his marriage, Wagner was conscious, in his relations with Liszt—and that, despite their tears of reconciliation—of a sadness that would not lift. They had ceased to correspond. The silence between them grew more and more impenetrable. And yet the abbé *did* expect an invitation. It came at last; but it came too late and he did not leave home. But it was worded as, in his heart, he had hoped it would be:

"Cosima will have it that you won't come, even if I ask you. So then we shall have to bear this, too, we who have already borne so much. Nevertheless, I intend to send you an invitation all the same. And you know what it means when I say, Come! You came into my life as the greatest man to whom I ever spoke in terms of loving friendship. You cut yourself off from me, perhaps because you had less confidence in me than I in you. In place of you, the most intimate part of you, a 'you' born a second time, comes to satisfy my ardent longing to know you wholly mine. You live then in full beauty before me and within me, and we are united even beyond the grave. You were the first who, by your love, ennobled me. I now proceed to a second and higher existence through her to whom I am wed, and so I am able to accomplish a task which, without her, I should have been powerless to fulfil. So it is that you have been all in all to me, while to you, I have always been of such little account. What immense advantages, then, you have given me over you. If I say to you, 'Come,' I mean by that: Come to your own home, for it is yourself that you will find here. Blessings be yours and love, whatever your decision may be."

Those indeed were fitting words to use; for the only possible mediator between them was the being who had sundered them and thanks to whom they now could, and *should*, be brought together again. And so the peerless player, striking triumphantly the strings of love, made this reply:

"Dear and Glorious Friend, I cannot reply in words to your letter, which has deeply moved me; but I fervently hope that the shadows and circumstances which keep me away will disappear, and that soon we shall meet again. Then you will understand how inseparable my spirit is from both of you, how it has found new life 'in that second and higher existence of yours in which you will be able to accomplish that which, alone, you could not have fulfilled.' I see, in that, a gift from Heaven. God's blessing be upon you, and with it all my love."

The festival began with a solemn performance of the *Ninth Symphony* in the old rococo opera-house of the Margraves. For, in default of the influential patronage of living friends, Wagner decided that his future temple should be dedicated to Beethoven. But in spite of the deep enthusiasm of the faithful, there was a hint that the veteran warrior was growing weary when, mounting the platform, he turned to the leading horn in the band and said, "Now not so much as a touch of feeling. . . . It must sound as if it were behind a veil." The hymn to gladness then burst forth, full of the sense of mystery which Wagner had breathed into it, at the time of the famous performance at Dresden in 1846. It was a splendid apotheosis of old German art, brought out into relief by the imponderable harmonies whereby the disciple contrived to infuse it with new blood. And more than that, it was a hymn of gratitude, of gratitude to the guide who had given aim and direction to the searchings of his successor and had brought him the assurance that an art both authentic and modern had uprisen from his toil.

The following day, the 22nd of May, it was raining. Under a lowering sky and a heaving sea of umbrellas the multitude watched the little wizard of this new Hill of Enchantment, as he made his way along in the mud. He grasped the hammer that was offered him. "Blessed be thou, my stone. Keep strong and hold fast." It sank into the soil, bearing the charm enclosed within it which began with these words: "Herein I seal up a secret; may time keep it inviolate." He also added a telegram, just arrived from King Ludwig. "From the bottom of my heart I send you, my very dear friend, my sincerest and warmest good wishes on an occasion fraught with such importance for the whole of Germany. Success and blessing to next year's great work. Today, more than ever, I am with you in spirit." Wagner was terribly pale when he got back again into his carriage with his wife and Nietzsche. Nietzsche, describing the incident later on said: "He was silent, communing within him with an expression on his face no words could tell. That day he was entering on his sixtieth year. All his past life had been a preparation for that moment. We know that men, in times of urgent peril, or at some important crisis of their existence, see their whole life as in a flash, beholding their past, whether recent or remote, with extraordinary vividness and detail. What sight did Alexander the Great behold when, at such a moment, he made Europe and Asia drink from the same cup? But what Wagner saw with his inward eye that day—what he had been, what he was, and what he would be— all that, we, his intimates, can up to a certain point, like him, discern; only that Wagnerian look will enable us to see his lofty deed—and that understanding will be our pledge of its fecundity."

After the ceremony the whole company returned to the Theatre of the Margraves and Wagner addressed the founders.

"Thanks to you," he said, "I find myself today in a position that has assuredly never been held by any other artist before me. You are believers in my promise to found for the Germans a theatre of their own, and you furnish me with sure means to erect it before your eyes. The temporary building whereof we have just laid the stone, will aid us in our task. When next we meet together in this spot a building will be here to welcome us, and in its lines you will read forthwith the story of the idea of which it is the incarnation. You will find that it has been wrought of the plainest materials. . . . You will note, perhaps with surprise, the absence of those fanciful decorations with which places of entertainment are usually adorned. On the other hand, you will find in the proportions, in the fittings and arrangement, of the place, the manifestation of an idea which, once you have grasped it, will transport you into a new and different order of things, that of the *Bühnenfestspiele*. . . . Such is my plan. . . . Since I am obliged to trust myself to carry out the artistic work to which I have alluded, I gather all my courage from the hope that has been breathed into me by my very despair."

There was a further and final reunion that same evening at the Sun Hotel. Wagner drank to his absent Parsifal, the king, whose lonely image haunted his mind, despite the disappointments which he had now been suffering for so long at his hands.

"It is usually one's duty," he said, "to offer thanks to the sovereign for the benefits received from him. But to me this prince is more, far more, than to anyone else in his kingdom. What he is to me far transcends his immediate person, for what he has required of me, inspired in me, and accomplished with me is bound up with a future which concerns us all, which extends far beyond what we understand by bourgeois and social life: a high spiritual culture, a stretching out towards the loftiest goal which a nation can set itself to attain. Such is the significance of the wonderful friendship of which I am here speaking. When permission was granted me to come back to Germany, and when nobody in the whole country, particularly the official academies, had any use for me, the king's generous voice called to me, saying 'I will protect you, artist whom I love. Your aims must be fulfilled. I will set you free from all material preoccupations.' That generosity it was that made possible the miracle of which you have just been witnesses."

So the guests drank the health of the royal recluse. Then they took their departure, and silence again descended upon Bayreuth. The masons set to work on the Wagnerian acropolis. At the other end of the town, on the fringe of the Margraves' park, there began to rise the dwelling in which Prospero designed to live out the rest of his days, and in which every third thought should be his grave.

PART FIVE

Chapter I

THE FIREBRAND OF VALHALLA

IF IT is a satisfaction to the mind, it is certainly a comfort to the heart, to note the progress of a man whose fortunes we have followed step by step as he fought his way first through poverty and hunger and the dangerous zone of middle-class, soul-killing self-complacency, till he reached those privileged regions where genius is welcomed as a relief to boredom and the work of a great artist as a pretext for luxurious display; if it is instructive to watch the stubborn fighter conquering successively the dim stretches of indifference to gain at length those heights where he may breathe at ease and taste the repose for which he craved and find that new equilibrium, that sort of ideal relationship between himself and the world, which had always figured in his imagination; if, in a word, there is pleasure in the thought that all his troubles have not been in vain, since the traveller has at last reached his goal—nevertheless our satisfaction is not wholly free from anxiety, not indeed as to the value of his enterprise, but, now that we know he has reached the end of the long road along which he has toiled with so much sweat and agony, sowing his masterpieces on the way, lest there should be nothing more left for us to discover in him, nothing more to admire, nothing more to fear. Our interest in one who attains the complete realization of himself is in danger of disappearing forthwith in the fierce glare which robs him of his mystery. Now, the years that still remained to Wagner he bestowed on Bayreuth. The story of the final triumph of his ideas and of his music, might, one would suppose, be summed up in a few pages. But such a man as he was not fated to enjoy undisturbed the honours of a renowned old age; nor must it be thought that the last fragment of his life was nothing else than an apotheosis. Wagner never enjoyed that direct homage which we call success, because a success of that sort was for him a thing impossible. "His madness was not of the head, but of the heart," says Byron in his *Lara*:

> In him inexplicably mix'd appear'd
> Much to be lov'd and hated, sought and fear'd.

But was Wagner's madness of the heart? Is it perfectly sure that he had a heart? If he had, is it discernible and, above all, was it ever a determining factor in a life that was apparently governed solely by the head? To estimate that "heart" at its true worth we must at the outset make up our minds that we shall not find it in its pure, elementary, and simple state, but mingled with all manner of alloy. Now this adventitious material, although foreign to his nature, was as strong as he, and gave him its colour and its weight. Inwoven with his heart, it controlled its magnetism, and dwelt in it, as a supplementary force. It is of little moment that we may discern in that heart various qualities, say, ambition, kindness, will-power, spontaneity, egoism, unscrupulousness, all that medley of things "we love and hate and seek and fear," as Byron has it. The very poise and firmness of Wagner's heart perhaps explain how it was that at the very height of his creative fervour he never neglected the business side of his work, and that he never gave of his love without exacting a sacrifice in return; and that, for all his artistic sensibility, he never went a-dreaming in the clouds, but reared his edifices on solid ground. The dreamer would bring his dreams to pass; the philosopher would be a man of affairs, the lover would wed his love. His aims were the aims of a captain of adventure. He would weigh the chances, reckon up the cost, and then, once his mind was made up, this lover of logic would risk his all on what he believed to be the winning card. As for fame, he cared not a fig for it, as he said over and over again. But he strove to bring his work to completion and to put the coping-stone on the edifice of his life, well knowing that the laurels would be added. He divided his career into two parts; one, artistic creation, the fiery demon, "God the Devil," as Nietzsche had it, in which he abandoned himself to the uncontrollable impulses of his genius; then came the other part, exploiting his creations, getting them put on, trying to make them pay, putting up, for fifty years, with humiliations, poverty, hunger, yet endeavouring—and with formidable success—to avenge himself for the mistrust, the incredulity, and the meanness of mankind. It was only now that he came to know himself, to judge himself, and to know and judge his fellows.

How should such a restless heart ever find repose? He had

named the house he was having built for him "Wahnfried" ("Peace of mind"). But that could only have been a motto for the benefit of its subsequent occupants. "Wahnfried," like the Festival Theatre, was but another of those illusions of which Wagner had need to nourish that tremendous energy till the task was over, till the third act of *The Twilight* and *Parsifal* were finished.

And that energy, mark you, never slept, for his adversaries were on the warpath. No doubt Wagner found in his new neighbourhood, in the municipality of Bayreuth, some excellent and strangely devoted friends, such, for example, as Burgo-master Munckler, Feustel the banker, the latter's son-in-law Adolph Gross, and the Pastor Ditmar. Artists they may not have been, those sturdy, sensible citizens, but they were all the better business men for that. Still, nothwithstanding all this, the anti-Wagner campaign showed no signs of abatement. A Munich spiritualist, pamphleteers in Berlin, Koenigsberg, and Cologne, vented their venom in the newspapers. Nietzsche was taken to task in his turn by a former pupil, the young philologist Wilamowitz-Maellendort. Wagner deemed that a reply was called for, and wrote an open letter to the press in which he took up the cudgels on behalf of his "literary lackey," as the *National Gazette* insisted on dubbing the Basle professor.[1]

Thus the world would not let Wagner rest. And Wagner did not rest. He was incessantly active during these years of prepa-ration for the Bayreuth efflorescence. He wrote his essay on *Actors and Singers*. He undertook tour after tour, going from Mannheim to Frankfort, from Strassburg to Darmstadt, from Cologne to Hanover, Magdeburg, Berlin—anywhere, in short, that they played his music and where he thought he might dis-cover his future interpreters, scene-painters, and stage-hands. He was always busy inspecting, selecting, writing. He got to-gether a number of useful records for the Bayreuth archives. He even established closer relations with King Ludwig and Liszt, with the object of gradually bringing them back to the fold.

Liszt was the first to return. On the 15th of October, 1872, he at last put in an appearance at Bayreuth and stayed with the Wagners in the rooms they were occupying while "Wahn-fried" was being built. The years of separation were over and the Wagner household became, or rather, again became, his

---

[1] Nietzsche, it will be remembered, was avenged by his friend Rohde, author of the famous *Psyche*. Moreover, Wilamowitz himself subsequently recanted.

own. And how was Liszt to do anything else but make it up with those he loved, despite the jealous resentment of old Princess Caroline? Liszt's real greatness lay in his kindness of heart. "Cosima is still 'my terrible daughter,' as I used to call her in the old days: an extraordinary and highly meritorious woman, far above the level of ordinary judgments and wholly worthy of the feelings of admiration she inspires in all who know her—Bülow, her first husband, to begin with." So wrote he to the recluse at Rome. "The foundations of the new theatre of the *Nibelungen* are beginning to arise. The enterprise is so extraordinary that it will probably succeed—despite the ill-natured, captious, carping, fault-finding things that are said about it. Wagner lives a very retired sort of life. Thursday night, however, he made an exception, and entertained about a dozen people or so. The other days and evenings the three of us have had entirely to ourselves. The five children are perfectly brought up and singularly charming. Cosima surpasses herself. Let who will judge and condemn her. For me she will ever remain a soul worthy of *il Gran Perdono* of Saint Francis, and my most admirable daughter." Wagner read aloud his sketch of *Parsifal*. The abbé was so overcome that the only way he could think of to express his emotion was to sit down at the piano and play some of Bach's fugues and *Tristan*. However, his daughter thought he looked very much aged, very worn out and depressed. He had attacks of nerves; a sort of feeling that he must get away from people. Just as Tolstoy, trying to escape from the effusive affection of his family, dropped down and died in a railway station, so Liszt went off to hide his distress in a city that happened to be on his line of route, to wit Ratisbon. He celebrated his birthday in the solitude of the cathedral; then he went back to Budapest, where he was now in the habit of spending a part of the year. There he, good Christian soul, ever eager to discover some outlet for his emotions, found again that peace and solace, without which he could not live. "The happiest hours of my life," he said, "are when I am kneeling with some poor old women in my parish church, Saint Leopold, or in the church of the Franciscans, during early Mass. I light my taper and pass it on to my neighbours with a royal delight, blessing the sweet yoke and light burden of Our Lord Jesus Christ."

It was at this time that Cosima became a Protestant. Love, no doubt, was the motive power. For the religious difference between Richard and herself was a terrible weight upon her heart. How could she endure the idea of an eternity in which she would be for ever separated from the man she loved? It was no doctrine, no point of dogma, nothing concerning the Blessed Virgin or the Pope, that was involved here. It was paradise and nothing less. And the only justification for such a step in the face of all the inborn instincts that restrain and hold one back is love, and one's faith in love. But Cosima, whom her husband's sorrow had not availed to deter, did not shrink from an act in which her very soul was at stake. Thus was her submission signed and sealed. But of the trials and troubles of which her diary is so full we find no traces in the entries of this date. On the contrary, the page that records her conversion to Protestantism is among the happiest of her intimate avowals, as though the very puissance of her resolution repressed the fluttering of her heart. "When we embraced each other, Richard and I, it seemed to me that our marriage had just been consecrated and that then, and not until then, were we one in Christ. May I, now that this solemn act has been performed, be born again! May it be granted me to give my heart to sorrow, to seek it out, and to shed joy around me! I am happy, for I yearned to belong to a Christian community, to feel that I was a Christian, and to be confirmed as such. And now that has been granted me. It was almost a greater thing for me to approach the communion table with Richard than to go with him to the nuptial altar. . . . All is goodness and grace, the grace of Heaven and the grace of love." Thus from the depths of her heart spoke the daughter, the "fearful and wonderful" daughter of Franz Liszt.

Before she reached her fortieth year, Cosima, swift to lay aside the distractions of youth, had discarded everything that did not strictly appertain to her duty. Secretary-general to the enterprise at Bayreuth; mother of six children (five little ones and Richard) such was the twofold mission to which she devoted her energies henceforth. She was an aristocrat and she thought a great deal more of order, dignity, and proper government than did her husband. If there was an implacable side to her nature, it was the uncompromising ambition with which she served the cause of an artist of whose strength and lack of judgment she was only too well aware. Everything she did was henceforth subordinated to that end. It was so even with her affections. Her love for her father, for example, suffered many an eclipse in the course of these later years, because the old *virtuoso* was too independent, too much of a Frenchman in heart and mind, too little of a Bismarckian, to suit her ideas. His later works, the *Christus* among others, betrayed that "Latin-

Roman" note which fell so strangely on Wagner's ear and filled him with a sense of discomfort which he found it impossible to dissemble. Cosima felt it, too, and it troubled her. But Liszt, all unsuspicious of his crime, paid no heed to their animadversions; the only voice to which he listened was the voice of his own heart. He came back again to Bayreuth, stayed on, acclimatized himself to the atmosphere, attended the little ceremonies that took place to mark the various stages in the building of his theatre and his house. He even thought of making his home there; for he had now no worldly possessions, no fixed abode, whether in Rome or Budapest or Weimar. And now he parted with one of the last of his treasures: he presented Cosima with the casket in which he kept the manuscript scores of *The Flying Dutchman, Tannhäuser,* and *Lohengrin,* which Wagner had given him twenty years before. Liszt, too, was a wayfarer, but a wayfarer who needed but little on the journey, a wayfarer who, unlike the Flying Dutchman, found his country and a home wherever he went. He had always been a wanderer; it was the only life that suited him, and so it came about that he was rarely seen except between two concert tours. And he was now giving concerts in aid of the Bayreuth funds.

It was a case now of looking to artists and friends to bring the Festival Theatre to completion, for music-lovers took small interest in it, and the public authorities none at all. A national subscription, opened in four thousand German bookshops, brought in six thalers (about twenty marks). Prince Bismarck, to whom Wagner made a direct application by letter, never answered at all. And Ludwig II, wholly taken up with his castles, his private performances, his new favourites, refused pointblank to sign the guarantee that would have enabled the work to be resumed. "The shower of gold" which followed the Peace of Frankfort gave an abnormal stimulus to trade and created all kinds of needs of which the people had hitherto been unconscious. But when the inevitable crash occurred this artificial prosperity came to a sudden end. The consequence was that for some time the Festival Theatre seemed doomed to come to naught. Wagner, in desperation, betook himself to Munich, hoping against hope that the king's humour would change. There he was informed of the latest royal eccentricities: the king hardly ever left his sleeping apartment and rarely rose before evening; would listen to no one save Hornig, his head coachman, and had thrown over all his former friends. It looked, then, as if the case were hopeless, when all of a sudden Ludwig came round and, on 25th of January, 1874, wrote to

Wagner as follows: "No, no, and again no! The thing must not end like this. We must come to your rescue." This time it was no empty promise, and the royal treasury opened a credit of 300,000 marks in favour of the Bayreuth management. Nevertheless, this was not a present, but an advance against future subscriptions, and it was made perfectly clear that His Majesty was to remain sole proprietor of all the assets of the undertaking. Wagner and his committee, fired with renewed hopes, gladly accepted the conditions. Thus the masons resumed their trowels and at last Wagner installed himself in his new abode.

It was a large square building in the romanesque style of architecture. In the entrance-hall, each on a pedestal of two steps, were a pair of marble columns supporting the busts of the master and his wife. Above them ran a frieze depicting all the heroes of the Wagnerian mythology. On the left was Cosima's drawing-room, in which she had collected all her personal mementoes, portraits of the family, of the king, the water-colour drawing by Semper of the Munich model theatre, which was never built, the various presentations, wreaths, gold and silver cups, etc. To the right of the hall was the dining-room; on the other side the great drawing-room looking out on to the garden beyond which lay the park of the Margraves. This spacious apartment contained the valuable collection of books, the concert-grand, the portraits of Schopenhauer, Wagner, and Cosima by Lenbach. On the landing above, opening out of a circular gallery, were the study, the bedrooms, and the children's quarters.

Thus Wagner's dream had come true; here were his temple, his dwelling, and his tomb. On the hill-top the theatre was nearing completion; he was living in a house which he himself had conceived and designed; and, finally, in the garden, facing the middle window of the drawing-room and scarcely concealed behind a clump of bushes, two graves had already been dug in which one day Senta would be laid to rest and, beside her, he who had been successively the Flying Dutchman, Loge the Spirit of Fire, Tristan, Wotan, and finally Prospero who could, by his art, set the wild waters in a roar, and, with his charm, allay them. On the night when they took up their quarters in their new abode, Richard and Cosima went out on to the balcony of their bedroom and looked with a friendly glance on the little budding pleasance newly planted on the fringe of the seignorial domain. "For our happiness," said Wagner, "our peace, our decline." He was right. A few months later, on the 21st of November, he wrote on the last page of his *Twilight*: "Finished at

'Wahnfried.' I add no comment." A quarter of a century had nearly gone by since he had dashed off a hurried outline of his vast Tetralogy at Zurich; and now, with Cosima weeping sad and bitter tears, he was bringing it to a close. Tears, for on that very day a quarrel arose between them, the cause of it a quite humble letter from Liszt. Had old Wotan grown jealous of his wife's affection for the old Saint Francis? Never think it for a moment. Liszt's letter was but a pretext. This outbreak of violence, this sudden explosion of brute rage, was but the foam of the wave that, in its breaking, shook the stanchions of his inmost being; was but the wrack and spume left upon the beach by the mighty billow which, rolling in from the deeps of his being, had now, after five-and-twenty years, come thundering down in the crowning catastrophic achievement of his life. The wave had broken at last, flinging at Wagner's feet a lifeless corpse, a heart as hard and smooth-rubbed as a pebble. And then when they tried to find a reason for this trouble between them, Wagner, summing it all up, exclaimed, "We love each other too much." Words, words, words! And Cosima inscribed this sad reflection in her diary. "That I have devoted my life to this work gives me no right to acclaim its completion with joyfulness. Therefore I celebrate it in sorrow and in tears. To whom shall I unburden my sorrow, for to Richard I must show no sign of it. To these pages, then, I will consign it. May they teach my Siegfried never to feel anger, or resentment, never anything but infinite pity for human misery. The children saw me weeping, wept awhile with me, and were soon comforted. Richard flung at me one last bitter word then turned and betook himself to bed. I went to the piano and essayed a few chords from *Tristan*, but my spirit could not brook the onrush of those themes. I could but seek solace in my own heart, and supplicate and pray. How could I celebrate the day more solemnly than this, how wish for aught save the utter annihilation of my individual self? Hail, day of fulfilment! How high soever genius wings its way to find its goal, what is left for a poor woman to do, but to suffer, to suffer, in love and exaltation?"

That year, 1874, and the beginning of the following one, death was busy among the friends of the solitaries of Bayreuth. There was Schott, the publisher, a careful and most capable collaborator. Then the beautiful Marie de Moukhanoff-Kalergis, the friend of Liszt, and Wagner's benefactress. And after her, Cornelius; then Albert Wagner, Richard's brother, and Wolfram, his brother-in-law, who, a few weeks later, was followed to the grave by his widow, Clara, the loyalest heart among all his sisters. Then came Russ's turn, the great Dane, which their Swiss servant, Vrenali, had bought in Geneva out of her savings ten years before. He was buried at the foot of the two graves in the garden. Thus vanished from the scene many of those to whom Wagner had so eagerly done the honours at Bayreuth. Nor were these farewells the only sad things that befell. Bülow sustained some severe financial losses, so they were given to understand; and he also had a slight stroke. And then he overworked himself, undertaking tour upon tour, in order to provide for his daughters, for he could not endure that they should be beholden to Wagner for anything. Friedrich Nietzsche cut himself off, living in strange and inexplicable isolation. Time after time they urged him to come and stay, but only once had he been to "Wahnfried." His health was getting worse, his eyesight was failing; well, but was not all that an excellent reason for coming and spending a holiday with his friends? The fact was Nietzsche was cooling off. "I have been thinking things out," he wrote to Erwin Rohde, "and I've had to make excursions into such distant regions that I have often wondered, when I got the proofs of my work (the second part of *Unzeitgemässe Betrachtungen*), when I could have written such a thing, and, indeed, if it was really I who had written it all. I am now engaged in rubbing the political and social virtues up the wrong way a little; I've even gone so far as to look a little beyond the 'national' idea sometimes—may God amend me, and it too. For Bayreuth, there's something new. I have addressed myself to studying with the utmost dispassionateness the reasons which caused the enterprise to misfire. I have learnt much in the process and I think I now know Wagner better than I ever knew him before. If the 'miracle' has come to pass today, it in no wise stultifies the results of my inquiry." Enigmatic words, but not without a hint of surprise, dissent, and disenchantment. The Wagnerian mystery was fading. Nietzsche had analyzed it; believed he had pierced it through and through, and thought to lay bare the secrets of the sorcerer. The alchemy of the thing, its pseudo-science, were now dissected and exposed on the table of the philosophical laboratory. Nietzsche pictured the artist palsied with age, about to cast himself at the feet of God. And that just when he himself deemed he was called upon to take up the challenge that had been flung down by history, tradition, and routine to the great deriders of the superstitions of mankind.

However, so far, all this was merely in the air. The memory of the founding of the Festival Theatre and the emotion that had thrilled him at the sight of Wagner triumphant were still strong upon him. If Wagner was a disease, as he came more and more every day to believe, he was not going to throw it off quite so easily as that. By way of a present for Christmas, 1872, he had sent Cosima the *Five Prefaces* to the works he was going to write—some day. It was weeks before she wrote to say she had received them. Whence Nietzsche inferred that the days of their mutual confidence, their intimate days, were past and gone. Nevertheless, he betook himself to Bayreuth the following year, arriving at Eastertide, when the financial crisis that was holding up the building operations was at its worst. He found the Wagners perturbed and anxious, read them his recent essay on *Greek Philosophy and the Tragic Age*, and felt somehow that he had disappointed them again. It was not what they expected from him, of course. Well, what then? Was it to be his sole duty henceforth to proclaim "the era of Bayreuthian civilization"? Were they going to quarrel with him for doing his own work? Henceforth there was nothing in common between them, any more than there can be between those who love the sea and those who love the mountain heights. They had come to live in different worlds. In Nietzsche's eyes Wagner came to be summed up as an actor of genius, an autocrat, and a politician suffering from arrested development. Thus, virtually without being aware of it, Nietzsche constituted himself Wagner's first real critic, being actuated by affection, by a desire to see into the true nature of things, and to help him. Moreover, he was mortified at finding him so little of a mystery and jealous of his disturbing and dominating influence. His reactions were the reactions of a man endowed with too clear a vision, a man who was trying to prevent his intellect surrendering to his feelings, fighting, too, against the Christian virus which imparted to Cosima's letters, so unfailingly delicate and seductive, a sort of feverish glow. And she even had the assurance, the rather high and mighty assurance, to draw his attention to some faults of style.

The following summer Nietzsche came and, on the piano at "Wahnfried," deposited Brahms's *Song of Triumph*. . . . It might almost seem as though some obscure idea of revenge was at the bottom of his mind. It may have been. Anyhow, Wagner was furious. The very binding, which was red, was like a red rag to a bull. "It's just bits of Handel, Mendelssohn, and Schumann bound in calf!" he shouted. Nietzsche was amazed at this outbreak, and never said a word; but, having questioned Wagner's intellectual greatness, it was borne in upon him that he had some serious defects of temper as well. Did this apparently cynical egoism cloak some serious shortcomings, such as insincerity, a tendency to vulgar resentment? Was this man, who had come so late into his spiritual inheritance, always going to display the explosive fanaticism of a rebellious schoolboy? If, in spite of all, there was something admirable about him, notwithstanding his uncouthness, his lack of proportion and moderation, was he entitled, with his lack of philosophic balance, and his latest craze, the moralizings of the repentant revolutionary— was he entitled to pose as a reformer, an apostle of the New Humanity? These were the questions Nietzsche asked himself, and wrote the finest of his "Intempestives," *Schopenhauer the Teacher*, in which he summed up his conclusions by saying that "virility of character, the precocious knowledge of man, the absence of a learned education and patriotic narrowness, freedom from all anxiety about making a living and from all connection with the government, in short, freedom first and last and all the time, are the conditions necessary for the creation of the new philosophic genius." Thus he used Wagner's own god to warn Wagner of his errors. He did not do so without a long inward struggle. But he had to make a momentous choice; he must either rescue Wagner from the impasse into which for ten years past he had been wandering in the train of Bismarck, Ludwig II, and Cosima, or else bid the most passionate friendship of his life a final and irrevocable farewell.

The summer of 1875 beheld the completion of the Festspielhaus and the rehearsals of soloists and orchestra at the summit of the hill, where the great red-brick amphitheatre and the neighbouring forest trees thrilled to the strains of the hidden music. In the interior of this mystic vessel darkness reigned supreme. Dimly visible in the surrrounding gloom were the shadowy figures of a few artists, or a sprinkling of friends scattered about on the tiers of the building, interested spectators of the scene. The instrumentalists were hidden from view, grouped together in a new mode, in a sunken space, in which even the conductor was invisible. On the stage, the singers were rehearsing under the direction of Hans Richter, while, standing at a table, on which was placed the score propped up against an empty packing-case, stood a queer-looking, oldish man, his strong, pale features lit up by the gleam of a paraffin lamp, in whose brain all those visionary forms, and all these wild and

passionate strains, had come to birth; all his life, in a word; or
to speak yet more accurately, all his lives. For he himself had
lived every one of all those parts. Proteus-like, he answered the
questions that they asked, changing his outward form each time,
and gave to those divers voices the appropriate accent—tender,
sarcastic, loving, wrathful, or careless—of his own proper
tragedy, the tragedy which he himself had lived. And he had
strange requirements to demand of his artists, in the matter
of looks and form, as to how they should live and move and
have their being. He insisted that they should import into their
everyday existence the sentiments and courtesy proper to
their parts, the grandeur or the subtlety of their characters, their
naïveté, pride, or cunning. Hardly ever did he pronounce himself satisfied, for he discerned the spirit behind the costume or
in the gesture, and this they could not see, wrapt up as they were
in themselves, despite the mask they wore. But the little man
beneath the paraffin lamp, he saw through them all. He would
stop the orchestra, explain, sing, compel his interpreters to forget that they were stars, that they were called Unger, Niemann,
Hill, Mme. Materna or Lilli Lehmann, and make them become
really and truly Brünnhilde, Wotan, Alberic, Siegmund, and
Siegfried, make them capable of hating, coveting, loving, and
created new souls for them, all aglow with the passions which
he himself had experienced.

Some French author, I cannot recall his name, has declared
that Wagner's music is a typical example of the sort of music
to which we are compelled to listen "with our heads in our
hands." That ironic appreciation leads me to infer that he has
never heard a Wagnerian opera. For it is a distinctive charac-
teristic of Wagner's music that you must listen to it with your
whole body—with the head certainly, but with the heart, too,
and the stomach, and, so to speak, with eyes and hands, as
though you were breasting a storm. It is never a bunch of for-
get-me-not or an exercise in harmony. All the dim, violent
yearnings it ferments within us intoxicates us like strong wine.
It is an overwhelming torrent against which we strive in vain.
One must either flee or suffer oneself to be carried away by it.
Who cares whether this music be fraught with hope or despair,
whether it be vulgar or distinguished, decadent or literary, or
whether you have to listen to it "with your head in your hands."
The fact of the matter is that the cries of Marsyas in his forest
filled all the countless little flute-players with alarm, and even
today they scamper off when they hear the trampling of the
satyr. For he is terrible and mighty, this solitary wanderer

of the Col de la Formazza, the Bois de Boulogne, and the pastures of Lucerne. His interpreters of 1875 looked on him with mingled feelings of love and awe. Little did they dream that that brow, encumbered with the vast Tetralogy which was just about to be born into the world, was even then big with the idea of *Parsifal*. The musician never laid aside his task, never wearied of weaving and reweaving the harmonies that told of a certain Good Friday twenty years before, when, on the terrace of "The Sanctuary" at Zurich, there had welled up in his bosom the eternal springtime of Buddha, Christ, and Richard Wagner.

So the months and the seasons went by. In February, 1876, Mme. d'Agoult passed away. "Sorrowful thoughts; a day of silence," wrote Cosima in her diary. A word or two suffices for an epitaph when we lose those who have long since been dead to us. Marie d'Agoult had brought her younger daughter into the world at Como, the elder one at Geneva, when her love-affair with Liszt was at its height. But these *enfants de voyage*, these wayside offspring, were fated ever to linger on the outskirts of their mother's love. It was Liszt, and he alone, who paid for their education and supplied their needs. When, therefore, the one-time rebellious and now repentant countess lay dying, with her legitimate family around her, the one daughter of her liaison that now survived could feel no more than a fleeting sadness. All her remaining capacity for bearing pain belonged to Wagner. He alone counted for her, and, doubtless, the hour was drawing near when she would be called upon to watch the homeless mariner as he sank at last into the sea of death. Naught would remain of him save his works and his fame. But were those the things she loved in him? No, what she loved was that man sitting on the stage there, gazing at his own unfettered soul, directing the long battle of his passions; that musician yonder, with the blanched hair, his face all lined and furrowed, with the profile of some old master of the Renaissance, a short and sturdy Adam who believed in love, in sorrow, in pity and in poetry—abstractions that bring a smile to the lips of men, but will continue to move the hearts of women for many a day to come.

Summer came; and with it the singers, the musicians, and the little army of workmen who had been picked and trained the year before. Work was resumed, and all through the months of June and July it went on merrily, albeit punctuated by countless unforeseeable little hitches. First one person fell ill, and then another; then there were little tiffs and quarrels, and this or that was not up to the mark, and some one's pride was wounded, or the stage carpenters were behindhand with their job. The same old troubles over again, as when he was producing the *Liebesverbot* and *Rienzi*. There was only one who knew how to put things right, and that was the old expert who knew every wheel in the machine, for he had designed it and superintended its construction. Somehow or other it was got into working-order, and it worked.

Then the personal friends put in their appearance, as they had done at Munich for *Tristan* and the *Meistersinger*: the Countess von Schleinitz, the mainspring of the Bayreuth finances; Malwida von Meysenbug and her former pupil, the daughter of Hertzen the revolutionary leader who was now Mme. Gabriel Monod; Edouard Schuré; Friedrich Nietzsche; and though Bülow was again absent (he was seriously ill at Godesberg on the Rhine), Liszt, at all events, was there this time. The presence of his old friend was immensely soothing to Wagner's mind. Even the Wesendoncks arrived to witness the triumph of their friend of other days. Then there were the Willes and the Sulzers. And Mathilde Maier also came, whom he had so delighted to make his *intendante* in Vienna; and Pecht, the painter, who had been through those hard times with him in Paris in 1840; and Pusinelli, in whose presence Minna had breathed her last. Old loves, old friends, old boon companions—all were gathered round him there. Nietzsche alone was sombre and taciturn. "When Richard Wagner was there," said Schuré, "he was shy, constrained, and almost always silent." A few days earlier, however, he had sent to "Wahnfried" his famous brochure, *Richard Wagner at Bayreuth*, a last token of seven years of admiration, dedicated to the man who, until that day, had been his guide. But the most high-minded of Wagner's disciples had come even then to deny his master in the spirit, and the man who stood thus motionless and silent in the musician's shadow was only waiting for the hour of deliverance to sound.

In the night of the 5th-6th of August, about one o'clock in the morning, a train consisting of only two coaches drew up in the open country, about three miles outside Bayreuth. It was the royal train. From it there alighted a very tall man. With rapid strides he made his way towards Wagner, who was waiting there to meet him, attired in evening dress. It had been their wish to be alone together at this, their first, meeting after eight years of separation. In silence they took their seats in the carriage and were swiftly borne to the Ermitage—the young king, lover of his Bavarian mountains, and that much-travelled mariner who, after roaming so many stormy seas, had at last come to anchor in that little haven of harmony. But what could they say to one another? For many a day now the flowers of their vocabulary had drooped and withered. However much Parsifal and his beloved may have thought themselves unaltered, they felt as though there was a glass wall between them. Everything seemed distorted, but neither of them could understand exactly how. Wagner spent two hours with the king and then returned home easy in his mind, and as he went the sun rose above the dew-drenched woods. But the days that followed, days that had brought back the royal dreamer from his home so far away, were not the old, happy days they once had known. Ludwig's eyes were no longer lit with the expression that tenderness of old had kindled there. He declined to see any people. In a word, he desired to take part in the festival no longer as a patron, but as an onlooker. Wagner wished to do him the honours of his house, but he refused the invitation and reached the Festival Theatre next evening by driving through the forest and avoiding the town. Crowds of people had gathered in the streets, which were all bedecked with flags. They were waiting to catch a glimpse of their handsome but enigmatic king, that they might greet him with their cheers. But Ludwig II eluded them, and while they were waiting for him to pass he took his seat in his box, with Wagner by his side, to witness the dress rehearsal of *The Rhinegold*. The theatre was empty. The two friends were soon deep in that water-world with which the Tetralogy opens, the whole of it on that "Curse of Gold" which had pursued the artist for so long and from which he had only won deliverance by grasping, first the slippery hand of this shadowy king, and then the firm arm of Brünnhilde-Cosima. And the Rhine Maidens, floating amid the waves, laugh their mocking laughter, laugh at the brutish appetites of man and at the unavailing ruses of the gods.

The king did not twice elude the demonstration of his people's affection. The rehearsal over, he drove in his calash through the gaily-lighted city, a pale face dimly seen behind the closed windows. "What, are they not completely Prussianized here?" he enquired in a tone of surprise. Next day he heard *The Valkyrie*, and the day after *Siegfried*; but no sooner had the curtain fallen on the last act of *The Twilight* than he set out again for his mountains. The reason was that old William had announced his arrival, and the King of Bavaria was in no mood to abase his crown before the Emperor of Germany.

The other disciple deserted a few days later. Nietzsche, who had so greatly looked forward to this festival, found it impossible to stay. He felt himself growing more and more angry and impatient with all the people who had come there out of idle curiosity, to see and to be seen. Every year he had kept the day he first met Wagner as a kind of intellectual anniversary, and now he could not repress a certain feeling of terror at the idea that he was illuding himself with a sort of pasteboard effigy, ignorantly applauded by the empty-headed crowd that flocked to fashionable first-nights because it was "the thing." The sensuality, nay, the sexuality of the *Nibelungen* music struck him in the face like an insult to real purity of soul. "Where am I?" he asked himself. "There is nothing, no one I recognize . . . not even Wagner." The little book he had just dedicated to him suddenly seemed to have grown leaden, like a sin, unpardonable as a lie. He rejected and repudiated it. It was nothing more to him now than a debt that he had paid, a debt of five years' standing.

How on earth could he ever have come to write that the *Nibelungen Ring* was "the most moral music that he knew?" How could he have come to believe that the essential feature of that morality was fidelity to the two currents which fought for supremacy in Wagner and was symbolized by the fidelity of Elisabeth to Tannhäuser, of Senta to the Flying Dutchman, of Isolde, Kurwenal, and King Mark to Tristan, and, finally, of Brünnhilde to the secret desires of Wotan. No doubt there were serious errors at the bottom of it all, but especially a hint of the comic and the grotesque. Wagner had undoubtedly understood the tragic quality in art, and its necessity as a *valeur de remplacement* for man involved in the infinitely more complicated problem of action and will. But thus travestied in erroneous symbols, art was but a mirage, a simplification without any real depth. Considered in itself, Wagner's art was no solution of any problem; it did not even square with modern social conditions. Wagner then in his attitude towards music was in the position of a comedian. Another mistake was that he only believed in himself, and anyone who only believes in himself cannot remain wholly honest with himself, since he exalts his failings. That brings one straight to the passions, that is to say to intellectual disorders. Thus for the Wagnerian, free-will goes by the board and there's nothing left but posturing, sublimity, demagogy, obscurantism, fascination. In building Bayreuth, Wagner was

running the same risk, and abdicated in the same manner as
Napoleon at Moscow; he was vanquished by himself.

Thus in Nietzsche's estimation Bayreuth was something positively harmful. He had a terrible attack of nerves. Everything
about this bookish mysticism, this sumptuous musical grandilo-
quence, struck him as false. A colossal philosophical error, he
thought, this cult of death, a religion for the aged or the hopeless. The young man in him revolted. He must get clear of it all.
"I am appalled at those long artistic evenings. . . . I am utterly
sick of them. Everything is a torture to me here." So he started
for the little spa at Klingenbrunn, but he did not stay long and
was back again for the first cycle. This time Nietzsche came in
for state processions, military pomp and circumstance, crowds
cheering the old Emperor William, the Emperor dom Pedro of
Brazil, the Princes of Würtemberg and Schwerin. This brilliant
and motley crowd pushed their way into the refreshment-room
of the theatre, and munched sausages and drank beer in the intervals. However, Nietzsche's old faith in his master protested
yet again. Was this all it led to—the music he had loved so
greatly, the music which, despite himself, still saturated him with
pleasure? All that he had put forth concerning the Greek tragic
spirit at last rerisen from the grave, his exposition of the drama,
the nakedness, the austerity of the classic spirit, standing out
with the shining purity of an antique statue—what had become
of all that in the face of this blatant beanfeast, this loutish
caricature.

But Wagner was up in the skies. The lion-tamer in him glowed
with triumph. With that blend of violence and cajolery which
has been imputed to him as a fault, he seduced, subdued, convinced his workers, riding the whirlwind and directing the storm,
aided, at will, by Ariel or Caliban. He entertained kings, joked
and jested, gave audience to all the artists in Europe, in batches
of a hundred at a time. Geyer's "Cossack" had come back again,
the child in the old man's guise. He played with himself as he
did with his guests. "Nietzsche is like Liszt," he said, noticing
his friend's ungentle look; "he doesn't like my puns." For
Nietzsche, indeed, was looking out for something else in the
man whom he could not help admiring—for an ironic word, a
shrug of the shoulders. But he looked in vain.

The last night, Wagner appeared on the stage and addressed
the crowd as follows: "What I should like to say to you may
be summed up in a few words, put into the form of an axiom.
You have just seen what we can do; it is for you, now, to make
up your minds to do it. If you do so, we shall have an art."

Lofty words. They were judged—as they still are—according as the hearer's heart was moved or no. But we must not lose sight of the sixty years of struggle which they crown, and the long ascent accomplished by Wagner from *Die Feen* to the funeral march in *Siegfried*. At the banquet which followed the performance, the composer rose to add a few comments to his previous remarks. "I did not mean," he said, "that we have had no art until now. But that what we Germans lacked was a national art, the sort of art which, in spite of weaknesses and temporary defects, the Italians and the French do possess." His art, he meant, was to be a starting-point for future achievements. For many it was a goal which they would never overpass.

But it was not so for Nietzsche, nor was it for Wagner. Nietzsche departed sad and sick at heart, but he was free! And Wagner saw that loneliness was to be his lot. No one would forgive him his greatness, not even his singers, some of whom never so far obeyed the Bayreuthian rule as to abstain from bowing to the audience at the end of the acts; and not a few of them went off in high dudgeon with the master. Richter, too, wilted now and again. Even that enthusiast Countess von Schleinitz cooled off a little. "Bayreuth," she remarked, "is the grave of friendship."

Nevertheless, at "Wahnfried" the receptions went on. But Wagner only showed himself with reluctance. He remained shut up in his room, exhausted with the effort he had just put forth, and thus he wrote his artistic will and testament. "Let not the oldest of men think of himself, but let him love the youngest for the love of that which he is bequeathing him." Love, desire, hope—such was ever the burden of his discourse. Among the foreign guests at Bayreuth was a woman who perchance had not come wholly and solely to catch a glimpse of the musician's evening glory, but for Wagner himself, for Wagner the man, for his strength and rugged energy, to fill her ewer at his quenchless spring. And that was Judith. He had seen her several times during the festivities, and now he wrote her thus: "Dear lady, I am sad. There is another reception tonight, but I shall not go down. I am reading over some pages of my life, things which I once dictated to Cosima. . . . Did I kiss you for the last time this morning? No. I shall see you again. I wish to—since I love you. Farewell. Think kindly of me."

Now, he knew perfectly well that he did not love her, but it was himself he did not want to lose. It was too soon to abdicate. He had forces in reserve; all the music of another work. This old man, with the blood of youth tingling in his veins, was not going to make Bayreuth his cemetery—not yet.

Chapter II

"PARSIFAL" AND THE FLOWER MAIDENS

I HAVE occasionally wondered, while penning this study, whether I was entirely justified, in commingling as closely as I have done, the artist's work with the circumstances and events of his life, in fusing together in the same narrative the reasoned actions of his mind and the subconscious impulses of his temperament, and in allowing that there was a constant connection, an absolute interdependence, between them. Is it then really true that heart and mind hold converse one with another? Is there some common denominator between a man's life and the works he produces? Alas! we all know, to our cost, how intractable, how wilful are our thoughts, how cunningly they elude our intentions, how subservient they are to forces beyond our control. And then, how can we help taking into account the tyranny imposed on man by the circumstance of his daily life? How should one fail to follow, step by step, as one weaving a romance rather than recording a history, the manifold influences exerted on him in his life's adventurous course, by those who shaped it with their hands.

Wagner denied that there was any congenital relationship between an artist's experiences and his creations. He claimed that the only thing that had driven him to create was the urge of nature and no desire to live his life again. His inward eye, he assures us, never turned its gaze on the gallery of his memories. He refused to allow that his *Tristan* was inspired by the drama unfolded at "The Sanctuary" and its Venetian sequel. The only work of his in which he acknowledged the imprint of his past, was the *Idyll of Tribschen*, which he afterwards rechristened the *Siegfried Idyll*. But these statements he flung out at a venture twenty years after the break with Mathilde, when the wound had long ago been cicatrized by Time. His music sounded in his ears no longer as the dolorous complaint for a sorrow past and gone, but rather as created music, displaying his technical development and the unbroken continuity of his art.

We, however, cannot share his illusions. Philosophic enquiry tends more and more to show that man's life and work form a single unity spiritual and material, conjoined in one indissoluble substance. And so the farther we advance in the story of Wagner's life, the larger the share we must assign, not indeed to theory and æsthetics, but to the personal and intimate events which crowd the margins of his *Collected Works*. For his works are the splendid efflorescence, grafted and regrafted, of his emotions. As M. Bergson[1] puts it, "A work of genius is usually the outcome of an emotion unique in its nature, an emotion which one might have deemed impossible to express, and which, nevertheless, insisted on expression." This emotion was not merely "an urge to create," but a fixed and definite urge which is satisfied as soon as that particular work has been brought to pass, and could have been satisfied in no other manner. That Wagner the man may sometimes seem to us inhuman rather than superhuman there is no denying, but it was above all when he was composing his last drama, the most mystical, and in many respects the most Wagnerian of all, that he showed how human he was, in the fullest acceptation of the word. If in Nietzsche's chastity there is something that suggests the keenness of a sword sheltering the all too vulnerable soul behind it, there is something no less deserving of our admiration in Wagner with his sixty-four years behind him, yielding himself without vain scruples, and none of an elderly man's misgiving, to the last promptings of the flesh which, for him, would never cool. Life gives all to those who refuse her nothing, and perhaps the day will soon be here when a man's greatness will no longer be measured by the things he renounces and the sacrifices he makes, but by the completeness with which he gives of himself, to the utmost limit of his powers. Gods as well as devils are born of man, and the great "affirmers" are always moulded in the likeness of Faust.

Now Wagner was a very genuine disciple of Goethe, so far, at least, as the art of life is concerned. He was indeed his superior in this, he either ignored or despised ridicule. Neither woman nor advancing years could make him abdicate. He is never ironic at his own expense. How, indeed, could he have been so when he was composing *Parsifal*. Wagner had not shed his will to conquer, and his instincts of domination were still intact. This Judith Gautier, a poet's daughter and herself no little of a poet, lured by his genius, was destined to give him that touch of fever which he needed to create his Kundry. Foaming

[1] Henri Bergson, *The Two Sources of Morality and Religion*.

and foundered at the feet of Parsifal, Kundry is the mythical representation of woman in thraldom to the poet, of the adulteress won over by divine love. In vain did Nietzsche deride the measureless *naïveté* of the tale; Kundry and Parsifal are not less moving than Zarathustra.

Thus I shall have no compunction in associating with Wagner's last musical poem this latest and last companion, this ultimate palpitation of desire, this woman's form clandestinely bending over him, even while the summons from Monsalvat fell upon his ears. Judith, as he writes, was the "abundance" from which he draws an overflowing and intoxicating measure. Not that Cosima had ceased to make him happy. On the contrary, never had he found more pleasure in his family and his peaceful surroundings than when he was composing the music for the Grail. But the real past-masters in the art of loving are always eagerly looking out for those intimate communions wherein they hope to find the image of themselves secretly enshrined. Whether there be any correspondence between such sentiments and the work wherewith they are in travail matters but little. An artist's work is to a great extent unconscious, and Wagner's especially so, though he knew it not. His instinct hurried him along with such tumultuous force that with him instinct and reason were as one; and many a time he deemed he was giving orders when in reality he was obeying them. But the important thing is that we should be under no misapprehension as to his sources. True, Judith never reached the deeps of Wagner's soul; nevertheless, she opened the floodgates of a stream of poetry in him, a final uprush of the sap within him. For a moment she personified the impossible, the unattainable, which, like veiled sunlight, had been his lure since youth, and towards which his branches, now bare of nearly all their leaves, had been unwearyingly aspiring. Was she Kundry? Was she Klingsor? Or a Flower-maiden of his magic garden; or simply a radiant morning shining on the Good Friday of one of those lay priests which every artist truly is? We know not. What is certain is that she gave to Wagner's eroticism its crowning stimulus.

Jenny Raymann had awakened it fifty years before. Next Minna Planer first gave it a definite meaning, revealing him to himself and goading him with torments which helped him to become what destiny would have him be. Jessie Laussot was a divagation, but a fertile one, and tempered his soul with scepticism. Lastly Mathilde Wesendonck brought him to the culminating point, to the zenith, of his puissance as a man. The mistresses who came after her hardly count at all. Mathilde Maier, Frederica, the little Viennese housekeeper, were merely friends or fancies of the fleeting hour. They prepared the way for Cosima, the completest, highest nature of all the women he loved, the mother of his children, almost a mother to him, his protectress, his colleague, his support. Then, last of all, came Judith. After all, that made no great number, seven or eight women in seventy years! Those who would make Wagner the chaste and sober husband of his two wives are just as wide of the truth as those who would make him a Don Juan or a passive partner, even a "Damen-imitator" as the Berlin Institute of Sexual Research has labelled him. Wagner was not lacking in ardour, that is certain. Nor in imagination. He retained his curiosity to the very end. But eroticism with him was never anything but an aspect of his talent. "What inspiration I find within your arms!" wrote he to Judith. "Oh, warm and gentle soul that you are!" It was his music that moved him to utter these caressing words, not love of a foreigner to whom love was, perhaps, anything but a new experience. What he liked in her was the proof she gave him that his prowess had not forsaken him. In the eyes of this beautiful young Frenchwoman he only sought a mirror in which, as he gazed, he might discern the lineaments of the Parsifal he fain would be, ageless, coming none knew whence, legendary even as himself. The words he spoke to her were the words of a shade holding converse with a shade.

The first Bayreuth Festival, then, ended in disappointment and a deficit. Disappointment because, in spite of all appearances to the contrary, the general public did not take to the Wagnerian style of art, and had no eyes or ears save for the brilliant and showy side of it. Wagner was under no delusion as to the value of the applause he got. As for the deficit, it was immediately evident that it would amount to 120,000 or 130,000 marks. The subscribers would not get paid, and it looked as if the enterprise were heading straight for the bankruptcy they had dreaded so long. The Wagners put their affairs into the hands of Feustel, the banker, and his son-in-law, Adolph Gross. Then they set out for Italy, visiting in quick succession Verona, Venice, Naples, and making a longer stay at Sorrento.

It happened that Malwida von Meysenbug had just become tenant of the Villa Rubinacci, where she was giving hospitality to a few friends who were in need of peace and quiet. Among them was Nietzsche, who was suffering much in his eyes and head, but worked hard all the same and was, as usual, rich in ideas. He was working on a new book, the one which he sub-

RICHARD WAGNER

sequently entitled *Human, Too Human!* "the record of a crisis. ·. . ." "In writing it [he said] I have freed myself from everything I had in me that was foreign to my real nature. Idealism of all kinds is foreign to me. The title of this book signifies, 'Where you see ideal things, I see human things, alas, too human!' That meant to say: The new musical genius whom you are celebrating is only an arrogant and dangerous play-actor; it behoves humanity to shake itself free of him at the earliest possible moment if it would avoid being inoculated by this maleficent doctor with poisons still more noxious than those of Christian humility, pity, and so-called necessary suffering, with which for centuries it has been sick unto death. Weakness all that and perilous illusion! These preachers of death are spiritual consumptives. It is their weakness which they worship and of which they make a virtue. The whole Wagnerian mythology is summed up in the old equalitarian chimera that bedazzled the revolutionary of 1848. There was danger that the higher would be submerged by the lower, that all distinctions would be lost, and that 'Parsifalism' would spread abroad over the face of the world, an appalling leveller of souls, that the will to conquer would grow feeble and finally disintegrate before this passion for resignation and renouncement."

Such were the conclusions at which Nietzsche arrived during these initial weeks of meditation and repose in Italy. And at the same moment Wagner arrived at Sorrento and took up his quarters at the Hotel Victoria. And so the musician and the philosopher met face to face. Wagner had got an idea of the kind of reproaches his disciple was, from this time onwards, to level at his head. They hardly spoke to one another, and exchanged no questions, and somehow realized that seven years had brought them along the road of confidences and veiled misunderstandings to the very borderline of friendship. Friendship indeed was no longer possible between them now. The hour of severance had come.

They went for a final walk together. It was a lovely day in late autumn. They skirted the margin of the bay, then went up through a forest of pines to the summit of a hill. Before them lay the sea. "'Tis a scene propitious to farewells," murmured the old musician in a low voice. And as though to bring out more clearly what was in his mind, he described the subject of his *Parsifal*, speaking of it as a grave and authentic religious experience, as an act of contrition. It was not now as of a work of art he spoke, but of a good deed, of a gesture at once difficult and full of joy, whereby the artist strives to accord, in what is almost a work of expiation, his long sinful past with a future made pure and holy by the Saviour. At the summit of his musical edifice, upon the dome of Monsalvat, he would fain set up the Cross of Christ. Not that the atheist had undergone any sudden and miraculous conversion; not that, in his heart, he had mounted the dolorous Calvary of the Christian convert. The soul of the Magician could not have been exorcised by a single thrust of Parsifal's spear. But it asked no more of life, that soul of his. It looked death in the face. It only lacked the adornment of kindliness, of pity, that rustic perfume of simplicity whereof so many artists have dreamed as of a crowning grace wherewith to confront posterity. Wagner did not win the faith. He did not enter into the bosom of the Church; but he had a profound sense of his sinfulness, of original sin, of that heritage of sorrow which is, as it were, the bitter yet rich-savoured almond of life's fruit, the secret marrow which imparts to man all his expressiveness, all his poetry. Therein lies his magic spell, his power of destruction. Thence he draws his wizard charms and all that mystery which lends to music a power of illumination which "passeth all understanding." Wagner's successive plunges into the waters of sensuality, followed by retreats into the heart of the forest rendered sacrosanct by Siegfried, created in his heart a chivalrous mysticism in which he beholds himself, at long last, in the virginal lineaments of Parsifal. This being, touched by God with divine madness, this "little one" of Christ called apart to heal the purulent sore of concupiscence—such is the human Christ whose saving priesthood he would fain establish ere he dies.

Now it was precisely this that the Nietzsche of Sorrento, the Nietzsche, new-born and free, had come to detest in his old master. This doctrine of redemption is only another form of the old cult of suffering proclaimed by the royal martyr of the Jews. It was not a thing pure and unalloyed; it was the product of wholesale pillaging among the oldest superstitions. A despot of genius, Wagner knows no other way of conquering men than by exalting their weaknesses. He has idealized their passions, that is all. He is preëminently the artisan of European decadence, the great corrupter of taste, the great sinner against the light. Nietzsche now was not even certain that music was indeed the direct language of the feelings. A blind rage took hold of him when he remembered that he had devoted a whole book—the first and hitherto most famous of all his books—to an idea that was perhaps quite false, to singing the praises of a man whose pride, whose theories, whose very art he now condemned. Doubt-

less there stole into his mind the memory of his first visit to
Tribschen when he heard Wagner at the piano playing that
passage from the third act of *Siegfried* when Brünnhilde cries,
"He hath wounded me, he who aroused me from slumber."
Wounded, too, Nietzsche had been. But he had recovered now.
He was awakening. The mists of the German forest were dis-
persing; the Mediterranean was opening before him broad and
clear. And, like Wotan taking leave of the Valkyrie, Nietzsche,
in his inmost heart, was bidding farewell to Wagner.

"Come, friend, you have nothing to say to me?" said Wagner,
turning to look at him.

Nietzsche could make no answer. Their ways parted here. But
neither the one nor the other suspected they were never to meet
again. Sometime later, Nietzsche made this entry in his notebook:

"When we are parting from some one for the last time, when
we are saying good-bye because our feelings and our convictions
no longer run easily in double harness, then it is that we are
nearest to one another. We are knocking at the wall which
Nature has raised between us and the being we are leaving."
As for Wagner, he had long since divined what was passing in
the mind of his hypersensitive friend. Henceforth he hardly
ever spoke of Nietzsche. When he received his copy of *Human,
Too Human!* he did not open it for a long time. Then he gave a
rapid glance at it and thought it was all made up of malice and
vexation of spirit. Angrily he tossed it aside. That plant so rare
had borne one solitary, unrivaled flower. All that now remained
was the bulb, decayed and sterile.

The Wagners decided to return to Germany by way of Rome
and Florence. At Rome, Cosima, in order to please her father,
called on the Princess von Wittgenstein in the smoke-begrimed
cell where the old lady was working on her *Mystical Theology*
in twenty volumes. Wagner went to St. Peter's, the Vatican, the
Sistine Chapel. But the pleasure he might have derived from all
his sight-seeing was ruined for him by the news from Bayreuth
which continued to be uncompromisingly bad. Nevertheless, it
was in Rome that he made the acquaintance of Comte de
Gobineau, a French diplomat whose literary and philosophical
works, introduced into Germany, were destined to achieve con-
picuous renown. Their meeting was marked by mutual courtesy,
but it was not until later on, at "Wahnfried," that the great
artist and this cultured gentleman of Normandy consolidated a
rich and fruitful friendship. Gobineau had spent his days in
Asia, Persia, Brazil, Greece, and Sweden. He claimed to be a

genuine descendant of the vikings. That excited Wagner's imagination and he set himself to read, one after another, all the books he had written. "Was it fated to be but now that I was to meet the only original writer I know?" he exclaimed. "I do not devour the *Nouvelles Asiatiques*, I roll them on the palate. I keep finding in them charms hitherto unknown in the French language."

From Rome they went on to Bologna. The civic authorities there had just awarded him the freedom of the city, and a performance of *Rienzi* was given in his honour. From Bologna they proceeded to Florence, saw the Uffizi, the Pitti, Fiesole, San Miniato and its terrace. But to these places, so dear to lovers, Wagner came too late, bringing a mind weighed down with care. All the same, the city of the Arno had a surprise in store for him, and that was nothing less than a meeting with Jessie Laussot, the friend of those far-off days at Dresden and Bordeaux. She had been a pupil of Bülow's and was an excellent musician. Though getting on in years, she was as alert as ever she had been, and was now about to begin life anew by marrying Professor Karl Hillebrand. It was he of whom Nietzsche said "he was the last German who knew how to hold a pen."

But Wagner was eager to get back to his solitude and his piano. Round about Christmas he was home again at Bayreuth and, on the 25th of January in the new year, 1877, he brought out and deposited on his writing-table the rough drafts of *Parsifal* he had sketched out long ago, and a supply of paper destined to receive the poem which he now intended to write straight off, without a break. Once more, and for the last time, inward anxiety, those misgivings regarding the future that weighed so heavily on him in the darker moments of his life, urged him to an act that should dispel the doubts and difficulties in which he found himself involved; and that was a creative act. In a single month (from the end of January to the end of February, 1877) the text of his poem was completely sketched out. By the end of April it was finished in detail. And all that was accomplished in spite of a number of financial problems which called for his decision. Vienna suddenly came along with an offer of 20,000 marks if he would put on *The Valkyrie*, and an English concert-agent made him a proposal for six grand concerts to be held at the Albert Hall, which, it was estimated, would bring him in enough to cover the deficit on the Festspielhaus. Tempted by the journey, Wagner closed with the offer and set out for London, accompanied by his wife. But, though he was welcomed everywhere like a king, and though ten thousand people went wild

with excitement when he appeared on the platform on the night
of the first concert, the second showed a marked decline in both
enthusiasm and receipts. After the eighth, the accounts were
totalled up. So heavy had been the expenses that there was only
a balance of £700 wherewith to wipe out his debts. Then once
more Wagner thought about quitting Europe, selling "Wahnfried" and going and settling down in America, whence he was
getting some wonderful offers. However, that was but a fanciful idea. Cosima offered to advance her husband 40,000 francs,
to be raised on her mother's estate; Richard came in with
another ten thousand or so, which had just been paid him,
and then they had to go round with the hat again.

The thing that kept him going through all these trying times
was his work on *Parsifal.* Cosima had begun to put it into
French and referred her difficulties to Judith Gautier. Wagner
wrote to her also, and in these terms: "Yes, the *Parsifal* music
—that's the thing now. I couldn't have gone on living without
plunging into some such enterprise as that. Help me. . . . Love
me, and don't let's wait for the Protestant heaven for that; it
will be a mighty dull place. . . . Dear, dear heart, never cease
to love me." And on the 27th of September he says: *"Parsifal,* oh! write and tell Cosima all you think about it. Only don't
be afraid of offending her. And don't imagine she has made a
literal translation. Oh, if you only knew how difficult it is to
give the faintest notion of this poetry, in a language so bound
down by convention as yours. The best Cosima has been able to
do has been to look out expressions as sober as death (hence
the stiffness you'll note) for the simple innocent things which
the French haven't got an idea of. . . . All the same it would
be all to the good if you and she were quite frank about the matter. . . . You will see in Act II the 'Charmers' of Klingsor,
flowers of his enchanted garden (tropical ones). . . . They
caress Parsifal, pat him on the cheek, chuck him under the chin,
like children at play: 'Come, come, young hero, beautiful boy,
etc. . . . Do you love me? I hope so. Oh yes! And if you don't
want to—I shall kiss you, all the same.'"

This time Wagner composed slowly, which was unusual with
him. Perhaps his creative powers had somewhat declined with
age (and yet the wonderful *Twilight* was not so very far away).
Love enveloped all his days, henceforth so smooth and tranquil
—Cosima's love in especial—and Judith's, a lesser thing, dis-
creet, and not without its good effects. But the well-spring of
his inspiration, which once had flowed so freely, now needed to

be coaxed. He had always taken a sensuous delight in rare and beautiful stuffs, and now he gave this taste full rein, to stimulate his sensations, for it was thus that he approached the realm of harmony. Others may fly to alcohol or drugs to pass the gateway of the Land of Miracles; what Wagner needed was silks and perfumes. Judith was commissioned to send them, in quantities, from Paris. He attached the most serious importance to these things, was for ever renewing his orders, and went into the minutest detail concerning his requirements. And if, in spite of his age, he sometimes still broke out with the lover's declamatory passion, he never lost sight of the practical object of his correspondence. His fair intermediary, since she could not give him back his youthful ardours, sent him, instead, cases of merchandise which he proceeded to unpack with all the eagerness of a devotee scanning the pages of a missive from his loved one.

"You can write me direct; I've made arrangements for that. I should like to have had a word from you, since I can always see you—from my writing-table—as you looked at me (God, with what eyes!) when I was writing souvenirs for our poor *cantatrices*. The absolutely extraordinary thing about it all is that you are the abundance of my poor life, which has been so calmed down and so sheltered since I have had Cosima. . . . You are my Lady Bountiful, my intoxicating 'over-and-above!' " (9th of December, 1877.)

A fortnight later he writes: "Now let's get to *business*. First of all as to the two cases which have not arrived. Well, they *will* arrive, and I shall be diving into the very soul of my Beneficent One. The satin brocade will be kept in reserve. I am disposed to place an order for thirty yards, but perhaps they will change the colours so as to be still more to my taste; I mean silver-grey instead of yellow, and pink, *my* pink (very pale and delicate) instead of the blue. And the Japanese dress? I am always looking at that splendid picture, with the dark hair. (Is it you?) You frighten me with your essences. I shall go and do something silly. On the whole I prefer powders, they are more easy to sprinkle on stuffs. . . . Now, once again, be prodigal, especially with those bath scents, the ambers, for example. I have the bathroom underneath my study and I love to smell the perfumes mounting. Well, don't be hard on me. I am old enough to permit myself these little indulgences. I have my three *Parsifal* years in front of me and nothing must be allowed to take me from the gentle quietness of this fruitful seclusion. Come . . . dear soul, beloved soul! Things are always so tragic, real things, I mean. But you still love me—and I couldn't help it even with the best will in the world. A thousand kisses. R."

". . . My Judith! *Meine Judith*, I say, *Geliebtes Weib!* (see dictionary). Everything has arrived safely. The Turkish slippers, the orris-water; first rate! But one wants a lot of it, a half-flagon for every bath, and I have one every day. Just imagine! Rimmel's *Rose de Bengale* is better than the White Rose. Let us adopt it and send me any amount—for I am extravagant. Anything else? Yes, I absolutely insist on your keeping well, for I very often go past that poor house in Bayreuth from which I was driven out by you. But above all, how goes it with your Japanese dress? Oh, magnificent idea! My soul loves me! In a few days I shall have finished the composition of Act I. You shall have some samples later on. Love me, my poor Beautiful, Bountiful One! Richard" (27th of January, 1878).

"Oh, you, soul warm and sweet, how inspired I felt within your arms! Must I forget it? No. But everything is tragic. Everything tends, in the best of cases, towards the Church!"

". . . Judith, oh, my Warm and Beautiful One! I love you ever. . . . I love to see you always standing up so valiantly for your country. I admire you all the more for your patriotism because I myself haven't got any at all; I look on myself as the sole German among all those stupid people they call Germans."

". . . I want satin, that's the only form in which silk pleases me, with the soft play of light in the folds."

". . . Sweet friend, Lovely spirit—I dream I am a refugee once more, trudging the muddy Paris streets, forsaken of everyone! Suddenly I meet you, *you*, Judith! You take me by the arm, you lead me home, you smother me with kisses! Ah, it's very touching, very touching! Oh, time and space—what foes you are! I ought to have found you then. How long ago it was, all that! I embrace you. Richard."

". . . Here's something I've forgotten, which compels me to write you again. Oh, my dear Judith, the slippers should be *without heels*! and then, here's something else. I want a cover for my lounge-chair, something utterly beautiful and out-of-the-common, which I shall call 'Judith.' Listen, try and get hold of some of that silk stuff they call *lampas* or some such name. A background of yellow satin—the palest possible—strewn with a network of pink flowers. . . . All that for *les bonnes matinées de Parsifal*. That name is Arabic. The troubadours of old did not understand it. 'Pars'—'fal,' signifies *parsi* (think of the Parsees who worship fire), pure; *fal* means mad, (*fol*), in a noble sense, that is to say, a man without learning, but endowed with genius. Adieu, ma plus chère, ma dolcissima anima. R. W."[1]

Thus was *Parsifal* brought to birth, "the pure and simple-hearted and transcendant madman," as Liszt called him, amid flasks of Rimmel, oriental silks and perfumed swaddling-clothes. Every morning at six Wagner was at work on it, continuing till two or three in the afternoon, and then, of an evening, he would bury himself deep in his books. We find him annotating the French version of the Bhagavad-Gita, the Gospels, St. Paul, and Renan's *Life of Jesus*. He constructs a theology of his own and attempts to superimpose the heroes of his own mythology on to the great prophets of India, Egypt, and Palestine. He documents his labours from the works of Goerres, San Marte, Gervinus and especially from Wolfram von Eschenbach and, though the sum-total of it all was poetry rather than history, there is no gainsaying that his doctrine of regeneration is certainly his own. . . . *Parsifal* is a transposition of the story of Jesus and Mary Magdalen, on the lines he had formerly sketched out in his *Jesus of Nazareth*, a parable of a renunciation brought about by the one act of faith of which he felt himself capable, namely pity. Wagner had at one time thought of removing the scene of his play to India so as to bring in Buddha's disciple, Ananda, who was beloved of Sawitri, the fair "untouchable," and won their twofold salvation by her chastity. This was the theme of the *Conquerors*. But as far back as 1857, that memorable Good Friday when, on the terrace of his Zurich home, Wagner felt the touch of a sort of mystic grace upon him, he had re-created his *Parsifal*, attaching him to a world at once heroic and sylvan, chivalrous and monastic—the world of King Arthur and his Knights of the Round Table, the world of Tristram and Iseult. That world of universal blossoming, home of the virgin soul, was very near to the country of *The Ring*. In both we find the same warring principles of good and evil, on the one hand, the Castle of the Holy Suffering of the Grail, on the other, Klingsor's abode of Sinful Pleasures. Once again, we see it all—Wagner's yearning for the pure and holy. Siegfried is there again under the lineaments of Parsifal—innocence bemocked, misunderstood, yet in the end triumphant alike over the cunning of the mind and the lures of the flesh. Klingsor, who has laid his curse on love, is another Alberic, who has

---

[1] These letters are as in the original. We have merely omitted a few passages and corrected a few grammatical errors which tended to obscure the meaning.

come·with his magic and introduced all the temptations of Satan
into this land of saints. Gurnemanz, the aged seer, is a Wotan,
all his hardness dissolved in tenderness and changed into a
poet full of meekness and love. Amfortas, King of the Grail, is
a transposition of Brünnhilde, condemned, like the Valkyrie, to
bear the weight of his sin till the day when he of the guileless
heart and pure shall redeem his guilt and heal, by his invincible
purity, the open wound in the sinner's side. Kundry alone in
this, the last of Wagner's dramas, appears as a new and enigmatic creation. This woman of the twofold countenance is now
the messenger of the Grail, the silent servant of the Knights
of the Holy Grail which held the Blood of Christ, and now the
spy of Klingsor, "the Nameless One, the world-old Temptress,
the Rose of Hell," Herodias burning with desire for the Prophet
of the Desert, who longed to print her burning kisses on the
bloody head of the saint who had spurned her. Kundry is at
one and the same time Mary Magdalen, the Woman taken in
Adultery, and the mystical lover of Jesus. She is symbolical
of Woman, the Eternal Feminine, good and evil in one, purity
and sin, sorrow and joy. "Time was when, with an impious
laugh, she mocked the sufferings of the Crucified One; but on a
sudden Jesus turned his eyes upon her, and from that day forth
she has been a wanderer on the face of the earth, seeking to
meet His eyes again and win His pardon." Love, she deems,
love alone can save her. Thus the curse and her redemption
are bound together in a single act of the will, in an instinct in
which her soul, lost in an ecstasy of carnal sin, is eternally
ransomed by repentance and the hope of forgiveness. In every
fresh lover Kundry looks for her Redeemer. And when she sees
that she is holding only another sinner in her arms—another,
yet ever the same—she breaks out once more into that pitiless
laughter which of old had rent the bosom of the Son of God.
Hungry for purity notwithstanding, consumed with passionate
longing for that beauty of soul she had beheld at the foot of
the Cross, Kundry tears herself away from the sorceries of
Klingsor and, putting on the most miserable disguise, turns
back to expiate her sin at the Gates of Monsalvat. She devotes
herself to a life of holiness and toil. She becomes again the
lowly servant. Her heart henceforth is all wrapt up in the
fulfilment of her innocent tasks—until the inexorable desire
again begins to stir within her. Then she starts up, as if from
a waking dream, utters a shrill cry, and rushes through the
woods to renew once more her secret life amid the Flower-
maidens, who bring her the fair prey whereof she has told them.

And so it is that one day these huntresses of love bring into her presence none other than Parsifal.

But if Kundry is the Eternal Feminine, Parsifal in no way symbolizes the Eternal Masculine; in the first place, because he has no conception of original sin. He knows not pity save what he has learnt of it from Gurnemanz, who made him feel ashamed of having killed a swan. He knows naught of pain save that he has seen the blood oozing from Amfortas' wound. Good and evil have never been revealed to him; and of desire he has not so much as a notion. Surrounded by the Flower-maidens, the Innocent beguiles himself with the fair and fragile sisterhood till Kundry suddenly appears and undertakes to instruct him. And how shall she, who reads so surely the secrets of the human heart, how shall she have her way with Parsifal more surely than by calling up to him his mother's memory? By this indirect approach his innocent soul is already ensnared and weakening, when Kundry, like Brünnhilde, imprints a kiss on the lips of him for whom she longs. And like Siegfried, who at that moment gets to know what fear is, Parsifal suddenly grows conscious, at the touch of that kiss, of the mystery of the world about him. He realizes what sin is. He remembers the wound of Amfortas. He has a vision of the sorrow which weighs upon mankind and from which he possesses the power to set them free. He realizes at a glance his past ignorance and his future responsibility. He perceives, moreover, that the only way to save the Temptress is to resist her. He thrusts her from him. He is victorious over her and over himself. He sets before the world a new philosophy, an idea of human sanctity, in the world and not withdrawn from it. For Parsifal in no sense upholds the cause of total renunciation. He is no recruiting agent for monastic life. Later on he will have experience of love and beget Lohengrin. But he is learning to master it, to be its lawgiver, and, for the first time in his existence, Wagner, in him, celebrates the victory of life over death.

What an amazing sight to contemplate this old man chanting in his crowning work a hymn of faith in Nature and in human effort. "For it is not the wretchedness of the weak to which pity is due," said he. "What we should aim at is the quality of mercy in the soul of the strong." There is no doctrine in *Parsifal*, but an example. When the Guileless One returns to the City of the Grail, when he heals the side of Amfortas by touching it with the spear which he has won back again from Klingsor and when all Nature in blossom sings the enchantment of Good Friday,

nothing in all this bears any resemblance to an Easter homily.
It is a new act of faith in man. The testimony of a grave and
grateful heart. Indeed and in truth it is not the chaste Parsifal
that is the chief character in this storied window. It is the im-
palpable presence of love, a peace that has descended from the
dome of Monsalvat upon the many-hued medley of human adventure. Amfortas remains the stake of the battle, the stricken
man condemned to life, he who unites in his heart the Satanism
of the Flying Dutchman, the sorrows of Tristan and the mysterious divinity of Lohengrin.

Amfortas—Wagner, there is no doubt about that. And Parsifal—Ludwig, he who knows not his name, the veritable Innocent
whose emotions shall continue to master him till the day when
he is brought face to face with reality. At the same moment as
Parsifal awoke to live his life, Ludwig II gave up the struggle
and hastened to his death. He never grew to manhood. He could
but personify the Parsifal of Act I and took no note of the example his master was setting before him from afar. The Child,
the Woman, the Man, the Demon, and Nature, such are the five
characters in this drama whereof a dove is the heart poised in
the void upon a ray of love.

The musical outline of *Parsifal* was completed on the 29th of
January, 1878; Act II on the 13th of October of the same year;
Act III on the 26th of April, 1879. His ideas once more welled up
in such profusion that his principal difficulty was to control them,
to regulate the flow. They pressed upon him, as the blood pressed
upon his bosom, laying him low sometimes in the very midst of
his labours. However, he did not trouble himself at the increasing frequency of these attacks of which he had had the first
warning experience at Moscow. All the same, he was haunted
by the feeling that there was no time to be lost. He made a fair
copy, in ink, of his drafts, developed them and put in the famous
syncopations, for he wanted his music to be as insubstantial as
the passage of the clouds. But he only managed between eight
and ten bars in a day. He re-read Plutarch, Xenophon's *Anab-
asis*, Shakespeare, Balzac, with his own family and a few intimate friends around him. Among the latter, Hans von Wolzogen
occupied a special place. He was a young man of good family
who had just founded, with the master's concurrence, and under
the title of *Bayreuther Blaetter*, a literary and musical review
dealing exclusively with Wagner's works and ideas, and the affairs of the Festival Theatre. Then there was Anton Rubinstein,
the celebrated pianist and composer and an ardent admirer of

Wagner's music. In the course of his frequent visits to "Wahn-fried," Rubinstein played through, of an evening, page after page of *Parsifal* just as it came from the composer's hand, and also *The Twilight of the Gods*. Malwida also came, and Liszt, who went from Weimar to Rome to the princess's; from Rome to Bülow's at Hanover; and from Hanover back again to Bayreuth. But the years were telling on him more and more and his noble face was covered with warts.

Indeed, everything seemed to be growing old, and apathy and languor to have descended on the subscribers and on the King. High up on the hill rose the great theatre, a huge eyeless red-brick building that looked like a cathedral fallen from grace. Everything slumbered, save Cosima's unquiet heart and Wagner's tireless spirit.

"What is Germany, and where?" That was the question Wagner was asking of himself, the question that every German always asks himself for whom the real drama lies in Germany's direct participation in the destinies of the world, that is to say in her value as a reformer. For such an one a comfortable income, a taste for art, Voltaire's "let us cultivate our gardens" has no significance. In an atmosphere of tranquillity and pleasure he droops and dies. It is not the enjoyment of good fortune that he wants, but the pursuit of it, even though it lead to death. A hundred years before Wagner, Goethe said, "The desire to exalt the pyramid of my existence as high as possible in the sky outrivals everything else; I hardly ever forget it for a single moment." For winning the game was far less important to him than the game itself. It was the same with Wagner. Quietude was nothing to him and did not even benefit his art. He refused to look upon his life's work as ended. Built up as it had been on the rocky heights, the plains of happiness were no fit place for it. And now that the ardours of the flesh importuned him no more, it behoved him to awaken the ardours of the mind. But he had lost his youthful idealism, and lost, too, his whole-hearted Schopenhauerian scepticism, and like so many men in the evening of their days whose earlier life prevents them from going back to their faith in religion because it would seem a stultification or an inconsequence, Wagner revived what Christian blood was left in him in the mysticism of his *Parsifal*. He even prided himself that he had strengthened the pure evangelical teaching by expelling from his musical confession of faith everything that recalled the old Jewish world. It was what he had already attempted in his *Das Judenthum in der Musik*. He now resumed the same theme, setting forth his theory of art, philosophy and religion, and to some extent basing his moral system on the ideas which agitated his whole spiritual existence: the tragic tyranny of poverty, the degeneration of the Western races under the influence of the Jews, whose aim it was to exploit the universal decadence; the excessive cult of the senses and the unsatisfactory nutritive régime of civilized peoples; the vices of institutional religion; the regeneration of man through vegetarianism, through art (sole intermediary between human and divine), and through the religion of pity. The titles of Wagner's writings at this period are sufficiently indicative of the trend of his ideas: *Know Thyself* (1879); *Religion and Art* (1880); *Heroism and Christianity* (1881).

Whither was Germany leading? Shall we go on hoping? Such were the questions which he felt were bound up with the problem of his destiny. But the new Reich only answered in terms of the barest and most official orthodoxy. The very significance of the spiritual as a positive value seemed lost. Even now the German no longer understood that, in the words of Carlyle, Shakespeare was worth more to England than all her colonies; and we may see pretty clearly what Wagner meant when he told Judith Gautier that he was entirely without patriotism. Bismarck himself no longer impressed him. His pan-Germanism seemed to him to be a dangerous error. Wagner cut himself adrift from humanity, from the heartless world of science when he became acquainted with the horrors of vivisection, that latter-day Inquisition, which was a blot on the nineteenth century. The modern world became more and more of an abomination in his eyes.

For the *Bayreuther Blaetter* he wrote an open letter to Ernst von Weber (against vivisection). "I do not believe in God," so the letter ran, "but in the divine as revealed to us in the person of a sinless Jesus. I believe in the divine which has, in a unique example, shown us the way of redemption, leading us beyond the ways of humanity along the path of perfect simplicity and purest beauty. That path leads to death, but Christ has set us the example of a beautiful death as the crown of a beautiful life!"

To live a beautiful life, that is what should be learnt and taught. Not the things which are read of in books and contained in the stupid curricula of schools. He would certainly never send his son to sit in the class-rooms of a school. He would have him brought up by a master who could teach him the meaning of Shakespeare and Cervantes, who was possessed of a pure mind, an honest will, a clean soul, and courage enough to couch his lance, like Don Quixote, against a windmill or two.

Seldom had the grey skies of Upper Franconia weighed more heavily on Richard Wagner than in this late autumn of 1879. The old heart-hunger for Italy suddenly awoke in him with that touch of intoxication which sometimes comes from the name of a town, the memory of a face seen in the dim light of a church, the pungent odour of some alleyway, or the perfume of a fruit. As Cosima was wont to say, "If one really feels called upon to earn the crown of martyrdom, one must live in Germany and die in Italy." And in truth Wagner did feel that vocation. For the hour of death was drawing near. If *Parsifal* was to be the last of his works, there was no time to be lost in completing its orchestration. And why shouldn't he work at it in Rome or Naples? Italia! How often had he not remeasured, in thought, the way he had fared in his youth, the way towards the country that was at once the oldest and the sanest in Europe. Was it not Liszt who had said, "Beautiful souls will always be homesick for Italy."

They fixed their choice on Naples. "Wahnfried" was to be shut up. They would forget all their professional worries. . . . After numerous negotiations and discussions, they took the Villa Angri on the Strada Nuova del Posilipo, and started on the last day of the year.

On the 4th of January, 1880, the whole family ascended the terrace of the villa, whence one could see the smoke rising up from Vesuvius. The cold was intense. Snow had fallen a few days before. What matter? The bay was sparkling. Yonder was Sorrento, Capodimonte, Ischia, Capri. . . . Ah, what a thing it was to be alive! Seated in the little tramway drawn by a pair of horses trotting along towards the city all athrill with gaiety, Wagner exclaimed: "To the devil with ruins! Naples is my city! Here everything has life in it!"

Chapter III

ITALIA

THE healthy, joyous paganism of Italy never fails to attract the artist and the voluptuary. It is through the eye, there, that the spell is laid upon the heart. In Italy more than anywhere else Wagner was alive to the passionate nature of the people, to the radiant skies, to the beauty of the women, to the charm of poetry. What he missed the least was his music. *Parsifal* came to a complete standstill. With his family and a few new friends around him, he took a simple, unaffected joy in the pleasures of being alive. Heinrich von Stein, a young German author, whom he would have liked to attach to his household as tutor to his son, and the Russian painter, Paul de Joukowsky, were frequent and welcome visitors at the Villa Angri. Joukowsky painted Frau Wagner's portrait. Stein wrote essays which afterwards brought him into prominence, and read aloud his translations of Giordano Bruno. Then they all went on excursions together. They went to Amalfi, and next, in caravan fashion, riding on donkeys, to Ravello, where they discovered the old Palazzo Raffoli built in the Moorish style. Wagner, when he saw the marble columns, the chapel all smothered in ivy, and the broad flight of steps leading down to a garden of roses, exclaimed, "I've found Klingsor's garden."

He took up going out early again, and went for early morning walks through the pinewoods and the vineyards. He soon began to feel like writing and dashed off rough drafts for his essay on *Art and Religion*, in which, still haunted with the nightmare of vivisection, he tried to establish that prehistoric man was a vegetarian and that his decadence dated from the time when he began to eat flesh.

In July he put his notes in order, and in a few weeks completed his new book, and this despite a general state of "nerves" and one or two attacks of chest pains which he succeeded in repressing by sheer willpower. Joseph Rubinstein arrived on a visit

to Naples, and in the evenings, played the later sonatas of Beethoven. These musical performances restored Wagner from the
agonizing but transient attacks of the malady to which he was
subject, but which no doctor seemed able to cure. He was recommended to try sea-bathing, but the effects were disastrous. Although the first few months at Naples had been beneficial (despite a recurrence of his facial eczema), it looked as though the
summer was going to be a trying time. Frau Wagner therefore
set to work to find a more bracing climate, and by the month of
August the whole household, Joukowsky included, departed to
take up their abode in the beautiful Villa Torre Fiorentina, at
the gates of Siena.

There they had a magnificent view over the hills and Wagner
slept in the bed of Pope Pius VI. Naples, well, Naples was
Africa; but Siena was the real Italy, sweet and radiant and
sparkling, and over all, over the natural landscape and the works
of men, brooded that incomparable atmosphere of tenderness
and love. Thus it was with the cathedral which looks down over
the city, with its mosaics, its multicoloured tiles, its busts of
the popes, and above all its dome poised aloft in the silent spaces
of the sky as a monument of eternal love. So profoundly was
Wagner impressed by it that he at once got Joukowsky to make
a drawing of the cupola to be used in the scenic designs for the
Temple of the Holy Grail. Thoughts of his unfinished opera now
began to steal into his mind again, and he set to work to rule
up some paper with a view to getting on with the work of
orchestration.

Then Liszt arrived for a ten days' stay. He was now over
seventy, but it seemed as though age were powerless to impair
the vivacity or the delicate sensibility of this indefatigable old
man who was still the cynosure of feminine eyes. Perpetually
going to and fro between Rome, Budapest, Weimar, and Paris, he
sometimes permitted himself a few days' rest at his daughter's,
playing the piano, inditing letters to his rival feminine admirers.
Then, packing his little wandering-minstrel's bag, off the old
virtuoso would go on his travels again. This time they took him
to see the dome at Siena, and in the evenings he played his
Three Sonnets of Petrarch, Beethoven's *Sonata quasi una fantasia*, several pieces by Chopin, his *Dante Symphony*, and, the
night before he left, nearly the whole of Act III of *Parsifal*,
Wagner standing up and singing it alongside of him. They tried
to make him stay on, Wagner lamenting the brevity of his
visits. He would have liked to keep this way-worn kinsman near
him. He was an old man now and needed care and tactful treat-

ment and loving attention. But Liszt slipped away from this happy domesticity. The once rich and splendid artist was growing daily more humble and timid, more "impersonal," as he put it in a letter to the Princess von Wittgenstein. He who had once played Mæcenas to Wagner cared for nothing so much as to be alone, to go and kneel down in some sequestered chapel corner, and to beseech his patron, Saint Francis, to chastise him with his rod for his too-numerous delinquencies.

From Siena Wagner wrote to King Ludwig to ask him one last boon, which was that he would lend his royal support to *Parsifal*, for he could not endure the thought that this "sacred mystery" should be profaned by being enacted on the same stage as the operettas of Offenbach. He longed to keep this work for Bayreuth alone. And when the king had given his assent to this petition and graciously promised to send, without any expense to his old friend, the Munich orchestra and choruses for the rehearsals in 1881 and the Festival performances in 1882, the Wagners set out again for Germany. They took in Venice on the way, stopping nearly a month at the Palazzo Contarini, and arriving at Munich on the last day of October. Without a trace of bitterness King Ludwig awaited the arrival of the one being in the world for whom he had really suffered. He commanded a private performance of *Lohengrin* and invited Wagner alone to come and sit with him in the royal box; Cosima and the girls were in another box by themselves. Then, two days later, Wagner, by command of the king, conducted the prelude to *Parsifal*. The composer was in a state of nerves. They had to wait a good quarter of an hour for the king to arrive. And when the prelude was finished—it was the first time Wagner had heard it on the orchestra and he was quite overcome—the king asked for it all over again, and then, after that, insisted on the prelude to *Lohengrin*. . . . Wagner handed over the bâton to Levi, went home in a frigid rage, and had another chest attack. That night at dinner the storm burst. Wagner cursed all the princes of the earth. "King, Emperor, Bismarck—they're all alike!" Lenbach, the painter, at whose house they were dining, attempted to defend his illustrious model. "Oh, I've had enough of your Bismarck!" cried Wagner. "If he had had any insight, he would have made peace with the French after Sedan. By carrying the fighting up to the very walls of Paris he has sundered the two nations for a whole century to come." As for the king, he certainly never guessed the fit of nervous rage that had overtaken the great man whom he feared as much as he admired. On returning to his palace, he took his diary and penned this reflec-

tion: "12th of November, afternoon, listened twice over to the
admirable and marvellous prelude to *Parsifal*, conducted by the
composer in person. Profoundly significant. . . . I have always
heard it said that between prince and subject, friendship was
impossible." He did not say what he thought himself. There follow some disconnected words . . . like the murmurs of a
troubled dream . . . ideas that will not piece together, landscapes in which "the moonlight" and "the waterfalls" remind
us that this shadow-haunted soul was rapidly descending the
slope at the foot of which, five and a half years later, he was to
be brought face to face with grim reality. Then perhaps, in a
gleam of lucidity, in that last hour, he saw that what men deem
reality is but bondage, and then and there resolved to die.

Be that as it may, neither Wagner nor the king had any notion
that on that November day in 1880 they had set eyes on each
other for the last time. Going back to "Wahnfried," on the contrary, Wagner thought that the clouds which had been accumulat-
ing for so long between Munich and Bayreuth had been completely dispelled. He at once returned to his score. Pressed into
the service as a scene-painter, Joukowsky was instructed to get
together sketches and models for *Parsifal*. The young composer,
Humperdinck, undertook to copy the manuscript, sheet by sheet,
as it left the composer's hands. And Wagner returned to playing
the old man, which was now the part he loved beyond all others.
He held forth on Shakespeare, Beethoven, Carlyle, and Parsifal.
Heroes who had become gods; the gods returning to earth as
pilgrims, servitors and pure in heart. Thus and thus only, he
thought, can man preserve whatever divinity he has in him:
love, kindness, and the sense of mystery, the cold analyses of
science deliberately put aside. Prospero, on his island, was preparing to lay down his magic.

> But this rough magic
> I here abjure: and, when I have requir'd
> Some heavenly music (which even now I do)
> To work mine end upon their senses that
> This airy charm is for, I'll break my staff,
> Bury it certain fathoms in the earth,
> And, deeper than did ever plummet sound,
> I'll drown my book.

The day's work done, Wagner would open one of his favourite
authors, now reinforced by the works of the Comte de Gobineau.
Indefatigable reader that he was, he read one after another,
*The History of the Persians, Three Years in Asia, Religions and
Philosophies in Central Asia, The Renaissance* and—his new

friend's master-work—the *Essay on the Inequality of Human Races*, all that moral geology, so to call it, in which the ideas in so many instances confirmed his own, fortifying them with a scientific knowledge of which Wagner, until then, had only had the barest notion. However, in the spring of 1881, this meditative existence had to be interrupted so as to allow him to go to Berlin to be present at the first complete cycles of his Tetralogy hitherto given outside Bayreuth. These performances of *The Ring* were a brilliant success, and the imperial family joined in the general applause. Wagner was compelled to appear on the stage and make a speech. But all this nervous strain brought on the inevitable return of his cardiac trouble. All he longed for now was the studious repose of "Wahnfried" and the silence of his library. He therefore delegated to Neumann the impresario, and to the conductors Seidl, Levi, and Richter, the task of doing what was necessary to his former works. Peaceful surroundings and loving care were more to him now than the performance of his music, for it had been yet again borne in upon him that even his most intelligent disciples and his most gifted singers would never reach those heights of perfection of which he had dreamed as an attainable ideal.

He invited Gobineau to come and stay with him. Gobineau came and stopped a month. An aristocrat and an exquisite, whose health had been seriously impaired by his long sojourn in hot climates, and who had been suffered by official stupidity to wear out his days in distant outposts, Gobineau got on well with Wagner from the very first; yet in almost every particular he was his exact opposite—a gentleman of ancient lineage, a royalist to begin with, and then an adherent of Bonaparte; a Catholic who sometimes lamented that his ancestors did not do their work more thoroughly on Saint Bartholomew's Eve; a conservative with a lofty idea of his race and his "house"; a foe to metaphysical theorizing; eighteenth century to the finger tips and to the point of knowing the finest prose passages by heart, and a wholehearted partisan of the privileged classes. . . . But he was an artist, a sculptor, an Orientalist, and a poet. Notwithstanding that, he was still, at sixty-five, waiting for the recognition which Europe seemed loth to bestow on him. For Wagner, too, recognition had been long in coming. But it was his at last. And Gobineau's turn would come. Both were passionately interested in the history of man and his origins, and in the greatness of the Aryan race. The gods of Wagner, Odin, Thor, and Frey, were the count's own ancestors. The spiritual bond thus forged was reinforced by a sentimental one, for Gobineau recollected that,

when he was French Minister in Greece, he had first heard
Wagner's music played on the piano by Mlle. Dragoumis, a beautiful young girl who had cast a glamour of enchantment over his
period of office at Athens. Who, then, was better qualified than
the Man of Bayreuth to savour the significance of the rather
disheartened utterance which Gobineau had made the motto of
his languishing ambitions. "In Life, there's love, and then work,
and after that—nothing!" Wagner, on his side, could not help
seeing in this brilliant but disillusioned *grand seigneur*, certain
traits that reminded him of Friedrich Nietzsche, the same pagan
loftiness of mien, the same indifference to worldly prosperity,
and that subversive originality of mind which distinguishes the
souls that are born of the spirit. They celebrated together the
master's sixty-eighth birthday, and then went back to Berlin
to hear the fourth cycle of the Tetralogy. Gobineau was profoundly impressed by it. On their return to "Wahnfried" he presented Wagner with a copy of *Religions et Philosophies dans
l'Asie Centrale*. It contained the following inscription: "A token
of sincerest admiration and most affectionate regard."

"Gobineau is my sole contemporary," said Wagner, who assigned him a niche in his mind very similar to the one which
Schopenhauer had filled nearly thirty years before. A trace of it
is visible in *Heroism and Christianity*, and it haunted Wagner
all the time he was finishing off the orchestration of the first two
acts of *Parsifal*. Gobineau was studied. Gobineau was expounded.
There were lessons in Gobineau. He was asked to write an article
for the *Bayreuther Blaetter*. Cosima wrote Judith Gautier, asking her to see Didot, the publisher, and get him to reprint the
Essay on the Inequality of the Human Races, which was out of
print, the Wagners offering to pay the cost of the new edition.
"Is it troubling you too much to ask for your good offices in this
matter? . . . My husband is much better this winter than last,
and Italy, particularly Siena, has done him a lot of good. Today
he has begun the orchestration of the second act of *Parsifal* and
we are in the midst of seeing about the scenery and dresses. I
doubt whether we shall leave home until the performances begin,
and it will then be six years since we saw each other."

But Cosima was wrong. She was destined to return to Italy
that same year, for it was now totally impossible for Richard to
endure the rainy climate of Bavaria. Never before had the call
of the south been so urgent with him. His nervous condition
was increased by hard work, and besides that, he now wanted
to adopt Bülow's two daughters, Daniela-Senta and Blandine, of
whom he was very fond. But Hans declined. At Wagner's request

Cosima decided to go and see her former husband. The interview took place during the summer at Nuremberg. It was eleven years since they had seen each other, and it was a sad and painful meeting. Outwardly, Hans had changed a great deal, but inwardly he was the same uncontrolled, unjust, feverish being he had always been, incapable of taking the large view. He accused Wagner of not knowing black from white, good from evil. All the same, Cosima was genuinely sorry for him, for he was a sick man and there was no cure for him. She wept, but it was clear she could find nothing to regret, and next day she went back to Richard, not, indeed, as one returning to peace and happiness, but with the satisfaction of knowing that she was all the peace and happiness of the man she loved. "I am going home after this meeting as though a new life were about to begin for me; a life without solace and yet a life of peace; happy in that he is happy, yet in my inmost heart conscious of an inexpiable sin. May God help me to value that peace, without ever forgetting the sin." All the tragedy of her life lay in her inability to forget.

This being the case, it was a happy event when the artists and choruses promised by the king arrived from Munich to give a practical idea of the still unfinished work which was to be produced the following summer. Therese Malten, Miss Brandt, and Messrs. Winckelmann, Gudehus, and Scaria arrived one after the other. Wagner plunged into action again, busied himself about the scenery and the stage machinery, and accompanied his singers on the piano. Liszt came in September, on his annual visit to Bayreuth, and found Judith Gautier there, "in the seventh heaven," as he put it to the princess. Thus, then, Richard's secret friend arrived just as he was orchestrating the Flowermaidens' garden of delights. "He's got to the end of the second act," was Liszt's report, "and there only remain between a hundred and two hundred long pages to be written. It takes more than mere care; it takes his genius and his tortured soul . . . M. de Joukowsky has done some fine pictures, illustrating *Parsifal*—temple, forest, and a weird garden." It was the dome at Siena and the garden at Ravello.

So it was still and always Italy, Italy where Wagner was dwelling so completely in the spirit that it was there he now placed the Burg of Monsalvat! And now came Rubinstein singing aloud the praises of Palermo. Once more Wagner opened his Baedeker, and in a moment all his thoughts were bent on getting away, away to the sunlight, for all his chest pains and his frequent attacks of dizziness he thought were rheumatic in origin. The doctors examined him. They told him that he was perfectly sound organically, but recommended a warm climate, a strict diet and plenty of air and exercise. And so, as happened twenty-two months before, the Wagners forthwith decided to go and spend the coming winter in Sicily. Once more they handed over the Festival Theatre and its affairs to Feustel and his son-in-law, Gross, and on the 1st of November the whole family set out *via* Munich, Verona, Ancona, and Naples, for Palermo.

Four days later they arrived, and took up their quarters at the Hôtel des Palmes. The next day but one Wagner was at work. The whole place acted like a tonic: the town, built like an amphi-theatre with its old palaces, its quiet streets, its gardens stocked with lemon trees, not to mention a cageful of monkeys on the terrace of the hotel itself. He did not waste a moment, for the fear was again upon him lest death should come before he had had time to finish his task, time to alter and alter again, time to note down, with the scrupulous care that was always his, the very last accents on the very last bar. But death was good-natured; it went on waiting, and gave him time. Cosima gave Judith an account of how the day was parcelled out: "Morning, work; midday, a stroll; one o'clock, dinners; two, a siesta; three, another stroll; five, work; seven, supper; and then bed." Fond as ever of sight-seeing, Wagner went to inspect the Duomo, which was Arabian in style, the Cloister of the Benedictines, the Palatine Chapel in the Palazzo Reale, the Villa Camastra, the owner of which, Count Tasca, soon became a friend. Then he would go back and resume his labours, with the geometrically regular outline of a palm tree before him with which to soothe his mind. Sometimes, too, he would go and visit a great owl which was kept a prisoner in the Florio garden. "That's nature, undisguised, cruel but sincere, and what a head, like an old lion's! The rascal's better-looking than a lion!" And when he saw people with nothing better to do teasing the poor old blind thing with the great round eyes, he would pull some copies of his anti-vivisectionist pamphlet from his pocket and hand them round among the bystanders. He now planned to spend every six months at Palermo. He forgot all about his old age. They saw him pull up outside a shop and look at himself in the glass, saying: "I don't know myself with this grey hair. Am I really sixty-eight?" Other expeditions, still further afield, were to be tacked on to this one: Egypt, Madeira, Ceylon. "What I need is blue sky." But still those frightful pains in the chest came on again, casting a sinister shadow over the future. Though he did not really believe there was anything serious the matter with him, Wagner increased the daily quota of work to such an extent that when Joukowsky arrived somewhere about Christmas-time, he found the work nearly completed.

On the 13th of January (1882), while they were all at supper, Wagner rose from the table, went up to his room, and returned with a voluminous parcel. It was his score: "There," he said, as he came in, "I finished my *Parsifal* just now." They uncorked a bottle of champagne. The master opened the piano and played through the overture to *Die Feen*, his first opera. It was just forty-nine years since he put his signature to the last page of it, adding, "*Finis, laudatur Deus.*" But now all he wrote at the end of his crowning work was just the famous initials R. W. Death might come now; it could not take away all that he had created in the course of the fifty years that sundered Wurzburg from Palermo, all that world of music which he had woven out of his dreams for a living; in a word, "the world that exists not."

Parsifal finished, the Wagners stayed on for several more weeks in Sicily. They were now in the villa belonging to Prince Gangi on the Via Monreale. They had got to know many more people, and although the boy Siegfried was suffering from an attack of paratyphoid, his sisters went about to dances. As soon as the child was well again, they entertained the Palermo Society at a farewell matinée, prior to going on to Acireale, and on that occasion Wagner conducted the band. Then Blandine, Cosima's and Bülow's second daughter, became engaged to a young naval officer, Count Biagio Gravina.

Almost at the same time Hans von Bülow himself got engaged to an actress at the Hamburg theatre. Thus, a situation which had been worrying Cosima for years and had been a continual wet blanket on Wagner and herself, suddenly cleared. The forlorn one had at last decided to start life anew. Appointed orchestral conductor by the Duke of Meiningen, he left Hanover, got together a group of instrumentalists that soon became famous, and gradually faded out from that sorrowful scene upon which passion had for so long been casting his restless shadow. And Prospero, from the foot of Mt. Etna, exclaimed:

> A solemn air and the best comforter
> To an unsettled fancy, cure thy brains. . . .

Halfway through April, they left for Naples and thence for Venice, the city which, of all others in Italy, was dearest to Wagner's heart, because, over and above its colouring and its movement, it was fulfilled of the calm repose wherein love and death most fittingly abide. It was the city of Byron and his escapades, of Casanova and his love-affairs, the city of Musset's despair and Leopold Robert's self-inflicted death, of Wagner's adieu to Mathilde Wesendonck. It was the grave of *Tristan* and the cradle of the *Meistersinger*. He loved its bells, its slow-moving waters, Saint Mark's, the lions, symbols in which the artist rediscovered the will to live and work, and in the oldest of the lions of the Arsenal, the very face and features of his Wotan. Yes, he must come back again to Venice next autumn, when *Parsifal* was over, come back and write some symphonies. No more operas in that theatre of a city; nothing but pure music, divested of every trace of literature. Here in this land, which knows not winter nor summer, it behoved the artist, now that old age had come upon him, to essay a spiritual antiphon to the silent, stone-wrought music of the Doges. Of a certainty it was at Venice he might look to find that balanced calm unmarred by feverish hope, that still repose wherein the old should seek their final home. And so they set themselves to find a palace they might rent for the season following *Parsifal*; and at length they fixed on the Palazzo Vendramini-Kalergi on the Grand Canal.

Hardly were they back again at Bayreuth, when the Comte de Gobineau arrived on a visit, joining in the family festivities—the traditionally brilliant affair—in honour of the 22nd of May, the master's sixty-ninth birthday. King Ludwig sent a pair of black swans. Gobineau, however, was seized with a sudden illness and Cosima fancied she discerned in the face of their beloved friend —for such he had become—the premonitory symptoms of apoplexy. He left to take the waters at Gastain, and soon after there arrived the host of soloists, chorus-singers and stage-hands, who, with Levi and Fischer in command, were to be responsible for the sixteen performances of *Parsifal*.

The theatre doors, which had been closed for six years, were again flung wide. All was stir and bustle on the Wagnerian hill. Within the mystic castle reigned a grave and solemn air, and even the most insignificant "super" swore passionate fealty to the new faith. Wagner flung himself unstintingly into the work, amid the ceaseless calamities born of the jarring rivalries among his artists. Then came the first disappointment. The King sent word to say he would not be there. He gave out that he was ill. But Wagner had a strong suspicion that other reasons were at work to account for his desertion, just when his *Parsifal* was about to take up the ideal position in the history of music which had been the common dream of both. What held Ludwig aloof from Bayreuth was his determination to be alone. He aimed at being no more to the world than a king that was dead, a statue. For a long time now he had severed himself from the commonplace crowd of *dilettanti*. He kept clear of their stupid activities. He had broken the bridges that linked his royal castles with the highways of the realm. His dreams, his everlasting dreams, dug a protecting moat around him, which he would not cross till the time came for him to die.

But Liszt at any rate was there, and Richard was so delighted that he said his old friend Franz was, in truth, his whole kith and kin. There came also some of his women friends of bygone days, among them his niece Johanna who created the part of Elisabeth in *Tannhäuser*, and Mathilde Maier. But Mathilde Maier absolutely refused to meet Wagner. She had grown deaf and shrank from letting him know of this shortcoming. Young Count de Gravina arrived, in due course, his marriage having been fixed for the 25th of August, the twofold anniversary of the King's birth and Wagner's wedding. Then followed a crowd of princes, friends, artists, and foreigners, among whom were to be seen the French composers Chausson, Léo Delibes, Vincent d'Indy, and Saint-Saëns. At the fifth performance, Scaria, on entering a little *salon* close to the wings, which Wagner reserved for himself, saw him suddenly turn livid, collapse on the sofa, and fall to beating the air with his clenched fists, as if he were struggling with death. When they had brought him round, for he had completely lost consciousness, he gasped, as he got on his feet again, "Another narrow escape!" Then he pledged everyone to silence about the matter lest it should in any way interfere with the subsequent performances. But the man was worn out. At "Wahnfried" he would sometimes fall asleep on the chair in his dressing-room. At night his wife would hear him talking in his sleep. "Good-bye, children!" he would exclaim. And she would say her prayers beside him and weep. But next day there would be nothing on the old, worn face to cause her any anxiety.

At his stepdaughter's wedding Wagner was full of life and spirits and made a long speech. At night the inhabitants of Bayreuth kindled bonfires on the neighbouring hills. Four days later, the sixteenth, and last, performance took place. Upper Franconia was shivering beneath a steady downpour of icy rain. Levi, who had caught a chill, was feeling very unwell, whereupon Wagner descended into the hollow where the musicians were concealed, and, taking the bâton, conducted the third act himself. Then when the curtain had fallen for the last time on the Temple of the Grail, Wagner spoke a few words of thanks to the musicians. "Till next year!" he cried. But his task was done. An infinite weariness weighed him down. He longed to get away from inhospitable Bavaria; longed to see Venice once again.

Chapter IV

PAN IS NOT DEAD

VENICE at last! The Palazzo Vendramini! The Wagners had taken the whole of the upper floor; eighteen rooms in all. The Duke della Grazia occupied the rest of this sumptuous building, which he had inherited from his mother, the Duchesse de Berri. In the Wagners' part, the furniture was Louis XVI, upholstered in red silk; the walls of the great hall were hung with Venetian leather; the bedrooms were quite simple. Wagner liked the place. It reminded him of the Palazzo Giustianini where, twenty-five years before, Tristan had kept watch across the lagoons for the coming of Isolde. All that was long, long ago. Now his wilderness had people in it, and the faces about him are none of them the same. He has created—and procreated—and the poet of lonely deaths has ended the song of his dreams. With most men their hearts are filled with regret when the objects of their dreams are slowly transformed into good sensible guardian angels. But with Wagner, who was endowed with an extraordinary faculty for living in the present, no such repining was there. He was one of the few human beings who have managed to ascend to a height level with his aspirations, without ever casting a glance on the void behind him, without the smallest tremor of dismay. Here in Venice, where all manner of romantic extravagances wander at will, where the air is heavy with the incense of decay and impregnated with the terrifying spell of passions spent, Wagner never felt any longing for the past. He was all for what was new, greedy of novelty. He loved the Piazzetta. He would mingle with the crowd, with the common people, observe their ways, and never grew weary of watching the youth of the world go by. He even chose the spot where death should come for him. It was to be in front of the porch of Saint Mark's, between a couple of pillars, on a stone seat. There it should come and take him as he sat watching the motions of the restless doves and the clouds go by like doomed and stricken things. Often his

378

thoughts turned upon Buddha, a brotherly god, and a friend to animals. "I dwelt in the forest; I made the lions and the tigers draw near to me by the power of my good will," he read of an evening in Oldenberg's book. As though his spirit were already disembodied, it left this Island of the Dead to stray among the oldest sages of the earth. It sought to refresh itself in the universal. Thanks to Gobineau's books, which he had been careful to bring with him, Wagner made his way into the country of the Brahmins and came upon the symbolical forest of Hindu metaphysics. He hearkened to the preaching of the anchorites. "We are of men the most august, and none here below can be compared with us. It is not without having merited it that we possess this supreme dignity. By virtue, and rising upwards step by step we have now reached the point where even kings grovel at our feet." His thoughts lingered on the august grandeur of the mind that is completely set free from matter. Is not his own mind somewhat in that case? Has not he too attained the heights whence man looks down on the sea of misery arising from the deep-rooted evil of property?

And now behold, as he was pursuing these meditations, there appears a new portent in the sky; as in the days when Julius Cæsar fell, as also when Tristan and his Isolde died, there blazed a comet on the night blackness of the Venetian sky. What presage, then, was this? For whom was it a warning? No apprehensions filled his mind and he could say then, as long ago he had said to Mathilde, "nothing can make me fear, since now nor hope nor future lies before me." Suddenly there came the news that Gobineau was dead, felled by a stroke in a hotel omnibus at Turin. That, then, was the prophecy of that golden tress in the heavens! "Our dearest friend. . . . Hardly has one fallen in with such an one, than he slips through one's fingers like water." Uhlig, Schnorr, Tausig, Nietzsche, Ludwig II of Bavaria, Gobineau—that all his friends should have thus escaped his hand, a hand too, which always held so firmly whatever came within its grasp. Of all the men whom Wagner had loved, one, and one only, stood by him still, and that was Liszt—and Cosima, his blood, the very heart of him. Ah, would that he might come full soon, the good old friend!

And come he did. On the 19th of November, at ten o'clock at night, Liszt alighted from the Milan train and stepped aboard Wagner's gondola. Wagner himself was waiting for him at the Palazzo Vendranimi, where every candelabrum held its blazing torch, waiting for him with that impatience, that joy, that frenzy one might almost call it, which always possessed him when his

Saint Francis, so poor and so radiant, was drawing near. He was conducted to his "princely lodging"—three rooms, including a drawing-room, and an antechamber facing his daughter's own apartments. And then life went on just as at Bayreuth. Liszt attended mass every morning at the parish church. At two o'clock the whole family sat down to dinner. In the afternoon he worked at his *Saint-Stanislas*, or else he would go with Cosima and call on any grandees who might be breaking their journey at Venice, while Wagner would go back and sit down on the stone bench at Saint Mark's. Richard's nerves were getting worse. Ever since Liszt had come, he had been growing more and more conscious of his inward isolation. Had they, when all was said and done, ever really understood each other? Were they not sundered by fundamental differences of nature which made any intimate union between them nothing but deliberate illusion? And now that Franz kept robbing him of Cosima, a sort of jealousy—perhaps it had been born thirty years before—began to seethe in his heart, he who had lived so long on Liszt and his lordly liberality. Wagner gave way to outbreaks of nervous irritation and Cosima was continually being forced to hide her tears. Liszt was the only one who never noticed that anything was wrong. He would take a hand at whist with the little girls, or sit down at the piano and play over his latest works, wholly unobservant of Wagner's fits of silence. And then it was a comical thing to see the pair of venerable masters talking both at once without listening to a word the other said, both having been accustomed to silence when they began to speak. And then it would happen they would find themselves alone together in Wagner's room. Liszt would sit down at the keyboard and play through a Beethoven sonata or one of Bach's fugues, and thus the secret path would be opened again whereby, years before, they had found the way to each other's heart.

For Christmas, Cosima's birthday, Wagner conducted his old Leipzig symphony, which was played by the Lyceum orchestra in the *salle du foyer* of the Phoenix. "It was the young Hercules overcoming the serpents and taking an Olympian pleasure in his task," wrote Liszt to Rome. "Following the example of the Bavarian king, there were no guests. We were a family party. . . . His genius hangs poised at art's very zenith." Franz's admiration showed no signs of abatement. But what strange presentiment was it that made him suddenly interrupt his *Saint Stanislas* in order to compose—which he did in a few days—the elegy of *La Gondole Funèbre*. And, as though to lend emphasis to the atmosphere, half smiling, half sad, which enveloped the dying year at Venice, he wrote, "I grieve not over-sorely at the death of people I have known. The one active and very lively feeling I retain is that of compassion, of sympathy with the throbbing heart-strings of suffering humanity. Sometimes, for a few brief moments, I feel the sufferings of sick folk in hospital, of the wounded in the war, and even of such as are condemned to torture or to death. It is something analogous to the stigmata of Saint Francis, minus the ecstasy, which belongs to the saints alone." But is it so certain that Liszt was not a saint in his way. And those stigmata of which he would have been so proud, are they not visible all through his life and works, humble yet glorious wounds in the artist's bleeding heart?

On the 13th of January, 1883, Liszt bade farewell to the Palazzo Vendramini and took train for Budapest. We know not what were the last words that passed between the two friends; no one has recorded them. Shortly after this Wagner received a copy of Nietzsche's new book, *The Joyous Wisdom*. "Nothing but Schopenhauer!" he exclaimed, disdainfully. Had he stumbled upon this passage: "It is certain that nothing is more contrary to Schopenhauer's spirit than whatever is especially Wagnerian in Wagner's heroes: I mean innocence of the highest love of self, faith in the *grande passion* as the highest good." Wagner flung the book angrily away from him, scorning the man whom he deemed devoid of all love, rotten and hollow like a tree that the first gust of wind will bring to the ground.

On Shrove Tuesday, Venice was crowded with revellers. Joukowsky arrived, and so did Levi, the conductor. Wagner took them and the children to look at the crowd outside Saint Mark's, the costumes, the illuminations, and the funeral procession of Prince Carnival—and his own stone bench. With the twelve strokes of midnight all the lanterns were extinguished and Ash Wednesday was ushered in in total darkness. That day Wagner set out in his gondola for the island of San Michele, the ancient burial-ground of Venice, but feeling unwell, he made a quick return to Vendramini. The next few nights he could talk of no one but Liszt. On Monday the 12th of February, after dinner he sat down at the piano, improvised a scherzo, and played through the lament of the Rhine Maidens. "I wish them well," he said, "those creatures of the watery deeps." And turning to his wife, he said, "Are you one of them, too?" That night he sat up late. They could hear him pacing up and down the room, talking to himself, as he usually did when composing poetry.

On Tuesday the 13th, Cosima sat down to breakfast with her husband, as usual, but Wagner was conscious of a sort of vague oppression. He felt that it was one of his attacks coming on and said to his man, "I shall have to be very careful today." He thought he would do a little work. Outside, it was raining in torrents. And his table was already littered with sheets of manuscript, the essay on *The Feminine Element in Man*, of which he had written some ten pages. He asked to be let alone all the morning. If the pain came on he would be able to manage all right. Silently the hours went by; outside the rain was still falling. About a quarter to two Joukowsky arrived for lunch and, to his great surprise, discovered Frau Wagner at the piano, playing Franz Schubert's song, *In Praise of Tears*. The master sent word that they were to begin without him, for he was not feeling well. Halfway through the meal, his bell rang twice, urgently. A moment later a maid appeared with a look of consternation on her face, and asked Frau Wagner to come at once. She rushed to his room, but he signed to her to go away. He had got over these attacks before and he would do so again. He was sitting at his writing-table, his cloak flung down beside him, and his groans were louder and more alarming than usual. Cosima went out of the room. But soon the bell rang again—violently. "My wife and the doctor!" he commanded, in an altered voice. Cosima came back and suggested the cold compresses which had usually given him relief. Wagner said no. He knew it was useless. He struggled to his feet, dragged himself as far as the little red-and-gold sofa in his dressing-room, and sank down with his head against Cosima's shoulder. The manservant got him undressed. "My watch!" he cried, faintly. It had fallen from his waistcoat pocket on to the carpet. Its ticking was audible, but Wagner's heart had ceased to beat.

Three days later, at the same hour, the massive coffin, adorned with the heads of lions, passed out of the Palazzo Vendramini. It was laid in the gondola whose funeral hymn Liszt had already composed. Maybe Ritter called to mind how, that far-off summer evening in 1858, the fugitive had been so deeply moved as he entered the dusky barge hung with the sombre trappings of Tristan. Cosima, erect and closely veiled, followed the body. She had cut off her hair so that the beloved one should bear with him that token of his faithful Senta.

Then began the triumphal progress of the dead across Italy and Germany. Deputations and bearers of wreaths awaited the mourners at all the stopping-places. At Innsbruck there was Levi. At Kuffstein, Herr von Burkell, secretary to the King of Bavaria, sent forth by His Majesty to greet his vanished Lohengrin. But, though at Munich an enormous crowd, forgetful of what had passed in former years, bore reverent and silent homage to the man who was now faring on his last journey through the capital of his hard-won fame, Ludwig II refused to attend the passing of one who in life had been the only being he had ever loved.

The train reached Bayreuth at dead of night. The whole town was awaiting it, and the obsequies took place the following day. The old revolutionary took his revenge on the "great ones" who for so many years had slighted him again and again. The funeral was on a royal scale, a crowd of functionaries on a dais, panegyrics and orations, flags at half-mast, sconces draped in black, representatives of the king and the Grand Duke of Saxony in full uniform, delegations of artists and of the Wagner societies, the corps of officers, the band of the 7th Infantry and of a regiment of Light Horse. On the hearse the only flowers were the two wreaths sent by the king. The procession passed right through the town. At the gates of "Wahnfried" stood the children, holding their father's two dogs in leash. Snow began to fall. The bier was lowered into the grave, the grave which for ten years had been waiting to receive it, and on which Wagner had been wont to turn a wistful glance every morning from his window.

Cosima alone did not appear.

And as for *Tristan* and the *Meistersinger*, Liszt, too, was absent from this supreme apotheosis. The news was brought to him at Budapest and he did not so much as lift his pen from the letter he was in the midst of writing. For a long time now, to die had seemed to him an easier thing than living. Three years later, in that same town of Bayreuth, as he was coming away from a performance at the Festival Theatre, the old eagle laid him down in his cassock to die, the name "Tristan" on his lips. In the delirium of death he had found no other name than that, the symbol of his loving soul. He also was destined to be interred at Bayreuth, but in the cemetery, like the rest of the folk, and, by his desire, no other memorial marked his resting-place than the plain cross of the disciples of Saint Francis.

Six months before Liszt's death, in the month of June, 1886, King Ludwig II lowered the curtain on the strange melodrama of his life, the melodrama that began when first he saw Tannhäuser escaping from the Venusberg and Lohengrin borne away by the swans to the land of illusions. For more than twenty years this prince, endowed with so rare a beauty, had striven to build amid the clouds a kingdom for his dreams to dwell in. But government officials have a mortal dread of poets. One day,

officers and ministers took by assault the inoffensive castle where
the lonely monarch held his shadowy court, amid the ghosts of
the kings and queens of France. They compelled him by force
to come down to earth. They maltreated him like any wandering
lunatic. But not even for forty-eight hours could he endure the
contact of reality. He seized his keeper, Doctor Gudden, by the
throat, dragged him as far as Lohengrin's lake, and the waters
closed over them in death.

There yet remained one more disciple, the last, he who had
forsaken Wagner in order to remain true to himself. He too was
stricken in his turn. Christmas Day, in the year 1888, Nietzsche
was in Turin, worn out with toil, almost blind and almost glorious; and on that day he too entered into the troubled realms
where madness wields the sceptre. There he was fated to drag out
a miserable existence for nearly twelve years, his memory gone,
his placid, short-sighted eyes fixedly gazing on the garden at
Weimar where his sister had installed him with every circumstance of material comfort, which, though he knew it not, the
fruits of his once brilliant mind ensured him.

As for the Wesendoncks, they had for some years been home
again in Germany. Otto died there in 1895. A young grandson of
the Willes'—Wagner's friends at Mariafeld—a student, used to
go of a Sunday and call on Mathilde, now an old lady, in her
beautiful Berlin home. She would rarely omit to get him to sit
down beside her easy-chair and talk to him at great length about
her belovèd past. And when they were alone, she would hand
him her note-books in which, long ago, she had written down
her recollections, together with copies of Wagner's letters, which
she never wearied of hearing read to her, over and over again.
Isolde died in 1902, twenty years after Tristan.

Alone, there remained at her post the woman who had sworn
fidelity to the homeless Wanderer of the sea. The moment Richard's eyes were closed, Cosima had vowed herself to death. For
many days they feared the worst might happen. Yet she was
fated to know the dread honour of surviving him for forty-
seven years and of bearing unaided the burden of her inheritance. She created Bayreuth anew, and for half a century
ordered and marshalled the almost preterhuman fame that clings
about the name of Wagner. She lived to behold the break-up of
the world, a world undone by the folly of the gods, a world which
had begun to perish the day they divided their power, founding
their empire upon pride and the abuse of force. For civilizations
have their day and come to naught, like any other creation of the
human mind. Nevertheless, it takes more than a season to com-

pass their overthrow. The vast Valhalla of nineteenth-century civilization in the West did not collapse because the warring nations sought by force or guile to win the gold accursed by Alberic. Its overthrow was determined long before that, for there is a slow patience in the maze of thought that works unseen and rises triumphant from the heaviest of tombs. The old edifice was doomed to fall from the day when its architects forbore to stop up the little fissures through which there crept into its foundations the dreams of justice and of love among men.

That Wagner knew. That is what all the poets know in their hearts. That is what the transient masters of that deceptive gold are beginning to discover, they whose kingdom today has no more substance than the air. Even those who mock at the things of the mind and profess no faith save in the world of matter are coming, at last, to see that theirs is but a wholly slavish version of Divine Law. It may be, indeed, as Nietzsche would have us believe, that the day will come when it will only be as an æsthetic phenomenon that the world will be able to justify its existence.

So ran my thoughts two years ago, upon the Indian Ocean. Our vessel was pursuing her course over a drowsy sea bounded on the west by castles of flame-girt clouds, while in our wake the night was descending upon Asia. That tiny fragment of Europe which was our ship, cleaving her way through the silent waters, seemed in very truth to have no geographical relationship with any quarter of the globe, but to be sailing as chance might ordain, upon the waters of Eternity. But, lo! upon a sudden there broke upon our ears the wondrous song of love and agony, the passionate outpouring of Tristram and Iseult! So then, round earth and sea there throb rank upon rank of ordered waves, and far out on the lonely deep there came to us the tidings that Pan was not dead, that Prospero had not succeeded in drowning his book. And in a moment we found ourselves again, each one of us a most distinct and individual personality. Noiselessly the passengers grouped themselves around those wondrous voices. One heard oneself in this complaint of a lover who a generation ago had gone to dwell among the shades. His music reopened a wound in everyone of us. It was as a voice calling us from the other end of the world, calling us back to our most precious sorrow. We found that the earth has but one homeland for each and all of us, the homeland of the heart. Tristram suddenly came upon us armed with our love and bearing in his hand his red heart, like a mystic flower. That heart became our emblem. It was our Hesperides, our Home. And meditating on the musician who had wooed from his pain so enduring a consolation, we said, in the words of the Umbrian people blessing the dead Saint Francis, "He gives ear to the prayers of those whom God himself has ceased to heed."

BIBLIOGRAPHY

In 1883, the year of Wagner's death, the number of items in a complete catalogue of "Wagneriana" was estimated at about 10,000. To-day, that figure would have to be doubled or even, perhaps, trebled. There is certainly nothing to rival it except the bibliographies of Napoleon and Shakespeare. Collectors, and other persons who are interested, will find, at the end of Max Koch's work on Wagner, a very up-to-date account of this vast literature. For the documentation of my own book I have had recourse to the Complete Edition of Wagner's works, to his own correspondence, and to that of his friends and to some recent works whose timely appearance has been the means of adding to, and occasionally of rectifying, the existing body of information on the subject. I need hardly say that I make no claim to have exhausted that subject. My endeavour has been to construct a true and living portrait of one of the most remarkable artists of his own or any other generation, an artist whose lineaments the fanatical exaggerations of his admirers and the no less fanatical denigrations of his enemies have combined most grievously to distort. A few unpublished letters of the utmost importance have been placed at my disposal by the Comtesse de Gravina, *née* von Bülow; and, thanks to the courtesy of M. Julien Cain, director of the Bibliothèque Nationale, Paris, I have had access to the original correspondence between Wagner, his wife Cosima, Liszt, and Judith Gautier. I have thus been enabled to throw considerable light on certain episodes connected with that luxurious period of Wagner's life. As I have no pretensions to an expert knowledge of music, I have refrained from discussing, analysing, and especially from passing judgment on Wagner's music. As in my previous biographical essays, my sole object has been to delineate the man, and to portray the events of a passionate life whose triumphs and agonies reverberated throughout a whole generation.

Glasenapp's monumental work, although a little out of date in style and method, remains, in spite of a partiality which is more comic than reprehensible, an invaluable mine of information in regard to Wagner's everyday existence. In addition we have two valuable volumes recently published by the Comte du Moulin Eckart on Cosima Wagner, studies by Julius Kapp, Paul Bekker, Max Koch, and Henri Lichtenberger, as well as Professor Charles Andler's admirable *Nietzsche*; Houston Stewart Chamberlain's *Richard Wagner* may also be consulted with advantage. I have purposely disregarded the pamphlet by Messrs. Hurn and Root, which received its full deserts not long ago at the hands of Mr. Ernest Newman, the distinguished English critic. Even if these authors had any revelations to disclose concerning Wagner's attitude to his first wife, it is scarcely to be expected that a collection, however voluminous, of letters exchanged between a distracted husband and a jealous wife would throw any new light on their respective characters.

Wagner's *Collected Works* have been translated into French by M. J. Prod'homme (Paris, Delgrave. 13 volumes).

The quotations from Liszt's letters are taken direct from the original text, which was frequently in French (Breitkopf and Haertel, Leipzig).

My Life (Mein Leben) has been published in a French translation by the Librairie Plon (Paris. 3 vols.).

I have myself translated the extracts from Wagner's letters, as well as the passages taken from the diary of Frau Cosima (as given by Comte du Moulin Eckart in the work above referred to). A full list of references follows:

REFERENCES

PART I

CHAPTER I

"The battles of 1813 . . ."	Chateaubriand, *Mémoires d'Outre-Tombe,* Vol. III
"A madman Napoleon undoubtedly was . . ."	Goethe, *Gespräche mit Eckermann,* (March 21, 1831)

CHAPTER II

"Hitherto, the God of Light . . ."	Glasenapp, *Das Leben Richard Wagners,* Vol. I

CHAPTER III

"When Zarathustra . . ."	Nietzsche, *Thus Spake Zarathustra*
"seeming to arouse the other instruments . . ."	R. Wagner, *My Life,* Vol. I
"in order to make the young girls . . ."	*Ibid.*
"Already I can hear the prancing . . ."	*Ibid.*
"I love those who despise greatly . . ."	Nietzsche, *Zarathustra*
"I knew what no one else knew . . ."	*My Life,* Vol. I

CHAPTER IV

"I pictured him . . ."	*My Life,* Vol. I
"The monetary difficulties . . ."	*Ibid.*
"A sublime and mystical monstrosity . . ."	*Ibid.*
"Fortunately I've got plenty of enemies . . ."	Glasenapp, *R. Wagner,* Vol. I
"What we wanted was high emotions . . ."	R. Wagner, *Gesammelte Werke,* Vol. IX
"felt its profound fascination . . ."	*My Life,* Vol. I
"I remember nothing . . ."	*Ibid.*

CHAPTER V

"intoxicating influence . . ."	*My Life*, Vol. I
"The main theme . . ."	*Ibid.*
"some impossible dream . . ."	*Ibid.*
"the graver problems that confront . . ."	*Ibid.*
"From that day onward . . ."	*Ibid.*
"There is no getting away from it . . ."	Glasenapp, Vol. I
" 'For my part,' says Gide . . ."	André Gide, *Un esprit non prévenu*

CHAPTER VI

"The cholera was there . . ."	*My Life*, Vol. I
"An ideal of beauty . . ."	R.W., *Jugendbriefe* (published by Kapp), Vol. I
"I grew harsh and bitter . . ."	*My Life*, Vol. I
"Two noble families . . ."	*Ibid.*
"My hero was Prince Arindal . . ."	*Ibid.*

CHAPTER VII

"It was said he did not know . . ."	Glasenapp, Vol. I
"Why not give him . . ."	*Jugendbriefe*, Vol. I
"We are not going to write like Italians . . ."	*Ibid.*
"the daring glorification . . ."	*My Life*, Vol. I
"to reveal the immorality . . ."	*Ibid.*
"the gracious aspect . . ."	*Ibid.*
"In all she did . . ."	*Ibid.*
"Oh, yes, preach away! . . ."	*Jugendbriefe*, Vol. I (letter of Dec. 7, 1834)
"Thank you, my golden friend . . ."	*Ibid.*
"as ladylike and well-dressed . . ."	*Ibid.*

CHAPTER VIII

"We spent some delightful days . . ."	*My Life*, Vol. I
"There comes a time . . ."	*Jugendbriefe*, Vol. I
"My music was merely . . ."	R. Wagner, *Gesammelte Schriften* and *Wagner im Bilde*
"One might have thought . . ."	*My Life*, Vol. I
"All my pent-up jealousy . . ."	*Ibid.*
"I was wandering in quest . . ."	*Ibid.*
"To prepare us for times . . ."	*Ibid.*

CHAPTER IX

"My grief was intense . . ."	*My Life*, Vol. I
"I was in a state of veritable enthusiasm . . ."	*Ibid.*

"She was depressed and demoralised . . ."	*Ibid.*
"And so it was that . . ."	*Ibid.*
" 'Wagner worried the life out of my staff! . . .' "	Max Koch, *Richard Wagner*, Vol. I
"Sing, sing, and yet again sing! . . ."	Glasenapp, Vol. I
"This centre of culture . . ."	*My Life*, Vol. I
"When I had in my hands . . ."	*Ibid.*
"There are more things in heaven and earth . . ."	Shakespeare, *Hamlet*, Act I
"A solemn music . . ."	*Ibid. Tempest*, Act V, Scene I
"For my part, I can only . . ."	R. Wagner, *Works*, Vol. VI
"From that moment began . . ."	*Ibid.*
"The Flying Dutchman . . ."	*Ibid.*
"I was delighted . . ."	*My Life*, Vol. I
"I am, so to speak . . ."	*Mozart's Letters*, Vol. I

Part II

CHAPTER I

"I loved music . . ."	Combarieu, *Histoire de la Musique*, Vol. III
"This young man's work . . ."	*Le Constitutionnel* (Oct. 3 and 7, 1839)
"We must honour Berlioz . . ."	*Works*, Vol. IV
"I cannot exist . . ."	*Ibid.*, Vol. VII
"that heaven-sent . . ."	*Ibid.*, Vol. IV
"I suddenly beheld . . ."	*My Life*, Vol. I
"into the world of light . . ."	*Works*, Vol. X

CHAPTER II

"Poverty and Privation . . ."	*Works*, Vol. I
"A Visit to Beethoven . . ."	*Ibid.*
"On being a Virtuoso . . ."	*Ibid.*
"On German Music . . ."	*Ibid.*
"A German Musician in Paris . . ."	*Ibid.*
"The human voice is a . . ."	*Ibid.*
"The 23rd June (1840), etc."	Glasenapp, Vol. I
"La Favorite, arrangement for piano . . ."	*My Life*, Vol. I
"Both these nations . . ."	*Works*, Vol. I
"I believe in God and Mozart . . ."	*Ibid.*

CHAPTER III

"What could Liszt be . . ."	Glasenapp, Vol. I
"The dead musician . . ."	*Ibid.*
"Diversions in Paris . . ."	*Ibid.*

"The Parisian Whirligig . . ." *Ibid.*
"The Musician and the press . . ." *Ibid.*
"I went wild with delight . . ." *My Life*, Vol. I
"During that period . . ." *Ibid.*
"A new world dawned . . ." *Ibid.*
"Oh! Paris! Oh, place of joy and
  suffering! . . ." Glasenapp, Vol. I
"in token of their appreciation . . ." *Jugendbriefe*, Vol. I
"The hour of deliverance sounded at
  last . . ." *My Life*, Vol. 1
"And we saw nothing . . ." *Ibid.*

CHAPTER IV

"I said to myself . . ." *My Life*, Vol. II
"Never was it so hard . . ." *Jugendbriefe*, Vol. I
"My excellent sister . . ." *My Life*, Vol. II
"He is a stranger to all . . ." Claudel, *Connaissance de l'Est.*
"I imagine I cannot . . ." Glasenapp, Vol. I
"Into an atmosphere . . ." *My Life*, Vol. II
"Paris remains unforgettable . . ." *Jugendbriefe*, Vol. I
"That he wanted to take stock . . ." *My Life*, Vol. II
"I jest, thought I . . ." *Ibid.*
"Yes, my dear Edward . . ." *Jugendbriefe*, Vol. I
"a piece of well-meant legerde-
  main . . ." *My Life*, Vol. II
"Greater than Donizetti . . ." Glasenapp, Vol. I
"I won't be robbed . . ." *My Life*, Vol. II
"I was obliged to recognize . . ." *Ibid.*
"which must shine pure . . ." *Works*, Vol. VI
"Think what I must . . ." *My Life*, Vol. II

CHAPTER V

"In Paris it is a common error . . ." Glasenapp, Vol. II
"Herr Wagner conducts . . ." *Ibid.*
"Richard Wagner has . . ." *Ibid.*
"A chaos of sounds . . ." *Ibid.*
"After suffering in Paris . . ." Berlioz, *Mémoires*, Vol. II
"The success of my operas . . ." *Jugendbriefe*, Vol. II
"We composers cannot . . ." *Ibid.*
"in a posture to brave . . ." *My Life*, Vol. II
"The nearer I grew to man's
  estate . . ." *Gesammelte Schriften*, Vol. IV
"the mysterious *Stimmung* . . ." Glasenapp, Vol. II
"The composer had taken excep-
  tion . . ." *Ibid.*
"for that parrot was . . ." *My Life*, Vol. II
"It was in a state . . ." *Works*, Vol. VI
"Until the final unfolding etc . . ." *Ibid.*, Vol. VII

"Behold a musician unrivalled . . ."   Nietzsche, *Nietzsche against Wagner*
"The whole set off with twelve . . ."   *My Life*, Vol. II
"I conduct merely with . . ."   *Ibid.*
"When I heard your *Rienzi* . . ."   *Ibid.*
"For heaven's sake . . ."   *Ibid.*
"Literally sparkle . . ."   *Ibid.*
"Certainly a witty fellow . . ."   Glasenapp, Vol. II
"mysterious pages . . ."   *My Life*, Vol. II
"by the make of the horns . . ."   *Works*, Vol. IX
"a tumultuous outburst . . ."   *Ibid.*
"A combat in the most exalted
    sense . . ."   *Ibid.*
"Renounce thou must . . ."   *Ibid.*
"Then with the clear-cut . . ."   *Ibid.*

CHAPTER VI

"Have you encountered . . ."   *The Flying Dutchman*, Act II
"That glowing fire . . ."   *Ibid.*
"The supreme incarnation . . ."   *My Life*, Vol. II
"God would be better advised . . ."   *Jugendbriefe*, Vol. II
"The hope of its realization . . ."   *Works*, Vol. VI
"At the height of the power . . ."   *Ibid.*
"Towards the intimate shadow . . ."   *Ibid.*
"Who should ask not . . ."   *Ibid.*
"In whom Lohengrin is drawn . . ."   *Ibid.*
"It was written . . ."   *Ibid.*
"The truth . . ."   Letters to Roeckel and Glasenapp
     Vol. II
"It is the truth towards . . ."   *Ibid.*
"Women are the music of life . . ."   Letters to Uhlig and Glasenapp
"The most profound anxiety . . ."   Glasenapp, Vol. II

CHAPTER VII

"were the natural consequence . . ."   Daniel Stern, *The Revolution of
    1848*, Vol. I
"But to the continental peace . . ."   *Ibid.*
"The effect was terrific . . ."   *My Life*, Vol. II
"The poorer a man is . . ."   Glasenapp, Vol. II
"*The Ninth Symphony* . . ."   *Ibid.*
"Things were going ill . . ."   *Letters of Wagner and Liszt*, Vol. I
    (June 23, 1849)
"Gave him back courage . . ."   *Letters* to Liszt (Feb. 20, 1849)
"Expression of this instinct . . ."   *Works*, Vol. VI
"A Barbarian reaching . . ."   *My Life*, Vol. II
"Bakounin claimed . . ."   *Ibid.*
"The annihilation of all . . ."   *Ibid.*
"But the well-fed Philistine . . ."   *Ibid.*
"Like a feeble being . . ."   *Ibid.*

"That is a marvellously fine thing . . ." — *Ibid.*

"Yes, everything will be destroyed . . ." — *Ibid.*

"Involuntary alarm . . ." — *Ibid.*

"It was a bright sunny afternoon . . ." — *Ibid.*

"Are you with us . . ." — Glasenapp, Vol. II

"Taking it all round . . ." — *My Life*, Vol. II

"Does not resist temptation . . ." — *Ibid.*

"The ball which is going to kill me . . ." — Glasenapp, Vol. II

"How gloriously shone the sun . . ." — *My Life*, Vol. II

"The tears of the Philistines . . ." — *Ibid.*

"War! War! . . ." — Glasenapp, Vol. II

"Dear Liszt . . ." — *Letters*, Wagner-Liszt (May 20 and June 5, 1849)

"Well, here I am . . ." — Glasenapp, Vol. II

"Nothing can compare . . ." — *Works*, Vol. VI

PART III

CHAPTER I

"My dear Friend . . ." — *Letters*, Wagner-Liszt, Vol. I (June 5, 1849)

"It is to you I am . . ." — *Ibid.*

"It will soon be four weeks . . ." — *Jugendbriefe*, Vol. II

"In my extreme poverty . . ." — *My Life*, Vol. II

"No more Socialist clap-trap . . ." — *Letters*, Wagner-Liszt, Vol. I

"To guide it into the way . . ." — *Works*, Vol. III

"These clumsy conquerors . . ." — *Ibid.*

"In a state of abasement . . ." — *Ibid.*

"Whose only grace . . ." — *Ibid.*

"Mercury, god of merchants . . ." — *Ibid.*

"Love of the weak . . ." — *Ibid.*

"The Christian idea . . ." — *Ibid.*

"Let us rear the altar . . ." — *Ibid.*

"Floats here and there . . ." — *Ibid.*

"Who then will be the judge . . ." — *Ibid.*

"The glorification of such a death . . ." — *Ibid.*

"About this time . . ." — *My Life*, Vol. II

"The dawn of the day . . ." — *Ibid.*

"I have broken the last . . ." — *Letters*, Wagner-Liszt (April 21, 1850)

"I can see you there . . ." — Glasenapp, Vol. II, and *Jugendbriefe*, Vol. II

"To be the axle on which . . ." — *My Life*, Vol. II

"I am no longer young enough . . ." Hurn and Root, *The Truth about Wagner*
"In a year, gracious heaven . . ." *Ibid.*

CHAPTER II

"I will carry out . . ." *Letters*, Wagner-Liszt, Vol. I
"My joy at having found you . . ." *Ibid.*
"Every bar . . ." *Ibid.*
"Your Lohengrin . . ." *Ibid.*
"This new and glorious name . . ." Liszt, *Gesammelte Schriften*, Vols. I and II

"Extraordinarily charming . . ." *Letters*, Wagner-Liszt, Vol. I
"When is Siegfried . . ." *Ibid.*
"Bülow was hysterical . . ." *My Life*, Vol. III
"Dear friend, you have here . . ." *Letters* to Uhlig, Feb. 16, 1851
"Ah! if I could only tell . . ." *My Life*, Vol. III, and *Works*, Vol. IV (Preface)

"Agreeable melodies . . ." Opera and Drama (*Works*, Vol. IV)
"In a phrase . . ." *Ibid.*
"It has only been given . . ." *Ibid.*
"Of which the principle is . . ." *Ibid.*
"She loved Polyneices . . ." *Ibid.*
"Saint Antigone . . ." *Ibid.*
"Pressed by need . . ." *Letters*, Wagner-Liszt, Nos. 57-59
"At last I saw . . ." *Ibid.*, No. 67
"Your letter, my friend . . ." *Ibid.*, No. 68
"Nature awakes . . ." *Letters*, Wagner-Liszt, Vol. I, and Glasenapp, Vol. II

"As if the Devil . . ." Glasenapp, Vol. II
"If so much loveliness . . ." *My Life*, Vol. III
"I've no longer got life in front of me . . ." *Letters* to Uhlig, and Glasenapp, Vol. II

"With me it is all a martyrdom . . ." *Ibid.*
"The aim of my life . . ." *Letters*, Wagner-Liszt, Vol. I, No. 82
"I am sinking ever deeper . . ." *Ibid.*, No. 88
"Oh, if you only knew . . ." J. Kapp, *Wagner and die Frauen*, p. 106

"Which contains all . . ." Glasenapp, Vol. II
"He is the height of intelligence . . ." *Letters* to Roeckel
"We must learn . . ." *Ibid.*
"I am a wilderness . . ." *Letters*, Wagner-Liszt, No. 96
"I have never been . . ." *Ibid.*

CHAPTER III

"Monsieur and Madame Wesendonck . . ." *Wesendonck Briefe*
"A sheet of white paper . . ." Glasenapp, Vol. II

"All the women . . ."	*My Life*, Vol. III
"For mankind, a state of indifference . . ."	*Letters*, Wagner-Liszt, Vol. I
"Richard is very delighted . . ."	J. Kapp, *Wagner und die Frauen*
"When you're working . . ."	*Letters*, Wagner-Liszt, Vol. I
"Havens for the harmonious calm . . ."	*My Life*, Vol. III
"The murmur of these waters . . ."	*Ibid.*
"To do or die . . ."	*Letters*, Wagner-Liszt, Vol. I, No. 127
"Paris resumed her sway . . ."	*My Life*, Vol. III
"It was not till I went to Paris . . ."	*Ibid.*
"Your wound will never be staunched . . ."	*Letters*, Wagner-Liszt, Vol. I, No. 105
"A sort of migration . . ."	*My Life*, Vol. III
"*The Rhinegold* is finished . . ."	*Letters*, Wagner-Liszt, Vol. II, No. 144
"I see in it . . ."	*Ibid.*, Nos. 144-145
"I was in a state of frenzy . . ."	*Ibid.*
"Where then shall I find energy . . ."	*Ibid.*
"I must have a thousand thalers . . ."	*Ibid.*, No. 162
"Dear Franz, beside . . ."	*Ibid.*, No. 168
"Thou shalt bear no arms . . ."	Glasenapp, Vol. III

CHAPTER IV

"I have ripped Siegfried . . ."	*Letters*, Wagner-Liszt, Nos. 244-245
"A solemn silence . . ."	Glasenapp, Vol. III
"It is through death . . ."	Comte du Moulin Eckart, *Cosima Wagner*, Vol. I
"You will I am sure allow . . ."	*Ibid.*
"Now I no longer hope . . ."	J. Kapp, *Wagner und die Frauen*
"I must make up my mind . . ."	*Ibid.*
"Because it would be impossible . . ."	*Letters* to Bülow
"Profound and calm . . ."	*Ibid.*
"Either absolute separation . . ."	J. Kapp, *Wagner und die Frauen*
"Oh no, no. It is not . . ."	Hurn and Root, *The Truth about Wagner*
"Mon enfant . . ."	*Wesendonck Briefe*
"The woman is furious . . ."	J. Kapp, *Wagner und die Frauen*
"I could not have felt . . ."	*Ibid.*
"My last night . . ."	*Wesendonck Briefe*

CHAPTER V

Extracts from Wagner's journal	*Wesendonck Briefe*
"The city of a hundred silences . . ."	Nietzsche, *Dawn*
"Even as Virgil . . ."	*Letters*, Wagner-Liszt, No. 289
"Am I recognized . . ."	*My Life*, Vol. III

"It has become quite evident . . ." *Wesendonck Briefe*
"It was a sad meeting . . ." *My Life*, Vol. III
"We could only bear to meet again . . ." *Wesendonck Briefe*
"Present, we see each other no more . . ." J. Kapp, *Wagner und die Frauen*
"Cannot we fix up an arrangement . . ." *Letters* to Otto Wesendonck, August 28, 1859

"If you agree . . ." *Ibid.*
"I have spent four days . . ." *Letters* to Bülow
"One day, however . . ." *The Flying Dutchman*
"Here am I once more . . ." *Letters* to Otto Wesendonck, Sept. 17, 1859

CHAPTER VI

"Let me be free . . ." *Ibid.*, Oct. 27, 1859
"You must be mistress . . ." J. Kapp, *Wagner und die Frauen*
"Far from it . . ." *Ibid.*
" 'That art,' he said . . ." *Wesendonck Briefe*
" 'Ah,' exclaimed he . . ." *My Life*, Vol. III
"The fact that I wrote . . ." *Letters*, Wagner-Liszt, No. 302
"All I hope is . . ." *Ibid.*, No. 308
"Mark my words . . ." *Ibid.*
"Heimatlos . . ." *Wesendonck Briefe*
"In what Baudelaire calls . . ." Baudelaire, *L'Art Romantique*
"People who imagine . . ." *Ibid.*
"You become all-powerful . . ." *Wesendonck Briefe*
"I have just heard . . ." Glasenapp, Vol. II
"I am enjoying a momentary sense . . ." *Ibid.*
"Liszt has become . . ." *Wesendonck Briefe*
"I haven't any object . . ." *Ibid.*
"Frightful weeks . . ." *Ibid.*
"She was and will remain . . ." J. Kapp, *Wagner und die Frauen*

CHAPTER VII

"My four happiest weeks . . ." Glasenapp, Vol. III
"She was the first person . . ." *My Life*, Vol. III
"The twenty-fifth anniversary . . ." J. Kapp, *Wagner und die Frauen*
"A naive and indefectible morality . . ." *Ibid.*
"Ah, child! . . ." R. Wagner, *Letters* to Mathilde Maier
"All that gives richness . . ." *Ibid.*
"Yes, and here's the audience . . ." Glasenapp, Vol. III
" 'Tis he in truth . . ." J. Kapp, *Wagner und die Frauen*

"What is he like . . ." — R. Wagner, *Gesammelte Schriften,* Vol. VIII

" 'I wish,' he said . . ." — Comte du Moulin Eckart, *Cosima Wagner,* Vol. I

"You see . . ." — *Ibid.*

"Cosima is a child of genius . . ." — Marcel Herwegh, *The Springtime of the Gods*

"The Schnorrs have come . . ." — *Letters* from Wagner to Minna, Vol. II

"What he felt was . . ." — *My Life,* Vol. III

"It might all be mystery . . ." — *Ibid.*

"What I lack . . ." — R. Wagner, *Letters* to Mathilde Maier

"I have decided . . ." — *Ibid.*

"Yes, I tell you . . ." — *Ibid.*

"I am still waiting . . ." — J. Kapp, *Wagner und die Frauen*

"I have no luck . . ." — *Wesendonck Briefe*

"The misfortune which . . ." — *My Life,* Vol. III

"Things might have been . . ." — Glasenapp, Vol. III, and fifteen letters to Elisa Wille

"Thank your friend Wagner for me . . ." — Glasenapp, Vol. III

"The ancients . . ." — *Ibid.*

"Friend, you know neither . . ." — *Ibid.*

"I'm finished . . ." — *Ibid.*

"The words were few . . ." — *My Life,* Vol. III

PART IV

CHAPTER I

"Though you know it not . . ." — Guy de Pourtalès, *Louis II de Bavière,* and Glasenapp, Vol. IV

"The unbelievable has come to pass . . ." — J. Kapp, *Wagner und die Frauen*

"I believe that if he came to die . . ." — *Letters* to Bülow, May 18, 1864

"What would be fine . . ." — *Ibid.,* June 1 and 9, 1864

"I am worried about Cosima's health . . ." — *Ibid.,* Sept. 30, 1864

"A new birth . . ." — Comte du Moulin Eckart, *Cosima Wagner,* Vol. I

"I have been here three days . . ." — *Ibid.*

"Dull people . . ." — Glasenapp, Vol. IV

"In their spite . . ." — *Ibid.*

"My only one . . ." — Guy de Pourtalès, *Louis II*

"Your letter gave me . . ." — E. Schuré, *Richard Wagner* (Introd.)

"Every man has a demon . . ." — *Ibid.*

"This night will end . . ." — Comte du Moulin, Vol. I
"Of a truth I am no longer alive . . ." — Glasenapp, Vol. IV
"If princes were better acquainted . . ." — Comte du Moulin, Vol. I
"This musicaster . . ." — Glasenapp, Vol. IV
"O my beloved one . . ." — *Ibid.*
"He would have to choose . . ." — Guy de Pourtalès, *Louis II*
"My very dear friend . . ." — Glasenapp, Vol. IV
"I look on myself as saver . . ." — R. Wagner, *Letters* to Mathilde Maier
"I've got to be deaf . . ." — Comte du Moulin, Vol. I
"Oh, she is to be envied . . ." — J. Kapp, *Wagner und die Frauen*

CHAPTER II

"Wagner's wife . . ." — Glasenapp, Vol. IV
"No one will turn me out . . ." — *Ibid.*
"In Germany . . ." — Comte du Moulin, Vol. I
"Otherwise, if we had to . . ." — *Ibid.*
"You seem to me . . ." — *Ibid.*
"We three . . ." — Glasenapp, Vol. IV
"Come, I ask you . . ." — *Letter* to Bülow, April 6, 1856
"I cannot and will not . . ." — Guy de Pourtalès, *Louis II*
"We hear and see nothing . . ." — Comte du Moulin, Vol. I
"I was greatly touched . . ." — *Ibid.*
"You know what sort of destiny . . ." — Guy de Pourtalès: *Louis II*
"Of all the women in the world . . ." — *Ibid.*
"For six months now . . ." — Comte du Moulin, Vol. I
"Whoso has enjoyed . . ." — *Ibid.*
"I most urgently beg you . . ." — *Ibid.*
"House packed . . ." — Liszt's *Letters*, Vol. VI
"Things that are regarded as right . . ." — Liszt's *Letters* to a Female Friend
"You may imagine . . ." — Comte du Moulin, Vol. I
"The Young Man of Germany . . ." — R. Wagner, *Ges. Schr.*, Vol. VIII
"Honour your German Masters . . ." — *Meistersinger*
"Gives utterance to the lament . . ." — Chamberlain, *Richard Wagner*
"I look on the hours . . ." — Comte du Moulin, Vol. I

CHAPTER III

"I am always . . ." — Comte du Moulin, Vol. I
"In my womb . . ." — *Ibid.*
"Blessed be the womb . . ." — *Siegfried*, Act III, Scene III
"I am grateful to you . . ." — Comte du Moulin, Vol. I
"You have had the kindness . . ." — *Letter* from Bülow to the Comtesse de Charnacé, Sept. 15, 1869 (unpublished)
"The calamities, public, latent . . ." — Nietzsche, *Ecce Homo*, Ch. 7
"Wagner is in reality . . ." — Foerster-Nietzsche, *Wagner und*

	Nietzsche zur Zeit ihrer Freund-schaft, p. 12
"His idealism is so great . . ."	Nietzsche, *Letter to Gersdorff*, Aug. 4, 1869
"The kiss of love . . ."	Comte du Moulin, Vol. I
"God the Father . . ."	E. Bertram, *Nietzsche*, p. 150
"Lit up with . . ."	Judith Gautier, *Le troisième rang du collier*, pp. 33, 40, 41, 111, 231
"Recited and sang . . ."	*Ibid.*
"Wagner caught me . . ."	*Ibid.*
"Whatever you do . . ."	*Ibid.*
"You are the people who . . ."	*Ibid.*
"But yesterday I found him . . ."	*Letter* from Cosima to Judith Gautier, Sept. 7, 1869. Bibl. Nat. (unpublished)
"I have been in such . . ."	*Ibid.*, no date
"The master goes on with his work . . ."	*Ibid.*
"The sister said it was . . ."	*Ibid.*
"I know I'm getting old . . ."	Comte du Moulin, Vol. I
"Richard Wagner gave me . . ."	Nietzsche, *Selected Letters* (Ed. Stock), p. 31
"Perhaps you could relieve me . . ."	Glasenapp, Vol. IV
"It vastly enriches . . ."	Nietzsche to Gersdorff, March 11, 1870
"The existence of the world . . ."	Nietzsche, *Origins of Tragedy*, Preface of 1886
"In good and evil days . . ."	Comte du Moulin, Vol. I
"When the weather is fine . . ."	*Ibid.*

CHAPTER IV

"It looks as if thunder . . ."	Glasenapp, Vol. IV
"You remember what you went through . . ."	R. Wagner to Judith Gautier, Bibl. Nat. (unpublished)
"The course civilization is taking . . ."	Nietzsche, *Selected Letters*
"A revelation . . ."	*Ibid.*
"German mission . . ."	*Ibid.*
"They looked long at one another . . ."	Comte du Moulin, Vol. I
"A noble sentiment . . ."	*Ibid.*
"Do you love me . . ."	*Ibid.*
"On every page . . ."	Foerster-Nietzsche, *Wagner und Nietzsche*, p. 86
"I have never read . . ."	*Ibid.*, p. 88
"For Wagner, Naxos . . ."	Ch. Andler, *Nietzsche*, Vol. II, p. 287

"One last word . . ."	Cosima to Judith Gautier, April 22, 1872, Bibl. Nat. (unpublished)
"What fate is awaiting us . . ."	Comte du Moulin, Vol. I
"Cosima will have it that . . ."	Glasenapp, Vol. IV
"Not a touch . . ."	*Ibid.*
"Blessed be thou . . ."	*Ibid.*
"He was silent . . ."	Foerster-Nietzsche, *Wagner und Nietzsche*
"Thanks to you . . ."	R. Wagner, *Ges. Schr.*, Vol. IX, and Glasenapp, Vol. IV
"It is usually one's duty . . ."	*Ibid.*
"Every third thought . . ."	Shakespeare, *Tempest*, Act IV

PART V

CHAPTER I

"Literary lackey . . ."	Nietzsche, *Selected Letters* (Oct. 25, 1872)
"Cosima is still . . ."	Liszt's *Letters*, Vol. VI
"The foundations . . ."	*Ibid.*
"The happiest hour . . ."	*Ibid.*
"When we embrace each other . . ."	Comte du Moulin, Vol. I
"No, no, a thousand times no . . ."	Glasenapp, Vol. V
"Finished at 'Wahnfried' . . ."	*Ibid.*
"That I have devoted . . ."	Comte du Moulin, Vol. I
"I have been thinking things out . . ."	Nietzsche, *Letter* to Rohde, Feb. 15, 1874
"It's just bits of Handel . . ."	Comte du Moulin, Vol. I
"The virility of character . . ."	Nietzsche, *Schopenhauer as Teacher*
"Heavy thoughts . . ."	Comte du Moulin, Vol. I
"When Richard Wagner was there . . ."	Glasenapp, Vol. V
"Where am I? . . ."	Foerster-Nietzsche
"I am scared . . ."	*Ibid.*
"The most moral music . . ."	Nietzsche, *Wagner at Bayreuth*
"Nietzsche is like Liszt . . ."	Foerster-Nietzsche
"What I should like to say to you . . ."	Glasenapp, Vol. V
"Bayreuth is the grave . . ."	Comte du Moulin, Vol. I
"Let not the oldest of men . . ."	Guy de Pourtalès, *Life of Franz Liszt*, p. 275
"Dear lady, I am sad . . ."	R. Wagner to Judith Gautier, Bibl. Nat. (unpublished)

CHAPTER II

"How inspired I was . . ."	R. Wagner to Judith Gautier, Bibl. Nat., Nos. 60 and 61
"A propitious landscape . . ."	Guy de Pourtalès, *Nietzsche in Italy*, p. 30

"At the last moment . . ."   *Ibid.*, p. 32
"Must it be that . . ."   Faure-Biguet, *Gobineau*
"The last German . . ."   Nietzsche, *Ecce Homo*
"Yes, it is a question . . ."   R. Wagner to Judith Gautier, Bibl.
                                               Nat. (unpublished)
"You may write to me direct . . ."   *Ibid.*, Dec. 9, 1877
"The pure and simple-hearted . . ."   Comte du Moulin, Vol. I
"The Nameless One . . ."   R. Wagner, *Ges. Schr.*, Vol. X
"Time was when . . ."   H. Lichtenberger, *Wagner*
"For it is not . . ."   H. S. Chamberlain, *Wagner*
"The creed of my barrack-room . . ."   Glasenapp, Vol. VI
"I do not believe in God . . ."   *Letter* from Wagner to von Weber
                                               (*Erinnerungen an Richard Wagner*, by H. von Wolzogen)
"If one really feels called upon . . ."   Comte du Moulin, Vol. I
"The devil may take the ruins . . ."   Glasenapp, Vol. VI

CHAPTER III

"I have found Klingsor's garden . . ."   Glasenapp, Vol. VI
"More 'impersonal' as he put it . . ."   Liszt's *Letters*, Vol. VII
"King, Emperor . . ."   Glasenapp, Vol. VI
"But this rough magic . . ."   Shakespeare, *Tempest*, Act V
"In Life, there's love . . ."   Faure-Biguet, *Gobineau*
"A token of sincerest admiration . . ."   Glasenapp, Vol. VI
"Is it troubling you too much . . ."   Cosima to Judith Gautier, June 6, 1881, Bibl. Nat. (unpublished)
"I am going home . . ."   Comte du Moulin, Vol. I
"In the seventh heaven . . ."   *Letters* from Liszt, Vol. VII
"He's got to the end . . ."   *Ibid.*
"Morning, work . . ."   Cosima to Judith Gautier, Nov. 13, 1881, Bibl. Nat. (unpublished)
"That's nature . . ."   Glasenapp, Vol. VI
"I don't know myself . . ."   *Ibid.*
"What I want is . . ."   *Ibid.*
" 'There,' he said, as he came in . . ."   *Ibid.*
"A solemn air . . ."   Shakespeare, *Tempest*, Act V
"Another narrow escape . . ."   Glasenapp, Vol. VI
"Good-bye children . . ."   Comte du Moulin, Vol. I

CHAPTER IV

"We are of men the most august . . ."   Gobineau, *Essai sur l'inégalité des races humaines*, Vol. I
"Our dearest friend . . ."   Comte du Moulin, Vol. I
"It was the young Hercules . . ."   Liszt's *Letters*, Vol. VII
"I grieve not over-sorely . . ."   *Ibid.*
"Nothing but Schopenhauer . . ."   Comte du Moulin, Vol. I
"It is certain that . . ."   Nietzsche, *The Joyous Wisdom*
"I wish them well . . ."   Glasenapp, Vol. VI

INDEX